CLEMENT OF ALEXANDRIA
AND HIS USE OF PHILO
IN THE *STROMATEIS*

SUPPLEMENTS TO

VIGILIAE CHRISTIANAE

Formerly Philosophia Patrum

TEXTS AND STUDIES OF EARLY CHRISTIAN LIFE
AND LANGUAGE

EDITORS

A. F. J. KLIJN – CHRISTINE MOHRMANN – G. QUISPEL
J. H. WASZINK – J. C. M. VAN WINDEN

VOLUME III

CLEMENT OF ALEXANDRIA AND HIS USE OF PHILO IN THE *STROMATEIS*

An Early Christian reshaping of a Jewish model

BY

ANNEWIES VAN DEN HOEK

E.J. BRILL

LEIDEN · NEW YORK · KØBENHAVN · KÖLN

1988

It has become clear to the publishers of *Philosophia Patrum* that the title of this series has misled some people into thinking that it treats the 'philosophy' of the Fathers in the technical sense, rather than their 'thought' in the most general sense of the word. For this reason it has been decided to change the title of the series.

We felt at the same time that it would be sensible to link the series closer to the journal *Vigiliae Christianae*, with which it shares an editorial board. It will thus now be known as *Supplements to Vigiliae Christianae*.

J. H. Waszink
J. C. M. van Winden
for the editorial board

Library of Congress Cataloging-in-Publication Data

Hoek, Annewies van den.
   Clement of Alexandria and and his use of Philo in the Stromateis : an early Christian reshaping of a Jewish model / by Annewies van den Hoek.
     p.   cm. — (Supplements to Vigiliae Christianae. ISSN 0920-623X ; v. 3)
   Bibliography: p.
   Includes Indexes.
   ISBN 9004087567
   1. Clement, of Alexandria, Saint, ca. 150-ca. 215.   Stromata.
2. Philo, of Alexandria—Influence. 3. Apologetics—Early church, ca. 30-600. I. Title. II. Series.
BR65.C65S7734 1988
239'.1—dc19   88-1026
                                              CIP

ISSN 0920-623X
ISBN 90 04 08756 7

PRINTED IN THE NETHERLANDS BY E. J. BRILL

Aan mijn kinderen
Joost, Pieter en Niklaas

CONTENTS

ACKNOWLEDGEMENTS

Writing a book is a prolonged ordeal. At the beginning, it is unclear how the problems will unfold and where the process will lead. At the end, the acquired knowledge and experience arouse the desire to redo the entire project. Fortunately, there was no time for that.

At the close of this process, my thanks go to Prof. Dr. P. F. Smulders, S.J. (Amsterdam), who unselfishly passed on knowledge and provided encouragement, both of which were indispensable for the project. He has lent a sympathetic ear as hypotheses were being formulated and has applied a critical eye to the results. I would like to thank Prof. Dr. A. J. M. Davids (Nijmegen) for his determination to see the project advance and for his willingness to brave the inevitable bureaucratic obstacles to its completion. I have good memories of the regular discussions in Nijmegen with both of them. Dr. J. J. Herrmann (Boston) has patiently sacrificed much time editing the English version and has relentlessly demanded clarifications whenever the theological thoughts flew too high for an archaeological ear to hear. He also introduced me to the fundamentals of word processing. Dr. P. van Litsenburg, S. J. (Den Haag) generously reviewed and checked the Greek, both in the manuscript phase and on the proofs of the book. Dr. J. J. S. Weitenberg (Leiden) has provided invaluable expertise by helping with the parallels in the 'Armenian' Philo. Prof. Dr. A. Méhat (Straßbourg) was kind enough to make his personal copy of his thèse complémentaire available to me. I thank him for our pleasant discussions of Clement, as I do Prof. Dr. E. F. Osborn (Melbourne) for his interest and for his welcome advice. Prof. Dr. J. C. M. van Winden (Leiden) has read through the manuscript critically, and I have gratefully made use of his notes. The same holds true for Prof. Dr. G. J. M. Bartelink (Nijmegen), Prof. Dr. Th. de Kruijf (Utrecht) and Dr. A. J. Vanderjagt (Groningen). A grant from the Netherlands Organization for the Advancement of Pure Research (Z.W.O.) made it possible to work calmly on this project for several years. Drs. H. C. van der Sar of the Stegon was very helpful. It is indispensable to work in good libraries, and several have provided hospitality; the U.B.(Amsterdam), the library of the K.T.H.A. (Amsterdam), the library of the Theological Institute (Nijmegen), the BUMA (Leeuwarden), the library of the Augustinianum (Rome) and the library of the Harvard Divinity School (Cambridge, Mass.). The Stichting Het Scholten-Cordes Fonds, the Stichting Aanpakken and the J. C. Warmoltsfonds generously financed the printing costs. Mr. J. G. Deahl of the publishing house E.J. Brill has been a foster-father to the manuscript through the publication process. He has introduced me to such advanced levels of word-processing that a home-made manuscript can roll almost directly from the most sophisticated printing presses; "et semel emissum volat irrevocabile verbum."

Schermerhorn/Dedham   Annewies van den Hoek
October 1987

ABBREVIATIONS

The translation by Wilson has been the point of departure for this rendering of the *Stromateis*, and the translation in the Colson-edition has had a corresponding role for Philo's works (see infra). For the abbreviations of periodicals and series, see S. Schwertner *International glossary of abbreviations for theology and related subjects*, Berlin/New-York, 1974. Some abbreviations related to Philo are taken from D.T. Runia, *Philo of Alexandria and the Timaeus of Plato*, Leiden, 1986.

Abbreviations throughout the study

C-W	Philo, Cohn-Wendland
Colson	Philo, Loeb Edition (Colson-Whitaker-Earp)
BiPatr	Biblia Patristica
BKV	Bibliothek der Kirchenväter
FE	Philo, French Edition (Arnaldez-Pouilloux-Mondésert)
GCS	Die Griechischen Christlichen Schriftsteller
PAL	*Philon d'Alexandrie; Actes du Colloque national Lyon 11-15 Septembre*, Paris, 1967
SPh	*Studia Philonica*
St-Fr	Clement, Stählin-Früchtel
SVF	*Stoicorum Veterum Fragmenta*

Abbreviations of Clement's works

Protr.	Protreptikos
Paed.	Paedagogue
Str.	Stromateis
Quis dives	Quis dives salvetur
Exc.	Excerpta ex Theodoto
Ecl.	Eclogae Propheticae
Hyp.	Hypotyposes
Fr.	Fragmenta

Abbreviations of Philo's treatises

Opif.	De opificio mundi
Leg.	Legum allegoriae
Cher.	De cherubim
Sacr.	De sacrificiis Abelis et Caini
Det.	Quod deterius potiori insidiari soleat
Post.	De posteritate Caini
Gig.	De gigantibus
Deus	Quod Deus sit immutabilis
Agr.	De agricultura
Plant.	De plantatione
Ebr.	De ebrietate
Sobr.	De sobrietate
Conf.	De confusione linguarum
Migr.	De migratione Abrahami

Her.	Quis rerum divinarum heres sit
Congr.	De congressu eruditionis gratia
Fug.	De fuga et inventione
Mut.	De mutatione nominum
Somn.	De somniis
Abr.	De Abrahamo
Ios.	De Iosepho
VM	De vita Moysis
Decal.	De Decalogo
Spec.	De specialibus legibus
Virt.	De virtutibus
Praem.	De praemiis et poenis
Prob.	Quod omnis probus liber sit
Contempl.	De vita contemplativa
Aet.	De aeternitate mundi
Flacc.	In Flaccum
Legat.	Legatio ad Gaium
Hypoth.	Hypothetica
Prov.	De providentia
Anim.	De animalibus
QG	Quaestiones et solutiones in Genesim
QE	Quaestiones et solutiones in Exodum

CHAPTER ONE

CONCEPTS AND METHODS

A summary of previous research and the aim of this study

1.1 Clement's sources and previous research

One of the characteristic features of the work of Clement of Alexandria is the presence of borrowed material, in other words phrases or passages, often extensive ones, taken more or less accurately from other authors. For this reason, Clement's work is, like that of Eusebius of Caesarea several generations later, a rich mine of fragments of Greek literature, some known from other appearances, others transmitted only by Clement. Within Clement's work, the *Stromateis* are preeminently the writings in which such borrowings are incorporated. While they have successfully served in this role as a source for the works of other writers, the *Stromateis* have long given difficulties as coherent compositions in their own right. Not only have scholars interpreted them very differently, but unwary general readers have also been discouraged by their heterogeneous texture. The abrupt shifts from Clement's own thoughts to the alien material, which is often rather awkwardly integrated into the flow of the text, make continuous reading a difficult task. Transitions are not always clearly distinguished, and acknowledgement of sources is scarce at best; most of the time Clement connects a thought 'from outside' by no more than a single word, a brief formula, a hidden allusion or a mere hint.

The various quotations, paraphrases and reminiscences are drawn from a colorfully disparate array of sources. In addition to the Bible and Early Christian and heretical writings, material is culled from every nook and cranny of the nearly thousand-year span of Greek literature, whether it be philosophy, history, rhetoric, tragedy, epic, lyric poetry, mythology or even tall stories, oracles and proverbs.[1] The indices to these borrow-

---

[1] W. Krause, *Die Stellung der frühchristlichen Autoren zur heidnischen Literatur*, 1958, p. 126, has given a numerical survey of quotations in the early Christian literature; it includes quotations from the Old and New Testament and Christian, Greek and Roman literature. Apparently, Clement offers an unusual picture, not only with regard to Greek literature, but also to his biblical usage.

ings have become very bulky in the course of the centuries, and they may
well be amplified by new discoveries in the future. Already in the second
edition of Clement's work published in 1592 in Heidelberg, Fr. Sylburg
included an inventory of quotations from the Bible and from profane
authors. The Oxford edition of 1715 by Potter infused a substantial
number of new references, particularly to Philo; it had an amplified and
improved version published in Venice in 1757, which was the basis for
Migne's edition, *PG* VIII/IX, Paris 1857 (reprinted 1890/1891).

When Otto Stählin was instructed by the Kirchenväter-Kommission
der Königlichen Preussischen Akademie der Wissenschaften to re-edit
Clement, he enlarged and enriched the identifiable borrowed material
with great erudition. In his first publications of the text, which appeared
from 1905 to 1909, this material was inserted in the annotations, and
ultimately it was brought together in an index volume, which came out
in 1936.[2] This extension of Clement's sources was greatly aided by
Stählin's contact with other contemporary editors of ancient authors;
Cohn-Wendland's work on Philo was particularly relevant for the present purpose.[3] He also was in touch with scholars engaged in identifying
borrowings in earlier Greek writers. Thus "entstand eine Ausgabe, die
höchsten Ansprüchen genügte und die Anerkennung der erfahrensten
Kritiker fand."[4] In the translation of Stählin in the 'Bibliothek der Kirchenväter', which appeared at the same time as his index, the river of
sources was swelled even further by more references. The process of identification continued in the later editions of Früchtel and Treu, which contained supplements to Stählin's index.

In studies on Clement, the problem of his sources has been examined
from different perspectives. When the influx of critical editions at the end
of the last century gave better access to texts of early authors, attention

	O. T.	N. T.	Christ.	Greek	Roman
Irenaeus	457	865	—	16	—
Hippolytus	194	269	61	118	—
Clement	1002	1608	152	966	1
Origen	552	934	6	39	—

The statistics in this survey, which includes many more authors, give only an approximation, because Krause has based his compilation on the indices of the various editions,
which are achieved in different ways, Krause, p. 125, (in my opinion his numbers of
Origen seem inaccurate). The survey offers, moreover, the direct quotations; for the relationship between direct and indirect quotations, see Krause, p. 128.

   [2] St-Fr, Einleitung, p. XII; Stählin, BKV 7, Einleitung, p. 42ff.
   [3] See p. 232.
   [4] St-Fr, Einleitung, p. XII.

was directed first to identifying pre-existing material in Clement.[5] Analysis then went on to the question of how this borrowed material had turned up in his work. Hypotheses were formulated about one or more writings that Clement had drawn on more or less consciously. For some, these writings would have formed the very backbone of his work; in this view, Clement became little more than a copyist.[6] The role of intermediary sources came into favor and was extensively discussed; in comparisons with other writers, groups of similar quotations could be identified, and it was conjectured that these parallel groups stemmed from a common source or sources. It was hypothesized that these sources were collections like handbooks, excerpts and florilegia. In this view, Clement, who would have made great use of these intermediaries, was not just a copyist but rather an independent compiler.[7]

The most provocative attempt to reconstruct the way in which this compendious material was transmitted to Clement was made by Wilhelm Bousset.[8] Discussion was long dominated by his theory of the so-called 'Pantaenus-Quelle': namely, that in parts of his work like the *Excerpta*, the *Eclogae* and the *Stromateis* VI and VII Clement used and published notes of his teacher Pantaenus. This 'Pantaenus-Quelle' was distinguished from another intermediary source that appears in *Stromateis* I and V and that is centered on the traditional theme of the 'theft of the Greeks' (in essence, the idea that Plato is dependent on Moses). In this theory, Bousset tried to bring forward a solution to the obvious contradictions and difficulties in composition found in Clement's work. The theory as such did not find favor in the eyes of later scholars and has been discredited, particularly by the dissertation of J. Munck.[9]

In the nineteen thirties, the study of Clement changed course and in a certain sense curved back to Clement himself by posing the questions of what purpose the borrowings served and how they function in Clement's thought. The change in viewpoint might have been caused by a more positive assessment of the symbolic way of thinking characteristic of Alexandrian writers in general. Not only their hermeneutical approach but also their attitudes toward spirituality and their ideas about the

---

[5] For a historical survey of the question of quotations and sources in Clement, see Stählin, BKV 7, Einleitung, p. 47ff. and with regard to the *Paedagogue*, P. J. C. Gussen, *Het leven in Alexandrië*, 1955, p. 5,8f.

[6] P. Wendland, *Quaestiones Musonianae*, 1886; in this book Wendland argues that *Paed.* II and III was simply a copy of a Stoic writing dedicated to Musonius. J. Gabrielsson, *Über die Quellen des Clemens Alexandrinus*, Vol. I 1906, Vol. II 1909, II p. 437, supposes one underlying source dedicated to Favorinus.

[7] A. Elter, *De gnomologiorum Graecorum historia atque origine*, Progr. Bonn (1893, 1894, 1895); H. Diels, *Doxographi Graeci*, 1879, p. 244ff.

[8] W. Bousset, *Jüdisch-Christlicher Schulbetrieb in Alexandria und Rom*, 1915.

[9] J. Munck, *Untersuchungen über Klemens von Alexandria*, 1933.

sacraments and the church were involved in this more favourable appraisal.[10] The books of Walter Völker on Philo, Clement and Origen form a monumental demonstration of this renewed theological interest.[11]

In the study of Clement's use of sources as well, the interest shifted from the form of the quotations and their derivation to the more authentic Christian content that Clement imparted to the material, a focus that appears in the book that F. Quatember wrote on the *Paedagogue*.[12] P.J.C. Gussen investigated the borrowings and their sources in the *Paedagogue* from a somewhat different angle but with similar presuppositions, namely that Clement should be treated within his own context and that it should be established how the borrowings function within his argumentation.[13] To this end he used the literary method of comparing the borrowings individually in form and content and meticulously defining the alterations of meaning in their setting in Clement. Gussen's approach, however, is not theological but cultural; everyday life in Alexandria is the focus in his work. In connection with this method, the studies of N. Zeegers-vander Vorst must be mentioned;[14] she drew Clement into her investigations of citations from Greek poets in Christian apologists and both established formal classifications and explored the usage and effect of the citations. F. Castincaud also distinguished an extensive system of categories to test and describe quotations from profane Greek writers in the *Paedagogue*.[15]

---

[10] H. Lewy, *Sobria ebrietas* (Beih. ZNTW 9), 1929; R. Arnou, Platonisme des Pères, in *DThC* XII, c. 2258-2392, 1933; H. U. von Balthasar, Le mystérion d'Origène, in *RSR* 26 (1936), p. 513-526; 27 (1937), 38-64; Idem, *Geist und Feuer*, 1938; R. Cadiou, *Introduction au système d'Origène*, 1932; Idem, *La jeunesse d'Origène*, 1936; Th. Camelot, Les idées de Clément d'Alexandrie sur l'utilisation des sciences et de la litérature profane, in *RSR* 21 (1931) p. 38-66; Idem, Clément d'Alexandrie et l'utilisation de la philosophie grecque, in ibid. p. 541-569; A. J. Festugière, *L'idéal religieux des Grecs et l'Evangile*, 1932; H. Koch, *Pronoia und Paideusis*, 1932; M. Lot-Borodine, La doctrine de la déification chez les pères grecs, in *RHR* 105-107 (1931-1933); E. Molland, Clement of Alexandria on the origin of Greek philosophy, in *Symbolae Osloenses* 15/16 (1936) p. 57-85; Cl. Mondésert, Le symbolisme chez Clément d'Alexandrie, in *RSR* 26 (1936) p. 158-180; H. Rahner, *Taufe und geistliches Leben bei Origenes*, in *ZAM* 7 (1932), p. 205-232; Idem, Die Gottesgeburt, in *ZKTh* 59 (1935) p. 313-418, see also his: *Symbole der Kirche*, 1964, p. 19-87; K. Rahner, Le début d'une doctrine des cinq sens spirituels, in *RAM* 13 (1931), p. 113-145. For a bibliography see A. Lieske, *Die Theologie der Logosmystik bei Origenes* (MBTh 22), 1938, p. VIIff. Literaturverz.; H. Steneker, *Peithous Demiourgia*, 1967, p. XIIIff.

[11] W. Völker, *Das Vollkommenheitsideal des Origenes* (BHTh 7), 1931; Idem, *Fortschritt und Vollendung bei Philo von Alexandrien*, 1938; Idem, *Der wahre Gnostiker nach Clemens Alexandrinus* (TU 57), 1952.

[12] F. Quatember, *Die christliche Lebenshaltung des Klemens von Alexandrien nach seinem Pädagogus*, 1946.

[13] Gussen, see note 5.

[14] N. Zeegers-vander Vorst, *Les citations des poètes grecs chez les apologistes chrétiens du IIe siècle*, 1972.

[15] F. Castincaud, *Les citations d'auteurs grecs profanes dans le Pédagogue de Clément d'Alexandrie*, (mémoire pour la maîtrise, Poitiers) 1976.

1.2 Studies in the relationship between Philo and Clement

The fact that Clement, particularly in the *Stromateis*, is dependent on Philo, was established in the critical editions of both authors and has been reconfirmed by many modern studies. This dependence has been described in various widely divergent ways. First of all, there have been general pronouncements which simply assert that Clement is dependent to an unspecified degree on Philo; these vague affirmations, which occur more than once, do little, of course, to illuminate the relationship.[16] Second, individual issues are discussed; philosophical concepts have been frequent points of comparison. One of the foci of attention has been the concept and description of God; another is the doctrine of the logos, a traditional meeting point in the relationship between the two writers.[17] Hermeneutics, biblical exegesis and allegorical interpretation have also been examined.[18] Philo and Clement are compared in studies of detail

---

[16] Völker, *Wahre Gnostiker*, points this out with some examples, p. 65 note 1.

[17] For the older literature up to 1956, see S. Lilla, *Clement of Alexandria, a study in Christian Platonism and Gnosticism*, 1971, p. 199 note 6; further: E. Molland, Clement of Alexandria on the origin of Greek philosophy, see note 10 above; H. A. Wolfson, Clement of Alexandria on the generation of the Logos, in *Church History* 10 (1951), p. 3-11; J. Quasten, Der gute Hirt in hellenistischer und frühchristlicher Logostheologie, in *Festschrift I. Herwegen*, 1938, p. 51-58. Further: A. Le Boulluec, *Clément d'Alexandrie, Stromate V*, t. II, p. 43, 85; H. Chadwick, *History and Thought of the Early Church* (a reprint of articles), 1982, earlier published in *The Cambridge History of later Greek and early medieval Philosophy*, (ed. A. H. Armstrong), 1967, p. 137-157 (Philo and the beginnings of Christian Thought), p. 168-181 (Clement of Alexandria); C. Colpe, Von der Logoslehre des Philon zu der des Clemens Alexandrinus, in *Kerygma und Logos* (Festschrift C. Andresen) 1979, p. 89-107; H. Dörrie, *Platonica Minora*, 1976; J. Egan, Logos and emanation in the writings of Clement of Alexandria, in *Trinification of the world* (Festschrift F. E. Crowe), 1978, p. 176-209; E. Fascher, Der Logos-Christus als göttlicher Lehrer bei Clemens von Alexandrien, in *TU* 77, 1961, p. 193-207; F. R. Gahbauer, Die Erzieherrolle des Logos Christus in der Ethik des Klemens von Alexandrien, in *MTZ* 31 (1986) p. 296-305; W. Kelber, *Die Logoslehre von Heraclit bis Origenes*, 1961; B. Mondin, *Filone e Clemente*, 1968; Idem, Fede cristiana e pensiero greco secondo Clem. Aless., in *Evangelizzazione e cultura* II, 1976, p. 132-142; E. F. Osborn, *The philosophy of Clement of Alexandria*, 1957; Idem, *The beginnings of Christian Philosophy*, 1981; H. Robberts, Christian Philosophy in Clement of Alexandria, in *Philosophy and Christianity* (ded.to Prof. H. Dooyeweerd), 1965; C. J.de Vogel, Platonism and Christianity, in *VigChr* 39 (1985), p. 1-62 (Philo, p. 1-17; Clement, p. 21-22); J. H. Waszink, Der Platonismus und die altchristliche Gedankenwelt, *Entretiens sur l'antiquité classique*, tome III, 1955, p. 137-179.

[18] W. den Boer, *De allegorese in het werk van Clemens Alexandrinus*, 1940; Idem, Hermeneutic problems in early Christian literature, in *VigChr* 1 (1947), p. 150-167; P. Th. Camelot, *Foi et Gnose*, 1945, p. 73ff.; I. Christiansen, *Die Technik der allegorischen Auslegungswissenschaft bei Philo von Alexandrien*, 1969; L. Copellotti, *L'influsso di Filone su Clemente nell'esegesi biblica* (diss. Torino),1956 (unfortunately after repeated requests not available); J. Daniélou, Typologie et allégorie chez Clément d'Alexandrie, in *StPatr.* IV (TU 79), 1961, p. 50-57; H. Dörrie, Zur Methodik antiker Exegese, in *ZNTW* 65 (1974), p. 121-138; R. P. C. Hanson, *Allegory and Event; a study of the sources and significance of Origen's interpretation of Scripture*, 1959; I. Heinemann, *Philons griechische und jüdische Bildung*, 1932; P. Heinisch, *Der Einfluss Philo's auf die älteste christliche Exegese*, 1908; H. de Lubac,

that describe either a single passage or a single book;[19] Wendland has used such a comparison in order to confirm the accuracy and coherence of the text of Philo and to establish the sequence of a number of his treatises.[20] Where the two writers have been brought together in studies of single words or concepts,[21] the relationship has rarely been projected systematically into a broader perspective.

It is self-evident that a hoard of valuable information can be found scattered in translations, introductions and commentaries.[22] Ever since Cohn/Wendland incorporated the close parallels in Clement in the notes to their edition of Philo , Philonic scholarship has continued to bring forward new perspectives on the relationship. Commentaries, monographs and articles in reference books like dictionaries also make valuable contributions.[23] Occasionally, comparisons are made from more remote fields of study. Valuable observations can be found for example in discussions of Pythagorean speculation on numbers, the Platonic idea of assimilation to God, the concept of 'anapausis' in Gnosticism or even the concept of 'darkness' in Dionysius Areopagita.[24] Many other examples

---

"Typologie" et "Allégorisme", in *RSR* 34 (1947), p. 180-226; B. L. Mack, Exegetical traditions in Alexandrian Judaism, *SPh* 3, 1974/75 p. 71-112; A. Méhat, Clément d'Alexandrie et les sens de l'Ecriture, in *Epektasis* (Mélanges J. Daniélou), 1972, p. 355-365; Cl. Mondésert, *Clément d'Alexandrie*, 1944; Idem, Symbolisme, in *RSR* 26 (1936) p. 158-180; R. Mortley, *Connaissance religieuse et herméneutique chez Clément d'Alexandrie*, 1973, p. 43ff.; J. Munck, Christus und Israel, in *Acta Jutlandica* XXVIII, 1956; V. Nikiprowetzky, L'exégèse de Philon d'Alexandrie, in *RHPhR* 53 (1973), p. 309-329; Idem, *Le commentaire de l'Ecriture chez Philon d'Alexandrie*, (ALGHJ 11), 1977; J. Pépin, *Mythe et allégorie, les origines grecques et les contestations judéo-chrétiennes*, 1976 (2e ed.), Philon, p. 231-242; Clément, p. 265-275; Idem, Remarques sur la théorie de l'exégèse allégorique chez Philon, in *PAL*, p. 131-167; C. Siegfried, *Philon von Alexandrien als Ausleger des Alten Testaments*, 1875; M. Simonetti, *Profilo Storico dell'esegesi patristica*, 1981; U. Treu, Etymologie und Allegorie bei Klemens von Alexandrien, in *StPatr* IV (TU 79), 1961, p. 191-211.

[19] For example: K. Prümm, Glaube und Erkenntniss im zweiten Buch der Stromata des Klemens von Alexandria, in *Scholastik* 12 (1937), p. 17-57; J. C. M. van Winden, Quotations from Philo in Clement of Alexandria's Protrepticus, in *VigChr* 32 (1978) p. 208-213; J. Daniélou, *Typologie*, p. 50-57.

[20] P. Wendland, Philo und Clemens Alexandrinus, in *Hermes* 31 (1896), p. 435-456.

[21] Dispersed examples may be found in the works of: P. Th. Camelot, *Foi et Gnose*, 1945; J. Daniélou, *Message Evangélique et culture hellénistique*, 1961, p. 100ff.,219ff.,300ff.; W. Völker, *Wahre Gnostiker*, see note 11.

[22] see p. 231.

[23] For example: V. Nikiprowetzky / A. Solignac, art. Philon d'Alexandrie / Philon chez les Pères, in *DSp* XII 1, col. 1352-1374, 1984.

[24] This is an arbitrary selection to show that the subject can be extended without limitations. For the above mentioned examples, see A. Delatte, *Études sur la littérature pythagoricienne*, 1915, p. 229-245; J. Helderman, *Die Anapausis im Evangelium Veritatis*, 1984; H. Merki, Ὁμοίωσις θεῷ; *von der platonischen Angleichung an Gott zur Gottähnlichkeit bei Gregor von Nyssa*, (Paradosis 7), 1952, p. 44-59 (esp. p. 51); Idem, art. Ebenbildlichkeit, in *RACh* 4 (1958), p. 467-479; H. Ch. Puech, La ténèbre mystique chez Pseudo-Denys l'Aréopagite et dans la tradition patristique, in *ÉtCarm* XXIII (1938), p. 33-53 (Clément, p. 46-48).

could be added to this arbitrarily selected handful. Strikingly, there have been separate studies on both Philo and Clement, like those of Pohlenz and Völker, that have dedicated little systematic attention to the relationship between the two.[25]

The following survey will generally leave out the above-mentioned categories of study and will concern itself with those that have attempted to analyze Clement's use of Philo thoroughly and consistently. The various methods and presuppositions of these studies will be discussed, and a comparison of their results will be attempted.

1.2.1 Heinisch

The first to make a major comparative study of both authors was Paul Heinisch in 1908.[26] Heinisch, originally an Old Testament scholar, gave his book the title: *Der Einfluss Philos auf die älteste christliche Exegese (Barnabas, Justin und Clemens von Alexandria)*, and as a subtitle: "ein Beitrag zur Geschichte der allegorisch-mystischen Schriftauslegung im christlichen Altertum." He built on a study of C. Siegfried dedicated to Philo's allegorical interpretation of the Bible, a work that had introduced the Fathers of the Church into the discussion in sketchy fashion.[27]

Heinisch deals first with the development of allegorical exegesis in Greek, Jewish and Christian writers.[28] The Christian series begins with Clement of Rome and continues through Barnabas, Justin, Theophilus of Antioch and Irenaeus to conclude with Clement of Alexandria. Some of these authors, like Barnabas and Justin, reappear regularly in the course of the book, although Clement of Alexandria is cited most frequently in comparisons with Philo. Heinisch then discusses Philo's influence on ancient Christian hermeneutics.[29] Important themes are the concept of inspiration, the various senses of Scripture and the hermeneutical rules; these rules include word-derivations, interpretation of proper names, symbolic interpretation of men, animals and lifeless things. An important principle is also the unity of Scripture. Finally, Heinisch

---

[25] M. Pohlenz, *Philon von Alexandreia*, [Nachr. von der Akad. der Wiss. in Göttingen, Phil.-Hist. Klasse], 1942,1; Idem, *Klemens von Alexandreia und sein hellenisches Christentum* [ibidem], 1943, 3; W. Völker, *Wahre Gnostiker*, p. 617ff., however, has given a brief appendix at the end of his book on the subject, where he gives a survey of various themes. See also J. Daniélou, *Sacramentum Futuri*, 1950; Idem, *Philon d'Alexandrie*, 1958; Idem, *Message évangélique et culture hellénistique aux IIe et IIIe siècles*, 1961; Idem, *Typologie*, cf. note 18.

[26] P. Heinisch, *Der Einfluss Philos auf die älteste christliche Exegese*, 1908.

[27] C. Siegfried, *Philo von Alexandria als Ausleger des Alten Testaments*, 1875.

[28] Heinisch, *Einfluss*, p. 1-42.

[29] Heinisch, *Einfluss*, p. 42-125.

delves into Philo's influence on the interpretation of the Old Testament, his special field of interest.[30] He describes this influence on concepts of God, the logos, creation, the patriarchs, the history of Moses and the law; Heinisch subdivides the last into ritual, moral and civil laws.

In his concise summary, a line of development is pursued from Philo through Justin and Clement up to Origen.[31] Heinisch concludes that Clement was entirely guided by his Jewish master. Clement renounced an independent exegesis of the Old Testament and satisfied himself with copying Philo's interpretation, which he often reproduced literally. In those passages in which Clement seemed to make his own contribution, he was dependant on Philo methodologically. In his allegorical explanation of the New Testament he manifested himself as a good pupil of Philo. Heinisch, however, appends rather weakly that Clement was not "ein blosser Plagiator"; apparently he directs himself to scholars of his time, like Wendland and Diels, who had an even lower opinion of Clement as an independent thinker.[32] Contemporarily with Heinisch's book, Gabrielsson published a study that passed an extremely negative judgement on Clement's originality.[33]

From a methodological point of view, several approaches are intertwined in Heinisch's work. On the one hand, in a method that might be called analytical, he bases himself on fragments, which he treats as unified 'blocks' and which he juxtaposes with passages from other authors. In his section on ritual laws,[34] for example, he pairs Philo's *De Vita Mosis* II with *Stromateis* V 32-38, or in dealing with the subject of civil laws,[35] he puts parts of *De Virtutibus* next to *Stromateis* II 84-100. In what might be called a thematic approach, on the other hand, Heinisch starts from a set of dogmatic conceptions for which texts are found as a kind of illustration. Examples can be found in the parts of his book that deal with God and logos, creation and matter, mankind and the Fall. Heinisch's agenda leads to a double track which proceeds analytically via the search for sources and the comparison of texts and at the same time systematically through the comparison of thoughts; a track that is pursued less convincingly than the first.

The ambiguity of his approach may be the reason why later scholars like Völker and Lilla have given such contrasting appraisals of Heinisch's work.[36] For Völker, Heinisch does not go beyond juxtaposing externals

---

[30] Heinisch, *Einfluss*, p. 125-291.
[31] Heinisch, *Einfluss*, p. 291-292.
[32] Wendland, Diels, see note 6-7.
[33] Gabrielsson, see note 6.
[34] Heinisch, *Einfluss*, p. 231ff.
[35] Heinisch, *Einfluss*, p. 281ff.
[36] Völker, *Wahre Gnostiker*, p. 65; Lilla, *Clement*, p. 199-200, especially about the concepts of the Logos.

and merely tacks together parallels. Lilla, on the contrary, is more positive; Heinisch's book offers "the most accurate and precise inquiry which has ever been made on the exact correspondances, in the single passages, between Clement and Philo."

1.2.2 Mondésert

In the course of the nineteen thirties the study of Clement took a different direction and focused more sharply on Clement's adaptation of his sources. In the vanguard of this movement was Claude Mondésert, who dedicated a systematical study to Clement's theology.[37] This publication was a pioneering effort to base a new understanding of Clement on his use of Scripture. Mondésert, who gives his book *Clément d'Alexandrie* the subtitle: "Introduction à l'étude de sa pensée à partir de l'Écriture", states, that when one considers the way in which Clement treats his borrowings from the Bible, one gains a better idea of the intention of his theological thinking in general.

With sharp and sensitive insight, Mondésert has shed light upon various aspects of Clement's theology, exemplified in numerous passages that he includes in translation. He discusses issues like the 'esoteric' character of Clement's work, Scripture as a continuous revelation and a living tradition, the role of the auditor and receiver of this tradition, the unity of the Old and the New Testament and other apologetic themes. He discusses symbolism and thinking in symbolic terms as well as more technical questions like the way in which Clement quotes, the biblical books he uses and the relationship between Clement's text and the Septuagint. He furthermore describes the distinctions between the various senses of Scripture and develops his own system of categories for this purpose. Mondésert concludes with a review of the main points of Clement's theology, which he groups around revelation, the incarnation of Christ, and salvation.

Within this framework, Mondésert has included a chapter on the relationship of Clement and Philo in which he investigates Philo's influence on Clement's use and interpretation of the Bible.[38] He inserts a marginal note on the opinion, which is as widespread as it is unnuanced, that Philo has been Clement's model, and he tries to formulate the relationship more accurately.[39] Delatte had already pointed out that not all the references in Stählin's edition were equally important. He had written a

---

[37] C. Mondésert, *Clément d'Alexandrie*, 1944.
[38] Mondésert, *Clément*, p. 163-183.
[39] Mondésert, *Clément*, p. 166.

study on Pythagorean literature published in 1915 that involved Clement in a passage dealing with speculations on numbers.[40] In a similar way, Mondésert expresses his doubts about Stählin's frequent references to philosophical formulae, which do not all represent direct or even indirect borrowings from Philo.[41] He applies the same prudence to biblical interpretations that run parallel in Philo and Clement in which a definite dependence is hard to establish. Even when the point of origin may be traced to Philo, it is not simple to decide if the material came directly or via an intermediate channel.

Mondésert, however, identifies unmistakable borrowings that are not mere quotations. As an example he has included a translation of the passage from the fifth book of the *Stromateis* in which the furnishing of the temple and the vestments of the high priest are described.[42] Clement's passage is projected against Philo's wording, and the different scriptural senses form the keys to the comparison. Thus he distinguishes historical, theological, prophetic, philosophical and mystical senses.[43] A second method of comparison, which is placed in the margin of the text just as the distinction of senses is, concerns itself with a distinction of themes; he makes a distinction between a Philonic theme, a Pauline theme and a Christian theme.

On the grounds of this comparison, Mondésert concludes that in the beginning of the passage Clement has close links with Philo but that he evolves gradually to a more mystical or even messianic level, an evolution that signifies an independent course. Mondésert explains that his chapter on Clement and Philo represents only the engagement of a starting gear in an exploration of the relationship between the two authors.[44]

Generally speaking, Mondésert is relatively sceptical about Philo's influence; he states that Clement might owe much to Philo in philosophical terms but that in the interpretation of the Bible his dependence on Philo is limited. It is confined to a few standard exegeses and allegorical interpretations, which may have been either copied or remodeled, some numbers and names, the decalogue and the above-mentioned passage

---

[40] Delatte, see note 24, cf. Chapter VII, p. 201-205.
[41] Mondésert, *Clément*, p. 167.
[42] Mondésert, *Clément*, p. 172-181.
[43] For Mondésert's distinction of the senses of Scripture, see p. 155-162: the 'historical' sense is related to the facts of the biblical stories; the 'theological' sense includes the ethical concepts; The 'prophetical' sense is distinguished in a merely prophetical and a typological component; the 'philosophical' sense can be understood as cosmical and psychological and the 'mystical' sense refers itself to the way of the soul to God.
[44] Mondésert, *Clément*, p. 182.

about the temple and the high priest. Mondésert, moreover, states that these subjects are not of great interest either for Clement or for us (!).[45]

As far as a comparison on a larger theological scale is concerned, Mondésert comes to similar conclusions, without, however, supplying much more evidence. Thus Philo reveals little historical sense; historicity is reduced in his writings to a few pieces of biblical data, just enough to be a law-abiding Jew. His religious philosophy is timeless and immaterial, according to Mondésert, "pure psychologie de la recherche de Dieu dans la prière et l'effort moral, dans la réflexion et par la pensée."[46] Clement is characterized as the contrary, as someone for whom the history of salvation is to be found in the Bible. It unfolds itself for both Greek and Jew in continuous stages from the divine revelation up to the incarnation of Christ. In Clement, the literal sense, therefore, is as important as the spiritual or mystical scriptural sense, or summarized: "Clément garde partout un sens historique; Philon ne l'a presque jamais. Clément est avant tout religieux et chrétien, Philo surtout philosophe et moraliste."[47]

Methodologically important is Mondésert's initiation of a more directed and critical kind of comparison of the two Alexandrians. He developed this technique by examining not only the text but also the context of a passage whose dependence on Philo was unmistakable. As a standard for the comparison he set up a system of categories formed by scriptural senses and themes. He, moreover, pointed out that Stählin's references should not be used without caution and that parallels did not necessarily equal dependence.

A difficulty in Mondésert's characterization of the relationship between Philo and Clement is his distinction between philosophical and biblical usage, which he alludes to more than once.[48] It is questionable if such a distinction is justified: that is, if one can detach the philosophical language from the interpretative biblical language in both authors to this extent. These problems will be brought up in the current inquiry, particularly when Clement's criteria of selection from Philo and his attitude toward him are discussed.

1.2.3 Wolfson

For this author for whom Philo had been the basis of interest but who in addition had described the church fathers, including Clement of Alex-

---

[45] Mondésert, *Clément*, p. 183.
[46] Mondésert, *Clément*, p. 170.
[47] Mondésert, *Clément*, p. 170.
[48] Mondésert, *Clément*, p. 144, 170, 183.

andria, the role of philosophy was of decisive importance. Harry Wolfson represents Philo as a philosopher, who, by his well-considered system, as it were a well-constructed building, used the important philosophical schools, based on Plato, Aristotle and the Stoa, as building material.[49] He considers Philo to be the embodiment of the Jewish version of Greek philosophy. In his preface to *The Philosophy of the Church Fathers*, Wolfson is quite explicit about the method he uses to compare Philo with Christian writers. Employing the systematical approach he developed to reveal the structure of Philo's thought, he analyzes the church fathers in order to describe the succeeding seventeen centuries of religious philosophy up to Spinoza.

Wolfson legitimizes his undertaking with the pronouncement that the material involved requires similar 'points of attack': "terms, formulas and analogies scattered throughout the writing in this case not of one but of many other men of successive generations. These we tried to piece together into a unified and continuous system".[50] Of special interest is Wolfson's idea that the person who has experience in the history of philosophy is better equipped than anyone else to survey the points at issue, even better than the very person who uttered the thoughts and took the effort to write them down; "words, in general, by the very limitations of their nature, conceal one's thought as much as they reveal it, and the uttered words of philosophers, at their best and fullest, are nothing but floating buoys which signal the presence of submerged unuttered thoughts."[51] The task of historical research then is to retrieve and co-ordinate these conceptions.

Wolfson can be eminently trusted with that kind of work; he describes his patristic subject with enormous erudition and with an eloquently clear argumentation. Yet he remains confined within the systematic structure that he had previously set up for himself.[52] Even the divisions which he made in his major book on Philo are adapted in *The Philosophy of the Church Fathers*. The first part of *The Philosophy...*, for example, is not only entitled "Faith and Reason", just as it had been in his book on Philo but is also treated in a generally similar way.[53] The chapters on the incarna-

---

[49] H. A. Wolfson, *The Philosophy of the Church Fathers*, 1956, Preface, p. V; cf. L. W. Schwartz, *Wolfson of Harvard; portrait of a scholar*, Philadelphia, 1978; D. T. Runia, History of Philosophy in the grand manner; the achievements of H. A. Wolfson in *PhRef* 49 (1984). p. 112-133.

[50] Wolfson, *Philosophy*, p. VI.

[51] Wolfson, *Philosophy*, p. VII.

[52] H. A. Wolfson, *Philo I/II*, 1947.

[53] Wolfson, *Philo* I, p. 87-289; various titles of sections reoccur in his book on the early Christian writers.

tion of Christ and the Trinity can, self-evidently, not be brought in a direct correspondance with Philo, yet because of the differentiation that Wolfson introduces to the problems surrounding the logos, the chapters are related to a Philonic background in an indirect way.

As for the relationship between Philo and Clement, in one sense, a great deal but, in another, very little can be found. The major comparable passages, like the description of the temple and the vestment of the high-priest, are present, located under the heading of the allegorical interpretation.[54] The story of Hagar and Sarah, which allegorically represents the relationship between philosophy and Scripture, is classified in a separate chapter entitled "Handmaiden of Scripture".[55] Most of the references, however, are scattered throughout the book.

A serious difficulty is that Wolfson has imposed Philo's influence on the other writers, whether it be Tertullian, Irenaeus, Origen, Eusebius or Arius, so strongly that all these authors, who are so different from one another, are pervaded by Philo. It is difficult for these reasons to come to a satisfactory definition of the relationship between these writers on the basis of Wolfson's discussion.

1.2.4 Méhat

In the nineteen sixties André Méhat had the courage to renew the attack on the literary and compositional problems of the *Stromateis*, which had been, to all appearances, exhaustively examined by De Faye, Bousset, Munck and Lazzati earlier in the century.[56] Two books were the result of his investigations: *Étude sur les Stromates de Clément d'Alexandrie*, published in 1966, and *Kephalaia, recherches sur les matériaux des Stromates de Clément d'Alexandrie et leur utilisation*, an unpublished complementary thesis of the same year.[57] The abundance of the material presented in these works competes to a degree with the voluminosity of the subject dealt with.

In his *Étude* Méhat uses various approaches. In the first part,[58] he discusses problems like the literary genre to which the *Stromateis* belong, the author's biographical background, the question of the trilogy, the title of the work and its table of contents; this section is largely based on

[54] Wolfson, *Philosophy*, p. 46ff.
[55] Wolfson, *Philosophy*, p. 97ff.
[56] E. de Faye, *Clément d'Alexandrie*, 2e éd., 1906; Bousset, see note 8 above; Munck, see note 9 above; G. Lazzati, *Introduzione allo studio di Clemente Alessandrino*, 1939.
[57] A. Méhat, *Étude sur les 'Stromates' de Clément d'Alexandrie* (Patr. Sorb.7), 1966. Idem, *Kephalaia; recherches sur les matériaux des 'Stromates' de Clément d'Alexandrie et leur utilisation*; Thèse complémentaire (dactyl.), 1966. The author was kind enough to send his copy to consult.
[58] Méhat, *Étude*, p. 23-175.

Clement's own words. In the second part,[59], which Méhat has called the 'tissue' of the *Stromateis*, he works primarily through literary insights. He thereby develops a method that is new to the study of Clement. He concludes his book with a third section in which his results are gathered together and brought into a more theological setting.[60] Special attention is given in this section to the didactic purposes and the character of the audience for which the *Stromateis* were intended.

Given the anthological character of the *Stromateis*, Méhat starts from the idea that the technical and literary problems are mostly formed by the transitions between the divers units that have been assembled. Méhat has developed a system of categories to distinguish between these differing parts. His technique is a detailed literary analysis; thus he recognizes words or groups of words that form transitions, that point out contradictions and that give explanations. He also identifies formulas that terminate or anticipate, and he studies the order in which the words or formulas occur.

Méhat distinguishes three literary categories that represent a progression according to their range; 'capitula' or 'kephalaia', 'séquences' and 'sections'. By 'capitula' or 'kephalaia' Méhat means a group of borrowings, either of biblical or non-biblical derivation, that offer a condensed formulation or summary and that have argumentative value. Within this category, the borrowings from Philo take up a special position.[61] The 'séquences' represent several 'capitula' together, which are interrupted but yet closely connected. As the longest and most homogeneous 'séquence', Méhat again gives an example derived from Philo: namely, the passage in which Clement has taken over parts of Philo's *De Congressu*, which are interrupted by quotations from Proverbs.[62] 'Section' forms the last category, which has an even larger frame of reference than 'séquence'.

The above-mentioned categories are worked out in Méhat's thesis, which is, moreover, given the title: "Kephalaia". His general objectives were to investigate the conditions under which and the methods by which the *Stromateis* were composed as well as the audience and purpose for which they were intended.[63] Thus with the 'capitula'-theory as a working method, the usage of the Bible, exegetical collections and profane authors

---

[59] Méhat, *Étude*, p. 179-279.
[60] Méhat, *Étude*, p. 283-522.
[61] Méhat, *Étude*, p. 200.
[62] Méhat, *Étude*, p. 233.
[63] Méhat, *Kephalaia*, p. 1.

are analysed; among the last are anthological collections from poets like Homer and Euripides and philosophers, above all, Plato. Two writers particularly, Tatianus and Philo, are distinguished because, in Méhat's opinion, they have been used in a more first-hand way. Méhat dedicates a separate chapter of his thesis to them.[64]. In the case of Philo, the usage has been direct, but not necessarily literal. Often a condensation, an abbreviation, a summary or a recombination of various lines may occur in Clement: processes in which the meaning often becomes enigmatic.[65]

Méhat characterizes Clement's way of working as recapitulation; sometimes this means reinterpretation. Borrowed material may be subtly altered, at times in connection with a polemical situation, at times to align it with a more up-to-date philosophical trend or again to give it a more Christian content. He exemplifies these various cases. In this way he observes that the Platonic distinction between body and soul has been emphasized less strongly in Clement than in Philo.[66] Méhat identifies several examples of relatively strong dependence on Philo. He observes that the examples in this category have a primarily biblical and exegetical line of connection. He cites the passages on the temple and the high priest in *Stromateis* V, on which he, like Heinisch and Mondésert, dwells extensively.[67] He also brings in the passages on the use of culture and philosophy[68] and on the life of Moses in the first book of the *Stromateis*.[69] He further cites the excerpts from Philo's *De Virtutibus* in the second book of the *Stromateis*.[70] In this last instance, he goes on to analyse the purposes of the selection closely. Beyond these passages, Méhat observes affinities to Philo in the realms of speculation on numbers and of psychology influenced by the Stoa, and, by extension, in ethical ideas culminating in apatheia.[71] Further kinships emerge in the Platonic concept of the assimilation to God, in the idea of following God, and in the various ways of speaking about God. Méhat considers Philo's ideas about the logos, on the other hand, of lesser influence on Clement.

Méhat observes that Clement has no constant working method in his adaptations of other sources but that he varies his technique according to the character of the borrowed material.[72] He thus distinguishes a difference between the sources on which Clement 'embroiders' and those

---

[64] Méhat, *Kephalaia*, p. 223-250.
[65] Méhat, *Étude*, p. 200; *Kephalaia*, p. 229-230.
[66] Méhat, *Étude*, p. 203.
[67] Méhat, *Étude*, p. 202; *Kephalaia*, p. 230-241.
[68] Méhat, *Étude*, p. 201; *Kephalaia*, p. 243-246.
[69] Méhat, *Étude*, p. 201; *Kephalaia*, p. 246-247.
[70] Méhat, *Étude*, p. 201; *Kephalaia*, p. 248-249.
[71] Méhat, *Étude*, p. 202-203.
[72] Méhat, *Kephalaia*, p. 4, 12.

against which he struggles. A similar observation had been made on Clement's usage of the Bible; quotations are put forward in different ways in accordance with different purposes. In approaching the question of the genre to which the *Stromateis* belong, Méhat suggests that they are a climax to their kind, which they almost seem to define. Few comparable writings can be found, although various lost books had the same title. Some of Plutarch's works might merit comparison for their eclectic composition. Plutarch, moreover, represents a fellow Middle Platonist, again among the few whose works survive.[73]

In contrast with De Faye, who considered the allegorical method characteristic of the *Stromateis*, Méhat has proposed the series of 'capitula' as the feature that offers the greatest insight into Clement's techniques and purposes. As far as working methods are concerned, Méhat has developed an excellent lens for viewing this material that has enabled not only him but also later investigators to bring many details into sharper focus. Concerning Clement's purposes in using Philo, Méhat is much more cautious. Why Clement takes over this material and how he adapts it and links it to his own argument is difficult to distil from the abundance of data that Méhat offers in his work.

1.2.5   Lilla

With the book of Salvatore Lilla,[74] the methodological problems in comparing Philo and Clement again come up, and the presuppositions behind such a comparison also need close examination. Lilla's book, which is marked by its clear style, deals with Clement as a representative of his time and his surroundings; in his view, Clement is a bearer of vestiges of Middle Platonism, Alexandrian Judaism and Gnosticism, especially the version associated with Valentinus. In three chapters he draws on Clement's ideas about the origin and value of philosophy, his ethics and his Christian philosophy; this last part takes the form of a compound chapter, entitled: "pistis, gnosis, cosmology and theology."

Clement emerges as an eclectic, although that does not imply that he borrows from Greek philosophy arbitrarily. His own contribution is valued positively, and Lilla describes him as a constructive thinker. "He wanted to transform his religious faith into a monumental philosophical

---

[73] Méhat, *Étude*, p. 104; cf. H. Dörrie, Die Stellung Plutarchs im Platonismus seiner Zeit, in *Philomathes* (in hon. P. Merlan). Den Haag, 1971, p. 36-56; J. Whittaker, Plutarch, Platonism and Christianity, in *Neoplatonism and Early Christian Thought* (in hon. A. H. Armstrong), London, 1981, p. 50-69.

[74] S. Lilla, *Clement of Alexandria, a study in Christian Platonism and Gnosticism*, 1971.

system, to which he allotted the task of reflecting the absolute truth.''[75]
It is not surprising to find a reference to a pronunciation of A. von Harnack in this context. In the process of hellenization, Philo has been Clement's teacher in many respects. Lilla not only traces Philo's influence
in the realms of philosophy, culture, biblical interpretation and
allegorical method, but also in ideas about the origin of the world, the
interpretation of Genesis, the logos as a metaphysical principle, the
transcendence of God and the concept of God.[76] Likewise Lilla points out
differences between Philo and Clement, as when, for example, Clement
represents a later and more advanced position in various lines of thought.

Clement seems to parallel Philo when he equates ἀπάθεια with ὁμοίωσις
as the ultimate objective.[77] With the idea of the resemblance or assimilation to God, moreover, the logos as a personal mediator becomes relevant. Unlike Philo, Clement has the logos intervene directly in the process that moves towards ἀπάθεια and ὁμοίωσις. Another change is detected
by Lilla in the passage in which the entrance of the high priest is described (Str. V 39,3ff.). Lilla draws the conclusion that Clement's formulation goes far beyond the realms of Philo's thought or of Platonism
and can be better explained in terms of Gnosticism.[78] In Clement's description of matter another significant variation occurs;[79] Philo had called
it οὐσία, while Clement, on the other hand, termed it μὴ ὄν, a terminology
which seems to reflect a more advanced phase of Platonism.

When we compare Lilla's book in broad terms (the only possibility here)
with other studies on Clement, a clear-cut difference emerges in the
various starting points. Lilla starts, as it were, on the opposite side from
Mondésert, Völker and Méhat. He does not take the elements in Clement's work related to the various philosophical schools as adventitious
but as integral. He puts them into a perspective in which they reinforce
each other; Philo, Middle Platonists and Neo-Platonists become
witnesses for the prosecution. Lilla states[80] that his objective is an exact

---

[75] Lilla, *Clement*, p. 232, 232 note 1.
[76] Lilla, *Clement*, p. 112f., 173, 227, 233.
[77] Lilla, *Clement*, p. 103-117. In our opinion Clement goes a step further than Philo.
Clement's idea of ἀπάθεια does not correspond with Philo's usage. Philo links ἀπάθεια and
ἀπαθής to the soul, the νοῦς or noetic things, τά ἀγαθά, φρόνησις, διάνοια or to the σοφόι
as personification of these concepts. The words can also be used in a less pregnant sense
as "unharmed" by diseases or disasters; see Leisegang s.v. ἀπάθεια/ἀπαθής. Philo never
links it to God as Clement does; cf. *Str.* II 40,2; 72,1; IV 151,1; VI 73,6; 137,4; see also
Chapter IV (2.2 p. 74-76). G. Bardy, art. Apatheia, in *DSp.* I, ccl.. 727-746; T. Rüther,
*Die sittliche Forderung der Apatheia in den beiden ersten christlichen Jahrhunderten und bei Klemens
von Alexandrien* (FThSt 63), 1949.
[78] Lilla, *Clement*, p. 181.
[79] Lilla, *Clement*, p. 193, 195, 196, 226, 230.
[80] Lilla, *Clement*, p. 7.

determination of Clement's relationship to others, but the question emerges if a method that attaches Clement so firmly to several disparate traditions does justice to Clement's own identity.

An underlying problem for this kind of comparative study also arises; what normative weight do the various sources have in an assessment of the author who is our point of reference; do these sources reinforce Clement's position and raise his standing as a Christian thinker or, on the contrary, do they weaken his position? A further difficulty is posed by the criteria for establishing a comparison. If the field of research is limited to common elements, the conclusions will tend to stress kinship, and the investigation will not produce more than the presupposition allows.

Lilla points out,[81] for example, that Philo's ideas about the relationship between philosophy and theology, described in *De Congressu*, influenced Clement directly in *Str.* I 30, 1-2. The observation is justified and can be supported not only by the word-for-word dependence in the individual fragments but also by the sequence in which the borrowings occur. In attempting to reinforce the relationship of dependence, however, Lilla argues that Philo gives exactly the same definition of philosophy and wisdom as Clement does. This definition is that "wisdom is the knowledge of divine and human things." Albinus is also drawn into the argument when Lilla says: "In Middle Platonism Albinus expounds practically the same views: in perfect agreement with Philo and Clement, he maintains that philosophy consists in longing for wisdom, defines wisdom as 'scientific knowledge of divine and human things', and considers theology as the highest part of philosophy."[82]

The definition in itself is a philosophical commonplace, which indeed had, in this case, been taken over by Clement from Philo. On other occasions, however, Clement used this topos outside a Philonic sphere of influence. It is possible that the commonplace was transmitted through Philo, but it is even more likely that Clement knew it quite well independently and that he—reasoned the other way around—has chosen the passage from Philo just because it contained an generally-accepted formula around which to build. A similar phenomenon can be observed when Clement takes passages from Philo that surround biblical quotations.[83] When these two categories of material, philosophical commonplaces and biblical citations, occur in Philo, they can function as 'eye-catchers' for Clement. In the case of a philosophical topos, particularly when several other possible sources for it are known, restraint must be showed in concluding influence or dependence.

---

[81] Lilla, *Clement*, p. 59.
[82] Lilla, *Clement*, p. 59.
[83] p. 108; 220ff.

Another methodological problem comes up in this connection; Lilla compares detached sentences so frequently that it seems as if, as Méhat pointed out,[84] Clement had been a writer of aphorisms. If one assumes, as Lilla does, that the *Stromateis* are well conceived and well composed works rather than a bundle of stray notes, then the context into which borrowings are absorbed should assert its rights and should cast light on the purpose of such borrowings.

In spite of the reservations that one may have, Lilla's study has clarified both by its many revealing references and by its clear style how much Clement had related himself to his cultural background, to the Platonic philosophy of his days and to contemporary currents in Gnosticism. Whether the many correspondences that Lilla has observed between Clement and writers like Philo, Albinus and Plutarch are indeed as 'unified' as he maintains, remains in our opinion an open question.

1.3   Method and objectives of this study

The overall problem that emerges from the literature discussed above is the variety of methods that have been devised for comparing Philo and Clement and the different results to which they lead. A first line of studies aims at demonstrating a common way of thinking in the two writers. Identical or at any rate similar material is detached from its context and put together in a process akin to stamp collecting, as Eric Osborn has called it.[85] A strong thematic tendency in the arrangement of material is related to this approach, and intentionality of intellectual patterns is emphasized; patterns tend to be interpreted so as to form a coherent philosophical system. In different ways Wolfson and Lilla are representatives of this 'systematic' approach.

Contrary to this is the approach of scholars like Méhat who work on the basis of literary rather than philosophical concepts. Méhat supposes a contextual and compository order in the *Stromateis*, but he does not understand this as a system of thoughts but as a structure of literary units. In this literary approach the systematic way of thinking recedes into the background. An intermediate position also emerges, represented first of all by Heinisch. This scholar presents a certain ambivalence in his study; he displays an interest both in literary exegesis and conceptual assemblage. While Heinisch does not achieve a satisfactory synthesis, Mondésert does manage to incorporate and integrate both approaches. He offers an extensive passage in Clement as an illustration of his method; the scope of his study, however, does not allow him to develop his views beyond the relatively few examples that he discusses in depth.

---

[84] A. Méhat, review in *RHR* 183 (1973), p. 73.
[85] Osborn, *Beginnings*, p. 279.

The problem that confronts any new investigation is to find a framework within which comparison between Clement and Philo may take place. Stählin's index with its additions has been chosen as the point of departure for this study. Because of the extensive material not all of Clement's works could be dealt with. The *Stromateis*, those 'bulky writings' that are less widely known but theologically more important appeared to be the most appropriate for an investigation. More than once, however, the question has come up of how best to exploit this multitude of references and of how to assess their value individually. In his preface to the German translation of the *Stromateis* in the 'Bibliothek der Kirchenväter' Stählin remarks[86] that, although Clement mentions Philo only a few times, "er ihn in weitem Umfang zu eigen gemacht hat", especially for the use of allegorical interpretations of the Old Testament. By Stählin's count, he used him on more than three hundred occasions, of which some are, at least in part, literal quotations.

Our study intends to review all the material from Philo that is included in the Stählin-edition, to reorganize it to reflect the perspective of Clement himself and to assess its importance for Clement. Attention will be directed towards the form of the borrowing and the technique of citation. The attempt will be made to recreate Clement's working methods: as it were, to look at him at his desk. It will be asked what books were on the desk at a given time, and how accurate or inaccurate was he in using them. What was his technique of writing when he adapted this material from 'outside'? Was it directly from outside or did it already belong to his cultural and intellectual baggage? Because we deal with one source here, namely Philo, and not a variety of authors, it is possible to develop a framework that is made to measure for the situation. In this case, an important part of the framework is testing for the degree of literality in a borrowing. The question is posed whether or not the borrowing represents a real quotation, one in which the adapted source is clearly recognizable even if not totally literal or a paraphrase.

In our definition, a quotation need not be entirely literal in the modern sense, but the wording should largely follow that of the source. The same words may be present in different cases, and equivalent words may be substituted. A paraphrase distinguishes itself from a quotation in that only a few (perhaps only one or two) words are unmistakably present. Reminiscences, in turn, are distinguished from paraphrases in that they present no literal correspondences but merely resemblances in theme or thought with the source. The different types of borrowing will be observed as they function and relate to one another in Clement's work;

---

[86] Stählin, BKV 7, p. 51f.

their usage will be investigated to see if they are associated with special situations. The context of the passage must be investigated, both in Clement and in his source.

If a literal or nearly-literal quotation is found, the size, the break-off point and the alterations must be considered. The structure and the tenor of the passage as a whole must be included in the discussion. It must be determined how Clement adapts the borrowing for its new context and if a significant conceptual difference is hidden behind even slight alterations. If a reminiscence rather than a quotation or paraphrase is involved, other data must be observed. It will be important to find out if parallels in other writers are known or if other references to Philo are present in the same environment. In the case of reminiscences, biblical texts play a considerable role in resolving doubtful cases; if, for example, a philosophical commonplace occurs in company with a biblical text that is common to both writers, the likelihood of dependence is much stronger.

By placing all the proposed cases of influence into this framework, it is hoped that a more fully objective comparison can be achieved. This method works differently from a comparative study of themes and thoughts in arriving at an understanding of Clement's dependence on Philo. By making an arrangement based on Clement's technique of borrowing, the material as a whole can be surveyed more conveniently from most points of view. It is a formal approach, however, that makes it impossible to go into every topic deeply; the material is too comprehensive and refractory for that. In theory, the arrangement recomposes traditional all-inclusive or undifferentiated inventories on the basis of methods of quotation.

The starting point is of course the most accurate quotations from Philo, which are a secure basis on which to work. These literal borrowings turned out to occur in such extended sequences that, as a practical matter, individual blocks of quotations are described in single chapters. Paraphrase and reminiscence are interleaved with quotation in these blocks, but the succession of borrowings occurs in such density and in such regular patterns that it seemed of overriding importance to maintain the unity of the blocks.

In these blocks similar structures are present, and consequently, the build-up of the chapters has been kept similar. A translation is given in which italicization designates the words taken over from Philo. A rough sketch of the context is given; then the passage is broken down into smaller units in which detailed juxtapositions of the two authors are made. The text from Philo will also be investigated in its setting. A conclusion accompanies the blocks and summarizes both the technical implications and the content of the passage. The isolated references from the index to Stählin's edition will be investigated separately in a *catalogue raisonné* found in chapter VII. Such a large percentage of these citations proved to be of dubious relevance that the group has been rated in terms of a scale of four possibilities. An A means certain dependence (quotation and paraphrase); a B signifies probable dependence (paraphrase and reminiscence with support from context); a C represents unprovable dependence (reminiscence) and a D non-dependence on Philo.

The method, as described above, tries to combine and adjust the two lines that were distinguished in previous writers on the relationship between Clement and Philo: the literary and the systematical. On the basis of the literary approach, an attempt will be made to answer the systematical question about the derivative character or the originality of the theological concepts involved. Several limitations are dictated from the beginning, first of all by the selection of the material itself. As mentioned above, the basis of the selection has been formed by the indices of Stählin/Früchtel/Treu, amplified by discoveries from recent literature or newly added here. In consequence, a systematic description of Clement's theology is not intended; the 'system' of Clement is only deepened as far as it appears from the parallels in Philo. If it is necessary to put the theological ideas under discussion into a broader setting, this has to be done either on the basis of comparable but non-Philonic passages elsewhere in Clement or of secondary literature.

In this way, the attempt will be made to learn more about how Clement uses Philo both in a technical and theological sense in the *Stromateis*. A background objective is to investigate a concrete example of the relationship between a Jewish and a Christian writer in the hellenistic tradition. This relationship between two authors a century and a half apart in time is a valid subject for comparison for more than one reason. There may be a special kinship in their common situation of confrontation with a surrounding culture that they simultaneously took seriously enough to encounter as a partner. This confrontation involved both resistance and rejection as well as an effort to appropriate and adapt useful elements.

CHAPTER TWO

THE HAGAR AND SARAH MOTIF

Str. I 28-32

1.1   Introductory remarks

The setting for the main themes

An important problem that Clement confronts in the first book of the *Stromateis* is to define the role that philosophy and Greek culture can play in faith. In the introductory paragraphs, he touches on the occasion that gave rise to his work, the difference between written and unwritten traditions and reminiscences of his own teachers. In paragraph 15 he then turns his attention to the main problem. He promises that he will make use of what is best in philosophy and other preparatory culture. In dealing with their role throughout this and the succeeding books, he evokes two pervasive images to illuminate the issue. First, there is the image of growth; watered with the thoughts of the Greeks, the earth will receive the spiritual seed cast upon it and cause that seed to grow. Clement compares his work to that of the farmers who direct this process.[1] In another passage, he compares preparatory culture and philosophy to showers; the rain falls everywhere, on good land and bad, and the resulting growth is correspondingly rich or meager; both weeds and grain spring up. Connected with this imagery, which illustrates Clement's idea of the role of philosophy, is the parable of the sower; there is only one sower, but through different ages his various seeds can bring forth a wide variety of plants.[2]

The second image in which Clement encapsules his theme is that of concealment. The *Stromateis* will, says Clement, contain the truth mingled with philosophy or rather, covered over and hidden by it, as is the edible part of the nut in the shell.[3] It is appropriate that the seeds of truth are kept only for the farmers of faith. Clement continues that he is not oblivious to the cackling of people, who in their ignorance are frightened by every noise and who say that one must occupy oneself with

---

[1] *Str.* I 17,4.
[2] *Str.* I 37,1ff.
[3] *Str.* I 18,1.

what is most necessary and indispensable for faith. They think that philosophy was introduced into life by the force of evil to ruin people. In this polemical setting, Clement tries to refute the arguments of his adversaries by saying that one cannot declare that something is useless or evil by nature without a basic knowledge of it. Philosophy is not put forward for its own sake but because it leads people to reflection and prepares them for comprehending the truth.[4]

Principal themes of the passage

This passage, which covers chapter 5 of the first book, describes in greater detail how philosophy functions as preparation for faith. In the construction of the passage, three components can be distinguished:[5] the theme, as described in Clement's own words, quotations from Proverbs, and quotations and reminiscences of Philo's *De Congressu*. The quotations from Proverbs are largely concentrated in a first group, the material from Philo in a second area. He precedes, separates and concludes these two groups of borrowings with exposition, adaptation and commentary in his own words.

Clement's theme

At the very beginning of chapter 5, the theme is announced; "Thus before the advent of the Lord, philosophy was necessary to the Greeks for justification, and now it becomes useful for piety, being a kind of preparatory training for those who reap the fruit of faith through proof by argument."[6] Shortly thereafter, he presents the following formulation: "For just as the law brought up the Hebrews, so this (philosophy) brought up the Greek world to Christ. Philosophy, therefore, is a preparation, paving the way for him who is perfected in Christ."[7]

Between the quotations from Proverbs and from Philo, we read "When Scripture says 'Be not much with a strange woman', it admonishes us, indeed, to use but not to linger and spend time with secular culture. For things that are bestowed at seasonable times on each generation for its advantage are a preliminary training for the word of the Lord." As a clear termination[8] of the passages from Philo, the theme

---

[4] *Str.* I 20,3; 80,5; 99,1; cf. Camelot, Idées, p. 51.
[5] See 1.2, schematic overview, p. 26-27.
[6] *Str.* I 28,1.
[7] *Str.* I 28,3; cf. II 37,2.
[8] *Str.* I 29,9: καὶ ταῦτα μὲν ταύτῃ...; cf. Méhat, *Étude*, p. 256.

returns.[9] "We say it now plain and simple: that philosophy has the task of searching for the truth and the nature of things (this is truth of which the Lord himself said 'I am the truth'): and again that the preparatory training for rest in Christ exercises the mind and stimulates the intelligence that generates an inquiring shrewdness, through true philosophy."[10]

In a development of his thought that was apparently evoked by a polemic situation, Clement defends the use of Greek philosophy. He calls philosophy as necessary for the Greeks before the advent of Christ as the law was for the Jews. Philosophy has been given to each generation in due time. After the advent, it becomes useful but is not indispensable; it is a kind of preparatory training that paves the way for him who will be perfected in Christ.[11]

Relationship of this theme to the borrowings from Proverbs and Philo's *De Congressu*.

One of Clement's arguments in support of philosophy is that it protects wisdom, rendering it inaccessible to the assaults of sophistry. He uses, therefore in *Str.* I 28,4, the image of the wall drawn from Proverbs;[12] in a later passage, *Str.* I 100,1, he employs the image of the fence and the wall, recalling the parable of the vineyard.[13] He continues that there is only one way of truth, but into it streams pour from all sides as into an ever-flowing river,[14] and he illustrates how wisdom takes on many forms and is prepared in different ways by quoting again from Proverbs. In his own words he explains how these preparatory approaches to wisdom are represented by the law, the prophets, and philosophy.[15] The advent of Christ rearranges this scheme and gives the law and philosophy a new position.

Clement's adversaries, who compare Greek paideia with a woman of pleasure and say, quoting Proverbs,[16] "Be not much with a strange woman", do violence to the text, according to Clement. One may use philosophy, but one should not waste too much time on it. From this train of thought, Clement comes to another image that he borrows from

---

[9] *Str.* I 32,4: φαμὲν τοίνυν ἐνθένδε γυμνῷ τῷ λόγῳ...

[10] *Str.* I 32,4.

[11] *Str.* I 28,3.

[12] Prov. 4:8a.9b: περιχαράκωσον αὐτήν, καὶ ὑψώσει σε...στεφάνῳ δὲ τρυφῆς ὑπερασπίσῃ σου.

[13] Mt. 21:33; Mk. 12:1, cf. note 19.

[14] *Str.* I 29,1.

[15] Méhat, *Étude*, p. 500.

[16] Prov. 5:3; 5:20; the last is a key text, cf. *Str.* I 29,6.9; 31,1

Philo's *De Congressu*. The relationship of the encyclical studies to philosophy and of philosophy to wisdom is expressed in terms of servant and
mistress. In *De Congressu* this relationship is linked to the Hagar and
Sarah story, which Philo turns into a long and sometimes difficult
allegory. Clement takes over some fragmentary elements from the text
of Philo but rearranges them; wisdom is mistress of philosophy, which
in turn has propaideia at her service. After a series of digressive elaborations on the different names of the patriarchs and their wives, into which
reminiscences of Philo are woven, Clement returns to the Hagar and
Sarah motif borrowed from *De Congressu*. He then concludes with his own
theme.

1.2   Schematic overview

Clement's own theme	Quotations from Proverbs		
Str. I 28,1	*Str.* I 27,2-3	—	Prov. 2:3-7
Str. I 28,3	*Str.* I 28,1	—	Prov. 3:23
Str. I 29,9	*Str.* I 28,4	—	Prov. 4:8a.9b
Str. I 32,1	*Str.* I 29,2	—	Prov. 4:10ac.11a.21a
Str. I 32,4	*Str.* I 29,3	—	Prov. 4:18a
	Str. I 29,6-9	—	Prov. 5:3.5.8.9.11.20
	Str. I 31,1	—	Prov. 5:20
	Str. I 32,2	—	Prov. 3:11-12

The following table gives an overview of the references to Philo. Here,
as in all such following tables, it is based on the index of Stählin and the
critical apparatus of the Stählin edition. Additions are indicated by an
asterisk. Material that is not referrable to Philo with a high degree of certainty is designed with a question mark. The first numbers (2.1; 2.2 etc.)
correspond to the numbers of the individual passages in section two.

Quotations and reminiscences of Philo

2.1	*Str.* I 28,4	—	*Agr.* 15f. ?
2.2	*Str.* I 29,4	—	*Somn.* II 250 ?
2.3	*Str.* I 29,10	—	*Congr.* 77-78
2.4	*Str.* I 30,1-2	—	*Congr.* 79-80
2.5	*Str.* I 30,3	—	*Congr.* 1 ?
2.6	*Str.* I 30,4	—	*Congr.* 20 ?
2.7	*Str.* I 31,1	—	*Congr.* 20 ?
			2 ?
2.8	*Str.* I 31,2-4	—	*Congr.* 35-73
			51 ?
2.9	*Str.* I 31,5	—	*Somn.* I 167
			Abr. 52 ?
2.10	*Str.* I 31,6	—	*Congr.* 124-125
2.11	*Str.* I 32,1	—	*Congr.* 153-154
2.12	*Str.* I 32,2	—	*Congr.* 158
2.13	*Str.* I 32,2	—	*Congr.* 177

Demonstrable sequence in:

2.3	*Str.* I 29,10	—	*Congr.* 77-78
2.4	*Str.* I 30,1-2	—	*Congr.* 79-80
2.8	*Str.* I 31,2-4	—	*Congr.* 35-37
2.10	*Str.* I 31,6	—	*Congr.* 124-125
2.11	*Str.* I 32,1	—	*Congr.* 153-154
2.12	*Str.* I 32,2	—	*Congr.* 158
2.13	*Str.* I 32,2	—	*Congr.* 177

2 Individual passages

2.1 *Str.* I 28,4 - *Agr.* 15f.

I 28,4 ''Now says Solomon: 'Defend wisdom and it will exalt you, and it will shield you with a crown of pleasure' (Prov. 4:8a.9b). For when you have *strengthened* it with a wall by *philosophy*, and with right expenditure, you also will keep it unassailable by *sophists*''.[17]

The idea that philosophy protects wisdom from the assaults of sophistry by forming a barrier around it is expressed by Clement in two later passages. In *Str.* I 100,1, he uses the image of a vineyard, recalling, as mentioned above, the parable of the vineyard, enclosed by a fence (φραγμός) and a wall (θριγκός) the very word that was employed in the passage under discussion.[18] In *Str.* VI 81,4, Clement discusses dialectics, which he compares to a wall that prevents truth from being trampled under foot by sophists.[19] For this passage, Stählin gives a reference to Plato's *Republic*.[20] In all three cases, the word θριγκός is found in connection with the defense against sophists.

Philo had developed this idea in his own way in *De Agricultura*. On the one hand, a reminiscence to that work in our text could be suspected in the form ὑπεροχυρώσας. Philo takes the position in *Agr.* 15 that the logical part of philosophy forms a φρουρὰ ὀχυρωτάτη for the other two parts, the ethical and physical, by refuting ambiguous approaches and false arguments. On the other hand, the key word θριγκός is missing in Philo, while he and other authors frequently use the terms ὀχυρός/ὀχυρόω. The composition ὑπεροχυρόω apparently occurs only in Clement.

---

[17] *Str.* I 28,4: αὐτίκα 'τὴν σοφίαν' ὁ Σολομὼν 'περιχαράκωσον' φησίν, 'καὶ ὑπερυψώσει σε· στεφάνῳ δὲ τρυφῆς ὑπερασπίσει σε', ἐπεὶ καὶ σὺ τῷ θριγκῷ ὑπεροχυρώσας αὐτὴν διὰ φιλοσοφίας καὶ πολυτελείας ὀρθῆς ἀνεπίβατον τοῖς σοφισταῖς τηρήσαις.

[18] Mt. 21:33; Mk. 12:1; cf. Pohlenz, *Klemens*, p. 111 note 1.

[19] Marrou, *History*, p. 210; 415 note 47.

[20] Plato, *Rep.* VII 534e.

In essence then, a reminiscence to Philo cannot be excluded in this passage, but the Platonic background is even more evident. From the time of Plato and Isocrates onward, as Marrou pointed out, philosophic tradition had continuously invoked the idea that dialectics or philosophy is a protection against rhetoric. Clement, furthermore, elaborates the idea in his own way. The word τρυφή of the quotation from Proverbs recalls the word πολυτέλεια in our passage, and these two expressions had long formed a regular combination in literature, an illustration of which can even be found in Clement himself in *Paed.* II 120,6.[21]

2.2   *Str.* I 29,4 - *Somn.* II 250

> **I 29,4**   "'Jerusalem, Jerusalem, how often would I have gathered your children, as a hen her chickens' (Mt 23:37; Lk 13:34). And *Jerusalem* is interpreted as *vision of peace*. He therefore shows prophetically, that those who peacefully contemplate sacred things are in manifold ways trained to their calling.''[22]

More than once, Philo had described Jerusalem as ὅρασις εἰρήνης and Israel as ὅρασις θεοῦ.[23] These etymologies could have been derived from certain passages in Ezechiel that speak of the prophets of Israel foreseeing visions of peace for Jerusalem.[24] A large part of the borrowings from Philo is formed by etymologies. Later on in this study we will deal with the importance of this category and its stereotyped use in Clement.[25]

Clement's 'Jerusalem quotation', which introduces this etymology, falls into the text in a strangely abrupt way. From time to time Clement repeats the quotation, but with a changing purpose.[26] Here he stresses that people can be trained for their vocation through many experiences. The idea of gathering (ἐπισυναγαγεῖν) and the image of the hen who collects her chicks in the Gospel quotation underline the multiform and encompassing character of vocation. A comparable interpretation of this 'Jerusalem quotation' may be found in Irenaeus, *Adv. Haer.* IV 36,8, where he cites the text and then writes that the same word of God that visited the patriarchs through the prophetic spirit also calls us by the advent of Christ. In Irenaeus, the multiplicity of vocation is stressed by this quotation, as it is in Clement.

---

[21] Stephanus s.v.; πολυτέλεια and τρυφή : Polyb.7,1,1; Xen. *Mem.* 1,6,10.

[22] *Str.* I 29,4: "'Ιερουσαλὴμ 'Ιερουσαλήμ, ποσάκις ἠθέλησα ἐπισυναγαγεῖν τὰ τέκνα σου ὡς ὄρνις τοὺς νεοσσούς''.'Ιερουσαλὴμ δὲ "ὅρασις εἰρήνης'' ἑρμηνεύεται. δηλοῖ τοίνυν προφητικῶς τοὺς εἰρηνικῶς ἐποπτεύσαντας πολυτρόπως εἰς κλῆσιν πεπαιδαγωγῆσθαι.

[23] *Somn.* II 254; *Ebr.*82; *Conf.*72; *Fug.*8.

[24] Not cited by Stählin: Ez. 8:3; 13:16; 40:2.

[25] Chapter VIII, p. 221f.

[26] *Paed.* I 14,4; 76,1; 79,2.

2.3   *Str.* I 29,10 - *Congr.* 77 (78)

I 29,10   a) *"For* already *some, ensnared by the charms of handmaids, have despised their mistress philosophy and have grown old,* b) some of them in music, some in geometry, others in grammar, most of them in rhetoric."[27]

This borrowing consists of a literal quotation (a) and a paraphrase (b), which is introduced by οἳ μὲν ... οἳ δέ, a construction that we encounter in Philo as well. The passage from which the literal quotation is derived treats one of the central themes in *De Congressu*. Philo describes the relationship between the ἐγκύκλιος παιδεία and philosophy in terms of servants and mistress.[28] It has been pointed out that behind this association lies a tradition of allegorical exegesis of Homer's myths. In Cynic-Stoic circles, those who stop at the preparatory schooling are compared to the suitors around Penelope, who settle for the servants instead of competing for the hand of the mistress herself.[29]

The wording of this passage is from Philo rather than from earlier sources; the proof lies in the words τοῖς φίλτροις δελεασθέντες. Philo uses these same words elsewhere to describe the relationship between encyclical studies and philosophy. In this other occurrence, *Ebr.* 50, he tells the story of Rachel, Lea and Laban. The difference in age between the two sisters, Rachel and Lea, and not the difference in rank, as in the Hagar and Sarah story, is the reference point in the treatment of the theme of subordination.

Clement attacks the position of those who are contrary to the study of philosophy. He introduces this quotation from Philo to illustrate his view that secular culture is useful as a preparatory training for the word of the Lord when this training is not over-prolonged. He inserts, however, the word 'already' in front of the quotation; we may hear an cautionary overtone in the word as if the situation had taken place and some people still remain irreparably fixed in their positions.

In the paraphrase (b), in which Clement makes a selection from the general formative studies, he cites music, geometry, grammar and

---

[27] *Str.* I 29,10: "ἤδη γάρ τινες τοῖς φίλτροις τῶν θεραπαινίδων δελεασθέντες ὠλιγώρησαν τῆς δεσποίνης, φιλοσοφίας, καὶ κατεγήρασαν" οἳ μὲν αὐτῶν ἐν μουσικῇ, οἳ δὲ ἐν γεωμετρίᾳ, ἄλλοι δὲ ἐν γραμματικῇ, οἱ πλεῖστοι δὲ ἐν ῥητορικῇ.

[28] The terminology varies; Philo: ἡ ἐγκύκλιος παιδεία; αἱ ἐγκύκλιαι ἐπιστῆμαι; αἱ ἐγκύκλιαι θεωρίαι; τὰ ἐγκύκλια προπαιδεύματα; τὰ ἐγκύκλια; ἡ ἐγκύκλιος μουσική; τὰ ἐγκύκλια μαθήματα; ἡ ἐγκύκλιος μελέτη; τὰ ἐγκύκλια παιδεύματα; ἡ ἐγκύκλιος χορεία τε καὶ παιδεία. Clement: ἡ ἐγκύκλιος φιλοσοφία; τὰ ἐγκύκλια μαθήματα; αἱ ἐγκύκλιοι μαθήσεις; ἡ ἐγκύκλιος παιδεία; ἡ κοσμικὴ παιδεία. Cf. Camelot, Idées, p. 41ff.

[29] Ariston of Chios in Stobaeus I, p. 246 (Hense) = *SVF* I 350, p. 78; Diog. Laert. II 79, *SVG* I 349, p. 78; see also Bion of Borysthenes in Plut. *Mor.* 7C; cf. Alexandre, *Congr.* (FE 16) Intr. p. 62f.

rhetoric. In the comparable passage, Philo mentions grammar, geometry, music and 'ten thousand other things'.[30] In the treatment of these general studies, neither Philo nor Clement establish a consistent catalogue.[31] Various choices were made and grouped differently, and the length of the lists varies. Grammar and rhetoric, geometry, which is occasionally supplemented with arithmetic, and the theory of music are the most frequently mentioned by both. Dialectic appears more often in Clement than in Philo.[32] Independent inclusions appear, as when Clement mentions the wisdom of magicians and the art of sorcery.[33] In the paraphrase, Clement emphasizes rhetoric by saying most of the people were spending their time in rhetoric.

Philo does not mention rhetoric explicitly, but in the following section, *Congr.* 78, he says that each art has its charms, its powers of attraction, by which some are beguiled (ψυχαγωγούμενοι). The word itself may allude to rhetoric, and the suggestion may well have influenced Clement's more compact formulation.[34] The surprising stress he puts on rhetoric justifies the question what function rhetoric has here and whether or not there is a negative overtone in its treatment.

In both authors, the context for ῥητορικός-ῥήτωρ usually has positive connotations.[35] Only in certain situations in Philo, as for example when rhetoric is associated with defending for payment, is the judgement negative.[36] Clement makes a similar distinction; rhetoric as such can be used in a neutral and technical way,[37] but when it is linked with sophistry and disputation, it takes on a negative charge.[38] In this case, however, it is difficult to prove that there is a pejorative flavor to the term. It may be no more than a simple statement that most people are devoted to rhetoric without implying any judgement whatsoever.

---

[30] Cf. Colson IV, p. 578 par. 77.

[31] Camelot, *Idées*, p. 41ff.; Bréhier, *Idées*, p. 281 note 5; Alexandre, *Congr.*(FE 16), Introd. p. 34.

[32] Camelot, *Idées*, p. 51.

[33] *Str.* II 2,3.

[34] Different opinion in Méhat, *Kephalaia*, p. 244: "l'idée est la même, sauf l'insistance sur la réthorique, marque d'une expérience personelle. Les deux phrases suivantes sont, chez Philon, une amplification oratoire de la précédente. Clément l'a omise, comme tout ce qui présente le caractère oratoire."

[35] Philo: *Cher.* 105; *Agr.* 13.18; *Congr.* 11.17.18; *Somn.* I 205; *Contemp.* 31; *QG* III 21; Clement: *Str.* I 39,3; 44,2; 79,3; II 49,2; VI 16,1. Alexandre, *Congr.* (FE 16), p. 37, 42, points out both the suspicion of rhetoric and praise (éloge) for it but she does not find this contradictory; cf. Bréhier, *Idées*, p. 289; Camelot, *Idées*, p. 54.

[36] *Agr.* 13.

[37] *Str.* II 49,2; VI 16,1.

[38] *Str.* I 39,3; 79,3; Clement often has contradictory viewpoints; for example about dialectics, cf. *Str.* I 39,4.5; VI 156,2; De Faye, *Clément*, p. 195.

2.4   *Str.* I 30,1-2 - *Congr.* 79.80

I 30,1   a) "But as *the cycle of studies contributes to philosophy*, their mistress, *so also philosophy* itself *co-operates for the acquisition of wisdom.* b) *For philosophy is the study* <of wisdom> *and wisdom is the knowledge of things divine and human and their causes.* c) Wisdom is therefore mistress of philosophy, as philosophy is of preparatory education.

I 30,2   d) For if *philosophy* promises us *control of the tongue and the belly and the parts below the belly*, and if it is to *be chosen on its own account; it will appear more worthy of respect* and of more authority *if practiced for the honor* and *knowledge of God.*"[39]

This entire block of borrowing touches the central issue of *De Congressu*. It is, in addition, a good example of the way in which Clement adapts Philo's text: partly quoting literally and partly by paraphrasing. Sentence a) is an almost literal quotation of Philo's description of the triad of encyclical studies, philosophy and wisdom. He thereby expresses the generally accepted idea that the encyclical studies form the appropriate preparation for philosophy.[40] At the same time, Philo adds a third factor, wisdom, which is not only the fullfillment of philosophy but also distinct from it in rank.[41] Encyclical studies stand in the same relationship to philosophy as philosophy stands to wisdom; the one is a preparation for the other. This scheme is taken over by Clement in an integral fashion. The distinction between encyclia and philosophy is accentuated further by adding 'their mistress'.

As amplification, sentence b) gives definitions of the concepts philosophy and wisdom; these definitions were traditional and had a wide area of diffusion in antiquity.[42] The definitions appear several times in Clement's work.[43] This is an extended version of the formula, but most generally

---

[39] *Str.* I 30,1-2: ἀλλ' ὡς τὰ ἐγκύκλια μαθήματα συμβάλλεται πρὸς φιλοσοφίαν τὴν δέσποιναν αὐτῶν, οὕτω καὶ φιλοσοφία αὐτὴ πρὸς σοφίας κτῆσιν συνεργεῖ. ἔστι γὰρ ἡ μὲν φιλοσοφία ἐπιτήδευσις <σοφίας>, ἡ σοφία δὲ ἐπιστήμη θείων καὶ ἀνθρωπίνων καὶ τῶν τούτων αἰτίων. κυρία τοίνυν ἡ σοφία τῆς φιλοσοφίας ὡς ἐκείνη τῆς προπαιδείας.
2. εἰ γὰρ ἐγκράτειαν φιλοσοφία ἐπαγγέλλεται γλώσσης τε καὶ γαστρὸς καὶ τῶν ὑπὸ γαστέρα, καὶ ἔστιν δι' αὐτὴν αἱρετή, σεμνοτέρα φανεῖται καὶ κυριωτέρα, εἰ θεοῦ τιμῆς τε καὶ γνώσεως ἕνεκεν ἐπιτηδεύοιτο.

[40] Colson IV, p. 452; Goodenough, *Light*, p. 247f.; Bréhier, *Idées*, p. 280f.; Alexandre, *Congr.* (FE 16), Introd. p. 28; Dillon, *Middle Platonists*, p. 141 note 1.

[41] Bousset, *Schulbetrieb*, p. 105; Pohlenz, *Philo*, p. 430; Alexandre, *Congr.* (FE 16), Introd. p. 71; Dillon, *Middle Platonists*, p. 141.

[42] Some parallels: Cicero, *De Off.* II 5; Seneca, *ep.* 88; 89,4; *SVF* II 35-36, p. 15; 1017, p. 304 (Aetius, *Placita* and Sext. Empt., *Adv. Math.*); Albinus 152,4; Plut. *Mor.* 874E; Aristobulos fr. 5 in Eus. *PE* XIII 12, 12-13. Philo: *QG* I 6; III 43; Alexandre refers to IV Macc. 1:16-17, Alexandre, *Congr.* (FE 16), p. 242; Völker, *Wahre Gnostiker*, p. 310 note 3.

[43] *Paed.* I 25,3; *Str.* I 35,3; 177,1; IV 40,3; 163,4; VI 54,1; 133,5; 160,2; VII 70,5; Alexandre, *Congr.* (FE 16), p. 241f.(X); Lilla, *Clement*, p. 73 note 1.

it is used in truncated fashion; wisdom is the knowledge of things divine and human. The formulation also varies, for example, by adding after ἀνθρωπίνων the nouns πραγμάτων or ἀγαθῶν or else amplifying θείων with οὐρανίων. Wisdom can be supplemented with τελεία or reinforced by γνῶσις.[44]

It is clear that Clement employs the nucleus of the formula not only in a variety of forms but also in various contexts. The question arises whether Philonic influence is always present. The answer must be negative; most of the time, nothing seems drawn from Philo specifically. It therefore does not seem justified to conclude that Philo was Clement's principal inspiration or that he transmitted the formula to Clement. He was, indeed, the source for the borrowings in this particular passage, but given the diffusion of the formula within Clement's work and far beyond it, one should not elevate this case into a general rule, as Lilla does.[45]

The situation may well be just the reverse; the presence of a commonplace in the Philonic passage may have led him to choose it. Moreover, may he not have made this choice in part because the commonplace would also have struck a responsive chord in his audience? After having put together this and many other examples of such 'double borrowings', as we will come to call them, we will address the question of what function they have and whether they contain any genuine expression of the thoughts of the writer himself. A similar question arises at the end of our passage, where biblical material dominates the block of quotations; presumably, the biblical texts in the stream of Philo's words caught Clement's eye. The principle seems to be the same as it had been in the philosophical commonplaces.

In sentence c) Clement gives a paraphrase in which he reverses the line of thought of Philo. While Philo starts at the bottom, designating preparatory culture as servant of philosophy, which in turn is servant of wisdom, Clement prefers to start at the top, calling wisdom mistress of philosophy and philosophy mistress of preparatory culture. The word χυρία stands out in this passage,[46] not only because it signifies a shift away from Philo, but also because in the last sentence d) σεμνοτέρα is reinforced by inserting the word χυριωτέρα. In itself the latter is a common enough term in a comparison,[47] but here it may echo χυρία, which is itself repeated in Str. I 31,5.

---

[44] For σοφία, ἐπιστήμη, γνῶσις as synonyms see Völker, Wahre Gnostiker, p. 308ff.
[45] Lilla, Clement, p. 59, stresses the dependence of authors on the basis of such formulas; cf. Méhat, Kephalaia, p. 245, who speaks of 'une définition banale'.
[46] Of the words δέσποινα, γυνή, ἀστή (γυνή), χυρία, Clement only lacks ἀστή.
[47] Cf. Arist. Eth. Nic. IX 8 1168 b 30.

In the last sentence d), one finds the greatest number of alterations, yet the structure of Philo's text is clearly recognizable. Clement makes a conditional construction by inserting εἰ at the beginning. He exchanges ἀναδιδάσκει for ἐπαγγέλλεται, which strengthens the conditional aspect of his interpretation.[48] As mentioned above, κυριωτέρα is added, and ἀρεσκείας is replaced by γνώσεως. It seems clear that Clement wants to avoid ἀρέσκεια here. The word occurs only once in his works, and then it has the meaning of coquetry.[49] Philo is one of the few who use the word ἀρέσκεια with a positive connotation as service to God.[50] This meaning, which is normal for the verb ἀρέσκω, gets a disreputable sound in forms derived from the present stem;[51] changing ἀρεσκείας to γνώσεως must be intended to avoid such overtones.

With another alteration Clement gives an entirely different perspective to the passage he borrows from Philo. Philo stated that philosophy teaches control, ἐγκράτεια. By repeating this word three times, he puts a very strong emphasis on it.[52] These powers of control attained as result of philosophy are said by Philo to be desirable in themselves but even more worthy of respect when practiced for the honor and service of God. In Clement it is not *control* but *philosophy* that determines the subject; philosophy is that which is more worthy of respect and of more authority, κυριωτέρα, if cultivated for the honor and knowledge of God. The major religious significance that is applied by Philo to 'control' is transferred by Clement to philosophy itself.[53]

Moreover, it becomes clear why Clement adds the conditional aspect *if* to this sentence; his own view is patently contrary to that which he takes over in adapted form from Philo. In *Str.* I 20,3; 37,1; 99,1, we can read that philosophy is not to be chosen for its own sake but rather as an aid in understanding truth.[54] Changes like adding the word *if* or substituting 'philosophy' for 'control' have more significance than appears at first sight. They intentionally alter the meaning and integrate the borrowings into Clement's own line of thought. Later we will return to this problem in dealing with the fact that when the concept 'virtue' crops up in *De Congressu*, Clement converts it to a concept derived from 'wisdom'.

---

[48] Méhat, *Kephalaia*, p. 246; *Étude*, p. 220.
[49] *Paed.* III 57,2.
[50] *Opif.* 144; *Sacr.* 37, 53; *Her.* 123; *Fug.* 88; *Somn.* I 66; *Spec.* I 176, 205, 297, 300, 317.
[51] Foerster in *TWNT* I, p. 455ff., s.v.
[52] Cf. Bréhier, *Idées*, p. 295 note 2.
[53] Cf. Alexandre, *Congr.* (FE 16), p. 158 note 3.
[54] But Méhat, *Étude*, p. 445; *Kephalaia*, p. 246: gnosis is preeminently desirable for its own sake.

2.5 *Str.* I 30,3-4 - *Congr.* 1 ?

I 30,3 "And Scripture will afford a testimony to what has been said by this; Sarah was at one time barren, being Abraham's wife. Having no child, Sarah assigned her maid, by name Hagar the Egyptian, to Abraham in order to get children.
I 30,4 Wisdom, therefore, that dwells with the man of faith (and Abraham was reckoned faithful and righteous) was still barren and without child in that generation....."[55]

Philo, whose program was to explain Genesis 16:1-6 on a word for word basis, begins *De Congressu* with the first two verses of Genesis 16. Clement takes up the same biblical text, but he restates it in his own words and fills it out with other material from Genesis.[56] There is no overt indication from the wording of the passage that he came to the biblical text by way of Philo. On the other hand, to avoid leaving the previous section dangling and to clarify who is meant by mistress and servant, Clement turns to the Hagar and Sarah story, with which Philo started his book. In that sense, it is fair to say that Clement leans on Philo. Formally, however, it is a free reminiscence drawn from memory.

Clement adds to this reminiscence an etymology of the name Abraham; Abraham, he says, means 'faithful and righteous'.[57] The background for the etymology comes from another passage of Genesis widely cited by Clement and his contemporaries (Gen. 15:6). The prominence of this text is clearly due to Paul's commentary on the righteousness of faith in Rom.4, where he draws on Gen. 15:6 for the example of Abraham's faith.

2.6 *Str.* I 30,4 - *Congr.* 20 ?

I 30,4 "By Egyptian the world is designated allegorically."[58]

This is an etymological reminiscence of Philo, who equates the word Egypt or Egyptian in various passages of his work with the body, senses or passions.[59] Probably Clement has in mind *Congr.* 20 because there, as

---

[55] *Str.* I 30,3-4: τῶν εἰρημένων μαρτυρίαν παρέξει ἡ γραφὴ διὰ τῶνδε·. Σάρρα στεῖρα ἦν πάλαι, 'Αβραὰμ δὲ γυνή. μὴ τίκτουσα ἡ Σάρρα τὴν ἑαυτῆς παιδίσκην ὀνόματι ῞Αγαρ τὴν Αἰγυπτίαν εἰς παιδοποιίαν ἐπιτρέπει τῷ 'Αβραάμ.
4. ἡ σοφία τοίνυν ἡ τῷ πιστῷ σύνοικος (πιστὸς δὲ ἐλογίσθη 'Αβραὰμ καὶ δίκαιος) στεῖρα ἦν ἔτι καὶ ἄτεκνος κατὰ τὴν γενεὰν ἐκείνην...
[56] Gen. 11:30; 15:6.
[57] Abraham has been called σοφός, τέλειος or πιστός by Philo, but not δίκαιος.
[58] *Str.* I 30,4: Αἴγυπτος δὲ ὁ κόσμος ἀλληγορεῖται. Cf. *Str.* II 47,1; 88,2; VII 40,2.
[59] Colson-Earp X, p. 303f.; U. Treu, Etymologie, p. 200; J. Munck, Christus und Israel, *Acta Jutlandica* XXVIII (1956) p. 49 Anm.

in Clement, a connection is made between Egypt and Hagar. In *Congr.* 20ff., Philo declares that encyclical studies are connected with Hagar, who is Egyptian. At the same time, preparatory schooling is associated with the sensible world or χόσμος αἰσθητός, which can only be perceived by the senses: the eyes, the ears and the other physical faculties. Sense perception, being the most bodily or physical part of the soul, is, according to Philo, riveted to the vessel of the soul, and this soul-vessel is symbolically called Egypt.

Clement does not equate Egypt with σῶμα but instead with χόσμος, a striking and significant change in usage. At first sight, it is not totally clear why Clement does not take up the relationship of Egypt and body established by Philo. There is a comparable passage in *Str.* V 7,4, where Clement, in opposing sensible to spiritual reality, does speak about earthly body, γεῶδες σῶμα. There he declares that we, bound to our earthly bodies, apprehend sensible objects with the body and spiritual objects through the intellectual faculty. An explanation for Clement's substitution of 'world' for 'body' in our passage could be that σῶμα in isolation (that is, not in the context of the antithesis sensible-spiritual) evokes a different meaning that the word often has in Clement: as body of Christ or the spiritual body representing the Church. Following a tradition that goes back to the New Testament, Clement can use χόσμος here with the meanings 'world of evil', transitoriness and hostility to God.[60]

In Philo, the situation is reversed; there, σῶμα is just the term from which passions, lusts and all manner of evil may derive,[61] while in his admiration for the unity, the beauty and the perfection of the universe, the word χόσμος cannot have this pejorative sense. Douwe Runia is struck by the fact that the Platonic concept σῶμα τοῦ χόσμου is rarely heard in Philo;[62] this strengthens the supposition that for Philo the word σῶμα is strongly connected to the terrestrial realm. It is hard to say from this single passage if the change of words actually represents a more substantial change in ideas about earthly reality. In examining passages that deal extensively with Clement's attitude towards the world and the origin of evil, it will be of value to keep this reminiscence in mind.

---

[60] Sasse in *TWNT* III, p. 889, s.v.; Mondésert, *Clément*, p. 198f., 203f.; for σῶμα in a positive sense cf. *Paed.* III 20,5; Méhat, *Étude*, p. 377 note 194; Pohlenz, Klemens, p. 131.

[61] Leisegang s.v. σῶμα; Völker, *Fortschritt*, p. 75

[62] Runia, *Philo*, p. 198; a similar alternation of χόσμος and χτίσις occurs, see *Str.* VI 142,4.

2.7 *Str.* I 31,1   -   *Congr.* 20 ?
                          Congr. 2 ?

I 31,1 "And Philo interprets *Hagar* to mean '*sojourning*'. For it is said in connection with this: 'Be not much with a strange woman' (Prov. 5:20). *Sarah* he interprets to mean '*sovereignty over me*'. He then who has received previous training is at liberty to approach to wisdom, which is sovereign, from which grows up the race of Israel."[63]

It is noteworthy that Clement mentions Philo as his source here, which he does only rarely, and also that this acknowledgement occurs in the middle of this group of borrowings rather than at the beginning.[64] These interpretations of the names Hagar and Sarah occur often in Philo.[65] As background for Hagar, one could think of *Congr.* 20, because there she is also combined with Egypt. For Sarah, *Congr.* 2 is a possibility because her name is connected with the increase of the people of Israel, as it is in Clement.

It is difficult, however, to prove Clement has these specific passages in mind. Etymological equivalencies like these, moreover, have already become so stereotyped in his work that they arise, as it were, spontaneously. In any case, the usage is based on reminiscences and loose associations of various Philonic elements.[66] A good example of how Clement himself plays with these words is his use of σοφία ἀρχικωτάτη in the following sentence, in which he echoes the idea of Sarah as ἀρχή. Also in repeating Prov. 5:20, an essential text for Clement, it appears how he is capable of weaving complex material from outside into the mainstream of his thought.

2.8 *Str.* I 31,2-4 - *Congr.* 35-37
                      Congr. 51 ?

I 31,2 "These things show that wisdom can be acquired *through instruction, to which Abraham attained,* passing from the contemplation of heavenly things to faith and righteousness according to God.

---

[63] *Str.* I 31,1: ἑρμηνεύει δὲ ὁ Φίλων τὴν μὲν Ἄγαρ παροίκησιν (ἐνταῦθα γὰρ εἴρηται· "μὴ πολὺς ἴσθι πρὸς ἀλλοτρίαν"), τὴν Σάραν δὲ ἀρχήν μου. ἔνεστιν οὖν προπαιδευθέντα ἐπὶ τὴν ἀρχικωτάτην σοφίαν ἐλθεῖν, ἀφ'ἧς τὸ Ἰσραηλιτικὸν γένος αὔξεται.

[64] *Str.* I 72,4; 153,2; II 100,3.

[65] Sarah: *Leg.* III 244; *Cher.* 3, 5, 7, 41; *Her.* 258; *Congr.* 6; *Mut.* 77; *Abr.* 99; Hagar: *Leg.* III 244; *Sacr.* 43.

[66] Chadwick, *Alexandrian Christianity*, p. 19: "The Miscellanies is a baffling and enigmatic work to read because Clement is constantly passing from one subject to another, leaving hints and allusions unexplained and undeveloped".

I 31,3   And *Isaac* is shown to mean '*self-taught*'; wherefore also he is discovered to be a type of Christ. He was the husband of one wife *Rebecca*, which they translate '*Patience*'.

I 31,4   And *Jacob* is said to have consorted with several, his name being interpreted '*Exerciser*'. *For many and various are the truths, in which practice finds its exercising ground*, whence also he is called *Israel* who is really endowed with the power of *seeing*, having much experience and being fit for exercise."[67]

The ingredients of this passage are to be found in the part of *De Congressu* describing Isaac. Clement uses the material freely and is inclined to continue the series of etymological equivalences that he had started with the interpretation of the name Egypt. These loose reminiscences can be traced back to *Congr.* 35-37 because they appear in combination. As always with these names, they occur elsewhere in Philo in isolation.[68] Curiously enough among all these fragments, one sentence is reproduced literally.[69]

In Philo the primary interest is evoked by the fact that Abraham and Jacob married various women while Isaac had only one wife and no concubines at all. Here as elsewhere in Philo the patriarchs personify attainment of virtue, and in a long and complicated allegory, the possession of women and concubines and the paths to virtue are linked to each other. The various ways of approach are formed by μάθησις (Abraham), φύσις (Isaac) and ἄσκησις (Jacob); Philo thereby adapts a scheme for reaching virtue through learning, nature and training that had a long previous history in Greek philosophy. The scheme ultimately goes back to Aristotle, but since the time of Antiochos it had been generally accepted in Platonism.[70]

Clement misses the point of this elaborate allegory and takes up only some disconnected explanations of a series of names. Philo's sequence

---

[67] *Str.* I 31, 2-4: ἐξ ὧν δείκνυται διδακτικὴν εἶναι τὴν σοφίαν, ἣν μετῆλθεν Ἀβραάμ, ἐκ τῆς τῶν οὐρανίων θέας μετιὼν εἰς τὴν κατὰ θεὸν πίστιν τε καὶ δικαιοσύνην.
3. Ἰσαὰκ δὲ τὸ αὐτομαθὲς ἐνδείκνυται· διὸ καὶ Χριστοῦ τύπος εὑρίσκεται. οὗτος μιᾶς γυναικὸς ἀνὴρ τῆς Ῥεβέκκας, ἣν ὑπομονὴν μεταφράζουσιν.
4. πλείοσι δὲ συνέρχεσθαι ὁ Ἰακὼβ λέγεται ὡς ἂν ἀσκητὴς ἑρμηνευόμενος (διὰ πλειόνων δὲ καὶ διαφερόντων αἱ ἀσκήσεις δογμάτων), ὅθεν καὶ Ἰσραὴλ οὗτος μετονομάζεται ὁ τῷ ὄντι διορατικὸς ὡς ἂν πολύπειρός τε καὶ ἀσκητικός.
[68] Isaac: *Sacr.* 6; *Det.* 30; *Deus* 4; *Ebr.* 94; *Sobr.* 65; *Conf.* 74; *Mut.* 1; *Somn.* I 168; Rebecca: *Leg.* III 88; *Sacr.* 4; *Det.* 30,45; *Plant.* 169; *Migr.* 208; *Fug.* 194; *Somn.* I 46; Goodenough, *Light*, p. 153ff.
[69] διὰ πλειόνων δὲ καὶ διαφερόντων αἱ ἀσκήσεις δογμάτων.
[70] Bousset, *Schulbetrieb*, p. 108; Völker, *Fortschritt*, p. 154; Pohlenz, *Philo*, p. 433; Wolfson, *Philo* II, p. 197; Bréhier, *Idées*, p. 273ff.; Lilla, *Clement*, p. 66f.; Dillon, *Middle Platonists*, p. 152.

Abraham-Jacob-Isaac is replaced in Clement by the usual chronological succession Abraham-Isaac-Jacob. When an etymological explanation like 'Jacob means exerciser' does not seem clear, he expands with a brief literal quotation from Philo. He inserts his own elaborations as well; thus Isaac is not described only by the Philonic etymology, τὸ αὐτομαθές, from which γένος is omitted, but he is also discovered to be a prefiguration of Christ. Abraham, who represents διδακτικὴ σοφία, is in addition the one who passes from contemplation of heavenly things to faith and righteousness.[71]

Here Clement alters the underlying idea; Philo says that Abraham pursues the virtue that comes through instruction. Clement substitutes wisdom for virtue. Even though we are dealing with a reminiscence and not an extended quotation, the change is unmistakable.[72] The concept of virtue, which plays such an explicitly important role in *De Congressu*, drops from prominence in Clement and is replaced by wisdom. The same kind of alteration had taken place in the previous section, and the phenomenon will occur again in the following passage.

The series of patriarchal names ends with a characterization of Israel as 'he who truly looks through' because of his experience and training. The word διορατικός is unparalleled in Philo, who associates Israel with ὅρασις or ὁρῶν or ὁρατικός.[73] Clement's image surely derives from Philo, but the compound is his own innovation, as is the use of πολύπειρος, by which he extends the etymology.

2.9   *Str.* I 31,5 - *Somn.* I 167 ?
              Abr. 52 ?

I 31,5 "Something else may also have been shown by the three patriarchs, namely that the seal of knowledge, which consists of nature, education and exercise, is sovereign."[74]

In his richly layered method of exposition, Clement follows the individual etymologies with a reminiscence of the three patriarchs as a group. The idea that these patriarchs represent nature, learning and training had already occurred in the previous passage.[75]

---

[71] Völker, *Fortschritt*, p. 177 note 4; cf. Chapter VII on *Str.* V 8,5; VI 80,3.
[72] Camelot, Clément, p. 556f.
[73] Cf. *Congr.* 51; Israel: Leisegang I, p. 13; Colson-Earp X, p. 334; for this passage cf. Clement, *Paed.* I 57,1ff.; for the etymologies: *Paed.* I 77,2; *Str.* II 20,2; IV 169,1; Den Boer, *Allegorese*, p. 96.
[74] *Str.* I 31,5: εἴη δ' ἄν τι καὶ ἄλλο δηλούμενον διὰ τῶν τριῶν προπατόρων, κυρίαν εἶναι τὴν σφραγῖδα τῆς γνώσεως, ἐκ φύσεως καὶ μαθήσεως καὶ ἀσκήσεως συνεστῶσαν.
[75] see note 70.

In Philo, the patriarchs and the three ways to reach perfect virtue are described in *Somn.* I 167 and in abbreviated form in *Abr.* 52. In *De Somniis* Philo says that virtue is attained through nature, training or learning and that for this reason all three patriarchs of the nation are described as wise. In *De Abrahamo*, Philo connects the tripartition with the Graces;[76] for, as he says, they are also three in number. He stresses that these three powers have been given as a gift of God's grace, χάρις.[77] In *De Somniis* Philo unobtrusively makes the link between virtue and wisdom by calling the patriarchs 'wise'; in *De Abrahamo* he stresses that not only human abilities are operative in attaining virtue but even more that these abilities are gifts. Both concepts are important for the comprehension of Clement's reminiscence.

Returning to Clement, the emphasis of the sentence is not on being trained for or having learned or being allotted virtue; he stresses the central part of the sentence (the indirect statement in the infinitive), in which Clement says that the seal of knowledge is sovereign. The repetition of sovereign (κυρία) has already been pointed out above in section 2.4.[78] In a similar construction, the seal of knowledge replaces the concept virtue, which had been used by Philo in *De Somniis*. It is not so easy to understand what Clement means with this central phrase.

The number three and the word seal (σφραγίς) launch us on a certain track. From other texts, it appears that Clement usually is thinking about Baptism when he uses the term seal. His point of reference is probably not so much the rite itself as it is the concept of Baptism as a starting point of Christian life.[79] In his book *The Seal of the Spirit*, Lampe gives an extensive survey of the various possible meanings for Clement's use of this term. The presence of the number three, which also occurs in Philo's allegories of the patriarchs and the Graces, seems to indicate that Clement has in mind a formula connected with that number. If this is the Trinitarian formula, which is convenient from many points of view, or some other cannot be resolved from the context. The expression of a formula as a stamp or a mark may have, as Lampe shows, a magical background.[80]

In a passage of Origen's *Contra Celsum*, the Old Testament titles God of Abraham, God of Isaac and God of Jacob are used in that very way:

---

[76] *Abr.* 54.
[77] Goodenough, *Light*, p. 136; Wolfson, *Philo* II, p. 198.
[78] p. 31ff.
[79] Lampe, *Seal*, p. 153ff.; Hanson, *Allegory*, p. 316-318.
[80] Lampe, *Seal*, p. 287.

as powerful names that were pronounced to overcome demons.[81] Whether connected with the names of the Father, the Son and the Holy Spirit or linked to an invocation formula, as in *Contra Celsum*, the meaning of Clement's sentence is that for the Gnostic or for the Gnostic soul, the seal of gnosis is primary (χυρία). Comparable texts in Clement clarify what is being said here in very compressed form;[82] people are capable through their natural capacities or by learning or training to make their own contribution. Primary and central, however, is the fact that wisdom or the truth are ultimately attained as a gift or through grace. Presumably, the seal of knowledge means that Baptism or the answer of the person who is baptized is considered a seal which confirms the act; it leads to knowledge in its first phase and opens the way to further perfection through ability, learning and training.

2.10   *Str.* I 31,6 - *Congr.* 124-125

> **I 31,6**   "You may have also another image of what has been said, in *Thamar sitting at the cross-roads and presenting the appearance of a harlot*, on whom the *studious* Judah (whose name is interpreted as 'powerful'), *who left nothing unexamined and uninvestigated*, looked; and *turned aside to her*, preserving *his profession towards God.*"[83]

The story of Thamar and Judah, which takes up a passage of Philo in fragmented form, is inserted by Clement to develop his stream of imagery at this point. The passage from Philo's *De Congressu* stands in the background unmistakably; Clement's words are more than a reminiscence or paraphrase, they are a compressed, edited version of his Philonic model. Philo discusses and digresses on Gen. 16:4: "he went in unto Hagar." After having compared this to the relationship between teacher and pupil, he comes to speak about Thamar. In order to identify and test inquiring minds, Thamar veils her face so that her beauty and her virginal modesty will be revealed to the lovers of learning who unveil her.

Scarcely anything of this allegory remains in Clement's version; why the Thamar story has been inserted here will be obscure for the reader who

---

[81] Origenes, *Cels.* 5,45.

[82] *Str.* I 34,1; 38,4; II 75,2; IV 124,1; VI 95,5; 96,3; VII 19,3; 64,6; cf. Pohlenz, *Klemens*, p. 116.

[83] *Str.* I 31,6: ἔχοις δ' ἂν καὶ ἄλλην εἰκόνα τῶν εἰρημένων τὴν Θάμαρ ἐπὶ τριόδου καθεσθεῖσαν καὶ πόρνης δόξαν παρασχοῦσαν, ἣν ὁ φιλομαθὴς Ἰούδας (δυνατὸς δὲ ἑρμηνεύεται) ὁ μηδὲν ἄσκεπτον καὶ ἀδιερεύνητον καταλιπὼν ἐπεσκέψατο καὶ "πρὸς αὐτὴν ἐξέκλινεν", σῴζων τὴν πρὸς τὸν θεὸν ὁμολογίαν.

does not know Philo. In this closing passage, it seems that Clement accelerates his flight across the text of Philo and, in a bird's eye view, gives a few more examples from *De Congressu* in highly abbreviated fashion. The etymology Judah equals δυνατός cannot be found in Philo; yet Philo terms Judah the highest military commander and king.[84] Clement takes over the complementary explanation that Judah preserves his profession towards God (cf. Gen. 29:35).

2.11   *Str.* I 32,1 - *Congr.* 153-154

I 32,1   "Wherefore also, when Sarah was jealous at Hagar, who surpassed her in favour, Abraham, as choosing only what was profitable in secular philosophy, said *'Behold, the maid is in your hands: deal with her as it pleases you'* (Gen. 16:6a), manifestly meaning: *I embrace secular culture as younger and your handmaid; but your knowledge I honour and revere as fullgrown mistress.*"[85]

Turning back to the first Hagar and Sarah allegory and to his original theme that only the useful part of philosophy must be chosen, Clement reinforces the position with some borrowings from the last part of *De Congressu*. Propaideia is called κοσμικὴ παιδεία, as it had already been in *Str.* I 29,9 and *Str.* I 30,4; in this passage, Clement also speaks about κοσμικὴ φιλοσοφία. A striking feature of these last borrowings is that they consist in large part of biblical quotations that had been used by Philo. They are technically comparable to the 'double borrowings' in 2.4b. Here they take the form of compressed notations in an almost telegraphic style centered on a biblical text.

2.12   *Str.* I 32,2 - *Congr.* 158

I 32,2   "*'and Sarah afflicted her'* (Gen. 16:6b); *which is equivalent to corrected and admonished her.*"[86]

Toward the end of *De Congressu*, the text of Gen. 16:6 was the occasion for Philo to elaborate the verb ἐκάκωσεν. Clement chooses only the biblical text and that part of the explanation that follows immediately, in which the position of ἐσωφρόνισε and ἐνουθέτησε is reversed.

---

[84] *Congr.* 125; *Somn.* II 44.

[85] *Str.* I 32,1: διὰ τοῦτο καὶ ὁ Ἀβραάμ, παραζηλούσης τῆς Σάρρας τὴν Ἄγαρ παρευδοκιμοῦσαν αὐτήν, ὡς ἂν τὸ χρήσιμον ἐκλεξάμενος μόνον τῆς κοσμικῆς φιλοσοφίας, "ἰδοὺ ἡ παιδίσκη ἐν ταῖς χερσί σου, χρῶ αὐτῇ ὡς ἄν σοι ἀρεστὸν ᾖ" φησί. δηλῶν ὅτι ἀσπάζομαι μὲν τὴν κοσμικὴν παιδείαν καὶ ὡς νεωτέραν καὶ ὡς σὴν θεραπαινίδα, τὴν δὲ ἐπιστήμην τὴν σὴν ὡς τελείαν δέσποιναν τιμῶ καὶ σέβω.

[86] *Str.* I 32,2: "καὶ ἐκάκωσεν αὐτὴν Σάρρα" ἴσον τῷ ἐσωφρόνισε καὶ ἐνουθέτησεν.

2.13   *Str.* I 32,2 - *Congr.* 177

> **I 32, 2** "It has therefore been well said '*My son, do not despise the correction of God; nor faint when you are rebuked by him. For whom the Lord loves, he chastens, and he scourges every son whom he receives*' (Prov. 3:11f.; Hebr. 12:5f.).
> **I 32,3** And the aforesaid Scriptures, when examined in other places, will be seen to exhibit other mysteries."[87]

Before Clement closes the passage he makes a last borrowing from *De Congressu*, which probably was evoked by the verb νουθετέω in the previous sentence. It is a double borrowing: a quotation within a quotation; Philo is citing two verses from Proverbs. The same two verses are also transmitted in the Epistle to the Hebrews, a coincidence that may well have captured Clement's attention. There is a difference between the Septuagint and the Philonic version of this text from Proverbs; the text of Hebrews follows the Septuagint.[88] In part Clement follows the Philonic version, by putting παιδείας θεοῦ at the beginning of the sentence; in part he draws on the Septuagint version by writing μηδέ and παιδεύει instead of καὶ μή and ἐλέγχει. In another passage, *Paed.* I 78,2, Clement cites the same text from Proverbs; there, however, he follows the Septuagint version exactly. This difference in wording shows conclusively that Clement came to the quotation in the section here via Philo's *De Congressu*.

As he does so often, Clement concludes by saying that there are more possible explanations; other mysteries can be pointed out. It is not right to take this as literally as Den Boer[89] does when he states that only the texts under discussion are subject to further elucidation and that it is unfortunate that Clement does not return to them. For Clement it is more a matter of method to interpret on every possible level; he not only declares this frequently, but he practices it systematically.

3   Conclusions

In surveying this extensive and complex material, a few recurrent patterns that are partly formal and partly thematic can be identified. First, a few conclusions about Clement's technique of borrowing can be drawn. Alterations of his sources will then be traced and the differences will be set in a somewhat broader context.

---

[87] *Str.* I 32,2 (continuation): εὖ γοῦν εἴρηται "παιδείας θεοῦ, υἱέ, μὴ ὀλιγώρει, μηδὲ ἐκλύου ὑπ' αὐτοῦ ἐλεγχόμενος· ὃν γὰρ ἀγαπᾷ κύριος παιδεύει, μαστιγοῖ δὲ πάντα υἱὸν ὃν παραδέχεται". 3. κατ' ἄλλους μέντοι γε τόπους ἐξεταξόμεναι αἱ προειρημέναι γραφαὶ ἄλλα μυστήρια μηνύουσαι παρίστανται.

[88] Heinisch, *Einfluss*, p. 191; Alexandre, *Congr.* (FE 16), p. 227 note 3.

[89] Den Boer, *Allegorese*, p. 121.

3.1 Technique of borrowing

In section 1.1 it has been pointed out that Clement fits the borrowings from Proverbs and Philo's *De Congressu* into his own line of thought.[90] He weaves this external material through his own themes, where it takes a subordinate position. This is an important fact when attempting to discover what the functional aspects of these borrowings are, not only in their technique but also in their content.

Borrowings generally stay in the sequence in which they occurred in the original source. This sequence is more clearly identifiable within the quotations from Proverbs than in the borrowings from *De Congressu*.[91] Yet even in the latter, a certain sequence can be discerned, as in the important borrowing from *Congr.* 77-80. These consistent sequences occur when the quotations are literal or almost literal. The sequence disappears when Clement quotes so loosely that he must be working from memory, as in the etymological equivalences, where only one sentence is reproduced literally from an earlier part of Philo's text, *Congr.* 35-37. At the end in the borrowings from *Congr.* 124, 154, 158, 177, the sequential principal emerges again. The biblical quotations within these last borrowings, it should be noted, are the determining element for Clement's selection.

Different kinds of borrowings were encountered simultaneously. While the material from Proverbs was quoted literally, that from Philo was absorbed in a variety of ways. More-or-less literal use, paraphrase and reminiscence could be identified. In our definition, the difference between paraphrase and reminiscence is that paraphrase is achieved intentionally while reminiscence comes up, as it were, spontaneously. Paraphrases usually occur in a context of and in combination with a literal quotation.

All along the line, Clement's choice of material seems to have been made for a definite purpose, but this purpose is not always easy to retrace. Quotations erupt frequently unexpectedly, as, for example, the Jerusalem quotation in *Str.* I 29,4 or the story of Thamar and Judah in *Str.* I 31,6. The associations Clement must have had and which must have been evident to his audience are rather obscure for us. Yet in other cases, it seems fairly apparent what Clement's intention was; this emerges most clearly in the additions, omissions and alterations that he makes in his borrowed material.

Addition, for example, was encountered in his 'widening' of an etymology. Isaac, who is connected with τὸ αὐτομαθὲς γένος in Philo, is

---

[90] p. 24f.
[91] Méhat, *Etude*, p. 233 note 77.

enlarged by Clement to become a type of Christ.[92] Judah, who is φιλομαθής for Philo, gets the added name δυνατός. Abraham is not only called πιστός but also δίκαιος. Sometimes Clement strengthens the terminology adapted from *De Congressu* with borrowings from other works of Philo, as in the case of the three patriarchs.

The omissions are more difficult to identify because Clement often takes over small fragments in which much is already left out. The most obvious omission is the background against which Philo puts his etymologies. In these etymologies, Clement applies the formula *a* equals *b* without indicating the context in which they occurred in Philo. The lost context is replaced by material of Clement's own composition. One of the underlying themes for Philo in *De Congressu* is that the wives of the patriarchs, especially Sarah, represent wisdom and virtue and the ways of achieving them. Clement does not make this theme explicit; only by etymologal equivalences are we reminded of it, as by a distant echo.

The alterations of the borrowed material confirm this view; in several cases, Clement avoided the term virtue and directed the concept into the realm of wisdom.[93] Sometimes the meaning of a sentence was shifted radically by a minor alteration of the wording, as in *Str.* I 30,2, where the verb was changed and the mood turned conditional by inserting *if*. By inserting such an apparently innocent word Clement seems to question his source. Alteration of a different kind occurred in translations of a word, as ἀρεσκεία by γνῶσις, and σῶμα by κόσμος. These alterations must be intentional, but the question must be left open whether the substituted word always incorporates a new or different meaning. It is quite possible that Clement's translation or interpretation, as in the case of σῶμα and κόσμος, gives what is to his ears a more appropriate verbal form for a similar underlying thought.

3.2   Changes in content

Comparison first reveals a difference in starting points. Clement moves in a polemical framework; he repeatedly indicates that there are people who resist the use of philosophy. The controversy is developed through the interpretation of certain biblical texts. Clement's opponents had apparently compared Greek paideia and its use with a woman who prostitutes herself. Clement adapts part of the quotations from Proverbs in refutation of this negative view: *Str.* I 29,6—Prov. 5:3; *Str.* I 29,9—Prov. 5:20; *Str.* I 31,1—Prov. 5:20. The story of Thamar in *Str.* I 31,6—Gen.

---

[92] Den Boer, *Allegorese*, p. 50, 94.
[93] *Str.* I 30,2; 31,2; 31,5.

38:14-16 can probably be related to this polemical position. As pointed out above, the stance is not peculiar to this passage alone but permeates the entire first book and the succeeding ones as well. When Greek paideia is under discussion, Clement seems to defend himself in a serious way from the attacks of his adversaries.[94]

Philo starts from a different situation.[95] His defense of philosophy against sophistry has polemical overtones, but this is a standard device drawn from the 'philosophical koine', as Henry Chadwick calls it.[96] Philo's program is primarily to give an exegesis of Scripture, in this case, six verses from the book of Genesis. He follows his chosen text step by step and after his many digressions takes it up again in orderly fashion. He tries to bridge the gap between paideia and the Jewish heritage. He describes with approval his own progress through the classical education that was proper for him as a member of a wealthy family. In such an enterprise of mediation, we can discern some pedagogical or protreptical elements but hardly anything truly polemical. With all his erudition and intellectual curiosity, Philo combines and adapts existing scholarly techniques and philosophic ideas and applies them to the interpretation of Scripture.

He found a tradition of allegorical interpretation of Homer, which he draws on when he adapts the Penelope motif to the Hagar and Sarah story.[97] Many attempts have been made to derive components of Philo's thought from individual philosophers or philosophical schools. Useful philosophical models were at hand in Middle Platonism, which had been influenced by Stoicism and Pythagoreanism and which already had a religious strain. This latter aspect is important for understanding the screen upon which Philo projects his concept of wisdom and the various stadia to obtain it. New is the choice Philo makes of these heterogeneous

---

[94] Camelot, Clément, p. 559; Völker, *Wahre Gnostiker*, p. 342 note 3; Chadwick, *Alexandrian Christianity*, p. 19; Méhat warns against a too 'massif' idea of this polemic; one must not mix it with other discussions. The attacks against the sophists are more important according to Méhat, *Étude*, p. 322ff.

[95] Wolfson, *Philosophy*, p. 99f.

[96] Chadwick, *Thought and Tradition*, p. 6: "As early as Philo, we see that the current intellectual coin of the more literate classes of society is this blend of Stoic ethics with Platonic metaphysics and some Aristotelian logic. Like the form of Greek spoken in the hellenistic world, it is a philosophical koine, and Philo simply takes it for granted."

[97] At the end of *De Congressu* Philo himself indicates that it is necessary to allegorize the story of Sarah and Hagar; otherwise, as he says, nothing is left but a story of two quarreling and jealous women. Involuntary one thinks of the one other known allegory on the Hagar and Sarah story, that of Paul in Gal. 4:21ff. He deals with the contrast between the slave and the free woman, between Ishmael and Israel, and ultimately between Judaism and Christianity. Except for the allegorization of the same story there are no similarities between Philo and Paul.

elements and the use he makes of them to interpret the Mosaic law. This process took place in a different context than that in which Clement moved a century and a half later, when he had to defend himself against people within his own circle who on principle entertained suspicions of or even rejected Greek culture.

Another major difference emerges within the concept of wisdom. As touched on above, in Clement virtue as an autonomous concept had to make way for wisdom. In Philo virtue and wisdom remain separate; the way to virtue, in fact, forms a fundamental issue in *De Congressu*. The two concepts are closely related through their religious component. True wisdom points toward true piety and the knowledge of God as its ultimate objective.[98] This process is represented by the word that came to Moses by way of revelation. This is the law or, as he also calls it, the beloved word in the life of believers; just as wisdom is connected with virtue, so it is also connected with the word.

In Clement virtue is not separate from wisdom but rather taken up within it. To express the idea of wisdom a row of synonyms emerge; wisdom and truth, true wisdom and true philosophy may be variously juxtaposed, but they are interchangeable. These concepts are ultimately extended in a Christological direction, and just as the logos is determined by Christ, so truth and true wisdom are. Wisdom is no longer, as in Philo, linked to the law but to Christ. Clement determines the rank of his concepts to a significant degree on the basis of time: that is, whether they are before or after the advent of Christ.[99] Law and philosophy are ranked together since they belong to the earlier phase. They are necessary before the advent and useful but not indispensable after it.[100]

Philo, as already noted, placed encyclical studies, philosophy and wisdom, expressed through the law of Moses, in an ascending series. The law of Moses, the keystone of Philo's structure, is devalued in a certain sense by Clement when he puts the law on the level of worldly culture as a preparatory phase and makes the two, so to speak, a pair of symmetrical buttresses for the essential edifice.[101]

Diagrammatically expressed:

Philo: ἐγκύκλιος παιδεία   —   philosophy   —   wisdom (law)
Clement: (ἐγκύκλιος παιδεία) —   philosophy and law — wisdom (Christ)

---

[98] Alexandre, La culture profane chez Philon, in *PAL*, p. 127.
[99] Pohlenz, *Klemens*, p. 109.
[100] *Str.* I 99,1; cf. *Str.* VI 159,9; VII 11,1f.; Pohlenz, *Klemens*, p. 110; G. Bardy, L'église et l'enseignement pendant les trois premiers siècles, in *RevSR* XII (1932), p. 5.
[101] Méhat, *Étude*, p. 395.

3.3 Reflections and prospects

In conclusion it seems clear that the themes of Philo and Clement are related. It could also be established that Clement stands in a Jewish apologetic tradition in which the polemic elements are stressed much more strongly than they had been in Philo. Clement uses this tradition in an independent way; he turns words and thoughts to his own purposes so that the results are related while showing substantial differences. There are, as it were, parallels at different degrees of latitude. Later on after examining other passages, his motives for inserting the Philonic material will be discussed.[102] Stated in extreme terms, the question is whether the borrowings dealt with here give direction to Clement's own line of thought or whether they merely form a flavorful filling for his capacious *Stromateis*.

---

[102] Cf. p. 217-220.

CHAPTER THREE

THE STORY OF MOSES

Str. I 150-182

1.1 Introductory Remarks

Summary of the contents and their relationship to the preceding section

Clement here deals with the life of Moses: the story of his birth, some details of his life up to early manhood, and aspects of the exodus from Egypt. In addition, titles and functions are attributed to him. Plato's relationship to Moses and an exposition of the law and its significance are also discussed. The passage continues a previous section,[1] in which Clement creates chronological tables interrelating the principal events of Greek and Jewish history. He compiles extended lists, for example, of judges, kings and prophets and connects not only Greek and Jewish events but also other historical facts like the dates of Persian and Macedonian kings. He concludes with the Romans up to the death of Commodus and calculates the birthdate of Christ. Between the chronological part and the story of Moses, Clement inserts the account of the translation of the Septuagint.[2] These units stand in a larger apologetic context, which intends to show that Hebrew philosophy is older than any other wisdom and that Plato is dependent on Moses or on the Jewish law written in Greek.[3]

Borrowings in general

Borrowings from Philo dominate our passage up to *Str.* I 165. Since Clement's *Stromateis* are pervaded by quotations, fragmentary quotes, paraphrases and reminiscences, everyone, who is acquainted with these writings, is aware that he rarely refers to one single source. Other extended borrowings, which appear simultaneously in this passage with

---

[1] *Str.* I 101-148.
[2] *Str.* I 148, 149. In Philo the story of the translation of the LXX is inserted in the course of *VM* II 25-41.
[3] *Str.* I 101,1; I 150.

those from Philo, draw on Eupolemos, Artapanos and the tragic poet
Ezechiel, while in the immediately preceding section Aristobulos had
been mentioned.[4] All these sources derive from a Jewish-Hellenistic
environment. As far as one can judge from these fragments, a similar
apologetic tradition already existed in which Moses was recognized as a
teacher of other nations: the Égyptians, the Phoenicians and the Greeks
in particular. After *Str.* I 165, Philo's influence recedes into the
background and that of Platonism becomes paramount.

1.2   Schematic overview[5]

2.1	*Str.* I 150,4(5)	—	*VM* I 1
2.2	*Str.* I 151-152	—	*VM* I 5-17
2.3	*Str.* I 153,2-3	—	*VM* I 23
2.4	*Str.* I 153,5	—	*VM* I 25
	Str. I 153,5	—	*VM* I 32
2.5	*Str.* I 156,3	—	*VM* I 60
	Str. I 157,1	—	*VM* I 143*
	Str. I 157,1	—	*VM* I 146
2.6	*Str.* I 157,2-4	—	*VM* I 141f.
2.7	*Str.* I 158,1	—	*VM* II 3 ?
2.8	*Str.* I 160,4-5	—	*VM* I 164 ?
2.9	*Str.* I 166,5	—	*VM* II 4* ?
2.10	*Str.* I 167,3	—	*VM* I 162; II 4 ?
2.11	*Str.* I 176,1(2)	—	*VM* II 2; II 46f. ?

2   Individual passages: *Str.* I 150-157 and 158-182

2.1   *Str.* I 150,4-5 - *VM* I 1

I 150,4   "And Numenius, the Pythagorean philosopher, writes explicitly:
for what is Plato but Moses speaking in Attic Greek? This Moses was a
theologian and prophet, *and as some say, an interpreter of sacred laws.*

---

[4] In the first century B. C. Alexander Polyhistor compiled anthologies of the works
of these three writers. Flavius Josephus, Clement and Eusebius have drawn from this
source. Eupolemos is a Hellenized Jewish writer of the second century B. C.; cf. F.
Jacoby, *Die Fragmente der Griechischen Historiker*, 1958, 3 C nr. 723; E. Schürer, *Geschichte
des jüdischen Volkes*, 1901(4), 3, p. 469, 474-477; P. Dalbert, *Die Theologie der hellenistisch-
jüdischen Missionsliteratur unter Ausschluß von Philo und Josephus*, 1954. Artapanos is an Alexandrian Jewish writer of the second century B. C., *Fr. Gr. H.* nr. 726; Schürer 3, p. 477-
480; Dalbert, p. 42-52; N. Walter, Jüdisch-hellenistische Literatur vor Philon von Alexandrien unter Ausschluß der Historiker, in *ANRW* II 20,12, 1987, p. 67-120, Artapanos,
p. 98-99. Ezechiel is an Alexandrian Jewish poet of the second century B. C. ; J.
Wieneke, *Ezechielis Judaei poetae Alexandrini fabulae quae inscribitur Exagoge fragmenta*, 1931;
A. Kappelmacher, *Zur Tragödie der hellenistischen Zeit* (Wiener Studien 44), 1924-25, p. 69-
96; Schürer 3, p. 469f, 500-503; H. Jacobson, *The Exagoge of Ezechiel*, 1983. N. Walter,
Jüdisch-hellenistische Literatur vor Philon von Alexandrien unter Ausschluß der
Historiker, in *ANRW* II 20,12, Ezechielos, p. 107-109. Aristobulos is an Alexandrian
Jewish writer, presumably of the second half of the second century B. C. ; N. Walter,
Der Thoraausleger Aristobulos (TU 86), 1964; Idem, Zur Überlieferung einiger Reste früher
jüdisch-hellenistischer Literatur bei Josephus, Clemens und Euseb, *StPatr.* VII (TU 92),
1966, p. 314-320.

[5] see p. 26.

I 150,5   His family and his deeds and life are reliably related by the Scriptures themselves, but have nevertheless to be stated by us also as briefly as possible."[6]

A direct quotation[7] is formed by the sentence "and as some say, an interpreter of sacred laws." This fragment comes from the very first sentences of Philo's *De Vita Mosis*. The beginning of this retelling of the life of Moses is divided into two parts: "Of Moses, whom *some* describe as a legislator of the Jews, *others* as an interpreter of sacred laws, I purpose to write the life." The division *some,...others* disappears in Clement's text and is preserved in a rudimentary form: *as some say*.

Before Clement goes on to speak of Moses separately, he mentions him as a fixed reference point in his historical tables.[8] The birth year of Moses and the year of the exodus were used to compare greatly divergent chronologies, whose apologetic intent has already been pointed out. Clement here describes Moses by some of his titles: theologian, prophet and interpreter of sacred laws. He will go on to develop the significance of these titles later in *Str.* I 158ff., and we will discuss them in connection with that passage. The only title of Moses that occurs uniquely here is that of theologian. There is another passage in the *Stromateis* where Orpheus is given the same designation.[9] Liddell and Scott, in fact, distinguishes two meanings of the word θεολόγος: a) one who discourses of the gods of poets such as Hesiod and Orpheus, of cosmologists like the Orphics, of diviners and prophets, and b) theologian equals Moses.

In Clement, both meanings are employed. The word comes into common, standardized use in Christian writers only in the fourth century.[10] Even in Philo, from whom the second usage derives, the title appears rarely; only twice the word *theologian* can be found in his works: in one case certainly, in the other probably applied to Moses.[11]

After the quotation from Philo, Clement alludes to the Holy Scriptures where the life of Moses is reliably recorded. That notwithstanding, Cle-

---

6 *Str.* I 150,4: Νουμήνιος δὲ ὁ Πυθαγόρειος φιλόσοφος ἄντικρυς γράφει· "τί γάρ ἐστι Πλάτων ἢ Μωυσῆς ἀττικίζων;" οὗτος ὁ Μωυσῆς θεολόγος καὶ προφήτης, ὡς δέ τινες νόμων ἱερῶν ἑρμηνεὺς ἦν.
5: τὸ γένος αὐτοῦ καὶ τὰς πράξεις καὶ τὸν βίον ἀξιόπιστοι κηρύσσουσαι αὐταὶ αἱ γραφαί, λεκτέον δὲ ὅμως καὶ ἡμῖν ὡς ὅτι μάλιστα <δι' ὀλίγων>.
7 Apart from the various cases required by the grammatical constructions.
8 *Str.* I 79,2; 101,1; 101,5; 102,4; 105,1; 106,2; 109,2; 113,4; 121,4; 124,4; 130,2; 136,3; 142,1; 147,2.
9 *Str.* V 78,4.
10 In Eusebius, Athanasius and Basilius, see Lampe s. v.
11 *VM* II 115; *Praem.* 53, cf. Colson VI, app. 609.

ment finds it worthwhile to recapitulate the facts. The allusion parallels an argumentation in *De Vita Mosis*. Philo, however, gives a clear explanation of why he begins with a biography. His argumentation is essentially an apologetic one; Philo asserts that the laws of Moses are spread over the entire inhabitable world, but that the man himself is scarcely known. Probably troubled by jealousy, learned Greeks refused to honor Moses, who was the greatest and most perfect person in every sense, and wasted their abilities on misguided undertakings. Drawing on written and unwritten sources, Philo retells the life to undo this maliciousness. Fusing both these sources, Philo believes he is giving a more correct picture of Moses's life.[12]

In stressing the venerable age of the law of Moses, Clement is apologetic in a general sense, but he does not take over Philo's apologetic argument here; he does not elaborate the question of why it is necessary to enter into the details of Moses' life, and the ὅμως dangles rather inexplicably.[13]

In conclusion, it can be said that in *Str.* I 150, 4-5 Philo's *De Vita Mosis* is quoted literally and that the use of the terms theologian and prophet is inspired by Philo; the mention of the Scriptures as an essential source for the life of Moses can also be traced back to Philo. The rationale for this material, however, remains in the background and can only be understood by turning to Philo.

2.2   *Str.* I 151-152 - *VM* I 5-17

I 151,1   "*Moses originally of a Chaldean family, was born in Egypt, his ancestors having migrated from Babylon into Egypt because of a protracted famine. Born in the seventh generation and having received a royal education, his story proceeded as follows.*
I 151,2   The Hebrews *having increased* in Egypt *to a large population, and the king of the country, being afraid* of a plot from the horde, *ordered all the female children* born to the Hebrews *to be brought up* (*women being unfit for war*) *but the male to be destroyed*, since he was suspicious of stalwart youth.
I 151,3   But being of noble family, the child was nursed secretly by his parents *for three months*, since natural affection was superior to the monarch's cruelty. But at last, *dreading lest they* should *be destroyed along with* the child, they made a basket of the papyrus of the region, put the child in it and *exposed it on the banks of the marshy river. The child's sister* stood *at a distance and watched what would happen.*

---

[12] *VM* I 1-5.
[13] λεκτέον δὲ ὅμως καὶ ἡμῖν ὡς ὅτι μάλιστα <δι' ὀλίγων> St., <διὰ βραχέων> Wi; cf. A. Méhat, *Étude*, p. 263, note 128. Méhat denies the necessity of Wilamowitz's correction, which has been taken over by Stählin; Méhat considers the sentence as a hidden transitional formula.

I 152,1   Then, *the king's daughter, who for a long time had not been pregnant though she longed for a child, came that particular day to the river for bathing and besprinkling,* and hearing the child cry, *she ordered him to be brought to her and touched with compassion,* asked for a nurse.

I 152,2   At that moment, *the child's sister ran up* and said that if she wished, she could procure as a nurse *a Hebrew woman, who recently had born a child.* And on her consenting and requesting her to do so, *she brought the child's mother* to be nurse *for a stipulated fee, as if she had been some other person.*

I 152,3   Thereupon, the princess *gave* the baby *the name* of *Moses, etymologically, because he had been taken up from the water—for the Egyptians call water 'mou'—in which he had been exposed to die.'*[14]

There can be no doubt that Clement uses Philo very directly in this section. Borrowing is often word for word, and at other times the constructions have changed but the words have the same stem or are cognate. Clement abbreviates Philo's story drastically, but he preserves the sequence of his model. Here and there he takes a word, borrows a whole sentence, or joins scattered sentences, thereby condensing the narrative without being incomprehensible.

Philo, on the other hand, tells the story verbosely and with a great feeling for detail and motivation. In short, he tells a midrash comparable to that of Flavius Josephus in his story of Moses in the *Antiquitates Judaicae.*[15] Typical of this expansiveness are his first chapters, where Philo digresses on the importance of the Nile for agricultural production before moving on to his subject proper.[16] The narrative around Moses's birth is spun out in all sorts of psychological reasonings. When, for instance, the parents begin to become apprehensive about possible betrayal, Philo

---

[14] *Str.* I 151,1-152,3: Μωυσῆς <οὖν> ἄνωθεν τὸ γένος Χαλδαῖος ὢν ἐν Αἰγύπτῳ γεννᾶται, τῶν προγόνων αὐτοῦ διὰ πολυχρόνιον λιμὸν ἐκ Βαβυλῶνος εἰς Αἴγυπτον μεταναστάντων. ἑβδόμῃ γενεᾷ γεννηθεὶς καὶ τραφεὶς βασιλικῶς περιστάσει κέχρηται τοιαύτῃ.

2. εἰς πολυανθρωπίαν ἐπιδεδωκότων ἐν Αἰγύπτῳ τῶν Ἑβραίων δείσας ὁ βασιλεὺς τῆς χώρας τὴν ἐκ τοῦ πλήθους ἐπιβουλὴν τῶν γεννωμένων ἐκ τῶν Ἑβραίων κελεύει τὰ μὲν θήλεα τρέφειν αὐτούς (ἀσθενὲς γὰρ εἰς πόλεμον γυνή), διαφθείρειν δὲ τὰ ἄρρενα εὐαλκῆ νεότητα ὑφορώμενος.

3. εὐπατρίδην δὲ τὸν παῖδα ὄντα τρεῖς ἐφεξῆς κρύπτοντες ἔτρεφον μῆνας οἱ γονεῖς νικῶσης τῆς φυσικῆς εὐνοίας τὴν τυραννικὴν ὠμότητα, δείσαντες δὲ ὕστερον μὴ συναπόλωνται τῷ παιδί, ἐκ βίβλου τῆς ἐπιχωρίου σκεῦός τι ποιησάμενοι τὸν παῖδα ἐνθέμενοι ἐκτιθέασι παρὰ τὰς ὄχθας τοῦ ποταμοῦ ἐλώδους ὄντος, ἐπετήρει δὲ τὸ ἀποβησόμενον ἄπωθεν ἑστῶσα τοῦ παιδὸς ἡ ἀδελφή.

152,1. ἐνταῦθα ἡ θυγάτηρ τοῦ βασιλέως, συχνῷ χρόνῳ μὴ κυΐσκουσα, τέκνων δὲ ἐπιθυμοῦσα, ἐκείνης ἀφικνεῖται τῆς ἡμέρας ἐπὶ τὸν ποταμὸν λουτροῖς καὶ περιρραντηρίοις χρησομένη, ἐπακούσασα δὲ κλαυθμυριζομένου τοῦ παιδὸς κελεύει προσενεχθῆναι αὐτῇ καὶ κατοικτείρασα ἐζήτει τροφόν.

2. ἐνταῦθα προσδραμοῦσα ἡ ἀδελφὴ τοῦ παιδὸς ἔχειν ἔφασκεν Ἑβραίαν γυναῖκα μὴ πρὸ πολλοῦ τετοκυῖαν παραστῆσαι αὐτῇ τροφόν, εἰ βούλοιτο· τῆς δὲ συνθεμένης καὶ δεηθείσης παρήνεγκε τὴν μητέρα τὴν τοῦ παιδὸς τροφὸν ἐσομένην ὥς τινα ἄλλην οὖσαν ἐπὶ ῥητῷ μισθῷ.

3. εἶτα τίθεται τῷ παιδίῳ ὄνομα ἡ βασιλὶς Μωυσῆν ἐτύμως διὰ τὸ ἐξ ὕδατος ἀνελέσθαι αὐτό (τὸ γὰρ ὕδωρ μῶυ ὀνομάζουσιν Αἰγύπτιοι), εἰς ὃ ἐκτέθειται τεθνηξόμενος.

[15] *Antiq. Jud.* II 217ff.

[16] *VM* I 5-6.

enlarges on their feelings of regret and guilt at having kept the child alive.[17] Another example is the state of mind of the princess: having no children and longing for them, particularly for a son, over a long period. Just this particular situation fits in so well with the adoption of the exposed child.[18] Philo seems to develop the whole story as the manifestation of a divine plan.[19] The idea of divine intervention is absent in Clement, but one finds it even more strongly emphasized in Flavius Josephus.[20]

In comparing Clement, Philo and the Septuagint, a certain 'synchronism' between the three seems evident. The parallel is a matter of the content and the course of the narrative rather than a literal one. In Philo, the basket is missing. Clement does not report the child's beauty, the presence of the slaves, or the child's identification as Jewish.[21] In Philo as in Clement, verses one, the end of nine and the beginning of ten of the Septuagint are missing.[22] In conclusion, it seems clear that Clement begins his Moses story in *Str.* I 151,1-2 borrowing exclusively from Philo. Thereafter, from *Str.* I 151,3 on, he continues to make use of the words of Philo but follows the biblical story closely. Scattered sentences from Philo are the means he chooses to fill out the framework supplied by the Bible.

---

[17] *VM* I 11; as a traditional theme, cf. Colson VI, app. 603 par. 11.

[18] *VM* I 13-14.

[19] *VM* I 12, 17: κατὰ θεὸν προμηθούμενον — ἐπινοίᾳ θεοῦ.

[20] *Antiq. Jud.* II 218,219, the promise of God; 219,220, the guarantee, that the promise is true; 221, salvation by God; 222, his divine completeness versus the human weakness; 223, the power of God; 224, God's care; 229, God's prediction.

[21] In Josephus, *Antiq. Jud.* II 226, the issue has a funny overtone, because the Jewish child refuses the breast of a non-Jewish mother.

[22] Ex. 2, 1-10:

		LXX	Clement	Philo
vs.	1	x	—	—
	2	x	x (— ἀστεῖος)	x (+ ἀστειοτέραν)
	3	x	x	x (— basket)
	4	x	x	x
	5	x (ἰδοῦσα)	x (ἐπακούσασα — slaves)	x (θεάσασθαι + slaves)
	6	x	—	x (+ Jewish child)
	7	x	x	x
	8	x	x	x
	9	x	x (— end)	x (— end)
	10	x	x (— beginning)	x (— beginning)

Heinisch's contention that Clement is closer to the text of the LXX seems questionable, Heinisch, *Einfluss*, p. 215.

2.3　*Str.* I 153, 2-3 - *VM* I 23

I 153,2　"Having reached the proper age, he was taught *arithmetic and geometry, rhythm and harmony as well as metrics and music by those who excelled in these arts among the Egyptians, and in addition, philosophy, which is conveyed by symbols, which they point out in hieroglyphics. The rest of the usual course of instruction, Greeks taught* him in Egypt, a royal child as he was, as Philo says in his Life of Moses;

I 153,3　in addition, he learned *the letters and documents of the Assyrians and the knowledge of the heavenly bodies from the Chaldeans and the Egyptians,* whence in the Acts he is said to have been instructed in all the wisdom of the Egyptians."[23]

This borrowing is in great part a reproduction of Philo's text; the sequence and much of the phraseology is the same even though Philo's text is more extensive. It is important to note that Clement refers to Philo explicitly here. There are few other places where Clement mentions him by name.[24] In this case, he acknowledges his debt well into the course of the borrowing.

The differences are a matter of detail; the learned Egyptians are called οἱ λόγιοι by Philo, but οἱ διαπρέποντες by Clement. When Philo comes to speak about Egyptian symbols, he mentions the 'so-called holy texts'. Clement echoes him with his 'hieroglyphs'. At the end of the passage, Clement states that the knowledge of the heavenly bodies derives from the Chaldeans as well as from the Egyptians. Philo only mentions the Chaldeans as experienced in these matters, but one sentence later, he remarks that Moses was taught μαθηματικήν by the Egyptians. Colson translates this as astrology; the French and the German translations as mathematics. In view of the dictionary definition of the word, both translations are acceptable, but Clement seems to confirm Colson's opinion by condensing the two sentences and taking the Chaldeans and Egyptians together.

2.4　*Str.* I 153,5 - *VM* I 25.32

I 153,5　"And moving himself eagerly toward his own origin, *he increased his wisdom, being ardently attached to the culture of his kinsmen and ancestors.*"[25]

---

[23] *Str.* I 153, 2-3: ἐν δὲ ἡλικίᾳ γενόμενος ἀριθμητικήν τε καὶ γεωμετρίαν ῥυθμικήν τε καὶ ἁρμονικὴν ἔτι τε μετρικὴν (ἰατρικὴν L) ἅμα καὶ μουσικὴν παρὰ τοῖς διαπρέπουσιν Αἰγυπτίων ἐδιδάσκετο καὶ προσέτι τὴν διὰ συμβόλων φιλοσοφίαν, ἥν ἐν τοῖς ἱερογλυφικοῖς γράμμασιν ἐπιδείκνυνται. τὴν δὲ ἄλλην ἐγκύκλιον παιδείαν Ἕλληνες ἐδίδασκον ἐν Αἰγύπτῳ, ὡς ἂν βασιλικὸν παιδίον, ᾗ φησι Φίλων ἐν τῷ Μωυσέως βίῳ,
3. προσεμάνθανε δὲ τὰ Ἀσσυρίων γράμματα καὶ τὴν τῶν οὐρανίων ἐπιστήμην παρά τε Χαλδαίων παρά τε Αἰγυπτίων, ὅθεν ἐν ταῖς Πράξεσι "πᾶσαν σοφίαν Αἰγυπτίων πεπαιδεῦσθαι" φέρεται.
[24] *Str.* I 31,1; 72,4; II 100,3.
[25] *Str.* I 153,5: εἰς δὲ τὴν ἀνδρῶν φύσιν ἄξας ἐπέτεινε τὴν φρόνησιν, τὴν συγγενικὴν καὶ προγονικὴν ζηλώσας παιδείαν....

In one sentence two short borrowings are put together. It is significant for Clement's method that he succeeds in fusing these widely-separated fragments into a unit.

The beginning of *Str.* I 153,5, εἰς δὲ τὴν ἀνδρῶν φύσιν, creates a problem which has consequences for the meaning of the sentence as a whole. The text of Stählin proposes ἀνδρῶν based on a conjecture of Hiller. Früchtel suggests αὐτοῦ (L αὐτῶν) in his critical apparatus. Hiller's reconstruction of Clement's text—"grown up to the age of boyhood"—seems defensible by comparison with Philo's—"when he was now passing beyond the term of boyhood."[26] If, however, this sentence of Clement is related to the Menander fragment, as Früchtel suggests, there is a new possibility. The comedy of Menander from which the borrowing could derive deals with a somewhat similar situation; a foundling is adopted and the possibility of his noble origin is discussed.[27] Früchtel's solution seems preferable for a number of reasons. It changes the text less than Hiller's does. It fits well into the narrative context. The verb ἀίσσω, moreover, comes up prevalently in poetic literature.

Between the passages *VM* I 25 and *VM* I 32, which Clement links so ingeniously, Philo digresses on the subject of good sense, temperance and self-control in contrast with unbridled lusts and passions. Moses is presented as a model of one who is able to control and reduce these powerful emotions to mildness. At this point, this material cannot be found in Clement, but later on he touches on it in a different context, and he calls the former virtuous qualities 'royal'.[28] These notions, however, are so commonly accepted that they can hardly be considered as example of immediate influence.

2.5 *Str.* I 156,3-157,1 - *VM* I 60, 143, 146

I 156,3 "He fled from there and *fed sheep, being thus trained beforehand for leadership by leading sheep. For the shepherd's life is a preparation for kingship, for one who is destined to command the tamest flock of men, just as also the chase is a preparation for those who are by nature warlike.* And God brought him from there to be commander of the Hebrews.

I 157,1 Then *the Egyptians,* often obtuse, *were admonished* many times; *the Hebrews, however, became spectators of the calamities which others suffered,* learning without danger the power of God."[29]

---

[26] *VM* I 25: ἤδη δὲ τοὺς ὅρους τῆς παιδικῆς ἡλικίας ὑπερβαίνων....

[27] Menander, *Epitrepontes* 105, 106 (Loeb p. 322, 323). A complicating fact is that in the Menander-fragment ἄξας is corrupt; for the conjecture see F. Leo, *Bemerkungen zu den neuen Bruchstücken Menanders* in *Nachr. Kön. Ges. Wiss. Göttingen, Phil. Hist. Klasse,* Berlin 1907, p. 320.

[28] *Str.* I 159,2f.

[29] *Str.* I 156,3-157,1: φεύγει δὴ ἐντεῦθεν καὶ ποιμαίνει πρόβατα προδιδασκόμενος εἰς

Three different borrowings from Philo can be discovered here. The first is a nearly literal quotation about Moses as a shepherd. The differences between Philo and Clement are minor: a synonym or a different case. Problematic, however, is the form ποιμενιχῇ. Given the close relationship to Philo's text, it might even be an error of transcription. Mangey, however, attaches so much value to Clement's text that he proposed ποιμενιχή in the text of Philo as a conjecture. In this short fragment, four functions of Moses are mentioned again; three of them are borrowed from Philo–the roles of leader, shepherd and king–while Clement himself adds the role of commander.[30]

The second borrowing, in which the Egyptians are summoned, can be a reminiscence of *VM* I 143, since the Septuagint does not make use of the verb νουθετέω. The plagues,[31] about which Philo is quite expansive, are scarcely discussed by Clement; they are touched on only in this sentence.

The third borrowing, which describes the Hebrews as spectators, is literal again except for the a.c.i. construction. Toward the end of the text of Philo there is a gap, which has been filled in by Cohn with Clement's reading. Mangey wants to insert only τοῦτο. Whatever the case may be, Philo goes on to state that the Hebrews learned piety (εὐσέβεια) from the events of which they were witnesses. This detail is missing in Clement; he only speaks about the power of God, which is learned painlessly by the Hebrews. This sentence again presents an example of how ingeniously Clement joins scattered quotes into a continuous sequence.

2.6 *Str.* I 157,2-4 - *VM* I 141f.

I 157,2 " ... and the Hebrews going away thereafter, departed *carrying off much spoil* from the Egyptians *not in avarice as their accusors say* (for God did not persuade them *to covet other people's property*),
I 157,3 *but, first of all,* they took *a just wage for all the time* they had served the Egyptians, and *then* in a way, they *vexed* the Egyptians in return, avaricious as they were, *afflicting* them by removing the booty, as they had afflicted the Hebrews by *enslaving* them.

ἡγεμονίαν ποιμενιχῇ· προγυμνασία γὰρ βασιλείας τῷ μέλλοντι τῆς ἡμερωτάτης τῶν ἀνθρώπων ἐπιστατεῖν ἀγέλης ἡ ποιμενιχὴ καθάπερ καὶ τοῖς πολεμιχοῖς τῇ φύσει ἡ θηρευτική. ἄγει δὲ αὐτὸν ἐντεῦθεν ὁ θεὸς ἐπὶ τὴν τῶν Ἑβραίων στρατηγίαν.
157,1. ἔπειτα νουθετοῦνται μὲν Αἰγύπτιοι πολλάχις οἱ πολλάχις ἀσύνετοι, θεαταὶ δὲ Ἑβραῖοι ἐγίνοντο ὧν ἕτεροι κακῶν ὑπέμενον ἀκινδύνως ἐκμανθάνοντες τὴν δύναμιν τοῦ θεοῦ.

[30] Cf. E. R. Goodenough, The political philosophy of hellenistic Kingship, in *Yale Classical Studies* 1 (1928), p. 55-102, p. 66; in a fragment of Diotogenes, preserved in Stobaeus IV p. 263-270 (Hense) the roles of the king are described in a threefold way as military leader, judge and priest.
[31] *VM* I 94f.

I 157,4 *One should say that this happened either as if in war, claiming under the law of victors their enemies' property*, as the stronger do from the weaker (and the cause of the war was justified; because of famine, the Hebrews came *as suppliants* to the Egyptians, but they, *reducing their guests to slavery*, compelled them to serve *them as captives*, giving them no recompense), *or as if in peace, taking the spoils as wages against the will of those, who for a long period had given them no recompense*, but rather had *robbed them.*"[32]

As a whole, *VM* I 141ff. is apparently present as a source for Clement. Many words are taken over in the same declension or conjugation, but also new forms appear. The order is changed a few times: in line 5, μισθὸν ἀναγκαῖον, and in line 8-13, εἴτε ... εἴτε. Some words are inserted in a different position, as ἀντιλυποῦντες in line 6 and καταδουλευσάμενοι in line 11.

Also the meaning of this last sentence is altered; Philo argues that the Hebrews take the spoils as compensation in spite of the fact that a real compensation is not possible for slavery and torture. Material damage and suffering, as Philo says, are quantities that cannot be compared to one another; they are of different natures. Connected with this, he stresses the idea of the justified and legitimate action of the Hebrews. These arguments do not reappear in Clement in the same form. The passage states baldly that the Hebrews take the spoils as compensation. As has been remarked above, Philo argues with more nuance and with more psychological sense. His observation, for example, that the Hebrews defended themselves not with weapons but with the shield of the Just cannot be found in Clement. The word ἠμύναντο, which had occurred at the end of the passage in Philo, is dropped in the middle of Clement's text (line 6) for no apparent reason.

In contrast with the previous borrowings, this entire passage gives an untidy impression. This may be caused by the alterations of εἴτε ... ἐν πολέμῳ, εἴτε ... ἐν εἰρήνῃ. From the point of view of both narrative technique and content, the passage seems confused.

---

[32] *Str.* I 157,2-4: ὕστερόν τε ἐξιόντες οἱ Ἑβραῖοι πολλὴν λείαν τῶν Αἰγυπτίων ἐκφορήσαντες ἀπῄεσαν, οὐ διὰ φιλοχρηματίαν, ὡς οἱ κατήγοροί φασιν (οὐδὲ γὰρ ἀλλοτρίων αὐτοὺς ἀνέπειθεν ἐπιθυμεῖν ὁ θεός),
3. ἀλλὰ πρῶτον μὲν ὧν παρὰ πάντα τὸν χρόνον ὑπηρέτησαν τοῖς Αἰγυπτίοις μισθὸν ἀναγκαῖον κομιζόμενοι, ἔπειτα δὲ καὶ τρόπον τινὰ ἠμύναντο ἀντιλυποῦντες ὡς φιλαργύρους Αἰγυπτίους τῇ τῆς λείας ἐκφορήσει, καθάπερ ἐκεῖνοι τοὺς Ἑβραίους τῇ καταδουλώσει.
4. εἴτ' οὖν ὡς ἐν πολέμῳ φαίη τις τοῦτο γεγονέναι, τὰ τῶν ἐχθρῶν φέρειν ἠξίουν νόμῳ τῶν κεχρατηκότων ὡς κρείττονες ἡττόνων (καὶ τοῦ πολέμου ἡ αἰτία δικαία· ἱκέται διὰ λιμὸν Ἑβραῖοι ἧκον πρὸς Αἰγυπτίους· οἳ δὲ τοὺς ξένους καταδουλωσάμενοι τρόπον αἰχμαλώτων ὑπηρετεῖν ἠνάγκασαν σφίσι μηδὲ τὸν μισθὸν ἀποδιδόντες), εἴτε ὡς ἐν εἰρήνῃ, μισθὸν ἔλαβον τὴν λείαν παρὰ ἀκόντων τῶν πολὺν χρόνον οὐκ ἀποδιδόντων, ἀλλὰ ἀποστερούντων.

2.7   *Str.* I 158,1 - *VM* II 3 ?

I 158,1 ''Moses then stands before us as a prophet, a legislator, skilled in military tactics and strategy, a politician, a philosopher.''[33]

Only the titles prophet and legislator are paralleled in the passage cited by Stählin. The other titles[34] are either not used by Philo or not used in the same sequence. In other words, this sentence could be compared with any other part of *De Vita Mosis II* since the book is built around the titles legislator, high priest and prophet. The title of high priest is missing altogether in the passage of Clement under discussion here. There is no clear-cut parallel and no evident borrowing in this passage. Clement's text may have been inspired by Philo in a general sense, but the development must be charged to Clement's account.

2.8   *Str.* I 160,4-5 - *VM* I 164 ?

I 160,4 ''Moses, on leading the people forth, suspecting that the Egyptians would pursue, left the short and direct route and turned to the desert and marched mostly by night.
I 160,5 For another purpose was also involved, namely, that the Hebrews were trained by great solitude and protracted time to believe in one God alone, having become accustomed by the wise discipline of endurance.''[35]

In this fragment a description of the journey through the desert is given. There seems to be scarcely any possibility of comparison between the two texts; there are no literal correspondences other than the fact that both authors describe the same events. Philo mentions two reasons for the Hebrews to depart from the most direct route; first, as precaution against meeting resistance and being forced to return, thereby exchanging one slavery for another. This is an argument that can also be found in the Septuagint. Next, Philo calls the journey a test of loyalty for the Hebrews. This idea can be found in Clement as well, but elaborated in a different way; educated by the expedition, the people will be trained and disciplined in their belief in God. As a sequel, both Philo and Clement have the account of the cloud. It might be noted that for the cloud,

---

[33] *Str.* I 158,1: Ἔστιν οὖν ὁ Μωυσῆς ἡμῖν προφητικός, νομοθετικός, τακτικός, στρατηγικός, πολιτικός, φιλόσοφος.

[34] Comparable passages in Clement with series of titles: *Str.* I 168,4; II 19,4 (in Stoic context).

[35] *Str.* I 160,4-5: Μωυσῆς τὸν λαὸν ἐξαγαγὼν ὑποπτεύσας ἐπιδιώξειν τοὺς Αἰγυπτίους τὴν ὀλίγην καὶ σύντομον ἀπολιπὼν ὁδὸν ἐπὶ τὴν ἔρημον ἐτρέπετο καὶ νύκτωρ τὰ πολλὰ τῇ πορείᾳ ἐκέχρητο.
5. ἑτέρα γὰρ ἦν οἰκονομία, καθ' ἣν ἐπαιδεύοντο Ἑβραῖοι δι' ἐρημίας πολλῆς καὶ χρόνου μακροῦ, εἰς μόνον τὸ πιστεύειν τὸν θεὸν εἶναι δι' ὑπομονῆς ἐθιζόμενοι σώφρονος.

Philo has νεφέλη, Clement στῦλος (*Str.* I 161,3), and the Septuagint στῦλος τῆς νεφέλης.

2.9   *Str.* I 166,5 - *VM* II 4 ?

I 166,5   "...in accordance with which, namely, good opinion, some have called law, right reason, which prescribes what is to be done and forbids what is not to be done."[36]

The fragment forms a Stoic commonplace, which occurs in both authors several times. It is hard to decide or to prove what role Philo plays in transmitting such a common expression to Clement.[37]

2.10   *Str.* I 167,3 - *VM* I 162; II 4 ?

I 167,3   "Now Moses, to speak comprehensively, was a living law, governed by the good word."[38]

Stählin refers to two passages in Philo where Moses is called the living law. The term originally seems to have come from Neo-Pythagoreanism and the Stoa of Chrysippos and was taken up by Philo , but it also relates to conceptions in Plato, Aristotle and Scepticism.[39] Philo does not link the concept of the living law uniquely to Moses; in *Abr.*5 he uses it in a more general sense.[40]

---

[36] *Str.* I 166,5: ᾗ τινες ἀκολούθως δηλονότι τῇ χρηστῇ δόξῃ λόγον ὀρθὸν τὸν νόμον ἔφασαν, προστακτικὸν μὲν ὧν ποιητέον, ἀπαγορευτικὸν δὲ ὧν οὐ ποιητέον.

[37] Cf. in Philo: *Praem.* 55; *Migr.* 130; *Deus* 53; *Jos.* 29; in Clement: *Paed.* I 8,3; 65,2; *Str.* II 34,4; III 84,1; Stoic sources: *SVF* III ns. 314-325; 332; Cicero, *De Leg.* I 18; Stobaeus, *Flor.* II 7, 11, (Wachsmuth) I p. 44; Colson VIII, p. 454 par. 55. Heinisch, *Einfluss*, p. 227, asserts without argumentation that Clement takes over this Stoic definition from Philo. Lilla, *Clement*, p. 75, agrees with this and sees Philo as intermediary in the use of ὀρθὸς λόγος. Lilla proceeds from the idea that Clement's definition of nomos is identical with that of Philo because in both authors the Mosaic law is merely a manifestation of the divine logos. A spark of this logos is left in the human mind; in defining φρόνησις Clement resorts to Stoic terms similar to those he used in clarifying nomos. Since φρόνησις is an intellectual activity and reason derives directly from the divine logos, the functioning of φρόνησις can be described by terms usually appropriate to nomos, as Lilla indicates (p. 76, λογισμοῦ γάρ ἐστιν ἐπιστήμη ὧν τε δεῖ ποιεῖν ὧν τε μή). Lilla discovers the same views in Philo and Clement; he points out, however, that similar definitions are available in the works of others (p. 76, esp. note 2). This last argument tends more, in our opinion, to tone down the interdependence of the two authors than to strengthen it. If one wants to prove dependence of Clement on Philo through such common ethical notions, it would be preferable to find more clear-cut points of comparison.

[38] *Str.* I 167,3: .... Μωυσῆς δὲ συνελόντι εἰπεῖν νόμος ἔμψυχος ἦν τῷ χρηστῷ λόγῳ κυβερνώμενος.

[39] Goodenough, Kingship, p. 63ff.

[40] W. Richardson, The Philonic Patriarchs as Nomos Empsychos, *StPatr.* I (TU 63), 1957, p. 512-525. Idem, Nomos Empsychos: Marcion, Clement of Alexandria and St. Luke's Gospel, *StPatr.* VI (TU 81), 1962, p. 191-196.

Clement certainly takes the words as a title of Moses from a Philonic
tradition, but they are not always employed in this sense and with this
derivation. Elsewhere, in *Str.* II 18,4, he puts the words 'living law' in
a Platonic setting, when the Eleatic guest declares a royal and political
man to be a 'living law'. The wording itself, however, is not to be found
in Plato.[41]

2.11   *Str.* I 176,1(2) - *VM* II 2; 46f. ?

> **I 176,1**   ''The Mosaic philosophy is accordingly divided into four parts:
> into the historic part, and that which is strictly called the legislative part,
> which two properly belong to ethics, and the third part, which relates to
> liturgy, belongs to physical science, and, above all,
> **I 176,2**   in the fourth place the theological part, the vision, which Plato
> says belongs to the truly great mysteries, while Aristotle calls this species
> metaphysics.''[42]

In Clement's analysis, Moses's 'philosophy' is divided into four
segments: a historical, a legislative, a liturgical and a theological part.
Stählin makes reference to *VM* II 2, which is concerned with the titles of
Moses; these titles of king, lawgiver, high-priest and prophet, however,
are the basis for the entire second book. One can make the same remark
as in 2.7 that a reminiscence is present in a general sense but that no
special point of reference is to be found and many other Philonic passages
could be cited. Stählin's second reference to *VM* II 46 shows a closer
point of comparison; Philo does make a division of the books of Moses,
but he distinguishes only a historical and a legislative part. Similar divisions can also be found elsewhere. For example in *Praem.* 1-2, he gives
a tripartite division of the words of Moses concerning the creation of the
world, history and legislation.

   In the literature, attention is often called to this passage in Clement.[43]
The problem for the reader is how to interpret the classification because
several schemes seem to be intertwined here. As mentioned above, Clement separates the Mosaic law into four sections, a division that seems
to be inspired by Philo. He substitutes theology for Philo's last category

---

[41] Cf. Stählin on *Str.* II 18,4.

[42] *Str.* I 176,1-2: Ἡ μὲν οὖν κατὰ Μωυσέα φιλοσοφία τετραχῇ τέμνεται, εἴς τε τὸ ἱστορικὸν
καὶ τὸ κυρίως λεγόμενον νομοθετικόν, ἅπερ ἂν εἴη τῆς ἠθικῆς πραγματείας ἴδια, τὸ τρίτον δὲ εἰς
τὸ ἱερουργικόν, ὅ ἐστιν ἤδη τῆς φυσικῆς θεωρίας·
2. καὶ τέταρτον ἐπὶ πᾶσι τὸ θεολογικὸν εἶδος, ἡ ἐποπτεία, ἥν φησιν ὁ Πλάτων τῶν μεγάλων ὄντως
εἶναι μυστηρίων, Ἀριστοτέλης δὲ τὸ εἶδος τοῦτο μετὰ τὰ φυσικὰ καλεῖ.

[43] Heinisch, *Einfluss*, p. 228-229; Den Boer, *Allegorese*, p. 54ff.,135; Camelot, *Foi*, p.
107; Wolfson, *Philosophy*, p. 52-55; De Lubac, *Exégèse médiévale*, I, p. 171-177; Méhat,
Kephalaia, 246ff.; Idem, *Étude*, p. 201; Idem, Clément d'Alexandrie et les sens de
l'Écriture, Ier Stromate 176,1-179,3, in *Epektasis* (mel. J. Daniélou), 1972, p. 355-365.

of prophecy and interrelates the four categories with a tripartite scheme of Platonic origin, which is divided into ethics, physics and dialectics. He connects the historical and the legislative parts with ethics, the liturgical part with physics. The theological part, which he first identifies with spiritual vision, is linked in the following passage with Plato's dialectics and then called true dialectics. He uses the names of Plato and Aristotle to endorse this last unit. Stählin observes that there is no literal borrowing from Plato and that Andronicos should be substituted for Aristotle.

We can visualize the divisions through the following diagram:

Philo	*Clement*	*Platonic*
historical	historical	
legislative	legislative	ethics
liturgical	liturgical	physics
prophetical	theological	dialectics

The first problem connected with this diagram is whether Clement uses a purely formal division, as Den Boer[44] suggests, in which the Mosaic philosophy merely reports historical facts, rules and prescriptions, the practice of sacrifice and spiritual experiences. Others, like Wolfson and Méhat, interpret the divisions as a hermeneutical scheme which is related to a dynamic movement and reflects the idea of progress from literal understanding up to spiritual knowledge.[45] In the latter case, the question arises of how to identify Clement's 'theological' with Philo's 'prophetical' part.

A related problem is the changing terminology of Clement in defining the different senses of Scripture, of which Mondésert says so strikingly: "S'il y a une terminologie compliquée et anarchique, c'est bien celle qui concerne les divers sens possibles de l'Écriture."[46] It is not so difficult to point out general correspondences and resemblances in the relationship between Philo and Clement, but this may do scant justice to Clement's own thought process. The term ἐποπτεία, for example, that has been used in this passage does not occur in Philo. Clement, indeed, appears to be a pioneer in the use of the term in a Jewish and Christian context.[47]

With regard to our comparison it seems safest not to claim too much for this passage or to use it as a basis for elaborate theoretical structures. In the course of his writing and speaking, Clement brings up a variety of schemes and is able to connect them with each other. Clement's

---

[44] Den Boer, *Allegorese*, p. 54-60.

[45] Wolfson, *Philosophy*, p. 56; Méhat, *Étude*, p. 201.

[46] Mondésert, *Clément*, p. 153.

[47] ἐπόπτης is used only once in *Apol. pro Jud.* (Hypothetica. Eus *P. E.* VIII 7,9), cf. *Praem.* 53-56.

scheme in the diagram above has clear Philonic overtones but he also holds on to his own distinctive topics: in this case ἐποπτεία, true dialectics and true philosophy.

3   Evolving methods

From the detailed study of individual passages above, a clearcut difference seems to emerge between the references to Philo in *Str.* I 150-157 and those in *Str.* I 158-182.

3.1   *Str.* I 150-157

In this part we come across extensive, often literal borrowings. It also seems clear that Clement follows the sequence of *De Vita Mosis* scrupulously, as the table on p. 49 makes clear.[48] We could not find noteworthy differences between the two authors. Most of the differences were matters of detail: the substitution of a word, the use of a related word or a synonym, or a change of construction. At times there were paraphrases. In all cases, a drastic abbreviation of the Philonic text could be observed; lesser or (more often) greater parts of the model were left out. It is difficult, however, to draw conclusions from quotations that an author does not make.

Sometimes the omissions have been indicated when they seemed obvious. The next question to be posed is whether the omissions are intentional amputations of inessential or unwanted material or if they are simply a product of the above-mentioned practice of shortening the Philonic text. It seems clear that Clement sets out to reproduce the birth story and the course of Moses's life concisely, for which he leans predominantly on Philo, but because the genre happens to call for an accumulation of sources, Clement tells without hesitation the same story of Moses again with the words of the tragic poet Ezechiel. If one counts all sorts of longer and shorter quotations from and allusions to Scripture in connection with Clement's own thoughts, then one knows why this work is called *Stromateis*: patchwork, indeed!

It is hard to explain why he made this selection from *De Vita Mosis*, why he admitted one detail but not another, why he left out most events and restricted himself to the titles, birth, paideia, ancestry, career as shepherd and a part of the exodus. Apart from the biblical story of the birth, a central element of course which he tells with Philo's words, the further selection seems arbitrary. Some of the options will return in the succeeding

---

[48] With exception of the last fragment, *Str.* I 157,2-4 - *VM* I 141f.

sections, where he dwells at length on the titles. The observation which Mondésert made about Clement's use of the Bible may also apply to these non-biblical borrowings. Mondésert states that when Clement quotes from a single book he gives the impression of unrolling a scroll.[49] In view of the sequential, literal borrowings from Philo, it seems quite evident that Clement had a copy of his work at hand. The state of affairs gives a remarkable opportunity to observe Clement practically in the act of writing.

In summary, it can be said that the distinguishing feature of the passage is a tendency to abbreviate Philo rather drastically while making a somewhat arbitrary choice of material. It is a narrative passage, extended with explanations and embellishments drawn from other sources, which, in view of Clement's own way of thinking, seem to be of no fundamental importance.[50]

3.2   *Str.* I 158-182

In this section, a comparison with Philo necessarily travels along different lines than it had previously, due, as noted above, to the absence of direct borrowings. It is, nevertheless, worthwhile looking at a number of themes that both authors have in common, particularly since this section is so clearly the continuation of the preceding. It is important to note not only the common elements but also the context in which these themes are employed. First, the comparison will be made between *Str.* I 158-165 and *VM* II 1-12, the preface of *De Vita Mosis* II, and then between *Str.* I 165-182 and *VM* II 12-66, the section that deals with Moses as legislator.

a)   *Str.* I 158-165 - *VM* II 1ff.

Starting from the Platonic train of thought[51] that argues that states can make progress only if kings become philosophers or philosophers kings, Philo speaks about Moses as legislator, high priest and prophet. All these functions are united in one and the same person, Moses. He explains this as follows; it is a royal task to command what is right and to forbid what is wrong. It belongs to the law to ordain what has to be done and to forbid what must not be done.

From this it follows that the king is a living law and the law a just king. A king and a legislator pay attention not only to human but also to divine

---

[49] Mondésert, *Clément*, p. 73.
[50] Méhat, *Étude*, p. 201.
[51] Plato, *Rep.* V 473d.

affairs. These matters are the proper concern of the high priest. Prophecy
concludes these functions of Moses because of the numerous matters
human as well as divine that are hidden from and inaccessible to the
human mind. Therefore a harmony of the four functions of king,
legislator, high priest and prophet is necessary, according to Philo.

In his typical fashion, Clement accumulates material, going on to add
several other functions to this list. Moses is not only prophet and
legislator but also strategist, commander and statesman.[52] After a bare
mention of the function of prophecy, Clement promises to speak further
about it in a later section.[53] The function of the high priest is conspicuously missing in this enumeration. If we survey the use of ἀρχιερεύς
in Clement, it appears that this is reserved for Christ or the logos. In one
other passage, the archangels are called by this appellation[54], but it seems
clear that Clement will not make use of the title of high priest for Moses
here.

Clement develops the idea of kingship further. As in Philo, this forms
not only the entry point, but all other functions are also dependent on
it. Several different types of king are distinguished. In a circular reasoning, Clement starts with divine kingship and goes on to characterize
good, mediocre and bad kings; the former have courageous spirits while
the latter are concerned only with their own desires. He connects, this
series of kings, especially the last, with a discussion of the passions and
their control by virtue. It is a royal gift to practice the virtues applying
them with intelligence, wisdom and tact. *The* kingship is reserved for
Christ and the end of the discussion thereby returns to its starting point.

This whole train of thought has little in common with Philo's introduction to his *De Vita Mosis* II. Yet Clement seems to use the Philonic scheme
of titles and functions of Moses as a basis for his ideas. Kingship, from
which all other functions depend, stays explicitly at the beginning, as in
Philo, but it receives an emphatically Christological interpretation. No
compelling point of comparison can be discovered in the following
passage (*Str.* I 160-165), in which Clement discusses Moses as a general
and points out how Greek generals imitated Moses's generalship. The
succeeding passage about pillars of fire (and other pillars), which is
illustrated with many poetical citations, must be charged entirely to Clement's account.

---

[52] see fr. 2. 5.
[53] *Str.* IV 2,2; 93,1; V 88,4.
[54] *Exc.* 27,3; B. Botte, La vie de Moise par Philon, in *Cahiers Sioniens* VIII/2-3-4
(1954), p. 60; Sagnard, *Exc.* (SChr. 23) Append. D, p. 220-223.

b) *Str.* I 165-182 - *VM* II 12-66

Clement's last paragraphs deal with lawgiving. They are thematically comparable with the corresponding part of Philo, in which Moses is described in his function as legislator. Three themes that are important for both writers will be discussed briefly: the role of Moses, the extraordinary and divine character of the law, and the concept of law in relationship to some philosophical currents.

The role of Moses

It may be clear in advance that in dealing with the role of Moses, Philo and Clement will go different ways. Philo dedicates a whole book to the subject, which is turned into the saga of a hero comparable to other ancient characterizations of ideal man.[55] In this connection the idea of a divine character or a messiah comes up. It is hard to say, however, to what degree messianic elements are present in Philo's description of Moses since the theme is not developed explicitly. Various complex questions are related to the messianic issue: the possibility of a divine element in Moses himself,[56] the logos as a personal power and the possibility of identifying Moses and the patriarchs with the logos. Wolfson correctly states that if there is a messianic element, it is connected more with the victory of the Mosaic law in the world than with the person of Moses.[57] Moses is clearly the mediator between God and man in Philo. He is the embodiment of the perfect man to whom the functions of king, legislator and prophet are allotted by divine providence. He forms a perfect model, and although there is no historical justification for some of the functions attributed to him (Moses was neither a king nor a high priest), he is turned into the exemplar of all these roles.

Clement takes over this inventory in part and extends it with the titles just, holy and friend of God.[58] The main difference is that for Clement

---

[55] Botte, loc. cit., mentions Plutarch's *Vitae Parallelae*; Dillon, *Middle Platonists*, gives examples of Neo-Pythagorean writers who could have been used as a model for Philo; see also Goodenough, *Light*, p. 223ff. ; idem, Kingship 64f. ; Bréhier, *Idées*, 18ff. The fragments of Diotogenes, Stenidas and Ecfantes are mentioned by the last scholars. These writings, however, are difficult to date and their relationship to Philo's concept is therefore hard to determine; see Dillon, *Middle Platonists*, p. 154.

[56] Goodenough, *Light*, 223ff., elaborates this question fully; see also H. Leisegang, *Der Heilige Geist*, 1919, p. 145; Bréhier, *Idées*, p. 6; Wolfson, *Philo* II, p. 415; Idem, *Church-fathers*, p. 177; W. A. Meeks, The Divine Agent and His Counterfeit in Philo and the Fourth Gospel, in *Aspects of Religious Propaganda in Judaism and Early Christianity* (ed. E. Schüssler Fiorenza), 1976, p. 43-67, esp. p. 45-49.

[57] Wolfson, *Philo* I, p. 419.

[58] 'Friend of God' is a term that is important in Philo as well as in various philosophical currents, cf. Y. Amir, *Die hellenistische Gestalt des Judentums bei Philon von Alexandrien*, 1983, 211ff.; see also below, chapter VII, p. 181.

Moses is not a unique and exclusive model for them. Clement says that
if we find these qualities in Moses, then we may truly call him wise.[59]
Both writers have in common that the legislative function is not concerned with punishment but with education and rehabilitation.[60] This
task, embodying the law among men and preparing people for virtue, is
connected by Clement with the task of the shepherd, a role previously
attributed to Moses.[61] The real shepherd is the good shepherd, who is the
good legislator of a unique herd. When he speaks about the just law, he
makes a connection with St. Paul's spiritual law, which leads to happiness. He who is the real lawgiver not only announces what is good and
noble, but understands it. The real lawgiver, as Clement concludes, is
the only-begotten Son.[62]

The extraordinary and divine character of the law

In both Philo and Clement, the extraordinary and divine character of the
law of Moses is emphasized; this uniqueness is acknowledged everywhere
by Greeks and non-Greeks alike.[63] There are clear-cut differences in the
views of the two authors. Philo underlines the idea that the law of Moses
is taken over by all nations at the same time that these nations reject each
others laws. In contrast with this 'positive' apologetic position, Clement
takes a negative stance. The law is given by God as κανών or θέσις, but
the Greeks misunderstood the law because of their lack of faith; they do
not recognize the truth. In both writers it is stated that the law has a
divine character. The emphasis in Philo is above all on the unity of
creator and lawgiver. The laws are given in order to live in consonance
with the harmony of the cosmos. Evil and injustice disrupt this universal
harmony. In Philo, the punishments are of cosmological nature like
floods or fire from heaven. In Clement, the divine character of the law
obliges man to be focused on one God and to act in a just way. Although
he mentions the cosmological harmony in this connection, he clearly con-
centrates on another point: looking to God.[64]

The law within a philosophical perspective

Philo and Clement both engage in an implicit dialogue with some of the
philosophical currents of their time, especially with Platonism and

---

[59] *Str.* I 168,4.

[60] *Str.* I 168,2-3; 172,2; *VM* II 50-51.

[61] The role of the shepherd is also connected with the role of the king in Plato, *Politicus*
265d, 268a; Goodenough, Kingship, p. 60ff., 84.

[62] For the relationship between Moses and Christ, see also *Str.* II 21,1.

[63] Wolfson, *Philo* II, p. 192.

[64] *Str.* I 165,2-3: πρὸς ἕνα θεὸν ἀφορᾶν, ... εἰς αὐτὸν ἀφορῶντας.

Stoicism. Philo first describes two kinds of legislator: those who establish what is allowed and what is forbidden and those who found a state according to the logos and fit it out with the appropriate laws. Moses chooses another direction; he does not act by commanding but by stimulating; he considers it beneath the dignity of the law to start with a state built by human hands, therefore he begins with the rise of the greater state, the universe, of which the law is an image. As already noted, the emphasis is placed on universal harmony. People who revolt against the virtues are not only enemies of humanity, but also of heaven and the universe. The punishments are analogous: cosmic punishments which return periodically like water and fire.

In this discussion Clement works in a more diffuse and less clearly defined way. Various disparate terminologies well up in his treatment. The law is called by him χρηστὴ δόξα and ἀληθής; both terms are clear reminiscences of Plato's *Minos*.[65] Some have interpreted this χρηστὴ δόξα as ὀρθὸς λόγος; a stoic vocabulary thereby emerges that had been taken over into Platonism well before Clement's time. Clement's interest is not cosmological, as it had been for Philo, who tried to make a synthesis between the Mosaic account of creation and various philosophical elements. Clement's point of orientation is spiritual vision or contemplation, the θεωρία. This orientation appears once again at the end of this passage when Clement has Moses function as a teacher of Plato in dialectics. For Clement, the aim of true dialectic, which is connected with true philosophy, is to ascend to God: that is to the God of the cosmos and to the knowledge of divine and heavenly affairs. This knowledge leads to real wisdom which is a godly power.

3.3   Final remarks

In viewing the relationship between *Str.* I 151-157 and 158-182 as a whole, a Philonic influence can be traced in both parts but in different forms. In the first part, which is narrative, material is borrowed quite literally from *VM* I. The borrowed material is transferred in highly condensed or reduced form, but its original sequence is respected. In the second part, literal borrowings could not be found, but philosophically tinted commonplaces and classifications could be identified in which a Philonic substratum is recognizable. A few themes from *VM* II, which is based upon the titles and functions of Moses, can also be retraced. The impulse to raise the exegesis of *VM* II to another level, namely, to make it more ethically and philosophically directed in contrast with the nar-

---

[65] Plato, *Minos*, 313c; 314e; 315a.

rative form that is a distinctive feature of *VM* I, is an impulse present in Clement as well.

Clement seems to use Philo in both the first and second part as a blueprint. In the first case he reduces the narrative of *De Vita Mosis* I to some identifiable fragments with the apparent intention of reproducing this 'historical novel' as briefly as possible.[66] In the second part he uses Philo only schematically. In content and development, however, the two writers go different ways. Philo operates within more readily surveyable limits within which all kinds of digressions are possible. Clement borrows some basic ideas, but his thought process tends to snowball; he accumulates more diverse and less tightly related kinds of material, which he takes up, returns to and digests as he encounters it in his criss-crossing path.

---

[66] Arnaldez a. o., *VM* I-II (FE 22), Introduction p. 14ff.

CHAPTER FOUR

THE LAW AND THE VIRTUES

Str. II 78-100

1.1   Introductory remarks

At the beginning of the second book of the *Stromateis*, Clement describes the task that he sets himself, saying that he will discuss faith, knowledge and science, hope and love, repentance and temperance and, above all, the fear of God (*Str.* II 1,1).[1] He places the virtues in a very broad context and he connects them with the opinions of various philosophers on final objectives and the principal good. Méhat points out that this arrangement presents all the traditional themes of ethics grouped in various blocks. For example, our passage (*Str.* II 78-100) is involved with virtues, a succeeding passage is focused on the πάθη (*Str.* II 105-127) and another with final objectives (*Str.* II 127-136).[2] In spite of a certain progression, Clement has not organized his material in as orderly a fashion as this scheme suggests; many digressions lead away from any underlying system. The digressiveness emerges, for example, when Clement anticipates themes that he will deal with more extensively later.

In this passage (*Str.* II 78-100), he repeatedly takes up the πάθη and leaps ahead to teleological questions, as in *Str.* II 80,5 and 97,1; both examples are, as it happens, connected with a borrowing from Philo. All these issues surrounding faith and knowledge or faith and virtues belong to the baggage of a person who is on the way toward true gnosis. As Clement himself points out, the profile of the Gnostic is defined by the exercise of θεωρία, the fulfillment of precepts and the preparation of good men (*Str.* II 46,1). Interconnections constantly erupt into Clement's discussions of individual points. The reader's attention is primarily directed to questions connected with faith and virtues because those issues emerge in all their ramifications in the second part of book two, and it is also there that Clement gives a cursory reading from Philo's *De Virtutibus*.

---

[1] This synopsis is a point of departure that applies to the first part but gives an incomplete view of the contents as a whole; the book is less transparent from a compositional point of view than Clement suggests in these few lines.

[2] Méhat, *Étude*, p. 373, note 172.

Much has been written about the various influences on Clement's ethical conceptions.[3] He is, indeed, able to elaborate his material with impressive erudition, and his descriptions of virtues often go back to pre-existing definitions or catalogues of definitions. These descriptions may be from one of the various philosophical traditions, whether Aristotelian, Chrysippian or otherwise, and there is a tendency in the literature to attach Clement to one of these traditions or influences above all others.

This passage is distinguished by individual descriptions brought together into 'lists of virtues': *Str.* II 78,1; 79,5; 80,1; 80,4-5; 84,5; 86,4; 87,2; 96,4; 97,1. Two of these lists are identified as direct, though fragmentary quotations from Chrysippus:[4] *Str.* II 79,5; 80,4-5. Two others derive via Philo: *Str.* II 84,5; 96,4; the rest may be credited to Clement himself. The identification of sources is only a step in assessing this material; the context must be investigated carefully to determine how these lists function in Clement's own line of thought.

Str. II 78-100 offers a cursory reading from Philo's *De Virtutibus*. The scheme in section 1.2 shows that Clement runs through his source from beginning to end in an orderly way. *De Virtutibus* consists of four separate treatises, which have courage, humanity, repentance and nobility as titles and of which humanity is the longest.[5] Although not originally counted among the virtues, the concept of humanity (φιλανθρωπία) appears to have come into prominence in Platonism and in the Stoa by

---

[3] J. Stelzenberger, *Die Beziehungen der frühchristlichen Sittenlehre zur Ethik der Stoa*, 1933; M. Spanneut, *Le Stoïcisme des Pères de l'église, de Clément de Rome à Clément d'Alexandrie*, 1957; W. Richardson, The basis of ethics: Chrysippus and Clement of Alexandria, in *StPatr.* IX (TU 94), 1966, p. 87-97; O. Prunet, *La morale de Clément d'Alexandrie et le Nouveau Testament* (*XHPhR* LXI), 1966; D. Paulsen, Ethical individualism in Clement of Alexandria, in *CTM* XLIII (1972) p. 3-20; R. Hoffmann, *Die Einheit von Theorie und Praxis bei Klemens von Alexandrien*, 1974; A. M. Ritter, Christentum und Eigentum bei Klemens von Alexandrien auf dem Hintergrund der frühchristlichen Armenfrömmigkeit und der Ethik der kaiserzeitlichen Stoa, in *ZKG* LXXXVI (1975) p. 1-25; D. J. M. Bradley, The transformation of Stoic ethic in Clement of Alexandria, in *Aug.* XIV (1974) p. 41-66; C. J. Classen, Der platonisch-stoische Kanon der Kardinaltugenden bei Philo, Clemens Al. und Origenes, in *Kerygma und Logos* (Festschr. C. Andresen), 1979, p. 68-88; R. Hoffmann, *Geschichte und Praxis, ihre prinzipielle Begründung durch Klemens von Alexandrien; ein Beitrag zum spätaniken Platonismus* (Die Geistesgeschichte und ihre Methode III), 1979; F. R. Gahbauer, Die Erzieherrolle des Logos Christus in der Ethik des Klemens von Alexandrien auf dem Hintergrund der (mittel) Platonismus und stoischen Anthropologie, in *MTZ* 31 (1980), p. 296-305.

[4] Marrou points out that Von Arnim attributes the stoicizing passages in Clement directly to Chrysippus, although there is not always a parallel text as evidence, *Paed.* I (SChr. 70), Introd. p. 50 note 8.

[5] φιλανθρωπία; Colson VIII, p. 194 note *a*, explains that 'humanity' seems the best word to describe the virtue in general but that in a number of cases 'benevolence', 'kindness' or 'charity' would be a better translation.

way of popular ethics. It also gains a certain significance in Hellenistic Jewish writings, in contrast to the New Testament, where the word appears only once (in Tit.3:4). Philo presents one of the earliest surviving efforts to integrate the presumably Hellenistic Greek concept of φιλανθρωπία into a larger context. Φιλανθρωπία is linked to the law in Philo, and it plays a role in his attempt to show that Jewish law and customs are not hostile to creation but congenial to it, an objective that he shares with Flavius Josephus.

It is not certain if Philo originally intended the four components of the treatise to be arranged in this order. In *Virt.* 1, Philo states that he has already discussed 'justice' elsewhere; the interrelationships between his various treatises on virtues is a question that has been discussed extensively but still remains open. By taking the fragments from *De Virtutibus* in this order Clement offers primary evidence for re-establishing Philo's sequence and grouping.[6] Wendland places as much weight on the one manuscript of Clement as he does on the rest of the Philo tradition.

From the point of view of content, Philo offers disconnected precepts from the law of Moses, which he amplifies and enlivens with case histories that illustrate the application of these principles. Rules are presented that not only prescribe proper behaviour toward brothers, foreigners and travellers but also respect toward slaves, animals and plants. The four virtues, courage, humanity, repentance and nobility form a convenient series of pegs on which he can hang various rules from Mosaic Law. Of decisive importance for the overall orientation of the four treatises are the passages from the Bible on which he draws and which he reproduces in his own words.

Clement's selection of material from *De Virtutibus* displays clear and consistent standards. The selection as a whole and the motivation for the continuous and progressive readings from *De Virtutibus* have to do with his vision of the law and his conception of God, and they are strongly propelled by a polemic directed specifically against Marcion. These issues will be dealt with further in the succeeding sections.

1.2   Schematic overview[7]

2.1	*Str.* II 78,2-3	—	*Virt.* 34-35
2.2	*Str.* II 80,5-81,2	—	*Virt.* 8-9
2.3	*Str.* II 81,3-4	—	*Virt.* 18-20
2.4	*Str.* II 82,1-83,1	—	*Virt.* 28-31

[6] Wendland, Philo und Clemens, p. 443ff.; Colson VIII, p. XII.
[7] see p. 26.

2.5	*Str.* II 83,3-84,1	—	*Virt.* (34)41.45
2.6	*Str.* II 84,4-5	—	*Virt.* 82-85
2.7	*Str.* II 85,1	—	*Virt.* 88
2.8	*Str.* II 85,2	—	*Virt.* 89
2.9	*Str.* II 85,3-86,2	—	*Virt.* 90-91
2.10	*Str.* II 86,3	—	*Virt.* 95f.
2.11	*Str.* II 86,5-86,6	—	*Virt.* 97.99.100
2.12	*Str.* II 87,3	—	*Virt.* 96
2.13	*Str.* II 88,1	—	*Virt.* 103
2.14	*Str.* II 88,2	—	*Virt.* 106
2.15	*Str.* II 88,3	—	*Virt.* 109
	Str. II 88,4-89,2	—	*Virt.* 110-115
2.16	*Str.* II 90,1-3	—	*Virt.* 116-119
2.17	*Str.* II 91,3	—	*Virt.* 122-124
2.18	*Str.* II 92,1	—	*Virt.* 126
	Str. II 92,2	—	*Virt.* 129
	Str. II 92,3-93,1	—	*Virt.* 131-133
2.19	*Str.* II 93,2-4	—	*Virt.* 134-140
	Str. II 94,1-2	—	*Virt.* 142-143
2.20	*Str.* II 94,3-5	—	*Virt.* 145-147
2.21	*Str.* II 95,1	—	*Virt.* 148-149
2.22	*Str.* II 95,1	—	*Virt.* 150
	Str. II 95,2-3	—	*Virt.* 156-159
2.23	*Str.* II 96,3-97,1	—	*Virt.* 165-168
2.24	*Str.* II 97,2	—	*Virt.* 168-172
2.25	*Str.* II 97,3-98,2	—	*Virt.* 183-185
2.26	*Str.* II 98,3-99,2	—	*Virt.* 201-210
2.27	*Str.* II 99,3	—	*Virt.* 211-219 ?
2.28	*Str.* II 100,2	—	*Virt.* 215-217

2   Individual passages[8]

2.1   *Str.* II 78,2-3 - *Virt.* 34-35

II 78,1   "It is then clear also that all the other virtues described in Moses supplied the Greeks with the starting point of their moral system; I mean courage and temperance and prudence and justice and endurance and patience and dignity and self-restraint; and over and above them, piety.

II 78,2   With reference to piety, it is clear to every one that it teaches *to worship and honor the highest and oldest cause*;

II 78,3   and the law itself puts justice and wisdom into the mind in an educative process, by abstinence from sensible idols and *attachment to the creator and father of the universe; from this notion as from a spring*, all intelligence increases."[9]

---

[8] The division of the various passages is made on the basis of Philo's *Virt.* , cf. Cohn I, p. LXXXIII. Méhat prefers a division based on the *Stromateis*, and he therefore distinguishes more individual passages, *Étude*, p. 238.

[9] *Str.* II 78, 1-3: Προφανεῖς μὲν οὖν καὶ πᾶσαι <αἱ> ἄλλαι ἀρεταί, αἱ παρὰ τῷ Μωυσεῖ ἀναγεγραμμέναι, ἀρχὴν Ἕλλησι παντὸς τοῦ ἠθικοῦ τόπου παρασχόμεναι, ἀνδρείαν λέγω καὶ σωφροσύνην καὶ φρόνησιν καὶ δικαιοσύνην καρτερίαν τε καὶ ὑπομονὴν καὶ τὴν σεμνότητα καὶ ἐγκράτειαν τήν τε ἐπὶ τούτοις εὐσέβειαν.
2. ἀλλ' ἡ μὲν εὐσέβεια παντί που δήλη τὸ ἀνωτάτω καὶ πρεσβύτατον αἴτιον σέβειν καὶ τιμᾶν [καὶ] διδάσκουσα.
3. καὶ δικαιοσύνην δὲ αὐτὸς ὁ νόμος παρίστησι παιδεύων τήν τε φρόνησιν διὰ τῆς τῶν αἰσθητῶν εἰδώλων ἀποχῆς καὶ τῆς πρὸς τὸν ποιητὴν καὶ πατέρα τῶν ὅλων προσκληρώσεως, ἀφ' ἧς δόξης οἷον πηγῆς πᾶσα σύνεσις αὔξεται.

Philo's first treatise within *De Virtutibus* deals with courage. He discusses the form of courage that is manifest in combat, and he declares that death is preferable to life without honor. In this connection he narrates the story of the Midianite women who seduced the Hebrews. As cause of the conflict between the Midianites and the Hebrews, Philo names the belief of the latter in the unique God. For strategic reasons, namely to disrupt the unity of their belief, the women were sent to ensnare the Hebrew men. Scriptural source: Num. 25:1-18; 31:1-12; cf. *VM* I 295-311.[10]

Clement points out in *Str.* II 78,1 that the virtues of the Greeks are dependent on the law of Moses. In the list of virtues he offers at this point, he names courage, temperance, prudence and justice, the four cardinal virtues, and he adds to them endurance, patience, dignity, self-restraint and piety toward God, a virtue on which he places special emphasis.[11] As a closer circumscription of the veneration due to God, Clement borrows from Philo the idea that piety teaches the worship and the honor of the highest and oldest cause. The law not only promotes piety but also educates in justice and prudence by abstaining from sensible idols and adhering to the creator and father of the universe.[12] This is again a borrowing from Philo, just as is the following words that "from this notion as from a spring" all intelligence increases.

Clement weaves scraps of Philo's text through his own theme in a paraphrase studded with literal components. We could characterize this, at best, as a cut and paste technique. At times it leads to strange results, as in the case of ἀφ'ἧς δόξης (p.154 line 5). Philo uses δόξα as 'honor of' the one God through which the Hebrews are united with an indissoluble bond. In Clement's version, the word is used in the less pregnant sense of 'notion' or 'opinion'. Clement connects δόξα not only with God, as did Philo, but even with the rest of his previous sentence (which points out that the law educates in justice and wisdom by abstaining from sensible idols and adhering to God). The borrowed image of δόξα as a spring has much less point in this new context.

Clement here is primarily interested in giving a description of God in Philo's words, but he does so in the framework of his own theses that the Greeks are dependent on the law of Moses and that the law educates in virtue. The context and the point of Philo's story of the Midianite women

---

[10] Cf. Colson VIII, p. 184a; p. 443 par. 34.
[11] Völker, *Wahre Gnostiker*, p. 298, note 3.
[12] προσκληρώσεως (based on Philo) Potter/Stählin; προσκλήσεως L; προσκλίσεως Sylburg; cf. Lazzati, *Introduzione*, p. 80.

is eliminated by Clement. Later he will again touch on the story as he re-encounters it in the course of his progression through Philo. Clement stresses the idea that it is the law itself that inculcates justice. The concept of justice also forms the connecting link to the quotations from Proverbs that follow this borrowing from Philo. This emphasis on justice is related to Clement's intention of demonstrating to his adversaries that the law is just and good and that the Scriptures as a whole form an integral manifestation of virtue.

2.2 *Str.* II 80,5-81,2 - *Virt.* 8.9

> **II 80,5** "...we are prepared for conduct of life that follows God consistently, *becoming like* the Lord as far as possible for us, mortal in nature as we are.
> **II 81,1** And this is being just and holy with prudence; *for the divinity needs nothing* and suffers nothing; and for this reason it is not, strictly speaking, self-restraint; for it is never subject to emotion, over which it has to exercise control, while our nature, being full of emotion needs self-control; thereby disciplining itself to need nothing, it tries according to its condition to approximate the divine nature.
> **II 81,2** *For the good man, who has few needs, stands at the boundary between immortal and mortal nature; he has wants because of his body* and his birth itself but is taught by rational self-control to have few needs."[13]

This borrowing from Philo stems from an earlier part of *De Virtutibus* than the previous fragment. Philo begins his treatise about courage with the statement that true courage is knowledge or wisdom (*Virt.* 1.5.8). There are many circumstances that demand courage: especially poverty or sickness. Sickness can be overcome by being contented with what nature offers, but higher wealth is bestowed by wisdom. Virtues free the soul from an inclination toward extravagance and engender in it a desire for assimilation to God. The difference between God and man is that God has no wants and is all-sufficient in himself. Man always longs for something more, but the man of worth has few wants, and he stands between mortality and immortality. Because of his mortal body, he has wants, but because of the virtue of his soul, which desires immortality, he can be satisfied with little.

---

[13] *Str.* II 80,5-81,2: τὴν ἑπομένην ἀκολούθως τῷ θεῷ πρᾶξιν στελλόμεθα, ἐξομοιούμενοι τῷ κυρίῳ κατὰ τὸ δυνατὸν ἡμῖν, ἐπικήροις τὴν φύσιν ὑπάρχουσιν.
81,1: τοῦτο δέ ἐστι 'δίκαιον καὶ ὅσιον μετὰ φρονήσεως γενέσθαι'. ἀνενδεὲς μὲν γὰρ τὸ θεῖον καὶ ἀπαθές, ὅθεν οὐδὲ ἐγκρατὲς κυρίως· οὐ γὰρ ὑποπίπτει πάθει ποτέ, ἵνα καὶ κρατήσῃ τοῦδε· ἡ δὲ ἡμετέρα φύσις ἐμπαθὴς οὖσα ἐγκρατείας δεῖται, δι' ἧς πρὸς τὸ ὀλιγοδεὲς συνασκουμένη συνεγγίζειν πειρᾶται κατὰ διάθεσιν τῇ θείᾳ φύσει.
81,2: ὁ γὰρ σπουδαῖος ὀλιγοδεής, ἀθανάτου καὶ θνητῆς φύσεως μεθόριος, τὸ μὲν ἐνδεὲς διά τε τὸ σῶμα διά τε τὴν γένεσιν αὐτὴν ἔχων, ὀλίγων δὲ διὰ τὴν λογικὴν ἐγκράτειαν δεῖσθαι δεδιδαγμένος.

Clement also discusses the difference between divinity and humanity and the role of the virtues in this connection. He particularly stresses the importance of self-restraint (ἐγκράτεια), which can curb emotions (πάθη). Divinity needs nothing (ἀνενδεές) according to Philo and is without emotion (ἀπαθές), as Clement himself adds, so that God, unlike man, never has to exercise self-control. By training man tries to come close to the divine nature within the limitations of his human condition.[14] Clement uses several terms to express the idea of homoiosis; he connects it here not with God, as Philo does, but with the Lord. As synonyms of ἐξομοιούμενος, we find μιμητικός (line 9) and ἑπόμενος (line 10); he also uses συνεγγίζω (line 16). As in Philo, the man who takes the consequences of this imitation seriously stands between immortality and mortality; because of his body and his created being itself he has needs, but by rational self-control he is taught to want little.

This reference consists of a paraphrase with literal components. Clement has changed some prefixes; ἀνεπιδεής becomes ἀνενδεής in line 13, and ἐπιδεής becomes ἐνδεής in line 18. Both Philo and Clement describe the difference between God and man, and the possibility for man to assimilate himself to God; yet it is notable that Clement replaces θεός with κύριος.[15]

A striking change turns up between the two authors. In Philo the soul desires immortality overtly while it is placed midway between mortality and immortality–a distinction with strong Platonic overtones. Clement takes over this distinction but is much more cautious in developing the idea of longing for immortality. When he says (with Philo) that man has wants because of his body, he alters the sentence by saying (unlike Philo) that man is, however, taught by rational self-control to want few things. The conception of the soul that desires immortality is entirely left out by Clement, and its place is taken by the theme of self-control and domination of emotions.[16] In addition, the words κατὰ τὸ δυνατὸν (line 11) show how carefully Clement touches on the concept of homoiosis. He says that, ''as far as possible for us'', we assimilate ourselves to the Lord, and he adds the further qualification, ''mortal in nature as we are''. The

---

[14] Méhat, *Étude*, p. 265, points out that this is an anticipation, as in *Str.* II 97,1 and II 100,3. The passage proper follows in *Str.* II 127-136; see also Marrou, *Paed.* I (SChr. 70), Introd. p. 37.

[15] Cf. Völker, *Wahre Gnostiker*, p. 288 note 2, who calls the attention to this shift and the related idea of following Christ.

[16] Völker, *Wahre Gnostiker*, p. 592; *La Tradizione dell'Enkrateia; motivazioni ontologiche e protologiche*; Atti del Congresso Internazionale Milano, 20-23 aprile 1982, pubblicati a cura di U. Bianchi, 1985.

restriction "as far as possible" (κατὰ τὸ δυνατὸν) derives from an important text of Plato that lies behind Clement's treatment here (*Theaet.*
176ab).

In this passage Clement plays on a pre-existing terminology and conceptual structure broader than that provided by Philo alone.[17] The
Platonic concept of homoiosis, which is offered, among others, by Philo,
is nuanced by the use of various synonyms and is limited by clear restrictions. Unlike Philo, he combines homoiosis with the Stoical concept of
the ἀπάθεια of God and stresses the human subjection to the πάθη.[18]

2.3 *Str.* II 81,3-4 - *Virt.* 18.20

> **II 81,3** "For what reason is there in the law's *prohibiting a man from wear-
> ing woman's clothing*? Is it not that it would have us to be manly, and not
> to be effeminate neither in person and actions, nor in thought and word?
> **II 81,4** For it would have the man who devotes himself to *truth to be
> masculine* both in acts of endurance and patience in life, conduct, word and
> discipline *by day and by night* even if the necessity overtook him of testimony
> by shedding his blood."[19]

As first of the sets of rules around which Philo has arranged his treatise
on courage, he speaks of the precepts governing clothing. He states that
the law desires to train the soul in courage[20] so much that it lays down
rules even about the kind of clothing to be worn. It severely forbids men
to wear women's clothes in accordance with nature, which makes it
obvious even in their outlines how different men and women are. The
'real' man is supposed to maintain masculinity in his clothes, which he
wears by day and by night, and he is not allowed to suggest anything
unmanly. Philo gives prescriptions for women in the same way, warning
again against commingling the attributes and behaviour of the sexes.
Scriptural source: Deut. 22:5.

---

[17] Völker, *Wahre Gnostiker*, p. 592 note 4; Méhat, *Étude*, p. 374ff.; Marrou, *Paed.* I
(SChr. 70), Introd. p. 41.

[18] ἀνενδεής of God: Clement *Str.* II 28,2; V 68,2; VII 14,5; *Quis dives* 27,5; Irenaeus
Adv. Haer. IV 14,1; *Od. Sal.* IV 9, Charlesworth p. 22; ἀπαθής of God: Clement *Str.* II
40,2; 72,2; IV 151,1; VI 73,6; 137,4; *Ecl.* 52,2; Spanneut, *Stoïcisme*, p. 248ff.; Völker,
Wahre Gnostiker, p. 183ff.; T. Rüther, *Die sittliche Forderung der Apatheia in den beiden ersten
Christlichen Jahrhunderten und bei Klemens von Alexandrien*, 1949.

[19] *Str.* II 81,3-4: ἐπεὶ τίνα λόγον ἔχει τὸ ἀπειπεῖν τὸν νόμον ἀνδρὶ γυναικὸς ἀμπεχόνην
ἀναλαμβάνειν; ἢ οὐχὶ ἀνδρεΐζεσθαι ἡμᾶς βούλεται μήτε κατὰ τὸ σῶμα καὶ τὰ ἔργα μήτε κατὰ
τὴν διάνοιαν καὶ τὸν λόγον ἐκθηλυνομένους;
81,4: ἡρρενῶσθαι γὰρ τὸν ἀληθείᾳ σχολάζοντα ἔν τε ὑπομοναῖς ἔν τε καρτερίαις κἂν τῷ βίῳ κἂν
τῷ τρόπῳ κἂν τῷ λόγῳ κἂν τῇ ἀσκήσει νύκτωρ τε καὶ μεθ' ἡμέραν καί, εἴ που μαρτυρίου δι'
αἵματος χωροῦντος ἐπικαταλάβοι χρεία, βούλεται.

[20] ἀνδρεία: both virility and courage.

In Clement the transition between this and the preceding sections is very abrupt and illogical, but the organization and meaning become somewhat clearer when the Philonic background is understood. Clement introduces the borrowing on clothing with a question about the sense of the prescription (ἐπεὶ τίνα λόγον ἔχει), as if he is opening a discussion with his source or his audience.[21] He adapts the passage on manly behaviour to the present by introducing ἡμᾶς and he varies Philo's ἠρρενῶσθαι with his own ἀνδρεΐζεσθαι.

He explains that someone who behaves in a masculine way is someone who devotes himself to the truth with an endurance and patience that can be sustained to the extreme of martyrdom. Various virtues are intertwined here, and Méhat has observed a method in this process, which he calls assimilation.[22] It seems more likely, however, that ἀνδρεία is not the link concept to martyrdom, as Méhat maintained, but rather that ἀνδρεία is assimilated to ὑπομονή and καρτερία. The last two concepts evoke martyrdom quite regularly in Clement, as in *Str.* II 103,1f.; IV 19,3f.; IV 78,2f.; IV 79,2; IV 104,1.

Technically, Clement has taken over two halves of disconnected sentences from Philo's discussion, in which the second fragment is curiously distorted. Philo states that a 'true' man has to behave in a manly fashion (ἠρρενῶσθαι γὰρ τόν γε πρὸς ἀλήθειαν ἄνδρα). Clement adapts this to read that the man who devotes himself to 'truth' behaves in a manly fashion (ἠρρενῶσθαι γὰρ τὸν ἀληθείᾳ σχολάζοντα).[23]

The refocusing underlines a general difference between the two writers in treating this material. Although Philo apparently presupposes in *Virt.* 18 that these disconnected rules were given to train the human soul and implicitly applies them to the soul, on the overt level he works differently, describing concrete situations more than he does in his other writings.[24] Allegory is excluded in these treatises, quite in contrast to his usual approach. Clement on the contrary, rises almost immediately to a different level of meaning, as we see quite clearly in his adaptation of this and many of the following regulations from the Old Testament.

Another difference of outlook is revealed in Philo's statement that the rules of the law are given according to nature; in Clement, we do not find this specific interest.

---

[21] see 3. 1, p. 110.
[22] Méhat, *Étude*, p. 362 note 97; Völker, *Wahre Gnostiker*, p. 470 note 5.
[23] Völker, *Wahre Gnostiker*, p. 472.
[24] Colson VIII, p. XVIII; Arnaldez, Delobre a. o. , *Virt.* (FE 26), p. 11.

2.4   *Str.* II 82,1-83,1 - *Virt.* 28-31

> **II 82,1**   "Again it (scripture) *says, 'if any one who has newly built a house and has not previously inhabited it, or cultivated a newly-planted vine and not yet partaken of the fruit, or is engaged to a girl and has not yet married her'*, the humane law orders that they *be relieved from military service*;
>
> **II 82,2**   for military reasons in the *first* place, lest, bent on their desires, we turn out sluggish in war; for they *encounter perils more boldly* if they are free *in their impulses*;
>
> **II 82,3**   and in the *second* place, *for motives of humanity, since, in view of the uncertainties of war*, the law reckoned it not right *that one should not enjoy* his own labours, and *another should, without incurring fatigue, receive what belonged to those who had laboured.*
>
> **II 83,1**   The law seems also to point out manliness of soul, *by enacting that he who planted should reap the fruit, and he who built should inhabit, and he who was engaged should marry; for it does not provide vain hopes* for those who train themselves to live according to the Gnostic word."[25]

After the prescriptions on clothing, Philo starts a new subject in *Virt.* 22: courage in wartime. After a description of cowardice, he goes on in *Virt.* 28 to discuss the exemptions from military service detailed in Deut. 20. Philo shows the humanity of the law with these three regulations: the exemptions for those who have just built a house, planted a vineyard or gotten married. He distinguishes two reasons for the exemptions. One (*a*) is that the issues of war are uncertain and that people should enjoy the fruits of their own labor. Another (*b*) is the interaction between body and soul; if the body fights, the soul must not be hanging back; both must be present and without distraction (cf. *Virt.* 27 and 32). Without an interval for enjoyment, the situation would be disturbingly tantalizing for the warrior. Scriptural sources: Deut. 20:5-7; cf. *Agr.* 148ff.

Clement moves on to the exemptions of Deuteronomy, signalling his change of topic with the transitional word πάλιν. To illustrate the humanity of the law, he also gives two reasons. The first (*b* in Philo), is strategic; people distracted by their desires serve in war unwillingly. He adds in Philo's words that those who have to confront perils without

---

[25] *Str.* II 82,1-83,1: πάλιν εἴ τις, φησί, νεωστὶ δειμάμενος οἰκίαν οὐκ ἔφθη εἰσοικίσασθαι, ἢ ἀμπελῶνα νεόφυτον ἐργασάμενος μηδέπω τοῦ καρποῦ μετείληφεν, ἢ παρθένον ἐγγυησάμενος οὐδέπω ἔγημεν, τούτους ἀφεῖσθαι τῆς στρατείας ὁ φιλάνθρωπος κελεύει νόμος,

82,2: στρατηγικῶς μέν, ὡς μὴ περισπώμενοι πρὸς τὰς ἐπιθυμίας ἀπρόθυμοι τῷ πολέμῳ ἐξυπηρετῶμεν (ἐλεύθεροι γὰρ τὰς ὁρμὰς οἱ ἀπροφασίστως τοῖς δεινοῖς ἐπαποδυόμενοι),

82,3: φιλανθρώπως δέ, ἐπειδὴ τὰ κατὰ τοὺς πολέμους ἄδηλα, ἄδικον εἶναι λογισάμενος τὸν μὲν μὴ ὄνασθαι τῶν αὐτοῦ πόνων, ἕτερον δὲ τὰ τῶν καμόντων ἀταλαιπώρως λαβεῖν.

83,1: ἔοικεν δὲ ὁ νόμος καὶ τὴν τῆς ψυχῆς ἐμφαίνειν ἀνδρείαν, δεῖν νομοθετῶν τὸν φυτεύσαντα καρποῦσθαι καὶ τὸν οἰκοδομησάμενον οἰκεῖν καὶ τὸν μνώμενον γαμεῖν, οὐ γὰρ ἀτελεῖς τὰς ἐλπίδας τοῖς ἀσκήσασι κατὰ τὸν λόγον τὸν γνωστικὸν κατασκευάζει·

hesitation must be free in their impulses. The second (*a* in Philo) is humanitarian; the uncertainty of battle might deprive hard-working men of the fruits of their labors. Clement adds that the law seems to indicate the manliness of the soul because it does not let the expectations go unfulfilled of those who train themselves according to the Gnostic teaching. The starting point of this thought comes from Philo, but Clement transforms it by introducing the issue of Gnostic teaching.

Clement gives a paraphrase with literal elements in which Philo's text is greatly compressed. As in the previous fragment, he gives his own explanation of what the law presents about the manliness of the soul. He adapts this to the expectation of the Gnostic. Because of an uncertainty in the manuscripts of Philo in *Virt.* 28 (all texts have φιλανθρωπίαν ὁμοῦ, except A, which offers φιλανθρώπως ὁμοῦ) Cohn, following Wendland, opts for the conjecture φιλανθρώπως ὁμοῦ <καὶ στρατηγικῶς> on the grounds of Clement's reading.[26] Colson thinks that this conjecture is based on a misunderstanding, a position that he supports with various arguments.[27]

From a close analysis of Clement's text, it is possible to reinforce Colson's point of view. Clement has articulated Philo's ἕνεκα δυοῖν by characterizing them as στρατηγικῶς μέν and φιλανθρώπως δέ then going on in a close approximation of Philo's words. The sequence of Philo's arguments (*a* and *b*) has been reversed. The reproduction of *b* is strongly abbreviated, while *a* (*Virt.* 29) remains highly recognizable. An inversion of arguments in a borrowing from Philo occurred also in *Str.* I 157,2-4.[28] For that reason it seems reasonable to follow Colson in attaching Philo's φιλανθρωπία νόμου to Clement's adaptation in *Str.* II 82,2: ὁ φιλάνθρωπος κελεύει νόμος.

2.5 *Str.* II 83,3-84,1 - *Virt.* (34f.) 41.45

> **II 83,3** "But I ask you? Did not the women of the Midianites by their beauty seduce the Hebrews who made war against them from prudence into godlessness *through incontinence?*
>
> **II 83,4** For having taken them as friends, they seduced them from a respectable mode of life into meretricious pleasures, and they made them insane to the point of idol sacrifices as well as foreign women; and overcome by women and by pleasure at the same time, they fell away from God and from the law, and the whole people was within a little of falling under the power of the enemy through female stratagem, until *fear by its admonitions pulled back those who were in danger.*

---

[26] Wendland, Philo und Clemens, p. 445.
[27] Colson VIII, p. 178 note 2, app. p. 442 par. 28.
[28] see p. 56f.

84,1   Then the survivors, *valiantly undertaking the struggle for piety*, began to dominate their adversaries.''[29]

After the regulations governing exemptions in war, Philo tells the story of the Midianite women; both are purportedly employed to support his position that body and soul have to be in good condition to take part in combat (*Virt.* 32). In Philo's extended narrative, the honor that the Hebrews render God (*Virt.* 34-35: see also fr.2.1) and the fact that God is their ally (*Virt.* 45-47) are given great emphasis.

The women are involved in the war for the strategic purpose of dissolving Hebrew unity, created by a common love of God; the tactic was seduction, to which the women were incited in a rousing adress. Elaborate rhetorical arguments are presented by Philo; the apparent prostitution involved could be justified since the souls of the female warriors would remain virgin, and the Midianite men, who feared a gruesome defeat, held out hope of a glorious female victory without bloodshed.

Philo is here at his best as a story-teller; he enriches the tale with rhetorical and psychological dimensions in a way that is comparable to his treatment of the birth and youth of Moses in *De Vita Mosis*.[30] Scriptural sources: Num. 25:1-18; 31:1-12; cf. *VM* I 295-311.

In Clement, the change of subject is abrupt; the transition is formed by the words τί δέ; He summarily states that the Midianite women distracted the Hebrews from their prudence and discipline so that they turned away from both God and the law and ran the risk of being totally lost. Fear, however, pulled them back from the brink of disaster. As reinforcement, Clement adds two quotations from Proverbs;[31] the association is made by two words θεοσέβεια and φόβος, which correspond to εὐσέβεια and φόβος in the borrowing from Philo.

In his own words, Clement gives a highly abbreviated summary of Philo's reworking of the story. He concludes the borrowing with two half sentences that are quoted almost literally; he alters only the tense of κινδυνεύω and changes φόβῳ to φόβος. In Philo, it is God who conducts the

---

[29] *Str.* II 83,3-4: τί δέ; οὐχὶ αἱ Μαδιηναίων γυναῖκες τῷ κάλλει τῷ σφῶν πολεμοῦντας τοὺς Ἑβραίους ἐκ σωφροσύνης δι' ἀκρασίαν εἰς ἀθεότητα ὑπηγάγοντο;
83,4: προσεταιρισάμεναι γὰρ < αὖ >τοὺς ἐκ τῆς σεμνῆς ἀσκήσεως εἰς ἡδονὰς ἑταιρικὰς τῷ κάλλει δελεάσασαι ἐπί τε τὰς τῶν εἰδώλων θυσίας ἐπί τε τὰς ἀλλοδαπὰς ἐξέμηναν γυναῖκας· . γυναικῶν δὲ ἅμα καὶ ἡδονῆς ἡττηθέντες ἀπέστησαν μὲν τοῦ θεοῦ, ἀπέστησαν δὲ καὶ τοῦ νόμου, καὶ μικροῦ δεῖν ὁ πᾶς λεὼς ὑποχείριος τοῖς πολεμίοις γυναικείῳ στρατηγήματι ἐγεγόνει, ἕως αὐτοὺς κινδυνεύοντας ἀνεχαίτισε νουθετήσας φόβος.
84,1: αὐτίκα οἱ περιλειφθέντες φιλοκινδύνως τὸν ὑπὲρ εὐσεβείας ἀγῶνα ἀράμενοι κύριοι κατέστησαν τῶν πολεμίων.
[30] see p. 51ff.
[31] Prov. 9:10; 19:23.

saving action (*Virt.* 40,41,45-50), but using φόβος as subject, Clement has the Hebrews themselves gain mastery over their enemies. In the sequel a motive for Clement's change emerges; he states polemically that people who suppose that the law produces fear are not able to understand the law and have in reality failed to comprehend it (*Str.* II 84,2). This statement is connected with Clement's conviction that the fear of God has a positive effect, a position that is developed more extensively in *Str.* II 32-40.[32]

2.6   *Str.* II 84,4-5 - *Virt.* 82-84

II 84,4 "In regard to sharing and contributing, though much might be said, let it suffice that the law *prohibits from lending to a brother on interest (designating as a brother not only him, who is born of the same parents but also one of the same stock* and one of the same mind and who has participated in the same word) *deeming it right not to take interest on money but to give graciously with open hands and heart to those in need.*
II 84,5 For God is the founder of such grace; now he who shares also takes suitable interest, namely *the most precious things among men, mildness, gentleness, magnanimity, an honourable name and a good reputation.*"[33]

The long treatise that begins at *Virt.* 51 deals with humanity or philanthropy, a virtue that, as Philo says, is the sister and twin of piety. Philo gives a series of examples of the virtue that are drawn from the latter part of the life of Moses and then from the Mosaic Law. Humanity, in the sense of kindness toward not only human beings but also animals and plants, is centered on prescriptions from the law. Lending money without interest forms the subject of *Virt.* 82-87. Biblical sources: Ex. 22:24; Lev. 25:36.37; Deut. 23:20; cf. *Spec.* II 74ff.

As introduction, Clement says that the following remarks about sharing and charitable contribution scarcely need to be made, and thereafter the borrowings begin. The law forbids asking interest from one's brother. For Philo a brother is not only someone of the same parents but also someone belonging to the same people. Clement largely accepts this

---

[32] Cf. *Str.* II 32-40; Völker, *Wahre Gnostiker*, p. 274; Pohlenz, *Klemens*, p. 139; Méhat, *Étude*, p. 414.

[33] *Str.* II 84,4-5: περί τε τῆς μεταδόσεως καὶ κοινωνίας πολλῶν ὄντων <λόγων> ἀπόχρη μόνον τοῦτο εἰπεῖν, ὅτι ὁ νόμος ἀπαγορεύει ἀδελφῷ δανείζειν (ἀδελφὸν ὀνομάζων οὐ μόνον τὸν ἐκ τῶν αὐτῶν φύντα γονέων, ἀλλὰ καὶ ὃς ἂν ὁμόφυλος ᾖ ὁμογνώμων τε καὶ τοῦ αὐτοῦ λόγου κεκοινωνηκώς), οὐ δικαιῶν ἐκλέγειν τόκους ἐπὶ χρήμασιν, ἀλλὰ ἀνειμέναις χερσὶ καὶ γνώμαις χαρίζεσθαι τοῖς δεομένοις.
84,5: θεὸς γὰρ ὁ κτίστης τοιᾶσδε χάριτος· ἤδη δὲ ὁ μεταδοτικὸς καὶ τόκους ἀξιολόγους λαμβάνει, τὰ τιμιώτατα τῶν ἐν ἀνθρώποις, ἡμερότητα, χρηστότητα, μεγαλόνοιαν, εὐφημίαν, εὔκλειαν.

definition (while omitting the term citizen, ἀστός), but he supplements it
with the amplification that a brother is like-minded and participates in
the same word (λόγος).

Following Philo, one has to give to those in need with a free hand and
an open heart because, as Clement adds, God is the originator of such
grace.[34] The one who shares will have as interest the most precious things
among men: mildness, gentleness, magnanimity, good name and
honorable reputation. This list is taken over from Philo with the omission
of the term charitable contribution (κοινωνία).

Technically speaking, Clement quotes almost literally; his expansions
are, moreover, related to the context in Philo. Philo does not say that
God is the originator of grace, but he does speak about the wealth of God,
which is contrary to wordly wealth. He elaborates as follows; the wealth
of virtue lies in the hegemonikon or sovereign part of the soul. The purest
part of existence, that is heaven, and God, the parent of all, claim it as
their own.

A similar interest in the soul in relationship to heaven and God is missing in Clement. He selects only material that can be paralleled in the
Bible, which he restates in Philo's words. He does adopt Philo's summary list of virtues, and he introduces two relatively minor
amplifications.

2.7   *Str.* II 85,1 - *Virt.* 88

II 85,1:   "Do you not think this *command* is characterized by *philanthropy*,
as is also *the following, 'to pay the wages of the poor on the very day'*? It teaches
the necessity *to discharge without delay the wages owed for service*; for as I think
the eagerness of the poor person *for the future* is paralyzed when he has suffered
lack of food."[35]

In connection with Deuteronomy, Philo provides two reasons for the
regulation that the wages of the poor have to be paid on the day the service was rendered: first, because of the work itself and second, to maintain the employee's willingness to perform hard physical labor. Scriptural
sources: Lev. 19:13; Deut. 24:14.15; cf. *Spec.* IV 195.

After his introduction with the words ἀρ'οὐ δοκεῖ σοι and in transition to
this fragment, Clement takes over bits of the beginning of *Virt.* 88 more

---

[34] Völker, *Wahre Gnostiker*, p. 487 note 2.
[35] *Str.* II 85,1: Ἆρ' οὐ δοκεῖ σοι φιλανθρωπίας εἶναι τὸ παράγγελμα τοῦτο ὥσπερ κἀκεῖνο,
'μισθὸν πένητος αὐθημερὸν ἀποδιδόναι'; ἀνυπερθέτως δεῖν διδάσκει ἐκτίνειν τὸν ἐπὶ ταῖς
ὑπηρεσίαις μισθόν· παραλύεται γάρ, οἶμαι, ἡ προθυμία τοῦ πένητος ἀτροφήσαντος πρὸς τοὐπιόν.

or less literally, and he paraphrases the rest. From the point of view of content, Clement chooses the most necessary elements centered around Philo's version of the biblical texts; while he leaves out Philo's psychological reasonings. The use of the verb διδάσκει gives a personal note of Clement's own; the law teaches and educates.[36]

2.8 *Str.* II 85,2 - *Virt.* 89

II 85,2 *"Further it says, 'let not the creditor enter the debtor's house to take the pledge with violence', but* let the former *ask him to bring it out, and let not the latter, if he has it, stay back."*[37]

Philo describes the prescription from Deuteronomy 24:10f. that a creditor may not enter the house of his debtor to take what is owed him violently.

Clement gives a paraphrase with literal elements in which he compresses the source material greatly. The transition ἔτι φησί is taken over from Philo.

2.9 *Str.* II 85,3-86,2 - *Virt.* 90.91

II 85,3 *"And in the harvest,* it (the law) prohibits the owners *from taking up what falls from the grasp,* as also in reaping, it enjoins *a part to be left unreaped,* thereby training excellently the proprietors for *sharing* and *good-heartedness, by giving up something of their own* to those who are in want, and thus providing means of nourishment for *the poor.*
II 86,1 You see how the law proclaims at the same time the *justice* and the goodness of God, who dispenses food to all ungrudgingly.
II 86,2 And in the vintage, it prohibits the grape-gatherers from going back *again* for what had been left and *from gathering the fallen grapes; and the same injunctions are given to the olive-gatherers.*[38]

A prescription about gleaning and picking follows; it is enjoined that fallen grain should be left ungathered and that a part of the field should

---

[36] see 3.2, p. 112.

[37] *Str.* II 85,2: ἔτι, φησί, δανειστὴς μὴ ἐπιστῇ χρεώστου οἰκίᾳ, ἐνέχυρον μετὰ βίας ληψόμενος, ἀλλ' ὃ μὲν ἔξω προφέρειν κελευέτω, ὃ δὲ ἔχων μὴ ἀναδυέσθω.

[38] *Str.* II 85,3-86,2: ἔν τε τῷ ἀμήτῳ τὰ ἀποπίπτοντα τῶν δραγμάτων ἀναιρεῖσθαι κωλύει τοὺς κτήτορας, καθάπερ κἄν τῷ θερισμῷ ὑπολείπεσθαί τι παραινεῖ ἄτμητον, διὰ τούτου εὖ μάλα τοὺς μὲν κτήτορας εἰς κοινωνίαν καὶ μεγαλοφροσύνην συνασκῶν ἐκ τοῦ προϊέναι τι τῶν ἰδίων τοῖς δεομένοις, τοῖς πένησι δὲ ἀφορμὴν πορίζων τροφῶν.
86,1: ὁρᾷς ὅπως ἡ νομοθεσία τὴν τοῦ θεοῦ δικαιοσύνην ἅμα καὶ ἀγαθότητα καταγγέλλει, τοῦ πᾶσιν ἀφθόνως χορηγοῦντος τὰς τροφάς;
86,2: ἔν τε αὖ τῇ τρυγῇ τὸ ἐπιέναι πάλιν τὰ καταλειφθέντα δρεπομένους καὶ τὸ τὰς ἀποπιπτούσας ῥῶγας συλλέγειν κεκώλυκεν· τὰ δ' αὐτὰ καὶ τοῖς ἐλάας συλλέγουσι διατάσσεται.

remain uncut; in that way rich people can share their wealth with and encourage the poor, who should be allowed to enter and gather the residue. The same principle governs the harvest of grapes and olives. Philo compares the law with a very loving and very just father, some of whose children live in wealth while others live in poverty. The father invites some of the latter to take property from their fortunate brethren without shame just as if the property was theirs as well. Scriptural sources: Lev. 19:9f.; 23:22; Deut. 24:19f.

The transition between this and the previous part is abrupt in Clement; he starts this new subject without any warning. The subordinate parts of this section are, on the other hand, linked by τε αὖ (line 13); Philo had used πάλιν (*Virt.* 91). The borrowing process greatly reduces the Philonic material in a way that shifts the center of gravity onto the text from Leviticus. In this paraphrase, which is once again studded with literal elements, Clement takes over the essential and eliminates the frills. He replaces κατασκευάζω with συνασκέω.[39]

The argumentation is somewhat different in Clement than in Philo; in Clement, the poor have the chance to get real food by gleaning the residue while in Philo their morale is improved. Clement continues in lines 11 and 12 with the explanation that the law proclaims the justice and goodness of a bountiful God. This explanation suits his purpose of maintaining the unity of the law, a central issue in his implicit polemical confrontation w'th the Marcionites. Cf. *Str.* II 86,5.

2.10   *Str.* II 86,3-4 - *Virt.* 95f.

> **II 86,3**   "Indeed, *the tithes of the fruits and the flocks* taught both to reverence the divinity and *to refrain from grasping everything greedily*, but to share with one's neighbour in a humane way. For from these first fruits, I believe, the priests were maintained.
> **II 86,4**   Therefore, do we thus understand that we are instructed in *piety* and in sharing and in justice and in *humanity* by the law? Isn't it?"[40]

Philo here describes the regulation on tithing agricultural products and animals; this is done to the honor of God and to refrain from turning everything to profit. Philo states that such action is ornamented with

---

[39] Cf. *Str.* II 98,3.

[40] *Str.* II 86,3-4: ναὶ μὴν καὶ αἱ δεκάται τῶν τε καρπῶν καὶ τῶν θρεμμάτων εὐσεβεῖν τε εἰς τὸ θεῖον καὶ μὴ πάντα εἶναι φιλοκερδεῖς, μεταδιδόναι δὲ φιλανθρώπως καὶ τοῖς πλησίον ἐδίδασκον. ἐκ τούτων γάρ, οἶμαι, τῶν ἀπαρχῶν καὶ οἱ ἱερεῖς διετρέφοντο.
86,4: ἤδη οὖν συνίεμεν εἰς εὐσέβειαν καὶ εἰς κοινωνίαν καὶ εἰς δικαιοσύνην καὶ εἰς φιλανθρωπίαν παιδευομένους ἡμᾶς πρὸς τοῦ νόμου; ἢ γάρ;

piety and humanity, the leaders of virtues. Scriptural sources: Lev. 27:30.32; Num. 18:21.24; cf. *Spec.* I 132f.

In Clement, the transition to the new subject is formed by ναὶ μὴν καί. The law does not order us, as in Philo, but teaches us. Clement adds that, in his opinion the priests were fed with these first fruits.[41] With the comment that the real interpretation of the prescription can 'now' be achieved ἤδη οὖν συνίεμεν, he extends the prescription to his own circle by saying that *we* are educated by the law in piety, sharing, justice and humanity. The borrowing is, as usual, a paraphrase that has been reduced to a bare minimum but that is punctuated with words quoted literally. The virtues involved are expanded; for Philo, the leading virtues had been piety and humanity. Clement shifts the direction significantly in his concluding comment; not only does he use a group of four virtues, but more significantly he alludes to the Pauline concept that the law educates us for Christ, as the wording makes clear.[42] He makes this reference more explicit later.

2.11 *Str.* II 86,5-6 - *Virt.* 97. 99. 100

> **II 86,5** "Does it not command *the land to be left fallow in the seventh year*, and did it not order *the poor* to use *the fruits that grow* by God's will *without fear*, for nature is farmer for all who want? How then is the law not *good* and a teacher of *justice*?
> **II 86,6** Again it orders *the performance of the same thing in the fiftieth year as in the seventh*, *restoring* to each one *his own land if by any circumstance* he had been deprived of it in the meantime, and setting bounds to *the desires* of those who covet possessions by measuring the period of enjoyment, and preferring that those who suffered protracted *penury* should not be *punished* for their entire life."[43]

From *Virt.* 97 on, Philo deals with the rules governing the seventh and the fiftieth years; land must lie uncultivated so that the poor can reap what fruit it naturally bears. Scriptural sources: Ex. 23:10.11; Lev. 25:3f.; cf. *Spec.* II 86-109.

---

[41] Cf. *Spec.* I 133.

[42] Völker, *Wahre Gnostiker*, p. 262, 266.

[43] *Str.* II 86,5-6: οὐχὶ διὰ μὲν τοῦ ἑβδόμου ἔτους ἀργὴν ἀνίεσθαι τὴν χώραν προστάττει, τοὺς πένητας δὲ ἀδεῶς τοῖς κατὰ θεὸν φυεῖσι καρποῖς χρῆσθαι ἐκέλευεν, τῆς φύσεως τοῖς βουλομένοις γεωργούσης; πῶς οὖν <οὐ> χρηστὸς ὁ νόμος καὶ δικαιοσύνης διδάσκαλος;
86,6: πάλιν τε αὖ τῷ πεντηκοστῷ ἔτει τὰ αὐτὰ ἐπιτελεῖν κελεύει, ἃ καὶ τῷ ἑβδόμῳ, προσαποδιδοὺς ἑκάστῳ τὸ ἴδιον εἴ τις ἐν τῷ μεταξὺ διά τινα περίστασιν ἀφῃρέθη χωρίον, τήν τε ἐπιθυμίαν τῶν κτᾶσθαι ποθούντων περιορίζων χρόνῳ μεμετρημένῳ καρπώσεως τούς τε πενίᾳ μακρᾷ ὑποσχόντας δίκην μὴ διὰ βίου κολάζεσθαι ἐθέλων.

The transition for Clement is formed by ἦ γάρ. In heavily paraphrased form he takes the essence of the prescriptions and adds that the law is both good[44] and also a teacher of justice. The same polemical idea occurred earlier in *Str.* II 86,1, where the good law as διδάσκαλος of justice leads in the direction of Christ;[45] this line of thought also anticipates the later passage, *Str.* II 90,1, in which Clement associates the precepts of the law with the Lord himself, and it becomes even more outspoken in *Str.* II 95,1, where he alters χρηστὸς νόμος into χρηστὸς λόγος.

Clement follows his material from Philo with a triple citation from Proverbs; he seems to center the citations around ἐλεημοσύναι/ἐλεῶν. This may be related to Philo's use of ἐλεεῖσθαι in *Virt.* 100: that is, in close proximity to the passage Clement borrows. Clement does not include the word in his paraphrase, but its presence nearby may have suggested a theme for his use of Proverbs. He reinforces the last quotation from Proverbs ("one who pities the poor shall be blessed") with the explanation that the one who shows love to one's fellow does so because of love for the creator of humankind. Again the tone is anti-Marcionite, as it had been even more explicitly in *Str.* II 91,1.[46]

The insertion of ἀγάπη, a word that finds no parallel in Philo, is expanded in *Str.* II 87,2, where it is found to be the underlying element in a number of virtues.[47] In a transitional sentence, *Str.* II 87,1, Clement suggests that other, more 'physical' explanations of the previous prescriptions exist;[48] he alludes to the ideas of rest and recovery of inheritance, but he postpones the discussion. To know more about these interpretations, we have to search the *Stromateis* to find passages like *Str.* V 40,1 or *Str.* VI 141,3.

2.12   *Str.* II 87,3-88,1 - *Virt.* 96

> **II 87,3**   *"Again it says, 'if you see a beast belonging to one of your relatives or friends or in general to anybody you know, wandering in the wilderness, take it back and restore it; and if the owner is far away keep it carefully with your own until he returns and restore it'. As a natural partnership*, it (the law) teaches to regard *what is found as a deposit* and not to bear malice to an enemy.

---

[44] Clement has χρηστός here, which he borrows from Philo (*Virt.* 97) and adapts for his own thoughts; cf. *Str.* II 86,1 (ἀγαθότης).

[45] διδάσκαλος, see Marrou, *Paed.* I (SChr. 70), Introd. p. 9, for the difference between διδάσκαλος and παιδαγωγός.

[46] Völker, *Wahre Gnostiker*, p. 487.

[47] Cf. *Str.* IV 53,1; 54,1; 55,3; these virtues have partly parallels in the N. T.: πραότης, χρηστότης, ὑπομονή, ἀφθονία. Not for ἀζηλία, ἀμισία, ἀμνησικακία (ἀμνησίκακος, I Clem. 2,5); Camelot, *Strom.* II (SChr. 38), p. 104 note 2; Méhat, *Étude*, p. 237.

[48] Den Boer, *Allegorese*, p. 60f.; Völker, *Wahre Gnostiker*, p. 317 note 5; Méhat, *Étude*, p. 201.

II 88,1 'The command of the Lord being a fountain of life' truly 'causes to turn away from the snare of death'."[49]

In relation to his treatment of first fruits and offerings of young animals, which included property rights connected with herds, Philo discusses lost animals. Biblical sources: Ex. 23:4; Deut. 22:1-3.

Clement adapts this passage almost literally from Philo, even taking over his transitional word πάλιν; the sequence, however, is interrupted; after a long progression he momentarily takes a small step backwards (cf. section 1.2, schematic overview). In line 22 of page 159, Clement's text is somewhat deformed; φυσικὴν κοινωνίαν might well need a preposition (διά, as is conjectured by Hiller) or else τὸ....λογίζεσθαι as subject, and φυσικὴν κοινωνίαν as object, as is suggested by Früchtel. A third solution could also be to consider φυσικὴν κοινωνίαν as a predicative acccusative, while the law is subject. The position of ἀπόδος (Philo: ἀποδίδως) has, moreover, been shifted. Again the verb διδάσκει is emphasized. Prov.14:27 concludes the borrowing, as usual with such biblical citations, to expand the implications.

2.13   Str. II 88,1 - Virt. 103

II 88,1 "But I ask you, *does it not command to love strangers not only as friends and relatives but as ourselves both in body and soul?*"[50]

In *Virt.* 102 a new subject appears: the foreigner. Foreigners who leave their country must be supported. First because they change their land for a better home, and second because they abandon idols to worship the "one and truly existing God". All are requested not only to regard the newcomers as friends but also to love them as one loves oneself. Biblical sources: Ex. 22:20; 23:9; Lev. 19:33f.; Num. 15:14-15; cf. *Spec.* IV 178.

Clement introduces the borrowing with τί δέ; and quotes in a literal fashion the most essential elements of his Philonic model.

2.14   Str. II 88,2 - Virt. 106

II 88,2 "Even more, it honors the gentiles and *bears no grudge against those who have done ill. Accordingly it says, 'You will not scorn an Egyptian, for you were*

---

[49] *Str.* II 87,3-88,1: πάλιν 'ἐὰν ἴδῃς' φησὶ 'τῶν οἰκείων ἢ φίλων ἢ καθόλου ὧν γνωρίζεις ἀνθρώπων ἐν ἐρημίᾳ πλανώμενον ὑποζύγιον, ἀπαγαγὼν ἀπόδος. κἂν οὖν τύχῃ μακρὰν ἀφεστὼς ὁ δεσπότης, μετὰ τῶν σαυτοῦ διαφυλάξας ἄχρις ἂν κομίσηται ἀπόδος.' φυσικὴν κοινωνίαν διδάσκει τὸ εὕρημα παρακαταθήκην λογίζεσθαι μηδὲ μνησικακεῖν τῷ ἐχθρῷ. 88,1: 'πρόσταγμα κυρίου πηγὴ ζωῆς,' ὡς ἀληθῶς, 'ποιεῖ ἐκκλίνειν ἐκ παγίδος θανάτου.'

[50] *Str.* II 88, 1: τί δέ; οὐχὶ τοὺς ἐπήλυδας ἀγαπᾶν κελεύει, οὐ μόνον ὡς φίλους καὶ σύγγενεῖς, ἀλλ' ὡς ἑαυτούς, κατά τε σῶμα καὶ ψυχήν;

a sojourner in Egypt', designating by the term Egyptian either one of that nation or anyone who belongs to the world.''[51]

In the course of discussing the precepts about foreigners, Philo distinguishes between foreigners who are co-religionists and those who are not, whom he terms 'co-habitants'. He explains that although it is a gift in itself to be admitted in a foreign country, the previous inhabitants do not have the right to treat the new people badly, no matter what their background is; in this connexion, Philo quotes Deut. 23:8.[52]

The transition in Clement is formed by ναὶ μὴν καί. He begins by saying that the law has also honored the gentiles. After the quotation from Deut. 23:8 borrowed from Philo, Clement interprets the name Egypt as a gentile or as a person who leads a wordly, i.e. a non-spiritual life.[53] Technically, Clement gives an almost literal quotation in which μνησικακεῖν is changed to μνησιπονηρεῖν. The etymology of Egypt is missing in this part of Philo although it can be found elsewhere throughout his works.

2.15   a) *Str.* II 88,3 - *Virt.* 109
        b) *Str.* II 88,4-89,2 - *Virt.* 110-115

> **II 88,3**   "And *enemies, even if they are standing before the walls* attempting to take the city, *are not regarded as enemies until they are summoned to peace by the voice of a herald.*
> **II 88,4**   Yes indeed, it forbids intercourse *with a female captive* as rape, but *'allow her'*, it says, *'thirty days to mourn* according to her wish, and later let her change her clothes and *come together with her as your lawful wife'*. For it regards it not right that this should happen either in wantonness or *for hire like harlots, but only for the birth of children.* Do you see humanity combined with continence?
> **II 89,1**   The master who has fallen in love with his captive maid is not allowed to gratify his pleasure, but it (the law) obstructs his lust by specifying an interval of time; and furthermore *it cuts off* the captive's *hair*, in order to discourage disgraceful *love*; for if it is *reason* that induces him to marry he will cleave to her even after she has become disfigured.
> **II 89,2**   Then *if one having satisfied his desire, does not care to consort any longer with the captive*, it ordains that it shall not be permitted *to sell* her, or *to have her any longer as a servant*, but desires *her to be free and released from service in the house, lest on the introduction of another wife, she bear any of the intolerable miseries caused by jealousy.*"[54]

---

[51] *Str.* II 88,2: ναὶ μὴν καὶ τὰ ἔθνη τετίμηκεν καὶ τοῖς γε κακῶς πεποιηκόσιν οὐ μνησιπονηρεῖ. ἄντικρυς γοῦν φησιν· 'οὐ βδελύξῃ Αἰγύπτιον, ὅτι πάροικος ἐγένου κατ' Αἴγυπτον,' ἤτοι τὸν ἐθνικὸν ἢ καὶ πάντα τὸν κοσμικὸν Αἰγύπτιον προσειπών·

[52] Philo quotes the LXX literally, a rare event; for the concept of πάροικος, R. A. Bitter, *Vreemdelingschap bij Philo van Alexandrië; een onderzoek naar de betekenis van* πάροικος, 1982.

[53] Cf. chapter II, 2.6 p. 34f.

[54] *Str.* II 88,3-89,2: τούς τε πολεμίους, κἂν ἤδη τοῖς τείχεσιν ἐφεστῶτες ὦσιν ἑλεῖν τὴν πόλιν

a) Philo indicates clearly in *Virt.* 109 that he progresses from one subject, treatment of foreigners, to another, treatment of captives. Here he discusses who is regarded as an enemy and what is the legitimate starting point for hostilities, and he sets very scrupulous and formal tests for suspension of the rules of peace and friendship. Biblical source: Deut. 20:10; cf. *Spec.* IV 219-221.

In Clement the introduction to this quotation, which is literal, is formed by τούς τε πολεμίους; a very abrupt way to introduce a new subject. The reflection of Philo is excessively abbreviated.

b) Philo dedicates an ample discussion to the relationships of captive women and their captors. A captive should be left alone for thirty days in order to mourn for the family from which she had been separated. To give expression to her mourning, her hair will be shaved. Probably from the same motive, her fingernails will be cut, and her former clothes replaced.

After the period of mourning, she can be taken as a lawful wife either for love and companionship or for the birth of children. Philo introduces various arguments to justify these regulations: to prevent unbridled lust, to test whether the man's love is inspired by passion or by reason, and to show pity for the captive, who has fallen into such unfortunate conditions. If the relationship should come to an end, her freedom and her right to depart must be granted. Scriptural source: Deut. 21:10-14.

The transition is formed by ναί μὴν καί. Clement takes over these regulations to show that they represent for him φιλανθρωπία μετ'ἐγκρατείας. The borrowing is a paraphrase that alters both the order and the wording of Philo's text. Among the differences, βασανίζω is replaced by δυσωπέω.[55]

πειρώμενοι, μήπω νομίζεσθαι πολεμίους, ἄχρις ἂν αὐτοὺς ἐπικηρυκευσάμενοι προσκαλέσωνται πρὸς εἰρήνην.

88,4: ναί μὴν καὶ τῇ αἰχμαλώτῳ οὐ πρὸς ὕβριν ὁμιλεῖν κελεύει, ἀλλὰ ''τὰς λ' ἡμέρας ἐπιτρέψας'' φησὶ ''πενθῆσαι οὓς βούλεται, μεταμφιάσας ὕστερον ὡς γαμετῇ νόμῳ συνέρχου·'' οὔτε γὰρ ἐφ' ὕβρει τὰς συνουσίας οὐδὲ μὴν διὰ μισθαρνίαν ὡς ἑταίρας, ἀλλ' ἢ διὰ μόνην τῶν τέκνων τὴν γένεσιν γίνεσθαι τὰς ὁμιλίας ἀξιοῖ. ὁρᾷς φιλανθρωπίαν μετ' ἐγκρατείας;

89,1: τῷ ἐρῶντι κυρίῳ τῆς αἰχμαλώτου γεγονότι οὐκ ἐπιτρέπει χαρίζεσθαι τῇ ἡδονῇ, ἀνακόπτει δὲ τὴν ἐπιθυμίαν διαστήματι μεμετρημένῳ καὶ προσέτι ἀποκείρ τῆς αἰχμαλώτου καὶ τὰς τρίχας, ἵνα τὸν ἐφύβριστον δυσωπήσῃ ἔρωτα· εἰ γὰρ λογισμὸς ἀναπείθει γῆμαι, καὶ γενομένης αἰσχρᾶς ἀνθέξεται.

89,2: ἔπειτα ἐάν τις τῆς ἐπιθυμίας κατάκορος γενόμενος μηκέτι κοινωνεῖν τῇ αἰχμαλώτῳ καταξιώσῃ, μηδὲ πιπράσκειν ταύτην ἐξεῖναι διατάττεται, ἀλλὰ μηδὲ ἔτι θεράπαιναν ἔχειν, ἐλευθέραν δὲ εἶναι καὶ τῆς οἰκετίας ἀπαλλάττεσθαι βούλεται, ὡς μὴ γυναικὸς ἑτέρας ἐπεισελθούσης πάθῃ τι τῶν κατὰ ζηλοτυπίαν ἀνηκέστων.

[55] p. 161 l. 1f.; cf. *Str.* II 92,3.

By his exclusions, Clement tends to emphasize control of the passions. A union is not based both on love and procreation, as in Philo, but exclusively on the latter.⁵⁶ Clement does not mention cutting the finger-nails and the explanation of the haircut is based on anti-esthetic reasons; her unattractiveness will put a brake on unbridled passion.

2.16   *Str.* II 90,1-91,1 - *Virt.* 116-119

II 90,1   "What more? The Lord *enjoins to relieve and raise up enemies' beasts when they are labouring beneath their burdens; teaching* us *from a distance not to indulge in joy at one's neighbour's misfortune,* or exult over our enemies in order to teach us, who are trained in these things, to pray for our enemies.

II 90,2   For he does not allow us either *to be jealous and to grieve at the good fortune of him who lives near us or to rejoice at our neighbor's ills. And if you find any enemy's beast straying, you are to set aside the incentives of your disagreement and take it back and restore it.* For forgetfulness *is followed by goodness, and the latter by dissolution of enmity.*

II 90,3   From this we are fitted for *concord,* and this conducts *to felicity.* And should you suppose one habitually hostile, and discover him to be unreasonably malicious either through lust or anger, turn him to goodness.

II 91,1   Does the law then which conducts to Christ appear humane and benign? And is not the same God good with justice from the beginning to the end dealing suitably with each generation to bring it to salvation?''⁵⁷

More injunctions that call for kindness are given by Philo. Beasts oppressed by their burdens must be raised up; one should not take pleasure in adversity, and even if it is an enemy's beast that is suffering, one is urged to relieve it so that more animosity and envy is not stirred up. Through all these regulations, the prophet (Moses) strives to create unanimity and an atmosphere of neighbourliness, which will then lead to happiness. Philo states that the rules live in 'our' prayers but that they will become reality if God grants them fruitfulness. Scriptural sources: Ex. 23:4ff.; Deut. 22:1ff.

---

⁵⁶ Cf. *Str.* II 137,1; Pohlenz, *Klemens,* p. 144; Marrou, *Paed.* I (SChr. 10), Introd. p. 57.

⁵⁷ *Str.* II 90,1-91,1: Τί δέ; καὶ ἐχθρῶν ὑποζύγια ἀχθοφοροῦντα συνεπικουφίζειν καὶ συνεγείρειν προστάσσει πόρρωθεν διδάσκων ἡμᾶς ὁ κύριος ἐπιχαιρεκακίαν μὴ ἀσπάζεσθαι μηδὲ ἐφήδεσθαι τοῖς ἐχθροῖς, ἵνα τούτοις ἐγγυμνασαμένους ὑπὲρ τῶν ἐχθρῶν προσεύχεσθαι διδάξῃ.
90,2: οὔτε γὰρ φθονεῖν καὶ ἐπὶ τοῖς πέλας ἀγαθοῖς λυπεῖσθαι προσῆκεν οὐδὲ μὴν ἐπὶ τοῖς τοῦ πλησίον κακοῖς ἡδονὴν καρποῦσθαι. "κἂν πλανώμενον μέντοι", φησίν "ἐχθροῦ τινος ὑποζύγιον εὕρῃς, τὰ τῆς διαφορᾶς παραλιπὼν ὑπεκκαύματα ἀπαγαγὼν ἀπόδος." τῇ γὰρ ἀμνηστίᾳ ἔπεται ἡ καλοκἀγαθία, καὶ ἡ ταύτῃ τῆς ἔχθρας διάλυσις.
90,3: ἐντεῦθεν εἰς ὁμόνοιαν καταρτιζόμεθα, ἣ δὲ εἰς εὐδαιμονίαν χειραγωγεῖ. κἂν τινα ἐξ ἔθους ἐχθρὸν ὑπολάβῃς, παραλογιζόμενον δὲ τοῦτον ἀλόγως ἤτοι ἐπιθυμίᾳ ἢ καὶ θυμῷ καταλάβῃς, ἐπίστρεφον αὐτὸν εἰς καλοκἀγαθίαν.
91,1: Ἆρα ἤδη καταφαίνεται φιλάνθρωπος καὶ χρηστὸς ὁ νόμος, "ὁ εἰς Χριστὸν παιδαγωγῶν," θεός τε ὁ αὐτὸς ἀγαθὸς μετὰ δικαιοσύνης, ἀπ' ἀρχῆς εἰς τέλος ἑκάστῳ γένει προσφυῶς εἰς σωτηρίαν κεχρημένος;

The transition in Clement is formed by τί δέ;, and the subject of the sentence is not Moses, as in Philo, but the *Lord*, who teaches *us*, while *we* are trained to pray for our enemies. In this section, Clement makes use of a number of words that are characteristic of his own vocabulary, as Méhat has pointed out and tabulated.[58] The position of ἕπεται is curious; Clement links it with ἀμνηστία, while in Philo's text it is part of the following sentence (*Virt.* 118). The pair of borrowed words is handled freely. In a paraphrase with literal components, Clement thus joins scattered words together to form new sentences, and yet the essence of Philo's text is preserved.

Clement adds a section, *Str.* II 91, 1-2, in which he maintains that the law, which educates to Christ is humane and good. As part of his polemic against Marcionite dualism, he goes on to say that the same God is good and just. Behind the unstated questions of why the law has a continuous influence and why the concept of the one God must be sustained, seems to lie the unstated answer that the same God works from the beginning to the end, from generation to generation. Thus he puts these concepts in the broad perspective of the history of salvation. He reinforces this argument with a synopsis of various gospel texts, which he had found in just this order in the first Epistle of Clement.[59]

2.17 *Str.* II 91,3 - *Virt.* 122-124

II 91,3 "Furthermore it (the law) prohibits those who are in servitude for their subsistence to be treated dishonorably, *and to those who have been reduced to slavery through money borrowed, it gives a complete release in the seventh year.* Further it prohibits *suppliants from being given up* to punishment."[60]

In *Virt.* 122 Philo starts a new section; the previous rules were applied to free men; here slaves and suppliants are discussed. A person reduced to a condition of servitude by poverty must be liberated in the seventh year, and even those who were born in slavery must not be rejected if they come as suppliants. Philo points out how fate is unpredictable and how respect must be showed even to those in a miserable condition. These rules are illustrated by applying them to various cases. Biblical sources: Ex. 21:2; Lev. 25:39-43; Deut. 15:12ff.; cf. *Spec.* II 79.

---

[58] ἀσπάζομαι, ἐγγυμνάζομαι, καρπόομαι, εὑρίσκω, ἀμνηστία, καταρτίζω, χειρογωγέω; Méhat, *Étude*, p. 220-221.

[59] 1 Clem. 13,2.

[60] *Str.* II 91,3: Ἔτι τοὺς <ἐπὶ> τροφῇ δουλεύοντας ἀτιμάζεσθαι κωλύει, τοῖς τε ἐκ δανείων καταδουλωθεῖσιν ἐκεχειρίαν τὴν εἰς πᾶν δίδωσιν ἐνιαυτῷ ἑβδόμῳ. ἀλλὰ καὶ ἱκέτας ἐκδιδόναι εἰς κόλασιν κωλύει.

In Clement the transition is formed by ἔτι, and the borrowing is embellished with a short anthology from Proverbs.[61] Slaves and suppliants must be treated well, and the latter are not allowed to be handed over (according to Philo) for punishment (added by Clement). Only a sentence and a half of Philo's text is recognizable, while the rest of the sentence is formed by a paraphrase with one addition.

2.18   a) *Str.* II 92,1 - *Virt.* 126
        b) *Str.* II 92,2 - *Virt.* 129
        c) *Str.* II 92,3-93,1 - *Virt.* 131-133

II 92,1 "And Pythagoras, in my opinion, derived his mildness towards irrational creatures from the law. For instance, it ordered abstention *from the immediate use of the young born in the herds of sheep, goats and cattle, not even under the pretext of sacrifice, both on account of the young and of the mothers.* It educates man to gentleness starting from below with the irrational animals.

II 92,2 'Resign accordingly', it says, 'the young one to its mother at least *for the first seven days*'. For if nothing takes place without a cause and if milk *comes in a shower* to animals that have given birth for the nourishment of the progeny, he who tears away the newborn from the supply of milk, dishonors nature.

II 92,3 Let the Greeks and whoever else inveighs against the law then feel ashamed if it shows mildness even in the case of irrational animals, while they expose the offspring of men, even though long ago and prophetically, the law in the above-mentionned commandment obstructed their cruelty.

II 92,4 For if it prohibits *the progeny of the irrational animals to be separated from the mother before sucking, much more* in the case of men does it provide beforehand a cure for *cruel* and savage mentality, so that even if they despise *nature*, they may not despise *teaching*.

---

[61] Cf. Prov. 17:3; 19:11; 14:23; 17:12; (9:6?); 16:8.

[62] *Str.* II 92,1-93,1: Ἐμοὶ δὲ δοκεῖ καὶ Πυθαγόρας τὸ ἥμερον τὸ περὶ τὰ ἄλογα ζῷα παρὰ τοῦ νόμου εἰληφέναι. αὐτίκα τῶν γεννωμένων κατά τε τὰς ποίμνας κατά τε τὰ αἰπόλια καὶ βουκόλια τῆς παραχρῆμα ἀπολαύσεως, μηδὲ ἐπὶ προφάσει θυσιῶν <λαμβάνοντας, ἀπέχεσθαι> διηγόρευσεν, ἐκγόνων τε ἕνεκα καὶ μητέρων, εἰς ἡμερότητα τὸν ἄνθρωπον κάτωθεν ἀπὸ τῶν ἀλόγων ζῴων ἀνατρέφων.

92,2: "χάρισαι γοῦν", φησί, "τῇ μητρὶ τὸ ἔκγονον κἂν ἑπτὰ τὰς πρώτας ἡμέρας". εἰ γὰρ μηδὲν ἀναιτίως γίνεται, γάλα δὲ ἐπομβρεῖται ταῖς τετοκυίαις εἰς διατροφὴν τῶν ἐκγόνων, <ὁ> ἀποσπῶν τῆς τοῦ γάλακτος οἰκονομίας τὸ τεχθὲν ἀτιμάζει τὴν φύσιν.

92,3: δυσωπείσθωσαν οὖν Ἕλληνες καὶ εἴ τις ἕτερός ἐστι τοῦ νόμου κατατρέχων, εἰ ὁ μὲν καὶ ἐπ' ἀλόγων ζῴων χρηστεύεται, οἳ δὲ καὶ τὰ τῶν ἀνθρώπων ἐκτιθέασιν ἔκγονα, καίτοι μακρόθεν καὶ προφητικῶς ἀνακόπτοντος αὐτῶν τὴν ἀγριότητα τοῦ νόμου διὰ τῆς προειρημένης ἐντολῆς.

92,4: εἰ γὰρ τῶν ἀλόγων τὰ ἔκγονα διαζεύγνυσθαι τῆς τεκούσης πρὸ τῆς γαλακτουχίας ἀπαγορεύει, πολὺ πλέον ἐπ' ἀνθρώπων τὴν ὠμὴν καὶ ἀτιθάσευτον προθεραπεύει γνώμην, ἵν' εἰ καὶ τῆς φύσεως, μαθήσεως γοῦν μὴ καταφρονῶσιν.

93,1: ἐρίφων μὲν γὰρ καὶ ἀρνῶν ἐμφορεῖσθαι ἐπιτέτραπται, καί τις ἴσως ἀπολογία τῷ διαζεύξαντι τῆς τεκούσης τὸ ἔκγονον· ἡ δὲ τοῦ παιδίου ἔκθεσις τίνα τὴν αἰτίαν ἔχει;

II 93,1 For they are permitted to satiate themselves with *kids and lambs*, and perhaps there might be some excuse for separating the progeny from its mother, but what cause is there for the exposure of a child?''[62]

a) In *Virt.* 125 Philo passes from the legislation about compatriots and foreigners, friends and enemies, slaves and free into rules in which he deals with moderation and kindness toward 'irrational' animals. Mother and off-spring must not be separated either for human nourishment or sacred sacrifice; the belly might be satisfied but the soul will be distressed by such an unnatural meal. Biblical sources: Ex. 22:29; Lev. 22:27.

As a preliminary remark Clement refers to Pythagoras; this suits his ongoing thesis that the Greeks in their conception of the virtues are dependent on the law of Moses. The borrowing proper is introduced by αὐτίκα: newborn animals are not allowed to be eaten, not even on the pretense of sacrifice.

The borrowing is literal with omissions. On the basis of Philo's text, editors have inserted <λαμβάνοντας, ἀπέχεσθαι>. As for ἀπέχεσθαι, the conjecture makes sense because of the genitive τῆς ... ἀπολαύσεως, which asks for a corresponding verb. Clement stresses the pedagogical idea by adding ἀνατρέφων. The contrast between belly and soul is omitted, as is the idea that the young animal is taken away for food; sacrifice is the only motivation that is left.

b) Kindness to animals includes respect for the natural provision of milk for the new born ; the offspring is to be left with its mother at least for seven days. Nature did not distribute these gifts to be destroyed; these are benefits prepared by a profound providence. Scriptural sources: Ex. 22:29; Lev. 22:27.

Clement takes over the ordinance to leave the young animal to its mother for a few days and amplifies to the effect that *if* nothing takes place without a cause, someone who interrupts a natural process dishonors nature. The borrowing is a smooth paraphrase that incorporates a few words taken over literally. Philo has connected nature with providence; Clement puts his source into question by inserting '*if*' (εἰ), without clarifying which way his own opinion leans.[63]

c) Threatening words and unflattering epithets are pronounced by Philo against people who expose their children and thus become the murderers of their own offspring. If nature does not, may teaching instil love of

---

[63] 3.1.4 p. 109.

family, sighs Philo. Nature has given the suitable means, and the lawgiver looks carefully to see that the gifts of God, which bring welfare and safety, will not be obstructed. Cf. *Spec.* III 108ff.

Clement juxtaposes the law of Moses against the 'Greeks'; the former is good and benign, while the latter are cruel in exposing their children. Clement characterizes the law as a guardian against a savage and unrestrained mentality. The borrowing is largely paraphrased, but some words can be traced back to Philo.[64] Both authors polemize; Philo does not mention an opponent by name while Clement levels his criticism at the Greeks. The correlation between nature and law is omitted by Clement while procreation as the most important function in marriage has been added.[65]

2.19 a) *Str.* II 93,2-4 - *Virt.* 134-140
b) *Str.* II 94,1-2 - *Virt.* 142-143

II 93,2 "Again the good law *forbids sacrificing the offspring and the mother together on the same day.* Thence also *if a pregnant woman* is condemned to *death,* Romans do not allow her to undergo punishment until she is *delivered.*
II 93,3 The law too expressly *prohibits the slaughtering of all pregnant animals until they have brought forth, from a distance restraining the unscrupulous conduct* of those who do wrong to man.
II 93,4 Thus also *it has extended its clemency even to irrational animals so that by training ourselves on creatures of different species we might practise humanity in a fuller measure toward beings like ourselves.*
II 94,1 Those too that kick bellies of certain animals before parturition, in order to feast on flesh mixed with milk, make the womb created for birth of the foetus its grave, although the law expressly commands, *'but neither shall you cook a lamb in its mother's milk'.*
II 94,2 *The nourishment of a living animal,* it says, *should not become the seasoning of the animal after its death, and that which is the cause of life may* not co-operate *in the destruction of the body.''*[66]

---

[64] 3.1.2 p. 108.
[65] see note 56 above.
[66] *Str.* II 93,2-94,2: πάλιν αὖ ὁ χρηστὸς νόμος ἀπαγορεύει ἡμέρᾳ τῇ αὐτῇ συγκαταθύειν ἔκγονον καὶ μητέρα. ἐντεῦθεν καὶ Ῥωμαῖοι, εἰ καί τις ἔγκυος καταδικασθείη τὴν ἐπὶ θανάτῳ, οὐ πρότερον ἐῶσιν ὑποσχεῖν τὴν τιμωρίαν πρὶν ἢ ἐκτεκεῖν.
93,3: ἄντικρυς γοῦν καὶ ὅσα τῶν ζῴων κυοφορεῖ, ὁ νόμος οὐκ ἐπιτρέπει ἄχρις ἂν ἀποτέκῃ σφαγιάζεσθαι, μακρόθεν ἐπισχὼν τὴν εὐχέρειαν τῶν εἰς ἄνθρωπον ἀδικούντων.
93,4: οὕτως ἄχρι καὶ τῶν ἀλόγων ζῴων τὸ ἐπιεικὲς ἀπέτεινεν, ἵνα ἐν τοῖς ἀνομογενέσιν ἀσκήσαντες πολλῇ τινι περιουσίᾳ φιλανθρωπίας ἐν τοῖς ὁμογενέσι χρησώμεθα.
94,1: οἳ δὲ καὶ περιλακτίζοντες τὰς γαστέρας πρὸ τῆς ἀποτέξεως ζῴων τινῶν, ἵνα δὴ γάλακτι ἀνακεκραμένην σάρκα θοινάζωνται, τάφον τῶν κυοφορουμένων τὴν εἰς γένεσιν κτισθεῖσαν μήτραν πεποιήκασι, διαρρήδην τοῦ νομοθέτου κελεύοντος "ἀλλ᾽ οὐδὲ ἐφήσεις ἄρνα ἐν γάλακτι μητρὸς αὐτοῦ"·
94,2: μὴ γὰρ γινέσθω ἡ τοῦ ζῶντος τροφὴ ἥδυσμα τοῦ ἀναιρεθέντος ζῴου, φησίν [ἡ σάρξ], μηδὲ τὸ τῆς ζωῆς αἴτιον συνεργὸν τῇ τοῦ σώματος καταναλώσει γινέσθω.

a) In *Virt.* 134, a new aspect of the law related to kindness to animals is developed; mother and offspring are not to be killed on the same day, neither as a sacrificial offering nor as simple nourishment. On the same principle, animals should not be killed while they are pregnant. Philo touches on other legislators who have forbidden pregnant women condemned to death to be executed before the child is born. He continues to say that Moses elevates the law further by extending this fair treatment even to irrational animals. Scriptural source: Lev. 22:28.

The transition in Clement is formed by πάλιν αὖ while the subject of the first sentence is ὁ χρηστὸς νόμος. The prohibition to slay pregnant animals is reinforced by the argument that the Romans did not execute pregnant women before delivery. By this elaboration Clement makes the theme of dependence on the law of Moses much more explicit. Clement extends the borrowing with an atrocious description of the killing of a foetus. This description is not taken from Philo but it can be paralleled in a tradition of which traces can be found in Plutarch.[67]

Of the three pages of text to which Clement refers, a mere three lines are taken over literally, and only one more reappears in a paraphrased form. Philo's generic mention of other legislators is given a definite label; for Clement the 'Romans' fill in the empty blank. According to the references that Cohn offers,[68] however, it appears that Clement gives too limited an idea of the diffusion of this law; in reality it must have been quite widespread.

b) The prohibition against separating the young from its mother or killing both of them on the same day is extended by a related law that forbids cooking the lamb in its mother's milk. If anyone wants to boil flesh in milk, he must do it without cruelty; he otherwise lacks a sense of compassion, which, according to Philo, is the most vital of emotions and most nearly akin to the rational soul. Biblical sources: Ex. 23:19; 34:26; Deut. 14:21.

Clement has chosen this fragment around the biblical passage, which he quotes more completely than Philo by including the word αὐτοῦ.[69] The borrowing is a fragmented paraphrase with literal components.

---

[67] Cf. Plut. *Mor.* 997A.
[68] Cohn V, p. 308 note 12; Colson VIII, p. 447 par. 139.
[69] Cf. 3.1.2. p. 108.

2.20   *Str.* II 94,3-5 - *Virt.* 145ff.

II 94,3   "And the same law commands *'not to muzzle an ox while it is treading out the corn'*; for also 'the worker must earn his food'.

II 94,4   *And it prohibits that an ox and an ass be yoked in the plough together, pointing* perhaps *to the dissimilarity of the animals*, and at the same time *it makes clear that wrong should not be done to any one of another race* nor bring him under the yoke *when there is no other cause to allege than difference of race, which is no cause at all, being neither wickedness nor the effect of wickedness.*

II 94,5   To me, the allegory also seems to signify that the farming of the word is not to be allotted equally to the clean and the unclean, the believer and the unbeliever; *for the ox is clean, but the ass* has been reckoned *among the unclean animals.*"[70]

From the law against muzzling the ox while treading out the corn, Philo discusses first the beneficial work of oxen in agriculture. Then he comes to another similar law that forbids yoking an ox and an ass together for ploughing. He interprets the dissimilarity of the animals not only as incongruity of nature, since the ox is clean and the ass belongs to the unclean, but also as disparity of strength, and he explains that the law has been given to protect the weaker. Finally Philo points out that for those whose souls have 'ears', it becomes clear that the ultimate meaning is not to do wrong to men of other nations. Biblical sources: Deut. 22:10; 25:4; cf. *Spec.* IV 204-206.

An abrupt transition from the previous to the present borrowing is formed by ὁ δὲ αὐτὸς νόμος διαγορεύει. Clement combines the Old Testamental text of the ox treading out the corn with the Gospel passage in which the labourer is worthy of his wages.[71] He found the two already linked in 1 Tim. 5:18, but the word wages (reward) is altered into food.

In dealing with Philo's idea that animals should not be yoked if they are of unequal strength, Clement inserts 'perhaps' (τάχα), as if he has reservations about it.[72] Philo's explanation not to do wrong to men of other nations is amplified with the consonant image of not bringing them under the yoke. That Clement is not completely satisfied with the allegory passed through Philo becomes clear from his concluding inter-

---

[70] *Str.* II 94,3-5: ὁ δὲ αὐτὸς νόμος διαγορεύει "βοῦν ἀλοῶντα μὴ φιμοῦν"· δεῖ γὰρ καὶ "τὸν ἐργάτην τροφῆς ἀξιοῦσθαι".

94,4: ἀπαγορεύει τε ἐν ταὐτῷ καταζευγνύναι πρὸς ἄροτον γῆς βοῦν καὶ ὄνον, τάχα μὲν καὶ τοῦ περὶ τὰ ζῷα ἀνοικείου στοχασάμενος, δηλῶν δ' ἅμα μηδένα τῶν ἑτεροεθνῶν ἀδικεῖν καὶ ὑπὸ ζυγὸν ἄγειν, οὐδὲν ἔχοντας αἰτιάσασθαι ἢ [ὅτι] τὸ ἀλλογενές, ὅπερ ἐστὶν ἀναίτιον, μήτε κακία μήτε ἀπὸ κακίας ὁρμώμενον.

94,5: ἐμοὶ δὲ δοκεῖ καὶ μηνύειν ἡ ἀλληγορία, μὴ δεῖν ἐπ' ἴσης καθαρῷ καὶ ἀκαθάρτῳ, πιστῷ τε καὶ ἀπίστῳ τῆς τοῦ λόγου μεταδιδόναι γεωργίας, διότι τὸ μέν ἐστι καθαρόν, ὁ βοῦς, ὄνος δὲ τῶν ἀκαθάρτων λελόγισται.

[71] Cf. Mt. 10:10; Lk. 10:7.

[72] Cf. 3.1.4, p. 110.

pretation.[73] In this, Clement states as his own opinion that the allegory points to the 'farming' of the word, a favourite image for Clement.[74] Not everyone participates in this farming to the same degree; some have been counted among the clean, others among the unclean animals.

Clement centers his selection around the material paralleled in the Bible. To a large extent, the borrowings are literal. In a certain sense Clement's exegesis deforms Philo's interpretation. The latter urges the necessity of an equal treatment in an unequal situation, and he focuses this on an interpretation with strong anti-discriminatory overtones. After borrowing the Philonic interpretations, Clement concludes, oddly enough, that inequalities are necessary, although not based on race but on belief.[75]

2.21 *Str.* II 95,1 - *Virt.* 148-149

II 95,1 "But the benign word, *abounding* in humanity, teaches that *neither is it right to cut down fruit trees nor to cut down the ear of corn before the harvest for the sake of mischief, nor to destroy* cultivated *fruit at all,* whether it is of fruit of the soil or of the soul. For *it does not even permit devastating the land of the enemies*" (cf. fr. 2.22).[76]

In the previous section, kindness to people and animals had been enjoined; in its continuation, Philo turns his attention to rules about vegetation. The transitions between the various subjects are lucidly and fluently handled. The treatment of fruit trees forms the first subject; Philo supports a wise administration of the environment, not only for an essential food supply but also for a comfortable life.

Clement plunges into this material without any introduction or transition and proceeds in a disconnected way. The subject of the sentence is not

---

[73] In this passage Méhat, *Étude*, p. 220-221, identifies Clement's own vocabulary in μηνύω, μεταδίδωμι, λογίζομαι, ἀλληγορία, πιστός, ἄπιστος, γεωργία. This is not quite correct because all the above mentioned words occasionally do occur in Philo as well. μετανοέω (*Str.* II 97,3 and passim) and τιμάω (*Str.* II 98,2) are even taken from Philo's passage directly. Methodologically it seems more secure to use the texts as a comparison and as a basis for looking for alterations or additions.

[74] Rather often Clement uses the image of γεωργία to refer to the growth and the harvest of philosophy, whether this is Greek or Christian. cf. *Str.* I 7,1; 37,1ff. (connected with the comparison of the sower); 43,1ff. (on occasion of John 15:1, the vine); VI 67,2. In *Str.* II 96,1 he summarizes by saying that the image of the farming (ὁ τῆς γεωργίας τύπος) is a way of teaching (διδασκαλίας τρόπος).

[75] Cf. *Str.* VII 109,1. The theme of secrecy and concealment occurs throughout Clement's works.

[76] *Str.* II 95,1: Δαφιλευόμενος δὲ τῇ φιλανθρωπίᾳ ὁ χρηστὸς λόγος μηδὲ ὅσα τῆς ἡμέρου ὕλης ἐστί, δενδροτομεῖν ταῦτα προσῆκον εἶναι διδάσκει, μηδὲ μὴν χείρειν ἐπὶ λύμῃ στάχυν πρὸ τοῦ θερισμοῦ, ἀλλὰ μηδὲ συνόλως καρπὸν ἥμερον διαφθείρειν μήτε τὸν γῆς μήτε τὸν τῆς ψυχῆς· οὐδὲ γὰρ τὴν τῶν πολεμίων χώραν τέμνειν ἐᾷ.

Moses or the law as in Philo, but surprisingly enough ὁ χρηστὸς λόγος; for Clement, the benign word teaches. He concludes with the amplification that the cultivated fruit is interpreted as either fruit of the soil or fruit of the soul.

The borrowing is an almost literal quotation composed of dismembered sentences. The law or Moses is altered to ὁ χρηστὸς λόγος, and πρὸ καιροῦ is replaced by πρὸ τοῦ θερισμοῦ (cf. *Str.* II 85,3). It is remarkable that Clement here refers to the fruit of the soul; on many other occasions when Philo had touched on the concept of the soul, Clement never adopted it. In this case, however, Philo did not mention the human soul.

2.22   a) *Str.* II 95,1 - *Virt.* 150
           b) *Str.* II 95,2-3 - *Virt.* 156-159

II 95,1 "For *it does not even permit devastating the land of the enemies.*

II 95,2 Indeed, even *farmers* derived advantage from the law in such things. *For it orders newly planted trees to be nourished three years in succession and the superfluous growths to be cut off to prevent them being loaded and pressed down and to prevent their strength being exhausted from want by the nutriment being frittered away; (it enjoins) tilling and digging round them so that nothing mischievous may spring up at their side and hinder their growth.*

II 95,3 *And it does not allow imperfect fruit to be plucked from immature trees, but only after three years, dedicating the first-fruits to God in the fourth year after* the tree has attained maturity.

II 96,1 This image of husbandry may be taken as a mode of instruction, teaching that we ought to eradicate the suckers of sins and the barren weeds of the mind, which spring up alongside the productive fruit, until the shoot of faith has matured and grown strong.

II 96,2 For in the fourth year, since time is also needed to instruct the person firmly, the quartette of virtues is consecrated to God, while the third stage already borders the fourth abode of the Lord.

II 96,3 And a sacrifice of praise stands above burnt offerings."[77]

---

[77] *Str.* II 95,1-96,3: οὐδὲ γὰρ τὴν τῶν πολεμίων χώραν τέμνειν ἐᾷ.
95,2: ναὶ μὴν καὶ γεωργικοὶ παρὰ τοῦ νόμου καὶ ταῦτα ὠφέληνται· κελεύει γὰρ τὰ νεόφυτα τῶν δένδρων ἐπὶ τριετίαν ἑξῆς τιθηνεῖσθαι τάς τε περιττὰς ἐπιφύσεις ἀποτέμνοντας, ὑπὲρ τοῦ μὴ βαρυνόμενα πιέζεσθαι καὶ ὑπὲρ τοῦ μὴ κατακερματιζομένης τῆς τροφῆς δι' ἔνδειαν ἐξασθενεῖν, γυροῦν τε καὶ περισκάπτειν, ὡς μηδὲν παραβλαστάνον κωλύῃ τὴν αὔξησιν.
95,3: τόν τε καρπὸν οὐκ ἐᾷ δρέπεσθαι ἀτελῆ ἐξ ἀτελῶν, ἀλλὰ μετὰ τριετίαν ἔτει τετάρτῳ καθιερώσοντα τὴν ἀπαρχὴν τῷ θεῷ μετὰ τὸ τελεωθῆναι τὸ δένδρον.
96,1: εἴη δ' ἂν οὗτος ὁ τῆς γεωργίας τύπος διδασκαλίας τρόπος, διδάσκων δεῖν τὰς παραφύσεις τῶν ἁμαρτιῶν ἐπικόπτειν καὶ τὰς συναναθαλλούσαω τῷ γονίμῳ καρπῷ ματαίας τῆς ἐννοίας πόας, ἔστ' ἂν τελειωθῇ καὶ βέβαιον γένηται τὸ ἔρνος τῆς πίστεως.
96,2: τῷ [τε] γὰρ τετάρτῳ ἔτει, ἐπεὶ καὶ χρόνου χρεία τῷ κατηχουμένῳ βεβαίως, ἡ τετρὰς τῶν ἀρετῶν καθιεροῦται τῷ θεῷ, τῆς τρίτης ἤδη μονῆς συναπτούσης ἐπὶ τὴν τοῦ κυρίου τετάρτην ὑπόστασιν.
96,3: Θυσία δὲ αἰνέσεως ὑπὲρ ὁλοκαυτώματα.

a) Not only one's own natural resources must be respected, but it is even forbidden to devastate the land and the trees of the enemy in wartime, since enemies may in the future turn into friends. Plants are not hostile but pacific and serviceable, and the cultivated kinds are particularly so since their fruits are essential for human life. Scriptural source: Deut. 20:19.

Clement quotes half of one of Philo's sentences literally.

b) From *Virt.* 155 onwards Philo gives an extensive description of the treatment and nursing of trees and fruit. After three successive years the newly planted tree is strong enough so that in the fourth year it will be able to bear perfectly (τελειογονεῖν), in harmony with the perfect number four. This first fruit must be dedicated to God. Scriptural source: Lev. 19:23f.; cf. *Plant.* 95,117.

The transition in Clement is made by ναὶ μὴν καί. He borrows according to the usual scheme; an almost literal part at the beginning is followed by a paraphrased continuation. Towards the end of the borrowing (*Str.* II 96,1ff.), Clement gives his own interpretation introduced by the phrase εἴη δ'ἄν, the standard opening words of one of his own allegories.

Clement explains first that the image derived from agriculture signifies a method of instruction[78] that teaches cutting off the proliferation of sin and the useless weeds of the mind until the shoot of faith has attained durability and strength. This explanation is continued by a cryptic last sentence in which Clement says: "For in the fourth year, since time is also needed to instruct the person firmly, the quartette of virtues is consecrated to God, while the third stage already borders the fourth abode of the Lord."

The period of three years and the number four, a perfect number according to Philo, may have been the hinges on which Clement's allegory turns. Two parts of the allegory can be distinguished; one that touches on the growth of faith by instruction and another that refers to Gnostic perfection. In the first, our attention is attracted by the combination of the fourth year, the neccesity of time and the word τῷ κατηχουμένῳ. From writers more or less contemporary with Clement, it is known that the first phase of the instruction in faith could have been a period of three years,[79] which was followed by a second, much shorter

---

[78] Cf. note 74; τύπος is connected to γεωργίας and τρόπος to διδασκαλίας. Differently Mayor and Stählin, see BKV XVII, p. 220.

[79] H. J. Auf der Mauer/J. Waldram, Illuminatio Verbi Divini-Confessio Fidei-Gratia Baptismi, in *Fides Sacramenti, Sacramentum Fidei* (Mél. P. Smulders), 1981, p. 51.

phase. The latter may correspond with Clement's term 'in the fourth year'. The longer period is not associated specifically with the number three, but the implication is clear. In the preceding borrowing from Philo, moreover, the period of three succeeding years had been mentioned explicitly. Furthermore, it is known that an essential part in this first phase was dedicated to instruction in and practise of the virtues.[80] Thus it appears that the first section of Clement's allegory alludes to the preparation connected with catechism.[81]

In the second part of the allegory, the idea of the number four surpassing the number three returns. According to Prestige, the term 'hypostasis' must not be understood as a philosophical concept but as a word that has the meaning of 'station' or 'stop'; in this sense it is paired with another word in the sentence: abode (μονή). This word occurs rather frequently in passages in which the ascent to Gnostic perfection is alluded to. Sometimes these 'homes' are characterized as heavenly or holy, in other cases, they are called the first 'home'. Biblical sources like Jn. 14:2 must have inspired the usage.[82]

The connection between the word 'abode' and the number three can be found throughout *Str.* VI 105-114. In *Str.* VI 114,1-3, for instance, various abodes are discussed, which differ according to the dignity of the believers. In the temple of God, there are lower parts, upper parts and a conceptual superlative part for the Lord. These three abodes are linked with the numbers thirty, sixty and one hundred.[83]

Another passage may be connected with the preceding; in *Str.* VI 107,2, Clement relates the ranks in heaven with the dignities of the church below; the grades of bishops, presbyters and deacons are imitations of the angelic glory. The link between the number three and the abodes is also apparent in *Str.* VII 40,4, in which Clement speaks about the union of the Gnostic and God through prayer. He says that those who are experienced in the threefold hours for prayer (the third, sixth and ninth hour), also know about the triad of the holy abodes.

The question arises of how the two parts of Clement's allegory are connected. In a comparable passage, *Str.* VI 109,1ff., the two segments, paideia and achievement, are mentioned within one movement. Clement

---

[80] Auf der Mauer/Waldram, ibidem, p. 53.

[81] C. L. Prestige, Clement of Alexandria, Stromata 2,8, and the meaning of 'hypostasis', in *JThS* XXX (1929), p. 270-272; Camelot, *Stromates* II (SChr. 38), p. 107 note 1 (end); Méhat, *Étude*, p. 221.

[82] Cf. *Str.* IV 166,1; VI 105,1; 109,1; 109,3; VII 9,4; 57,5; 88,3. In *Str.* IV 37,1 Clement links the theme with Plato, *Phaedo* 114bc.

[83] Cf. Irenaeus, *Adv. Haer.* V 36,2.

is working in a two-phased structure, in which he makes a distinction between πίστις and γνῶσις that parallels the difference between being saved and the highest honor after being saved. In a similar way in our passage, *Str.* II 96,1-2, two phases are described in one rising movement; the first is connected with the preparatory instruction for faith and the second moves into the Gnostic perfection of faith. The number four and the concept of perfection form the binding elements between the two.[84]

Clement's statement that a sacrifice of praise[85] is superior to burnt offerings seems lost in this context. At first sight it is not at all clear if the sentence is meant to be conclusive or introductory; the latter choice is made by Stählin, judging by his layout of the text. The biblical allusions behind the passage, however, suggest that the sentence is a conclusion. The treatment of the trees, taken over by Clement in Philo's wording, is based on Lev. 19:23. The following verse, Lev. 19:24, makes mention of the fourth year in which all the fruit " shall be holy *to praise* the Lord" (... πᾶς ὁ καρπὸς αὐτοῦ ἅγιος αἰνετὸς τῷ κυρίῳ). In another place in Philo, *Plant.* 95, the two biblical verses also occur together. Whether Clement's concluding phrase has been inspired by the Septuagint directly or by way of Philo must be left an open question.

2.23   *Str.* II 96,3-97,1 - *Virt.* 165-168

II 96,3   " 'For he', it says, 'gives you strength to get power'. And if *your affairs are enlightened, get and keep strength and acquire power* in knowledge.

II 96,4   For thereby it is shown that both good things and gifts are supplied by God, and that we, becoming ministers of the divine grace, ought to sow the benefits of God and *make those who are near us* noble and good; so that *as far as possible, the temperate may make others continent, the courageous make them noble,* the wise may make them intelligent, and *the just may make them just.*

II 97,1   This is the Gnostic, who is after the image and likeness of God, *who imitates God as far as possible, deficient in none of the things which contribute to the attainable likeness,* practising self-restraint and endurance, living righteously, reigning over the passions, *sharing* what he has as far as he can, and doing good both in word and deed."[86]

---

[84] Marrou, *Paed.* I (SChr. 70), Introd. p. 31.

[85] θυσία αἰνέσεως, Ps. 49:23 / Hebr. 13:15 (both θυσία αἰνέσεως and καρπός).

[86] *Str.* II 96,3-97,1: "οὗτος γάρ σοι", φησί, "δίδωσιν ἰσχὺν ποιῆσαι δύναμιν". ἐὰν δὲ φωτισθῇ σοι τὰ πράγματα, λαβὼν καὶ κτησάμενος ἰσχὺν ἐν γνώσει ποίει δύναμιν. 96,4: ἐμφαίνει γὰρ διὰ τούτων τά τε ἀγαθὰ τάς τε δωρεὰς παρὰ τοῦ θεοῦ χορηγεῖσθαι καὶ δεῖν ἡμᾶς, διακόνους γενομένους τῆς θείας χάριτος, σπείρειν τὰς τοῦ θεοῦ εὐποιίας καὶ τοὺς πλησιάζοντας κατασκευάζειν καλούς τε καὶ ἀγαθούς, ἵνα ὡς ὅτι μάλιστα ὁ μὲν σώφρων τοὺς ἐγκρατεῖς, ὁ δὲ ἀνδρεῖος τοὺς γενναίους συνετούς τε ὁ φρόνιμος καὶ δίκαιος τοὺς δικαίους ἐκτελῇ. 97,1: Οὗτός ἐστιν ὁ "κατ᾽ εἰκόνα καὶ ὁμοίωσιν", ὁ γνωστικός, ὁ μιμούμενος τὸν θεὸν καθ᾽ ὅσον οἷόν τε, μηδὲν παραλιπὼν τῶν εἰς τὴν ἐνδεχομένην ὁμοίωσιν, ἐγκρατευόμενος, ὑπομένων, δικαίως βιούς, βασιλεύων τῶν παθῶν, μεταδιδοὺς ὧν ἔχει, ὡς οἷός τέ ἐστιν, εὐεργετῶν καὶ λόγῳ καὶ ἔργῳ.

In accordance with the words from Deuteronomy—"he gives you strength to make power"—Philo gives an explanation of the gift of power. He distinguishes two possibilities in using power; the first deals with people who become rich themselves and make others poor, while the second refers to the opposite: wise, good and worthy people who impart these qualities to others. Philo describes what he understands by real δυνάμεις and what their aim is; they appeal to the rational part of the soul in its attempt to imitate God and to leave nothing undone that could promote such assimilation. Scriptural source: Deut. 8:18.

Clement moulds Philo's concept of 'strength for power' to his own ideas. The new focus appears from the alterations in wording: εὐρωστῇ becomes φωτισθῇ while ἐν γνώσει is added.[87] Other manifestations of his point of view appear in a word like χορηγεῖσθαι and the explanation that *we* as ministers of divine grace must show the benefits of God. He also inserts the words συνετούς τε ὁ φρόνιμος in the double series of virtues. When this elaborate structure of adaptation and addition is sorted into its separate components, it becomes evident how skillfully Clement makes Philo's thoughts shade off into his own; the process is one of editing not copying. The element of intentional reworking becomes even more clear when Clement, referring to Gen. 1:26, gives a description of the Gnostic;[88] he is not only, in Philo's words, imitating and assimilating, but also, in his own words, self-restraining, enduring, living justly, king over his emotions, sharing and doing good.

The passage is a paraphrase with various literal elements, which are woven into Clement's own line of thought in a complex way. This method of work is necessitated by the different approaches of the two authors. For Philo, the rational nature is the central point around which his attention revolves; Clement, on the other hand, focuses himself on the Gnostic, understood within a Christian framework.

2.24   *Str.* II 97,2 - *Virt.* 168-172

II 97,2   " 'He is the greatest', it says, 'in the kingdom, who shall do and teach', *imitating God by freely bestowing benefits of the same kind; for God's gifts are for the common good.* "[89]

God gives his benefits to men, and men themselves are able to do likewise. The benefits must be used and enjoyed but not misused by harming

---

[87] Cf. Prümm, Glaube und Erkenntnis, p. 50 Anm. 50.
[88] Marrou, *Paed.* I (SChr. 70), Introd. p. 41; Völker, *Wahre Gnostiker*, p. 111ff.
[89] *Str.* II 97,2: οὗτος "μέγιστος", φησίν, "ἐν τῇ βασιλείᾳ ὃς ἂν ποιῇ καὶ διδάσκῃ" μιμούμενος τὸν θεὸν τῷ παραπλήσια χαρίζεσθαι· κοινωφελεῖς γὰρ αἱ τοῦ θεοῦ δωρεαί.

others. In continuation, Philo touches on arrogance and pride, vices that had been mentioned earlier in *Virt.* 161; to reinforce this theme he quotes Num. 15:30.[90]

Clement adds to the passage about the imitation of God a verse from the gospel of St.Matthew; "He is the greatest in the kingdom who shall do and teach (Mt. 5:19)." This biblical text joins and amplifies the previous sentence. Philo's definition of God as ὁ πρῶτος ἡγεμών is concisely replaced by θεός. As the end of Philo's treatises comes into sight, the borrowings become more and more abrupt. This is evident in *Str.* II 97,3 from μετανοεῖν onwards; these words are borrowed from Philo's next treatise *De Paenitentia* (corresponding with *Virt.* 183), while the previous part of Clement's sentence refers to *De Humanitate* (corresponding with *Virt.* 171-172); in an ingenious way, the two fragments are combined in one sentence. The last fragments testify once again how biblical references catch Clement's eye in making a selection.

2.25   *Str.* II 97,3-98,2 - *Virt.* (171-172) 183-185

II 97,3   "'*Whosoever sets his hand to do anything with presumptuousness provokes God*', it is said. For arrogance is a vice of the soul, of which as of other sins, he commands us *to repent, by adjusting our lives from a state of derangement to a change for the better by these three things: mouth, heart and hands.*
II 98,1   *These are symbols: the hands of action, the heart of volition, the mouth of speech.* Beautifully, therefore, *has this word been spoken* about penitents; '*You have chosen God today to be your God, and the Lord has chosen you today to be his people*'. For him who is eager to serve the Existent, being a suppliant, God adopts to himself.
II 98,2   *And though he be only one in number*, he is honored equally with the people. For being a part of the people, he becomes complementary of it, being restored from what he was, and the whole is named from a part."[91]

In this treatise, or perhaps sermon, about μετάνοια,[92] Philo insists that repentance is within reach. He calls for conversion from disobedience to

---

[90] See also fr. 2.25.
[91] *Str.* II 97,3-98,2: "ὃς δ' ἂν ἐγχειρῇ τι πράσσειν μεθ' ὑπερηφανίας, τὸν θεὸν παροξύνει," φησίν· ἀλαζονεία γὰρ ψυχῆς ἐστι κακία, ἀφ' ἧς καὶ τῶν ἄλλων κακιῶν μετανοεῖν κελεύει ἁρμοζομένοις τὸν βίον ἐξ ἀναρμοστίας πρὸς τὴν ἀμείνω μεταβολὴν διὰ τῶν τριῶν τούτων, στόματος, καρδίας, χειρῶν.
98,1: σύμβολον δ' ἂν εἴη ταῦτα, πράξεως μὲν αἱ χεῖρες, βουλῆς δὲ ἡ καρδία καὶ λόγου <τὸ> στόμα. καλῶς οὖν ἐπὶ τῶν μετανοούντων εἴρηται τὸ λόγιον ἐκεῖνο· "τὸν θεὸν εἵλου σήμερον εἶναί σου θεόν, καὶ κύριος εἵλετό σε σήμερον γενέσθαι λαὸν αὐτῷ." τὸν γὰρ σπεύδοντα θεραπεύειν τὸ ὂν ἱκέτην ὄντα ἐξοικειοῦται ὁ θεός.
98,2: κἂν εἷς ᾖ τὸν ἀριθμόν, ἐπ' ἴσης τῷ λαῷ τετίμηται· μέρος γὰρ ὢν τοῦ λαοῦ συμπληρωτικὸς αὐτοῦ γίνεται, ἀποκατασταθεὶς ἐξ οὗ ἦν, καλεῖται δὲ καὶ ἐκ μέρους τὸ πᾶν.
[92] See note 73.

obedience to the law, which according to the words from Deuteronomy is not far off, not too high, nor at the other side of the sea, but nearby in our mouth, hand and heart. The choice made by an individual person is done in interaction with God, according to another passage from Deuteronomy, in which it is said that mankind chooses God and God chooses mankind to be his people. Philo explains that one honest and sincere person has a value equal to that of a whole nation. He adopts for this purpose the image of a pilot on a ship, or a general in an army, who alone is worth as much as all the others together: his failure may be equivalent to the destruction of the entire force. Biblical sources: Deut. 30:11-14; 26:17.

Clement reflects Philo's thoughts in a paraphrase colored with literal components. The transition is ingeniously fitted in (cf. fr. 2.24), and the selection is defined by the passages from Deuteronomy. Clement diverts Philo's explanation of the second biblical reference by leaving the ethical realm and moving into an eschatological dimension. Philo's concept of singularity and multitude is adapted by Clement to the idea of the restauration of mankind.

The additional words ἀποκατασταθείς, μέρος and συμπληρωτικός make this evident[93]. Other comparable passages in Clement clarify his purpose in using these terms, cf. *Str.* II 134,2; IV 132,1. Especially close correspondences are found in the latter passage, in which the building of the body of Christ, the unity of the faith and the fullness of Christ are discussed as a commentary on Eph. 4:11ff. Clement thereby describes the Gnostic on his way to perfection and his return to the fullness of Christ.

Thus Philo's concept of singularity and multitude, applied to one wise person who is in worth equal to a whole nation, is transposed by Clement to the unity and diversity of the believers and the admission in the fullness of Christ. The connection between εὐγένεια (see *Str.* II 98,3, fr. 2.26) and ἀποκατάστασις is made in *Str.* IV 132,1 as well as when Clement says εἰς τὴν ἀποκατάστασιν τῆς τῷ ὄντι τελείας εὐγενείας...

2.26   *Str.* II 98,3-99,2 - *Virt.* 203-210

II 98,3 ''But nobility itself is exhibited in choosing and practising what is best. For what benefit to Adam was such nobility as he had? *No mortal was his father*; for he himself was father of men that are born.
II 98,4 Following his wife *he readily chose the dishonourable things* and neglected what is true and good; *on which account he exchanged his immortal life for a mortal life*, but not for ever.

---

[93] A. Méhat, "Apocatastase", Origène, Clément d'Alexandrie, Act. 3,21, in *VigChr* 10 (1956), p. 196-214; Wyrwa, *Platonaneignung*, p. 188.

II 99,1 And Noah, whose origin was not the same as Adam's, *was saved* by divine care. For he took and consecrated himself to God. And Abraham, *who had children by three wives, not for the indulgence of pleasure, but in the hope, as I think, of multiplying the race,* was at first succeeded *by one alone who was heir of his father's blessings, while the others were separated* from the family; **II 99,2** and *of the twins who sprang* from him, *the younger* having won his father's favour *became heir and received his prayers, and the* elder *served him.* For *it is the* greatest *benefit to a bad person not to be his own master.''*[94]

Philo's brief treatise about repentance ends in *Virt.* 186; from *Virt.* 187 onwards the value of the nobleness of birth forms the topic. True nobility is based on wisdom and cannot be transmitted by virtuous ancestors to their offspring. There is no justification for nobility since we do not inherit these gifts. In *Virt.* 203 the first human beings appear; although their parent was not mortal but the eternal God, they went wrong, and Adam had to exchange his immortality for mortality. Philo continues his theme of inheritance with various examples of good parents and degenerate sons, as also of malicious ancestors and virtuous descendants. The conclusion in *Virt.* 226/227 is that everyone will be judged by his conduct and not by his descent.

Giving a kind of bird's-eye view, Clement makes excerpts from various passages of Philo's last treatise, which is illustrated with stories about the patriarchs. Clement makes his selections around Adam, Noah, Abraham and Abraham's descendants. εὐγένεια is demonstrated by choosing and practising excellence.[95] He omits Philo's idea that this virtue is found in the sovereign part of the soul and is directed toward wisdom. With Philo's words, Clement acknowledges that Adam made the wrong choice, but in his own words he adds that Adam had followed his wife and neglected what was true and good. Adam's choice, however, was not definitive, and he was not abandoned for ever.[96] Noah dedicated himself to God, and Abraham had only one successor. ἀποδείχθη is altered to διαδέχεται.

---

[94] *Str.* II 98,3-99,2: αὕτη δὲ ἡ εὐγένεια ἐν τῷ ἑλέσθαι καὶ συνασκῆσαι τὰ κάλλιστα διαδείκνυται. ἐπεὶ τί τὸν Ἀδὰμ ὠφέλησεν ἡ τοιαύτη αὐτοῦ εὐγένεια; πατὴρ δὲ αὐτοῦ θνητὸς οὐδείς· αὐτὸς γὰρ ἀνθρώπων τῶν ἐν γενέσει πατήρ.
98,4: τὰ μὲν αἰσχρὰ οὗτος προθύμως εἵλετο ἑπόμενος τῇ γυναικί, τῶν δὲ ἀληθῶν καὶ καλῶν ἠμέλησεν· ἐφ' οἷς θνητὸν ἀθανάτου βίον, ἀλλ' οὐκ εἰς τέλος, ἀνθυπηλλάξατο.
99,1: Νῶε δὲ ὁ μὴ οὕτω γενόμενος ὡς ὁ Ἀδὰμ ἐπισκοπῇ θείᾳ διασῴζεται· φέρων γὰρ αὐτὸν ἀνέθηκε τῷ θεῷ. τόν τε Ἀβραὰμ ἐκ τριῶν παιδοποιησάμενον γυναικῶν οὐ δι' ἡδονῆς ἀπόλαυσιν, δι' ἐλπίδα δέ, οἶμαι, τοῦ πληθῦναι τὸ γένος ἐν ἀρχῇ, εἰς μόνος διαδέχεται κληρονόμος τῶν πατρῴων ἀγαθῶν, οἱ δὲ ἄλλοι διωχίσθησαν τῆς συγγενείας·
99,2: ἔκ τε αὐτοῦ διδύμων γενομένων ὁ νεώτερος κληρονομεῖ εὐάρεστος τῷ πατρὶ γενόμενος, καὶ τὰς εὐχὰς λαμβάνει, δουλεύει δὲ ὁ πρεσβύτερος αὐτῷ· ἀγαθὸν γὰρ μέγιστον τῷ φαύλῳ τὸ μὴ αὐτεξούσιον.
[95] Cf. *Str.* II 98,3.
[96] See also Irenaeus, *Adv. Haer.* I 28,1-2; III 23,1-8; Bradley, Transformation, p. 48.

2.27   *Str.* II 99,3 - *Virt.* 211-219 ?

> **II 99,3**   "And this arrangement was prophetical and typical. It clearly
> indicates that all things belong to the wise when it says 'Because God has
> had mercy on me, I have all things'. For it teaches that we are to desire
> one thing, by which are all things and that what is promised is assigned to
> the worthy."[97]

In the context of bad parents and good children Philo speaks about
Abraham being a descendant of parents who were astrologers and
idolaters; his life and personality, however, are standards of virtue and
nobility.

Clement focuses on the idea that everything belongs to the wise and links
this idea with Gen. 33:11. No immediate parallel to and hardly any
reminiscence of the Philonic passage presents itself. Clement's use of
Gen. 33:11, which is the earliest in the Christian tradition, however,
reveals a more distant influence from Philo (cf. *Str.* II 20,1; the same
biblical verse is quoted in Philo, *Sacr.* 42).

2.28   *Str.* II 100,2 - *Virt.* 215-217

> **II 100,2**   "and again, teaching that the wise man is king, it introduces
> people of different race saying to him (Abraham) 'you are a king before
> God among us'; since the subjects obey the good man voluntarily because
> of his desire for virtue."[98]

Abraham who is regarded as a king represents the faithful and virtuous
man. Philo alludes to Gen. 23:6 (cf. *Mut.* 152; *Somn.* II 244; *Abr.* 261,
where he quotes this part of the biblical verse literally). Abraham is not
a king by appearance but because of the greatness of soul. Philo says that
his spirit is the spirit of a king.

Clement seems to reflect Philo's passage in his own way. Some words like
ἀρχομένων, ἀρετῆς, ὑπακουόντων and τῷ σπουδαίῳ may have been taken
over from the Philonic context. Clement quotes Gen. 23:6 more overtly
than Philo has done in the texts that parallel *Virt.* 215-217. Clement is
again the earliest in the Christian tradition to quote this biblical verse.

---

[97] *Str.* II 99,3: ἡ δὲ οἰκονομία αὕτη καὶ προφητικὴ καὶ τυπική. ὅτι δὲ τοῦ σοφοῦ πάντα ἐστί,
σαφῶς μηνύει λέγων· "διότι ἠλέησέν με ὁ θεός, ἔστι μοι πάντα." ἑνὸς γὰρ δεῖν ὀρέγεσθαι
διδάσκει, δι' οὗ τὰ πάντα γέγονεν καὶ τοῖς ἀξίοις τὰ ἐπηγγελμένα νέμεται.

[98] *Str.* II 100,2: πάλιν τε αὖ βασιλέα τὸν σοφὸν διδάσκων τοὺς μὴ ὁμοφύλους ποιεῖ λέγοντας
αὐτῷ· "βασιλεὺς παρὰ θεοῦ σὺ ἐν ἡμῖν εἶ," ἐθελουσίῳ γνώμῃ τῶν ἀρχομένων διὰ ζῆλον ἀρετῆς
ὑπακουόντων τῷ σπουδαίῳ.

Unlike the previous section, a clear reminiscence of Philo's treatment is present.

Clement concludes with a Christian elaboration; a heir is a good person who takes the citizenship of the kingdom seriously. The people who lived in a just way under the law and before the law was given also have a chance. This explanation concludes the sequence of borrowings from Philo and forms the transition to a new subject, the description of the 'final objective' according to various philosophical schools. The name of Philo turns up in this transitional section; Clement evokes him as a supporter of Pythagoras, cf. *Str.* I 72,4. The reference is unexpected because it had been so conspicuously absent in the entire previous passage. The transitional section itself is inserted in chapter VII (cf. sub *Str.* II 100,3), because no special reminiscence to *De Virtutibus* is apparent.

3. Conclusions

3.1 Technique of borrowing

3.1.1 Frequency and sequence

Clement's borrowings from Philo's *De Virtutibus* fall into a standard, almost rhythmic pattern from a technical point of view. In the previous units we already saw this technique, but nowhere had it been carried through as steadily as here.[99] Underlining the parts of Philo's text that Clement takes over first the frequency of the borrowings appears, then their regular spacing and finally and perhaps most strikingly, their progressive sequence. On almost every page of a modern text, some lines have been used in a continuous reading. The first selection is made at a point halfway through the treatise on courage, but then Clement jumps back to the beginning of the treatise to continue borrowing from there. This 'anticipatory technique' has already been noted in previous chapters. Mondésert's suggestion about Clement's use of the Bible, namely, that he seems almost to be scrolling and unscrolling the source manuscript before him as he works on his own text, functions equally well for Clement's use of Philo.[100] The schematic overview in 1.2 demonstrates this method quite clearly. After a relatively brief 'anticipation', he returns to the beginning of his scroll and advances steadily through it thereafter.

[99] Méhat, *Étude* p. 234, 238.
[100] Mondésert, *Clément*, p. 73.

3.1.2 Focus of the selection

Of the four treatises of Philo on virtues, which are entitled courage, humanity, repentance and nobility, the largest is that on humanity.[101] From this treatise, Clement has taken over almost all the prescriptions; only the introduction, which describes the last days of Moses, has been omitted from consideration.[102] A limited harvest has been taken from the first treatise on courage, and his collection from the last two on repentance and nobility are progressively sparser. A similar method of exploitation with varying degrees of intensity has been seen earlier.[103]

Clement's choice seems to be centered on the biblical prescriptions submerged in Philo and which he takes over in Philo's words. The text of the Bible may not always be present literally in the Philonic passage, but a biblical content and structure lies in the background unmistakably. When the biblical content fades too far into the distance, for example by conflation of several scriptural passages, as in the story of the Midianite women, then Clement's adaptation seems to be much freer (cf. *Str.* II 83,3-84,1). It is striking that at times Clement seems to pursue the thought of the biblical passage even farther than Philo does, as in *Str.* II 96,3, where he probably goes into the verse of Leviticus beyond the one used by his model. In one case where Philo quotes the Septuagint literally, Clement quotes the passage even more fully (in *Str.* II 94,1).

Clement has given this cursory reading from Philo to reinforce his position that there is one law, which is good and just throughout. He treats the well-sorted and well-adapted material that he finds in Philo as essentially equivalent to a direct reading from the Bible, and he gratefully uses it as a reliable biblical synopsis convenient for his purposes.

3.1.3 Formal structure

Clement moves rapidly across his model detaching scraps of sentences from their original contexts.[104] It is obvious that the product of this kind of a working method will often be fragmented and difficult to interpret. Only after comparison with the original source, can transitions, development and conclusions of the borrowings be seen in their intended perspective. In a number of cases, transitions are very abrupt. These harsh juxtapositions of abbreviated thoughts are partly caused by Cle-

---

[101] see note 5, p. 70.
[102] This is considered to be an appendix on *VM*.
[103] see p. 43.
[104] Méhat, *Kephalaia*, p. 248; Colson VIII, p. XIIa.

ment's disconnected manner of excerpting, but they are also caused in part by the rich complexity of the source material itself, since Philo brings so many different biblical rules under one common denominator. Abrupt transitions were observed in *Str.* II 81,1; 83,3; 85,3; 88,3; 90,1-2; 94,3; 95,1; 96,3.

Still, Clement regularly gives these abbreviated fragments an introductory phrase; he does this in a declarative form: for example, παντί που δήλη (*Str.* II 78,2); or περί τε τῆς μεταδόσεως ... ἀπόχρη μόνον τοῦτο εἰπεῖν (*Str.* II 84, 4); ἐμοὶ δὲ δοκεῖ (*Str.* II 92,1). He may also use an interrogative form of introduction: for example, ἐπεὶ τίνα λόγον ἔχει (*Str.* II 81,3); ἆρ' οὐ δοκεῖ σοι (*Str.* II, 85,1); τί δέ; (*Str.* II 88,1; 90,1); ἢ γάρ; (*Str.* II 86,5).[105]

Clement also employs single transitional words like πάλιν (*Str.* II 82,1; 86,6; 93,2; αὐτίκα *Str.* II 84,1; 92,1); αὖ (*Str.* II 86,2); ναὶ μὴν (καί) (*Str.* II 86,3; 88,2; 88,4; 95,2); ἔπειτα (*Str.* II 89,2); ἔτι (*Str.* II 91,3). Sometimes these transitions are taken over from Philo's text, like ἔτι (*Str.* II 85,2); πάλιν (*Str.* II 87,3). In some cases Clement introduces his subject by using 'headlines' like περί τε τῆς μεταδόσεως καὶ κοινωνίας (*Str.* II 84,4); τούς τε πολεμίους (*Str.* II 88,3); Νῶε δέ (*Str.* II 99,1); τόν τε 'Αβραάμ (*Str.* II 99,1).

The borrowing itself may be of varying degrees of fidelity, but the different types may well be combined in a single passage. Their sequence, moreover, tends to fall into a regular pattern within a passage. A distinction must be made between literal use, paraphrase with literal components and reminiscences. These categories form a diminishing progression in which the Philonic substratum is less and less recognizable. The paraphrase with literal components is the most common technique, and within this technique, a certain development takes place; Clement often starts literally and finishes by paraphrasing.

The dilution of the Philonic content also takes place in a broader context; as we approach the end of *De Virtutibus*, Clement's borrowings often become looser and more abrupt. Loosening of form is broadly characteristic of Clement's working methods; his attention is attracted by the core, which he adapts carefully, while he is relatively indifferent to its trappings. Not only the beginning and the development, but also the conclusion of a borrowing have characteristic forms.

Often Clement gives his borrowing an additional explanation, mostly in the form of an allegory. He can allegorize with a short formula, as in *Str.* II 81,2; 81,4; 88,2; 93,1; 94,5; 95,1; 98,2; sometimes the form is more extensive: *Str.* II 96,1/2; 99,3. In a few cases, Clement explains the

---

[105] Méhat, *Étude*, p. 232 identifies spoken language here.

borrowing with an etymology or thought that he may have derived from
a different passage in Philo: *Str.* II 84,5; 86,3; 88,2.

A different kind of conclusion is formed by the quotations from Proverbs, which are seeded throughout the *Stromateis*; in this passage, they
occur in *Str.* II 78,4; 83,2; 84,1; 86,7; 88,1; 91,4.[106] The reference to
Barnabas, as the N.T. 'dossier' from the first epistle of Clement, is a
similar sort of concluding element. These scriptural and post-scriptural
references are introduced to reinforce the material from Philo. Sometimes the link to the previous material may be evident, but on other occasions the connection is very tenuous.[107] Sometimes Clement accompanies his conclusion with a final phrase like ἤδη οὖν συνίεμεν (*Str.* II
86,4); ὁρᾷς (*Str.* II 89,1); ἄρα ἤδη καταφαίνεται (*Str.* II 91,1).

3.1.4   Alterations in general

The Philonic model can be altered in various ways. In the previous section, 3.1.3, examples have been given of supplementary explanations
concluding a borrowing. These comments, which usually transpose the
material onto a Christian level, can occur not only at the end of the borrowing but at almost any point during its course as well. Clement puts
his example in a different light either with a single word or with a more
elaborate thought. He does this not only by rephrasing in his own words
but also by introducing reminiscenses of the N.T. In addition to the
places mentioned in 3.1.3, examples of this phenomenon occur in *Str.* II
83,1; 84,4; 86,1; 86,4; 86,7; 89,1; 90,1; 90,3; 91,4; 96,2; 96,4; 97,1.

A special position is occupied by the additions in which Clement seems
to question his source: ἐπεὶ τίνα λόγον ἔχει (*Str.* II 81,3); εἰ (*Str.* II 92,2);
τάχα (*Str.* II 94,4). The alterations that arise by compression or abbreviation have already been touched on in the preceding section; the omission
of themes that are essential for Philo will be discussed in the following
section since this is more a matter of content than technique. Substitu-
tions remain to be considered; these verbal transpositions can involve the
use of synonyms in which no significant shift of meaning occurs.
Examples of this appear in *Str.* II 81,1/2; 81,3; 85,3; 88,2; 89,1; 90,2;
90,3; 95,1; 97,2. Intentional alterations of meaning by the use of another
word or, more subtly, by the use of the same word in another case or as
another part of speech occur in *Str.* II 78,3; 80,5; 81,4; 83,4; 96,3/4;
99,1.

---

[106] These biblical texts reveal no sequence.
[107] Méhat, *Étude*, p. 237.

3.2 Alteration of content and points of comparison

The many changes that appear in Clement's handling of material taken from Philo have their roots in the different starting positions of the two authors. These positions influence the course of each author's thought continuously. The theoretical problem is therefore one of comparing two different categories. Philo's intentions are, moreover, uncertain to some degree; his four heterogeneous treatises, which cover in Cohn's edition about seventy pages, may not necessarily have been intended by the author to be arranged as they are at present.

Clement does not adapt more than one seventh of Philo's text and, moreover, infuses it with all sorts of material of his own and from other sources. Yet in spite of dissimilarities of purpose, background and sheer length, there is one important binding factor, which is objectively demonstrable; both writers have numerous partial or complete sentences in common, and these common elements are, in fact, substantial enough to form a good basis for a comparison even though their contexts may be different.

Philo's point of departure seems to be an apologetic one; this intention generally emerges between the lines rather than overtly, but in *Virt.* 141, he protests openly against slanderous ideas to the effect that Jewish laws were asocial and particularistic. His book is in large part occupied with giving examples to demonstrate the contrary. Bringing many, often unrelated laws under the common denominators of a few virtues must have been motivated by these outside attacks.

Just as Clement does, Philo focuses on general virtues like justice, prudence, temperance, courage and self-restraint, to which he adds piety and humanity. Philo develops a kind of doctrine of virtues from apologetic motives on the basis of the law of Moses. The concept of doctrine must be understood in a restricted sense, however, since the above-mentioned virtues are an arbitrary series that can be extended or abbreviated at will. Most of the biblical texts are lodged under the title of humanity. The prescriptions of the law represent the virtues and not vice versa; the virtues are attributes of the law, labels that make the qualities of the law recognizable in broader terms. The law offers people a primary training that leads them on their way to God.

It is striking that Philo in *De Virtutibus* did not find an occasion to allegorize in the way that is so familiar from his other works. He does not find it necessary to transpose the law onto any other level. The law as such incorporates the virtues and leads to knowledge. A few general philosophic concepts like this are stated unobtrusively or lie semi-hidden between the lines.

At the very beginning, he points out that courage is identical with knowledge (*Virt.* 1). In other places, the equation between the virtues and wisdom reappears; for example in *Virt.* 190, where he uses the image of the fool, who has no home nor city and is expatriated from virtue, the native land of the wise. Knowledge leads the wise on his search for God. Philo uses several terms to designate God: generally, 'the one', but also 'the oldest', 'uncreated', 'creator of all', 'father of all spiritual and visible things', 'highest and oldest cause'.

A human being, who consists of body and soul, is directed along the highest part of the soul, now called λογικὴ ψυχή or λογικόν now ἡγεμονικόν, to know and imitate God. These various thougts, here briefly touched on, are the general philosophical substratum of Philo's exposition in *De Virtutibus*. His essential orientation, however, is determined by the rules of the law, along which he has grouped his treatises and which he transmits in his own words. The entire composition is an attempt to pull the law of Moses out of its isolation and to give it a respected position within the thought of his time and environment.

Clement, on the other hand, has a motivation that is more polemical than apologetic. He wants to show that law and faith form a unity. No separation is allowed since God is simultaneously good and just;[108] this identity is valid from beginning to end. The concept that the same law is just and good forms a recurrent refrain: *Str.* II 78,3f.; 86,1; 86,6; 91,1; 95,1. In order to maintain this unity within the law, Clement actualizes it for his audience and on the other hand develops allegorical interpretations of it. Clement says explicitly that *we ourselves* are addressed by the law. The use of the first person plural is an intentional and necessary element in Clement's transposition; *Str.* II 81,3; 82,2; 86,4; 90,1; 96,4; 100,1.

To give form to this actualization and to develop his initial polemic theme, he goes on to say that the law educates for virtue; the verbs παιδεύω/παιδαγωγέω and διδάσκω are employed for this end. In the first pair, he employs the Pauline idea (Gal. 3:24) that the law educates unto Christ. διδάσκω is repeatedly inserted to reinforce the prescriptions from the law; the law teaches: *Str.* II 78,2; 85,1; 86,3; 86,5; 87,3; 90,1; 95,1; 96,1; 97,2; 99,3. Clement thereby offers a variation on Philo, who in addition to διδάσκω makes regular use of verbs that express a command. Not only does the law educate to Christ but a reversal also takes place in which it is the Lord himself who teaches (*Str.* II 90,1) and in which the χρηστὸς λόγος takes the place of the χρηστὸς νόμος (*Str.* II 95,1); the

---

[108] Marrou, *Paed.* I (SChr. 70), Introd. p. 33; H. J. Horn, Antakoluthie der Tugenden und die Einheit Gottes, in *JAC* 13 (1970), p. 5-28, esp. p. 22-24.

benign word is rich in humanity and teaches the prescriptions of the law, in this case, the rules for cultivating and pruning trees.[109]

In addition to his efforts to actualize, Clement applies the technique of allegory to the individual rules, which he takes over so abundantly from Philo, in order to transpose them into a new spiritual context. Thus as indicated in 3.1.3, he can do this in several ways; he may use a short supplementary phrase; in *Str.* II 81,4, for example, he alludes to martyr- dom in connection with courage, or in a more elaborate allegory in *Str.* II 96,1/2, he makes a link occasioned by the numbers three and four, with the time of preparation and accomplishment of faith.

The role of the virtues is not easy to characterize in the passage centered on Philonic material. Clement has not developed a coherent system of virtues any more than Philo had. The virtues alternate with each other in various series: cf. 1.1. He does, on the other hand, have distinct preferences, and he applies combinations that tend to fall into fixed patterns, as Méhat has started to map out.[110] In our passage, ἐγκράτεια and σωφροσύνη, ὑπομονή and καρτερία occur prominently; in a more polemical setting, δικαιοσύνη is an important notion, and in connec- tion with *De Virtutibus*, εὐσέβεια, κοινωνία and φιλανθρωπία are dominant.

It seems too easy to suggest, as some authors do, that for Clement the virtues represent a lower stage in the development of the believer while knowledge prevails on a higher level.[111] Knowledge (γνῶσις) is too much a matter of both head and heart for him, and it is, therefore, not easy to detach from other important elements of his theological thought.

Our passage subtly reveals Clement's conception of the role of the vir- tues in the development towards gnosis. In *Str.* II 86,7; 87,2, he gives an interpretation in which ἀγάπη, love for one's neighbour, forms the key- word. Clement explains this concept of love, expanding it with synonyms like χρηστότης and with other words in order to flavour the concept. Apparently this key word has an over-all function, and it is defined by Clement as undivided (ἀμέριστος), undistinguished (ἀδιάκριτος) and com- municative (κοινωνική). In *Str.* II 87,2, Clement has, as it were, gathered and elevated the various virtues to the level of ἀγάπη, where there is no longer any need to distinguish them. The question whether individual virtues are fused together and assimilated to other concepts similar to ἀγάπη (like faith and hope) would be interesting to investigate, but answers lie beyond the present passage.

---

[109] For γεωργία, see note 74, p. 97.
[110] Méhat, *Étude*, p. 362f.
[111] Classen, see note 3, p. 80, 81.

When Clement's adaptation is held up to the light of its Philonic source, it becomes evident that Clement uses Philo's treatises entirely in service of his own objectives: that is, to show within a Christian polemical situation directed against Marcion and his followers that law and faith cannot be detached from one another.[112] He has chosen *De Virtutibus* as characteristic examples of the law extracted from their original setting, and he treats this extract as equivalent to a direct and continuous reading of the Bible. The Philonic borrowings represent a useful synopsis of essential material that lies ready to hand. Because Clement's attention is centered on the biblical texts lying behind Philo's words, he eliminates the peripheral Philonic material. Philo had developed his argument around these biblical concepts for the purpose of showing the outside world that the law of Moses stands in harmonious connection with the ideas and customs of the Hellenistic world.

The differences in perspective obviously lead to other differences, like the attitudes of both authors toward the philosophical currents of their days. Both have lines of communication with the Stoa that are evident in their lists of virtues and in the way that the virtues are mutually engaged. Clement, however, emphasizes the idea of conquering the πάθη by ἐγκράτεια; this relationship, although not entirely absent, is played down in Philo. The latter, on the other hand, describes the human being along Platonic lines with special stress on the subdivision of the soul; the articulation of the soul plays almost no role in this part of Clement. Similar observations can be made with regard to Philo's interest in describing the function of divine providence, the role of the one God and the concept of national community; the link he makes between law and nature is also missing in Clement.

The most important difference between the two Alexandrians, however, lies in their conception of the law and the relationship between virtues and knowledge within it. For Philo it is the unallegorized law that incorporates the totality of the virtues and that leads in a dynamic movement to knowledge. Virtues and knowledge, although distinguished, are at the same time interchangeable. In Clement, a different relationship emerges between law, virtues and knowledge. The law and the virtues, which are incorporated in the law, form an essential condition to travel the way that leads to knowledge, which stands at a higher stage. To express this progressive relationship, Clement needs the allegorical inter-

---

[112] Harnack, *Marcion*, p. 102f.; 245ff.; Mondésert, *Clément*, p. 146; B. Aland, Marcion, Versuch einer neuen Interpretation, in *ZThK* 70 (1973), p. 420-447; R. Riedinger, Zur antimarkionitischen Polemik des Klemens von Alexandreia, in *VigChr* 29 (1975), p. 15-32.

pretation, here passed over by Philo; only in this way can Clement move from the precondition for travelling the way up to its result, or in other words, bridge the gap between possibility and final realisation.

CHAPTER FIVE

THE TEMPLE, VESTMENTS AND THE HIGH PRIEST

Str. V 32-40

1.1   Introductory remarks

Clement's description of the temple and the vestments of the high priest
stands in a long tradition, whose Old Testament background is formed
mainly by Ex. 26-28. The first chapters of this passage of Exodus
carefully detail the framework and covering of the tabernacle and the
screens that separate its various parts. Colors and kinds of materials, and
measures, sizes and quantities are specified; these numerical specifica-
tions form a striking aspect of the description. The liturgical furnishings
and finally the vestments of the high priest with their elaborate and
precious ornaments receive a similar detailed and colorful treatment.

Philo and Flavius Josephus seem to follow an established tradition in
taking up this subject matter and giving it a symbolic development not
found in Exodus.[1] Already traditional is the use of the tabernacle and the
priest's vestments as an image for the surrounding universe with stars
and planets, evoked by the gold and the variety of colors in the original
biblical text. The treatments of this in Philo and Josephus, however, differ greatly. Josephus's description of the construction is extensive while
his symbolic interpretations are, in contrast with Philo, rather meager.
The most important passages in Philo dealing with this material are *VM*
II 71-135, the background text of Clement's passage, *Spec.* I 66-97 and
QE II 51-124. In addition, there are shorter passages like *Leg.* II 56; III
119; *Cher.* 101-106; *Ebr.* 87; *Migr.* 102f.; *Her.* 215f.; *Congr.* 117; *Fug.*
108ff.; *Somn.* I 214f.; *Spec.* I 296f. The Epistle to the Hebrews carries the
theme into the specifically Christian realm.[2] As in Jewish writers, the
heavenly high priest and his heavenly sanctuary appear; in this case, the
high priest is fully identified with Christ. In the Apostolic Fathers,[3] in

---

[1] Josephus, *Antiq.* III 102-224; *Bell.* V 184-237; next to Philo and Josephus see also
Sap. 18:24; Sir. 45:6-13.

[2] For the literature see Herbert Braun, *Handbuch zum NT* 14, 1984, Exc. 17 p. 71,
Jesus der himmlische Hohepriester, (Test. XII and Qumrantexts are included).

[3] 1 Clem. 36,1; 61,3; 64,1; Ign. *Phld.* 9,1; *Pol.* 12,2; *Mart. Pol.* 14,3; cf. Schrenk, in
TWNT III, p. 284.

Justin and in various Gnostic teachings the tradition lives on, basically nourished by the Epistle to the Hebrews.[4]

Clement stands in this line of descent and manages to incorporate material from all these radiating traditions and, at the same time, is able to make his own distinct contribution to them. He provides symbolic interpretations of the temple and the vestments both as a whole and in their different parts. The passage of Exodus lies in the background of his treatment, but he introduces another descriptive theme, namely the entrance of the high priest, whose basis is supplied by Leviticus 16.[5] In Clement's interpretation of this liturgical action, the high priest represents Christ who becomes visible to the world by the creative power of the logos and by his coming into human being. At the same time, the high priest represents the Gnostic who moves upward to an unceasing contemplation.

Philo's description of the temple and the vestments is propelled by a cosmological preoccupation; he develops a scheme in which the universe in its totality is ruled by God and revolves around God and his powers. The way in which God reveals himself to men like Abraham and Moses is also determined in cosmological terms. In Marguerite Harl's formulation, "Le savoir cosmologique est le plus haut enseignement de la révélation divine."[6] Cosmology and anthropology are extensions of each other; mankind as the most important element of creation is compared to a sanctuary. The human soul represents a second sanctuary after a first sanctuary, which is the universe; the second sanctuary is transformed into a microcosm in tune with the cosmic harmony.[7] The purpose of God for the world as a whole and his intention for mankind are two related sides of the same principle; insight into the origins and the harmony of the cosmos may provide man knowledge of God himself.

In Clement, the emphases are different; he avails himself of cosmological models and terms but puts the accents elsewhere. Ultimately his motivation is the idea that the faithful rise up to a spiritual reality above time and space, to which Christ gives the dimension. The reverse of this rising movement is the incarnation of Christ; the ascent of man is only possible through the descent of Christ. Cosmology is pres-

---

[4] See *BiPatr* I, 519-524.

[5] Lev.16:4.

[6] M. Harl, Cosmologie grecque et représentations juives dans l'oeuvre de Philon d'Alexandrie, in *PAL*, 1967, p. 189-203; H. F. Weiss, *Untersuchungen zur Kosmologie des hellenistischen und palästinischen Judentums* (TU 97), Berlin 1966.

[7] Cf.*Cher.* 101-106; *Ebr.* 87; *VM* II 135; *QE* II 51.

ent but transformed since the creative power of the logos is simultaneously the redeeming power of Christ.

1.2   Schematic overview[8]

2.1	*Str.* V 32,2	—	*VM* II 118?
2.2	*Str.* V 32,3	—	*VM* II 87*-88
2.3	*Str.* V 33,1-3	—	*VM* II 101 105?
2.4	*Str.* V 33,4	—	*VM* II 81? 101*
2.5	*Str.* V 34,4-7	—	*VM* II 114f.? 101*
2.6	*Str.* V 34,8-9	—	*VM* II 102-103
2.7	*Str.* V 35,3	—	*VM* II 104
2.8	*Str.* V 35,5	—	*VM* II 82.95?
2.9	*Str.* V 35,6	—	*VM* II 97ff.?
2.10	*Str.* V 37,1	—	*VM* II 117?
2.11	*Str.* V 37,5-38,1	—	*VM* II 131?
2.12	*Str.* V 38,2	—	*VM* II 130? 122
2.13	*Str.* V 38,2-3	—	*VM* II 122
2.14	*Str.* V 38,4	—	*VM* II 124

Demonstrable sequences in:

2.2	*Str.* V 32,3	—	*VM* II 87-88
2.3	*Str.* V 33,1-3	—	*VM* II 101
2.4	*Str.* V 33,4	—	(*VM* II 101)
2.5	*Str.* V 34,4-7	—	(*VM* II 101)
2.6	*Str.* V 34,8-9	—	*VM* II 102-103
2.7	*Str.* V 35,3	—	*VM* II 104
2.12	*Str.* V 38,2	—	*VM* II 122
2.13	*Str.* V 38,2-3	—	*VM* II 122
2.14	*Str.* V 38,4	—	*VM* II 124

2.   Individual passages

2.1   *Str.* V 32,2 - *VM* II 118?

V 32,1 "It would lead too far to go through all the prophets and the Law, picking out what is expressed through enigmas; for almost the entire Scripture speaks through inspiration in this way. For any one of intelligence it may suffice, I think, to select a few examples to prove the point at hand. **V 32,2** Now, connected with concealment is the special meaning of what is told among the Hebrews about the seven circuits around the old temple, and also the equipment on the robe, whose multicolored symbols allude to celestial phenomena, which indicates the agreement from heaven down to earth."[9]

---

[8] See p. 26.

[9] *Str.* V 32,1-2: Μαχρὸν δ' ἂν εἴη πάντα ἐπεξιέναι τὰ προφητικὰ καὶ τὰ νομικὰ τὰ δι' αἰνιγμάτων εἰρημένα ἐπιλεγομένους. σχεδὸν γὰρ ἡ πᾶσα ὧδέ πως θεσπίζεται γραφή. ἀπόχρη δ', οἶμαι, τῷ γε νοῦν κεκτημένῳ εἰς ἔνδειξιν τοῦ προκειμένου ὀλίγα τινὰ ἐκτεθέντα παραδείγματα. 32,2: αὐτίκα ὁμολογεῖ τὴν ἐπίκρυψιν ἡ περὶ τὸν νεὼν τὸν παλαιὸν τῶν ἑπτὰ περιβόλων πρός τι ἀναφορὰ παρ' Ἑβραίοις ἱστορουμένη ἥ τε κατὰ τὸν ποδήρη διασκευή, διὰ ποικίλων τῶν πρὸς τὰ φαινόμενα συμβόλων τὴν ἀπ' οὐρανοῦ μέχρι γῆς αἰνισσομένη συνθήκην.

In *VM* II 66-187, Philo describes Moses in his function as high priest. Of particular interest in this connection is the first part, *VM* II 66-140, in which Philo deals with the construction of the sanctuary and its furnishings, the ark, the altar of incense, the candlestick, the table and the altar of offerings. Subsequently, he describes the vestments of the high priest and their meaning, and he concludes with an exposition on the construction of the bronze basin. In presenting the clothing of the high priest, Philo first describes the elements that make up the outer appearance: the gown or tunic,[10] the cape that covers the shoulders,[11] their colors, their materials and their ornamentation (109-116).

He then proceeds to their meaning (117-135);[12] the costume has to be considered both as a whole and in its components as a representation of the cosmos and its parts. The full length gown is violet because it is an image of the air, which is naturally black. The air stretches out everywhere from below the moon to the ends of the earth, the gown therefore covers the entire body from the chest to the feet (118). The relationship between the cosmic elements, earth, water and air, is brought in; Philo states (119ff.) that they are mutually interdependant and that they are in harmony with the all.[13]

Clement continues the theme of hidden meanings that had occupied him in the previous section by introducing the seven circuits around the temple and the ornamentation of the clothing of the high priest as examples of hidden meanings in Scripture. Strikingly, he does not give any further mention of the tantalizing seven circuits. They do not appear in any other source known to us,[14] but in *Str.* V 33,3, he refers to a circuit as a place for people who are excluded from the temple's interior. The vestment of the high priest symbolizes both the heavenly bodies, and by extension the covenant (συνθήκη) between heaven and earth. This might have been inspired by the Epistle to the Hebrews, in which Christ, who is called the high priest, will make a new covenant (διαθήκη) with the house of Israel.[15]

---

[10] Philo gives several words for this gown: ὁ ὑποδύτης (*VM* II 109); ὁ ποδήρης (*VM* II 117); ὁ χιτών (*VM* II 118); it appears from *VM* II 117,118, that for Philo ποδήρης is equivalent to χιτών. In the LXX these two are considered to be different, cf. Ex. 28:4.

[11] This is also called 'ephod'.

[12] In Josephus a similar way of treatment occurs: first the external description and then the symbolic meaning.

[13] Background text: Ex. 28. Parallels in Philo: *Spec.* I 85-95; *Migr.* 102f.; cf. Josephus, *Antiq.* III 184.

[14] Cf. Le Boulluec, *Str.* V (SChr. 279), p. 135.

[15] Hebr. 8:8.10; 9:15; also in Clement is the term διαθήκη as covenant with God a more common term than συνθήκη; cf. Stählin, *Clemens Al.* IV (GCS 39), 1936, s.v.

No literal material passes from one author to the other. At most it could be called a distant echo. διὰ ποικίλων τῶν πρὸς τὰ φαινόμενα συμβόλων (p. 347 l. 5/6) can be associated with Philo's entire passage connecting the vestments with the cosmic elements, while ἀπ᾽οὐρανοῦ μέχρι γῆς (p. 347, l. 6) forms a comparison with ἄνωθεν ἀπὸ τῶν μετὰ σελήνην ἄχρι τῶν γῆς ... περάτων (C-W IV, p. 227, l. 20). A major variation on the distant Philonic model is formed by Clement's reference to the covenant between heaven and earth in order to explain the priest's colorful clothing. While Philo does not speak about such a covenant, he does give an extended cosmological speculation on the three elements, their mutual interdependence and their relationship to living creatures that is missing in Clement.

2.2   Str. V 32,3 - VM II 87*-88

> **V 32,3** "The *covering* and the *veil* were stitched with various colors, *with blue and purple and scarlet and linen*; these hinted at the revelation of God, since the nature of the elements contains them.[16] *For purple comes from water, linen from earth, blue being dark is like air, as scarlet is like fire.*"[17]

In his description of the building of the tabernacle, Philo speaks of the multicolored fabrics lavished on it (*VM* II 88-89). Not only does he repeatedly mention the four colors blue, purple, red and white, but he also calls attention to the numbers 4, 5, 9, 10, 28 and 40. The enumeration of both colors and numbers form important elements in the background text (Ex. 26). While he follows the biblical text for the colors, Philo goes off on his own in mentioning the numbers 9 and 40, which are missing in Exodus. The Septuagint, on the other hand, uses the numbers 11 and 50, which are not found in Philo.

In the terminology of the various fabrics, Philo also diverges from the Septuagint.[18] As a general term, he uses woven work (ὑφάσμα(τα): *VM*

---

[16] ἐπέχει with the meaning of 'containing' according to the reading of L; cf. Méhat, *Kephalaia*, p. 231; Le Boulluec, *Str.* V (SChr. 279), p. 135; for more examples of this meaning see *Str.* IV 39,3; VI 138,2.

[17] *Str.* V 32,3: τό τε κάλυμμα καὶ παραπέτασμα ὑακίνθῳ καὶ πορφύρᾳ κόκκῳ τε καὶ βύσσῳ πεποίκιλτο, ἠνίττετο δ᾽ ἄρα, ὡς ἡ τῶν στοιχείων φύσις περιέχει, τὴν ἀποκάλυψιν τοῦ θεοῦ· ἐξ ὕδατος μὲν γὰρ ἡ πορφύρα, βύσσος δὲ ἐκ γῆς, ὑάκινθός τε ὡμοίωται ἀέρι ζοφώδης ὤν, ὥσπερ ὁ κόκκος τῷ πυρί.

[18]

Ex. 26:1ff.	αὐλαίαι	(idem Philo)
Ex. 26:7	δέρρεις	
Ex. 26:14	κατακάλυμμα	
	ἐπικαλύμματα	
Ex. 26:31	καταπέτασμα	(idem Philo)
Ex. 26:36	ἐπίσπαστρον	(κάλυμμα Philo)

cf. A. Pelletier, Le grand rideau du vestibule du Temple de Jérusalem, in *Syria* XXXV (1958), p. 218-226; Idem, La tradition synoptique du Voile déchiré, in *RSR* 46 (1958),

II 84,93); subsequently, he distinguishes the curtains (αὐλαίαι: *VM* II 84, 85, 86, 87), of which there are ten according to the Septuagint, as well as the covering (χάλυμμα: *VM* II 87) by which the outer part of the sanctuary is shielded from view, and the veil (καταπέτασμα: *VM* II 80, 86ff.) with which the inner part of the sanctuary is covered.[19] All these textiles have the four above-mentioned colors that allude to earth, water, air and fire because, as Philo concludes, the fabric of the temple built by human hands refers to the basic elements from which the Creator has made the cosmos.[20]

Without any real introduction to the theme of the tabernacle, Clement launches himself into the covering and the veil; his terms are χάλυμμα and παραπέτασμα. As in the Septuagint and Philo, these textiles are worked with four colors, and in the footsteps of Philo, they are linked with the elements, which are characterized by just these tints. In Clement, however, the nexus of colors and elements stands in the sign of the revelation of God; this theme gives a new direction to the Philonic model.

Technically, Clement gives a paraphrase with literal components from *VM* II 87-88. The sequence of Philo's text is preserved. Almost literal is the mention of the colors (p. 347, ll. 7-8), but he varies κόκκινος (Septuagint and Philo) with κόκκος, and he reverses the order of βύσσος and πορφύρα on their second appearance (p. 347, ll. 9-10).

p. 161-180. The temple schematically presented by U. Früchtel, *Die kosmologischen Vorstellungen bei Philo von Alexandrien*, 1968, p. 77:

---

[19] The similar terminology easily caused confusion; cf. Le Boulluec, *Str.* V (SChr. 279), p. 136, in which παραπέτασμα and καταπέτασμα are confused. Clement speaks on p. 347 l. 12 of παραπέτασμα (Aquila's version of Ex. 37:3) and on p. 347 l. 15 of καταπέτασμα. Philo only uses καταπέτασμα, according to the LXX, (see previous note) in *VM* II 80, 86, 87 (2x), 95, 101.

[20] Background text: Ex. 26; for the color scheme in this order, cf. Ex. 37:3. Parallels: *Congr.* 117; *Fug.* 110; *QE* II 85; cf. Josephus, *Bell.* V 212-213; *Antiq.* III 124, 183.

In the distinction of covering and veil (p. 347, l. 7) Clement follows Philo very closely but varies the Philonic κατάπετασμα with παραπέτασμα in accordance with Aquila's version of Ex. 37:3.[21] The reference to the cosmic elements is paraphrased in Clement; comparable is τοῖς στοιχείοις ἰσαρίθμους ἐξ ὧν ἀπετελέσθη ὁ κόσμος (C-W IV, p. 221, ll. 1-2) to Clement's adaptation: ἠνίττετο δ'ἄρα ὡς ἡ τῶν στοιχείων φύσις περιέχει (p. 347, ll. 8-9). A variant can also be distilled from ποικίλλειν (p. 347, l. 8) (to embroider with various colors) and the Philo's συνυφάνθαι (VM II 87) (weaving together), to which can be added ποικίλοις ὑφάσμασι as a reminiscence (C-W IV p. 219, ll. 20-21). The explanation ζοφώδης ὤν (p. 347, l. 10)[22] is a variation on Philo's φύσει γὰρ μέλας οὗτος (C-W IV p. 221, ll. 4-5).

Clement opts for a description of κάλυμμα and παραπέτασμα according to the Philonic version of the Septuagint material; he abbreviates it strongly and leaves out the speculations on numbers entirely. A theologically significant shift in content is the emphasis on the idea of revelation. For Philo with his interest in the creation of God, the cosmological context is of primary importance, but for Clement, cosmology is downplayed, and the revelation of God[23] is the center of attention.

2.3   Str. V 33,1-3 - VM II 101
105?

V 33,1   "In the midst of the covering and the veil where the priests were allowed to enter was situated the altar of incense, as a symbol of the earth placed in the middle of this cosmos, from where the vapors came.
V 33,2   And that place intermediates between the inner veil, where on prescribed days the high priest alone was permitted to enter, and the external curtain surrounding it,[24] accessible to all Hebrews; they say that this is the middlemost point[25] of heaven and earth. But others say it is the symbol of the intellectual and sensible world.
V 33,3   The covering then, as a barrier against popular unbelief, was stretched over the five pillars, keeping back those in the surrounding space."[26]

---

[21] Cf. Méhat, Kephalaia, p. 232.
[22] Cf. Str. V 37,1 (fr. 2. 10). Stoic theme, for sources see Le Boulluec, Str. V (SChr. 279), p. 136.
[23] Identified by Méhat as term from Clement's vocabulary, Méhat, Étude, p. 220.
[24] Stählin has translated αὐλή instead of αὐλαία, BKV XIX p. 146.
[25] According to L.
[26] Str. V 33,1-3: ἀνὰ μέσον δὲ τοῦ καλύμματος καὶ τοῦ παραπετάσματος, ἔνθα τοῖς ἱερεῦσιν ἐξῆν εἰσιέναι, θυμιατήριον [τε] ἔκειτο σύμβολον τῆς ἐν μέσῳ τῷ κόσμῳ τῷδε κειμένης γῆς, ἐξ ἧς αἱ ἀναθυμιάσεις.
33,2: μέσος δὲ καὶ ὁ τόπος ἐκεῖνος τοῦ τε ἐντὸς τοῦ καταπετάσματος, ἔνθα μόνῳ τῷ ἀρχιερεῖ

Philo treats the several units that are mentioned in Exodus systematically without, however, following the sequence of Exodus. The discussion of the colorful fabrics is extended in a catalogue of the furnishings of the tabernacle. After the ark and its covering, called the mercy seat, he deals with the other three articles of furnishing from *VM* II 101 onward: the altar of incense, the candlestick and the table. These three objects stand in the space called the πρόναος, which is between the four and five pillars and is shut off by the two woven screens, the κάλυμμα on the outside and the παραπέτασμα on the inside.

The altar of incense is, according to Philo, placed in the middle as a symbol of thankfulness for what earth and water bring forth. These elements, earth and water, have been assigned a position in the middle of the cosmos. In *VM* II 105, Philo interprets the candlestick and the altar of incense as a representation of heaven and earth; the candlestick had earlier been called a symbol of the sun, and here he designates the altar of incense as the earth, from which vapors arise.[27]

Clement also gives a connected but concise discussion of the furnishings of the temple. At the basis of his approach are the following distinctions; there is a space for priests, which borders both the holy of the holies, the space that only the high priest may enter, and the place assigned to the Hebrews, who he elsewhere identifies as the λαϊκή ἀπιστία (p. 347, l. 19). His interest in the various ranks and restrictions also appears in words like: ἐξῆν εἰσιέναι (p. 347, l. 12); ἔνθα μόνῳ .. ἐπετέτραπτο εἰσιέναι (p. 347, l. 15); the play on words κάλυμμα - κώλυμα (p. 347, l. 19); εἶργον ... (p. 348, l. 1). This interest derives from Clement's theme: the necessity to conceal truth that is intended only for insiders.[28] Different sources can be distinguished, as is made clear by φασί (p. 347, l. 17) and ἄλλοι λέγουσιν (p. 347, ll. 17-18). In the latter, θυμιατήριον is explained as symbol of the intellectual world and world of sense.

In this section Clement apparently has in mind Philo's *VM* II 101 since the symbolism of the altar of incense as cosmic centerpoint does not exist in the other sources known to us, the Septuagint and the Epistle to the Hebrews. In elaborating this reminiscence, however, Clement proceeds

---

ἐπετέτραπτο ῥηταῖς εἰσιέναι ἡμέραις, καὶ τῆς ἔξωθεν περικειμένης αὐλαίας τῆς πᾶσιν ἀνειμένης Ἑβραίοις· διὸ μεσαίτατον οὐρανοῦ φασι καὶ γῆς· ἄλλοι δὲ κόσμου τοῦ νοητοῦ καὶ τοῦ αἰσθητοῦ λέγουσιν εἶναι σύμβολον.

33,3: τὸ μὲν οὖν κάλυμμα κώλυμα λαϊκῆς ἀπιστίας ἐπίπροσθε τῶν πέντε τετάνυστο κιόνων, εἶργον τοὺς ἐν τῷ περιβόλῳ.

[27] Background text: Ex. 30:1f. Parallels: *Her.* 218ff.; *Spec.* I 285ff.; *QE* II 91ff.; cf. Josephus, *Antiq.* III 147.

[28] Cf. Den Boer, *Allegorese*, p. 134ff.; Méhat, *Étude*, p. 492ff.; Lilla, *Clement*, p. 144ff.

in his own direction. In Philo, the altar of incense symbolizes thankfulness for earth and water. Clement takes over the symbolism of earth but leaves water out, and earth is characterized not by fruitfulness but by vapors, an attribute mentioned slightly later by Philo (cf. *VM* II 105). αὐλαία (p. 347, l. 16) is a variation of Philo's κάλυμμα (*VM* II 101). Clement has adapted the idea of the centerpoint for a different purpose; Philo means it as a cosmological center: τὸν γὰρ μέσον ταῦτα τοῦ κόσμου τόπον κεκλήρωται. Clement, on the contrary, seems to speak about a more exclusively spiritual locus, which is accessible in varying degrees. He calls this the centerpoint of heaven and earth, but this characterization is connected less with cosmological position than with human position; people are related to that middle point as insiders and outsiders.[29]

This 'esoteric' element is missing in the corresponding context in Philo. When he speaks about the hierarchy of priests, the division of tasks and obligations is primarily at issue (cf. *VM* II 174ff.). Clement's second level of interpretation of the altar of incense as image of the sensible and intellectual world is difficult to attribute to a specific source. The paired concepts represent a familiar Platonizing distinction which may be little more than a commonplace both in Clement and in Philo. Clement, indeed, suggests that he has taken various sources into consideration, but it is hard to determine if they are in the form of documents on his table or recollections in the back of his mind.

2.4   *Str.* V 33,4 - *VM* II   81?
(101*)

V 33,4 "So, very mystically, five loaves are broken by the Saviour and fill the crowd of the listeners. For great is the crowd that adheres to the things of sense as if they were the only things in existence.
V 33,5 'Cast your eyes round and see', says Plato, 'that none of the uninitiated listen. Such are they who think that nothing else exists but what they can hold tight with both hands but do not admit as part of existence actions and processes of generation and the whole of the unseen'.
V 33,6 For such are those who cling only to the five senses. Inaccessible to the ears and similar organs, however, is the perception of God."[30]

In the course of his speculation on the numbers fifty and five, Philo explains five as the number of the senses, which are directed to two sides,

---

[29] Den Boer, *Allegorese*, p. 69ff.

[30] *Str.* V 33,4-6: ταύτῃ τοι μυστικώτατα πέντε ἄρτοι πρὸς τοῦ σωτῆρος κατακλῶνται καὶ πληθύνουσι τῷ ὄχλῳ τῶν ἀκροωμένων. πολὺς γὰρ ὁ τοῖς αἰσθητοῖς ὡς μόνοις οὖσι προσανέχων. 33,5: ''ἄθρει δὴ περισκοπῶν,'' φησὶν ὁ Πλάτων, ''μή τις τῶν ἀμυήτων ἐπακούῃ. εἰσὶ δὲ οὗτοι οἱ οὐδὲν ἄλλο οἰόμενοι εἶναι ἢ οὗ ἂν ἀπρὶξ τοῖν χειροῖν λαβέσθαι δύναιντο, πράξεις δὲ καὶ γενέσεις καὶ πᾶν τὸ ἀόρατον οὐκ ἀποδεχόμενοι ὡς ἐν οὐσίας μέρει·'' 33,6: τοιοῦτοι γὰρ οἱ τῇ πεντάδι τῶν αἰσθήσεων προσανέχοντες μόνῃ. ἄβατον δὲ ἀκοαῖς καὶ τοῖς ὁμογενέσιν ἡ νόησις τοῦ θεοῦ.

namely, inside and outside (*VM* II 81). According to Philo, this is the
reason why the five pillars are placed on the boundary between inside
and outside. They symbolically represent the border between the realm
of mind and the realm of sense.[31]

The five columns in the description of the furnishings of the tabernacle
are connected by Clement with the five loaves in the miracle of the
multiplication of the loaves and fishes[32] and, further on, with the five
senses.[33] The passage exemplifies well Clement's way of piling on extra
material, in this case through association with a number, while he sticks
to his themes. Alain Le Boulluec characterizes this practice as 'discur-
sive', but it could also be termed 'association on different levels'.

On the first level, there are insiders and outsiders; on the second, contrasting sensible and noetic realms; on the next level is the description of
the temple, and finally come numbers. In Clement, all these different
layers flow into one another. The distinction between sensible and noetic
reality, to which Clement alluded in V 33,2 (fr. 2.3), has a continuation
here in a quotation from Plato's *Theaetetus*.[34] Clement's particular
interest in the 'insiders' who have access to the noetic world and the 'outsiders' who cling to the sensible world is reinforced by the use of the
Platonic text; further on, Clement will call on St. Paul as support for the
same idea.[35]

In *Str.* V 34,1-3, Clement elaborates the idea that the Son as πρόσωπον
of the Father became flesh for the five senses;[36] he is the logos who voices
the specific character of the Father. This is already a prelude to the
important concluding part of the whole passage from *Str.* V 38,5
onwards, in which Clement gives a Christian construction to some of the
elements under discussion and in which the references to Philo recede in
favor of citations of St. Paul. The apostle is also quoted in this section
(V 34,2) to reinforce the concepts of living according to the spirit and
walking by faith as opposed to walking by sight.

The number that emerges through the discussion of the five pillars is
for Clement the stimulus to continue further on other arithmetic

---

[31] Parallels: *Op.* 62; *Plant.* 133; *Migr.* 201ff. (five senses); *Somn.* I 27.

[32] Mk. 6:38; Jn 6:9.

[33] Cf. *Str.* VI 134,2.

[34] *Theaet.* 155e; Le Boulluec, *Str.* V (SChr. 279), p. 137, indicates the 'ironic' overtone
of this text, which has been adapted by Middle Platonism in a serious way. Wyrwa,
Platonaneignung, p. 255, wrongly maintains that the quotation serves "die Vorläufigkeit
des Glaubens in einem Nebengedanken fest zu halten. "

[35] Gal. 5:25; 2 Cor. 5:7.

[36] Cf. *Paed.* I 57,2; *Str.* VII 58,3 (Ps. 23:6 πρόσωπον equals Christ); *Exc.* 10,6;12,1;
23,5; Le Boulluec, *Str.* V (SChr. 279), p. 138.

examples: five loaves, five senses. In *Str.* V 34,4, the four pillars introduce a similar sort of speculation and accumulation. The connection of
the number five with the five senses is widespread; we can find many
other examples both in Philo and Clement. The link between five pillars
and senses may have Philo (*VM* II 81) as its source, but no firm evidence
supports the idea. In any case, Clement elaborates this quite
independently on the basis of the theme of the sensible and noetic world
connected with the idea of the insiders and outsiders.

Philo treats the concept of αἴσθησις differently in *VM* II 81; he says
expressly that it has a double function in man; it works not only exter-
nally but also internally, that is, toward the realm of the mind, to which
it is subordinate by the laws of nature.

2.5   *Str.* V 34,4-7 - *VM* II   114f.?
            (101*)

V 34,4 "Back to the veil of the entrance into the holy of holies there are
four pillars, a sign of the sacred tetrad of the ancient covenants.
V 34,5 Furthermore there is the mystic name of four letters, which was
affixed to those alone to whom the adytum was accessible; it is called Jahwe,
which is interpreted as 'Who is and shall be'.
V 34,6 Among the Greeks too the name of God contains four letters.
V 34,7 He alone will come into the intellectual world who has become
lord over his emotions,[37] reaching the knowledge of the ineffable and ascending above every name that is made known by the sound of a voice."[38]

In *VM* II 114f. Philo speaks about a gold plate in the form of a crown
in which four letters are engraved; it shows a name which may be heard
or pronounced only in the holy place by those whose ears and tongues
are purified. Philo connects the letters with the numbers one, two, three
and four, with the geometrical categories and with the harmonies in
music. In a parallel-text, *VM* II 132, Philo also speaks about the golden
plate above the turban of the priest. The graven shapes of four letters
indicate, "as we are told", the name of Him who is. This means that it
is impossible for anything that is to subsist without invocation of Him.[39]

---

[37] Reading according to L, without the conjecture 'ἀρχιερεύς' Ma and 'διά' Po; cf.
Méhat, *Kephalaia*, p. 234; Früchtel in St-Fr Nachträge p. 534/348,20f.
[38] *Str.* V 34,4-7: πάλιν τὸ παραπέτασμα τῆς εἰς τὰ ἅγια τῶν ἁγίων παρόδου, κίονες τέτταρες
αὐτόθι, ἁγίας μήνυμα τετράδος διαθηκῶν παλαιῶν,
34,5: ἀτὰρ καὶ τὸ τετράγραμμον ὄνομα τὸ μυστικόν, ὃ περιέκειντο οἷς μόνοις τὸ ἄδυτον βάσιμον
ἦν· λέγεται δὲ Ἰαουε, ὃ μεθερμηνεύεται ὁ ὢν καὶ ὁ ἐσόμενος.
34,6: καὶ μὴν καὶ καθ' Ἕλληνας θεὸς τὸ ὄνομα τετράδα περιέχει γραμμάτων.
34,7: εἰς δὲ τὸν νοητὸν κόσμον μόνος ὁ κύριος <ἀρχιερεὺς> γενόμενος εἴσεισι, <διὰ> τῶν
παθῶν εἰς τὴν τοῦ ἀρρήτου γνῶσιν παρεισδυόμενος, ὑπὲρ "πᾶν ὄνομα" ἐξαναχωρῶν, ὃ φωνῇ
γνωρίζεται.
[39] Background text: Ex. 39:30. Parallels: *Migr.* 103; cf. Josephus, *Bell.* V 235; *Antiq.*
III 178.

Schematically Clement develops παραπέτασμα in combination with the number four, as in the previous part, *Str.* V 33,3-34,4, he had set forth κάλυμμα connected with the number five. In fact the scheme goes back to Philo's *VM* II 101, in which the four and the five pillars, shut off by two woven screens, inside and outside, are mentioned. πάλιν (p. 348, l. 15) indicates that Clement takes up this schematic line. He applies the number four to the four covenants, the tetragrammon and the name of God in Greek, θεός, which consists of four letters as well.

The associations are concluded by an allegorical explanation of the 'insider'; only the person who masters the emotions or passions, the Gnostic, is allowed to enter the noetic realm. The allegory may be evoked by πάθη, which, as counterpart of the four virtues, traditionally is linked to the number four.[40] This sequence fits into Clement's usual pattern of concluding with a Christian allegory, after mentioning a number of other examples.

The point of comparison between Philo and Clement is the four letter inscription on the gold plate of the turban of the high priest. The Hebrew name of God is engraved in the plate as if on a seal; according to the Septuagint tradition in Greek, the name is replaced by (ἁγίασμα) κυρίου (Ex. 28:36). The explanation that Clement gives of the tetragrammon corresponds to Philo's words in *VM* II 132 and ultimately goes back to Ex. 3:14, which may be the most commented text of the Old Testament: ἐγώ εἰμί ὁ ὤν. The addition that Clement gives, ὁ ἐσόμενος, could be a reminiscence of Apoc. 1:4.8; 4:8, (cf. Is. 41:4), ὁ ὢν καὶ ὁ ἦν καὶ ὁ ἐσόμενος, but the verb in the Apocalypse is ἐρχόμενος. Another solution for the addition of ἐσόμενος can be that Clement supplements the Septuagint version of Ex. 3:14 with the translations of Aquila and Theodotion; both have ἔσομαι (ὅς) ἔσομαι. The use of these revised versions, if this is the case here, probably came to Clement by way of an earlier Christian or Judeo-Christian source, as it had in other such cases.[41]

Philo is, therefore, unlikely to be Clement's source here. Another reason for excluding Philo's influence at this point is the connection of the four pillars with the four ancient covenants. In Christian tradition, these convenants with Adam, Noah, Abraham and Moses represented the sum of preceding humanity.[42]

---

[40] Cf. *Paed.* I 98,2; Orig., *Sel. in Jer.* 51,21; also according to gnostic traditions, see Hippol., *Haer.* 6 32,5.

[41] Méhat, *Kephalaia*, p. 232; for a detailed study of Clement's use of the LXX and the revised versions, see O. Stählin, *Clemens Alexandrinus und die Septuaginta* (Gymn. Progr.), Nürnberg 1901; Idem, BKV VII, p. 50 note 1.

[42] Cf. Clement, *Ecl.* 51,2; see A. Luneau, *L'histoire du salut chez les Pères de l'église* (ThH 2), 1964, p. 111-112; a different development in Irenaeus, *Adv. Haer.* III 11,8; Le Boulluec, *Str.* V (SChr. 279), p. 140 also mentions Aphraates, *Demonstr.* 11,11.

2.6   *Str.* V 34,8-35,2 - *VM* II 102.103

V 34,8 "*The candlestick*, too, was placed *to the south* of the altar of incense, which shows *the motions of the seven light-bearing stars that perform their revolutions towards the south*.

V 34,9 For three branches rose *on either side of the candlestick* and on them were *lights; since* also *the sun, like the candlestick, set in the middle of the other planets dispenses the light to those above and below it according to a kind of divine harmony*.

V 35,1 The golden candlestick has another enigma of the sign of Christ, not only by its form but also by its casting light at many times and in many ways on those who believe and hope in him and look at him through the service of the 'first-created' beings.

V 35,2 And they say that the seven eyes of the Lord are the seven spirits resting on the rod that springs from the root of Jesse."[43]

After describing how the altar of incense, the candlestick and the table were placed in the vestibule of the temple (cf. fr.2.3 *VM* II 101), Philo elaborates further on the candlestick. It is placed in the south, thereby figuring the movements of the stars, because the sun, the moon and the other celestial bodies run their courses in the south. Because of this same astronomical parallel, the candlestick has six arms, three on each side; they issue from the central lampstand, which brings the number up to seven. On all these are set seven lamps, symbols of the planets. The sun, like the shaft of the candle, has the fourth place in the middle of the six other heavenly bodies and spreads light to the three above and the three below it, so tuning to harmony an instrument of music truly divine.[44]

Clement gives an abbreviated version of his example, downplaying Philo's cosmology and advancing a christological interpretation; the golden candlestick represents the sign of Christ, not only in form but also in the illumination it sheds on believers. This radiance is made possible —Clement continues with a cryptic addition—because of the service of those who are first created; he means the so-called 'protoctistes', higher

---

[43] *Str.* V 34,8-35,2: ναὶ μὴν ἥ τε λυχνία ἐν τοῖς νοτίοις ἔκειτο τοῦ θυμιατηρίου, δι' ἧς αἱ τῶν ἑπτὰ φωσφόρων κινήσεις δεδήλωνται νοτίους τὰς περιπολήσεις ποιουμένων.
34,9: τρεῖς γὰρ ἑκατέρωθεν τῆς λυχνίας ἐμπεφύκασι κλάδοι καὶ ἐπ' αὐτοῖς οἱ λύχνοι, ἐπεὶ καὶ ὁ ἥλιος ὥσπερ ἡ λυχνία μέσος τῶν ἄλλων πλανητῶν τεταγμένος τοῖς τε ὑπὲρ αὐτὸν τοῖς τε ὑπ' αὐτὸν κατά τινα θείαν μουσικὴν ἐνδίδωσι τοῦ φωτός.
35,1: ἔχει δέ τι καὶ ἄλλο αἴνιγμα ἡ λυχνία ἡ χρυσῆ τοῦ σημείου τοῦ Χριστοῦ, οὐ τῷ σχήματι μόνῳ, ἀλλὰ καὶ τῷ φωτεμβολεῖν "πολυτρόπως καὶ πολυμερῶς" τοὺς εἰς αὐτὸν πιστεύοντας ἐλπίζοντάς τε καὶ βλέποντας διὰ τῆς τῶν πρωτοκτίστων διακονίας.
35,2: φασὶ δ' εἶναι "ἑπτὰ ὀφθαλμοὺς" κυρίου τὰ "ἑπτὰ πνεύματα", <τὰ> ἐπαναπαυόμενα τῇ ῥάβδῳ τῇ ἀνθούσῃ "ἐκ τῆς ῥίζης Ἰεσσαί".

[44] Background text: Ex. 25:31ff.; 38:13ff. Parallels: *Her.* 218ff.; *Spec.* I 296ff.; *QE* II 73ff.; cf. Josephus, *Antiq.* III 144.

spriritual beings, who are put in a hierarchy above angels and archangels and contemplate the Son directly as the face of the Father.[45]

We can interpret the role of the seven 'first created' or 'seven spirits' from a parallel in Clement, *Exc.* 10, in which the celestial hierarchy is discussed. The association of these seven spirits with the candlestick here has more than one text in the background. In Apoc. 5:6, the lamb with the seven horns and the seven eyes represents the seven spirits of God sent out into the earth (cf. Apoc. 1:4). In Zech. 4:2.10, which had already been of influence on the Apocalypse, the seven-branched candlestick (!) is called the seven eyes of the Lord.

The number seven and the images of light and radiance form the connecting links between the borrowing from Philo and the Christological aenigma. Clement uses the number as a guide that leads him to the idea of the protoctistes, who are here mentioned for the first time in the *Stromateis*. A variety of biblical overtones accompanies the images.[46] The whole allegory is centered on Christ, as appears from the traditional images of the lamb and the root of Jesse.[47]

The original text of Philo is clearly recognizible in Clement; technically, it is a paraphrased borrowing with literal components and omissions. The introduction and the transition back to his Philonic source is formed by ναὶ μὴν. Clement preserves the original order, but some alterations occur; in *Str.* V 34,8, he has δεδήλωνται while in *VM* II 102, Philo has αἰνίττεται. Clement uses the word αἴνιγμα, but places it in a new setting in his Christological interpretation in *Str.* V 35,1. Another difference appears in numbering. Philo has an extensive series; besides the numbers three and seven, the six arms of the candlestick and the fourth place of the sun are mentioned. Clement restricts himself to three and seven; the latter is directly applied to the light-bearing stars; Philo had introduced it as the sum of the three double arms plus the middlepart of the candlestick.

Clement returns to Philo as a guide for the description of the temple furnishings and the vestments of the high priest, which he passes over as quickly as possible in order to move on to his own interpretation. For that purpose he minimizes the strong cosmological setting of this part of *Vita Mosis* II. Even in *VM* II 133-135, where Philo introduces a human ele-

---

[45] The imagery of the "Protoctistes" might come from a Jewish-Apocalyptic background, see Le Boulluec, *Str.* V (SChr. 279), p. 143-144; cf. Hermas, (SChr. 53 bis) *Vis.* III 4, 1, p. 108f.; *Sim.* V 3, p. 236; also J. Daniélou, *Message*, p. 221-222; Idem, *Théologie*, p. 139; Sagnard, *Exc.* (SChr. 23), p. 77 note 2.

[46] Heb. 1:1; Apoc. 5:6; Zech. 4:10; Is. 11:1f.

[47] Parallels: *Exc.* 10-12; 27,3; *Ecl.* 51,1-52,1; 56,7; 57,1.

ment, man remains attached to the greater surrounding universe. Clement has a much stronger human focus. He interprets the candlestick as Christ in his relationship to men, who are described as believers hoping and watching. The higher spiritual beings, who are ranked in a divine hierarchy, render assistance to mankind. Thus Clement uses Philo's cosmological ideas but turns them into a history of salvation.

2.7   Str. V 35,3 - VM II 104

V 35,3   "*North* of the altar of incense *was placed a table on which was* the exposition of *the loaves; for the most nourishing winds are those of the North.*
V 35,4   Seats of churches might possibly be signified, which 'breath together' to form one body and one assembly.
V 35,5   And the things recorded of the sacred ark signify the noetic realm which is hidden and closed to the many.
V 35,6   Indeed, those golden figures, each of them with six wings, signify either the constellations of the two Bears, as some will have it, or rather the two hemispheres. And the name cherubim meant 'much knowledge'.
V 35,7   But both together have twelve wings and by zodiac and by time, which moves on it, point out the world of sense."[48]

In *VM* II 104.105, Philo declares that the table with the bread and salt, is put at the north. This position is related to the north winds, which bring rain and thereby provide food. Alain Le Boulluec points out a text in Porphyrius, *Antro* 28, in which there is a play on the words βόρεια-βορά (food). The association may therefore have been traditional.[49] Philo explains that because food comes from heaven and earth in the form of rain and seeds, symbols of heaven and earth were set on the sides of the table; heaven is signified by the candlestick and earth by the vapors of the altar of incense.[50]

Clement uses Philo's wording on the position of the table in the north without specifying the functions of the north wind. Of the ingredients on

---

[48] *Str.* V 35,3-7: πρὸς δὲ τοῖς βορείοις τοῦ θυμιατηρίου τράπεζα εἶχε τὴν θέσιν, ἐφ' ἧς ἡ παράθεσις τῶν ἄρτων, ὅτι τροφιμώτατα τῶν πνευμάτων τὰ βόρεια.
35,4: εἶεν δ' ἂν μοναί τινες εἰς ἓν σῶμα καὶ σύνοδον μίαν συμπνεουσῶν ἐκκλησιῶν.
35,5: τά τε ἐπὶ τῆς ἁγίας κιβωτοῦ ἱστορούμενα μηνύει τὰ τοῦ νοητοῦ κόσμου τοῦ ἀποκεκρυμμένου καὶ ἀποκεκλεισμένου τοῖς πολλοῖς.
35,6: ναὶ μὴν καὶ τὰ χρυσᾶ ἐκεῖνα ἀγάλματα, ἐξαπτέρυγον ἑκάτερον αὐτῶν, εἴτε τὰς δύο ἄρκτους, ὡς βούλονταί τινες, ἐμφαίνει, εἴτε, ὅπερ μᾶλλον, τὰ δύο ἡμισφαίρια, ἐθέλει δὲ τὸ ὄνομα τῶν Χερουβὶμ δηλοῦν ἐπίγνωσιν πολλήν.
35,7: ἀλλὰ δώδεκα πτέρυγας ἄμφω ἔχει καὶ διὰ τοῦ ζῳδιακοῦ κύκλου καὶ τοῦ κατ' αὐτὸν φερομένου χρόνου τὸν αἰσθητὸν κόσμον δηλοῖ.; cf. Daniélou, *Message*, p. 221ff.
[49] Le Boulluec, *Str.* V (SChr. 279), p. 148.
[50] Background texts: Ex. 25:30; 29:23f.; Lev. 24:5-9 (salt); Num. 4:7; cf. Josephus, *Antiq.* II 139.

the table, he mentions the bread but not the salt. The bread, however, is touched on in the phrase 'exposition' of the loaves, παράθεσις τῶν ἄρτων, a term used only once by Clement with this meaning.[51]

From the Philonic borrowing, Clement jumps on to the interpretation of the bread; it signifies the one body and the joining together of the individual churches.[52] τινες should probably not be translated as 'some' but with a more indefinite term like the Latin 'fere' or the German 'etwa'. A variety of biblical passages lie behind the brief remark that 'the shew-breads signify the body of Christ'.[53] Parallels within Clement clarify this concise allegory and show how Clement brings together the eucharistic bread and the spiritual church in harmony with the terrestrial church.[54]

Comparison reveals that this is a rather short borrowing from Philo that is absorbed into Clement's own allusive way of thinking; it occurs in the same sequence in Clement as in Philo. Technically, it represents a paraphrase with literal components, in which Clement alters and varies a few words like: εἶχε τὴν θέσιν instead of τίθεται and ὅτι for ἐπειδή. Clement does not mention the salt and stresses the shewloaves; it is possible, as Alain Le Boulluec suggests, that various Septuagint-texts are evoked in this connection. Clement may here have been influenced by the New Testament, especially Hebr.9:2, where the presentation of the loaves is mentioned in the description of the temple.

2.8   *Str.* V 35,5 - *VM* II 82.95?

(For the translation see fr. 2.7)

Stählin refers to *VM* II 95ff., in which the ark is described; the symbolic meaning that Philo gives to it is the gracious power of God. In *QE* II 68ff., in which the relationship between God, the divine logos and the other powers is discussed, Philo calls the ark, as Clement does here, symbol of the noetic world.[55]

Although a Philonic echo is present in Clement, this borrowing is not directly from him. Clement has the noetic world shut off from the multitude; thus he projects the imagery from his own viewpoints.

---

[51] The term is uncommon; one would expect πρόθεσις τῶν ἄρτων cf. Ex. 29:23f.; Lev. 24:8; Mt. 12:4; Mk. 2:26; Lk. 6:4; Heb. 9:2; also Philo in *Congr.* 168; *Fug.* 185. παράθεσις is linked to texts like 4 Ki 6:23; 2 Chron. 11:11; Prov. 6:8.

[52] C. Mondésert, A propos du signe du Temple, un texte de Clément d'Alexandrie, in *RSR* 36 (1949) p. 580-584.

[53] Eph. 4:4; Jn 2:19-21; Col. 1:21; 1 Petr. 2:5; *Didache* 9,4.

[54] Cf. fr. III *Contra Jud.*, Stählin III p. 218, 24ff.; also *Str.* VII 32,4; 88,3.

[55] Background text: Ex. 25:10-22. Parallel: *QE* II 6.

2.9   *Str.* V 35,6 - *VM* II 97ff.

(For the translation see fr. 2.7)

Two winged creatures, called cherubim in Hebrew, are placed on the cover of the ark (*VM* II 97f.). Philo gives what is presumably a traditional terminology in Greek, ἐπίγνωσις καὶ ἐπιστήμη πολλή, and adds a symbolic meaning; the two creatures signify the two hemispheres, one above the earth and one below it. This interpretation is attributed by Philo to others (τινες μέν φασιν). His own allegorical explanation (ἐγὼ δ'ἂν εἴποιμι δηλοῦσθαι) is that the two cherubim represent the two highest powers of God, which he distinguishes as a creative and a kingly power.[56]

In *Cher.* 21ff. Philo alludes to a similar image; the cherubim and the flaming sword between them represent the revolution of the entire vault of heaven, in which the stars have their position and in which the planets have their course. In addition, Philo offers alternative interpretations of the cherubim as the two hemispheres (*Cher.* 25) or as the highest divine powers; the latter is a more personal or, as he calls it, more inspired reading ἤκουσα .... μαντεύεσθαι) (*Cher.* 27); this time he distinguishes the powers as ἀγαθότης and ἐξουσία, which are kept together by a third power, called logos, symbolised by the sword. In *QE* II 62 the etymology ἐπίγνωσις πολλή is used, and the two powers are distinguished as creative and royal, a symbolic meaning similar to what they had in *VM* II 99.[57]

Clement allots six wings to the cherubim, thereby introducing the number twelve, and gives a tightly-packed capsule of allusions;[58] the two superior beings suggest the Great and the Little Bear and the two hemispheres. He gives the etymology of the name, ἐπίγνωσις πολλή as it occurs in Philo, and the number twelve of the wings is applied to zodiac and time, which together signify the visible world. The passage is concluded and embellished with a quotation from a tragedy.[59]

No text of Philo can be clearly identified in the background of Clement's words; only some parallels in general ideas occur. Both writers have in common the etymology of the name and the reference to the two hemispheres; Philo, however, attributes the interpretation of the hemispheres to 'others', so that it has to be considered as 'common property'. Etymologies of names also have to be treated carefully; they may

---

[56] M. Harl, Cosmologie, p. 193.

[57] Früchtel, Griechische Fragmente, p. 114. Background texts: Ex. 25: 18ff.; parallels *Cher.* 25-27; *QE* II 62.

[58] Cf. Is. 6, where the Seraphim have six wings.

[59] Eurip. *Pirith.* fr. 594, A. Nauck / B. Snell, *TrGF* I p. 171; cf. Le Boulluec, *Str.* V (SChr. 279), p. 147.

well be traditional. The constellation of the two Bears and the explanation of the twelve wings are missing in Philo, but he does have the zodiac: for example, in the description of the branches of the candlestick in *QE* II 76 and with the stones on the vestments of the high priest in *Spec.* I 87; *VM* II 124. The last passage mentions the zodiac in connection with the two hemispheres. The images and allegories are intertwined and interchanged. In Philo, for example, the two cherubim signify God and his powers; Clement, on the contrary, applies this idea to the ark (*Str.* V 36,3).

Both writers have in common that they mention a variety of interpretations in a tentative way, expressing their own preferences and indicating which interpretations are their own inventions. Philo offers a more coherent picture while Clement chops his up with manifold alternative interpretations, sometimes contradicting himself in the process. In *Str.* V 35,7 he explains that the cherubim, because of their twelve wings, signify the realm of sense. In the next paragraph, in *Str.* V 36,4, however, the same beings seem to be identified with the noetic realm; their face is the rational soul, the wings are powers and the voice is glory in ceaseless contemplation.

The fragments 2.8 and 2.9 are closely related to the (non-Philonic) passage *Str.* V 36,3-4, where Clement discusses the ark and says that the Hebrew word for κιβωτός is θηβωθά. He interprets this word as one instead of one in all places (ἓν ἀνθ᾽ ἑνὸς πάντων τόπων). This interpretation is apparently unique in Clement.[60] Clement also suggests alternative meanings; "Whether it (the ark) is the eighth region and the world of thought or God, all-embracing and without shape and invisible, we may for the present defer." In any case, as Clement states, it signifies 'anapausis' that dwells with the adoring spirits, the cherubim. Clement makes an attempt to draw the contours of an eschatological reality evoked by the ark and the cherubim. As he frequently does, he only touches on the various interpretations without developing his underlying idea fully. The technique may even be a rhetorical means of leaving the interpretation loose, open and yet opaque.

It has been pointed out that the ark is also a symbol of the noetic world in Philo but is not related to the number eight. In Philo, the number seven has similar significance, while eight is not of any special interest. Clement, on the contrary, attaches great importance to eight, an interest that is paralleled in various Gnostic traditions, particularly the Valenti-

---

[60] Le Boulluec, *Str.* V (SChr. 279), p. 148.

nians, to whom he is opposed.[61] In terms of space, it refers to the eighth heaven, in time, to the eighth day, the day of the Lord and the day of the resurrection. Beyond space and time, it signifies the summit and the terminus of repose and beatitude. In Clement, the number eight is usually connected with the number seven; seven has to be traversed to reach eight.

To summarize, Clement seems to reflect a Philonic influence in the opening of his interpretation of the ark, which, as in Philo, represents the noetic world; schematically, the imagery of the supercelestials has correspondences. Yet Clement develops the theme in such a different way that he seems here to be essentially independent; echoes may reflect only a broadly common tradition.

2.10 *Str.* V 37,1 - *VM* II 117.118* ?

V 37,1 "Let it suffice that the mystic interpretation has advanced so far. The high priest's robe is the symbol of the world of sense, and the seven planets are represented by the five stones and the two carbuncles, for Cronos and Selene. The former is southern, moist, earthy and heavy; the latter aerial, whence she is called by some Artemis, because she is aerotomos (cutting the air);[62] and the air is dark.

V 37,2 And co-operating as they did in the production of things here below, those that by divine providence are set over the planets are rightly represented as placed on the breast and the shoulders; and by them was the work of creation, namely, the first week. The breast is the seat of the heart and soul.

V 37,3 Differently, the stones might be the various phases of salvation; some occupying the upper, some the lower parts of the entire saved body.

V 37,4 The three hundred and sixty bells suspended from the robe are the space of a year, 'the acceptable year of the Lord', proclaiming and sounding the magnificent epiphany of the Saviour.

V 37,5 But also the gold cap that points upward indicates the regal power of the Lord, since 'the head of the church' is the Saviour.

V 38,1 The cap on the head is, then, a sign of most absolute power; and otherwise we have heard it said: 'The head of Christ is the God and Father of our Lord Jesus Christ'."[63]

---

[61] Cf. *Str.* VI 108,1; 138-141; VII 57,1-5; *Exc.* 63,1. F. J. Dölger, Die Symbolik der Achtzahl in der sonstigen Literatur des christlichen Altertums, in *Antike und Christentum* 4, 1934, p. 175ff.; R. Staats, Ogdoas als ein Symbol für die Auferstehung, in *VigChr* 26 (1972), p. 29-52; A. Quacquarelli, *L'ogdoade patristica e suoi reflessi nella liturgia e nei monumenti*, Bari, 1973.

[62] Artemis: ἀεροτόμος, cf. Le Boulluec, *Str.* V (SChr. 279), p. 154.

[63] *Str.* V 37,1-38,1: ᾿Απόχρη μέχρι τοῦδε προχωρῆσαι τὴν μυστικὴν ἑρμηνείαν· τοῦ δὲ ἀρχιερέως ὁ ποδήρης κόσμου ἐστὶν αἰσθητοῦ σύμβολον, τῶν μὲν ἑπτὰ πλανητῶν οἱ πέντε λίθοι καὶ οἱ δύο ἄνθρακες διά τε τὸν Κρόνον καὶ τὴν Σελήνην· ὁ μὲν γὰρ μεσημβρινὸς καὶ ὑγρὸς καὶ γεώδης καὶ βαρύς, ἡ δὲ ἀερώδης· διὸ ῎Αρτεμις πρός τινων εἴρηται ἀεροτόμος τις οὖσα, ζοφερὸς δὲ ὁ ἀήρ.
37,2: συνεργοῦντας δὲ εἰς γένεσιν τῶν τῇδε τοὺς ἐφεστῶτας τοῖς πλανήταις κατὰ τὴν θείαν

After having described the clothing of the high priest according to its out-ward appearance (*VM* II 109-116), Philo passes on to its symbolic mean-ing; it represents the world in the totality of its individual parts.[64]

Clement first allegorizes the furnishings of the tabernacle, and then moves on to the clothing of the high priest, which he links to the visible or sensible world. Mentioning the five stones and the two carbuncles, which together represent the seven planets, has no parallel either in Philo or in Exodus; the latter is followed more closely by Philo than by Cle-ment. Philo only discusses two stones that he identifies as costly emeralds. Only shortly thereafter, in *Str.* V 38,2ff, Clement takes up Philo's two stones in his description of the breast and the shoulder of the vestments (see fr. 2.12-2.14). Clement has no apparent compunctions about placing different interpretations of the same thing next to one another.

This passage is centered on the number seven; as he has done else-where, Clement connects it with the seven ruling archangels,[65] the seven planets, and the seven days of creation. A second focus is formed by the chest and shoulder areas of the clothing, which are associated with activity and which ultimately point to creation. In the next section, *Str.* V 38,2.4, Clement explains that the shoulder is the beginning of the arm or hand, the limb with which work is done. Clement then offers a Chris-tian interpretation of the stones; they are fixed in a hierarchical position on the upper and the lower parts of the body that has been saved.

The idea that the variegated stones represent ways of salvation accord-ing to the rank of members of the spiritual body, that is, the church, fits well into an underlying theme of the passage; throughout, Clement has stressed the different grades of 'insider'. The number of the bells, 360, finds no correspondance in other writers; Justin and Irenaeus mention

---

πρόνοιαν ἐπί τε τοῦ στήθους καὶ τῶν ὤμων εἰκότως ἱδρῦσθαι διαγράφει, δι' ὧν ἡ πρᾶξις ἡ ἐπιγενεσιουργός, ἡ ἑβδομὰς ἡ πρώτη· στῆθος δ' οἰκητήριον καρδίας τε καὶ ψυχῆς.

37,3: εἶεν δ' ἂν καὶ ἄλλως λίθοι ποικίλοι σωτηρίας τρόποι, οἳ μὲν ἐν τοῖς ὑπεραναβεβηκόσιν, οἳ δ' ἐν τοῖς ὑποβεβηκόσιν ἱδρυμένοι παντὸς τοῦ σῳζομένου σώματος.

37,4 οἵ τε τριακόσιοι ἑξήκοντα κώδωνες οἱ ἀπηρτημένοι τοῦ ποδήρους χρόνος ἐστὶν ἐνιαύσιος, "ἐνιαυτὸς κυρίου δεκτός", κηρύσσων καὶ κατηχῶν τὴν μεγίστην τοῦ σωτῆρος ἐπιφάνειαν.

37,5: ἀλλὰ καὶ ὁ πῖλος ὁ χρυσοῦς ὁ ἀνατεταμένος τὴν ἐξουσίαν μηνύει τὴν βασιλικὴν τοῦ κυρίου, εἴ γε "ἡ κεφαλὴ τῆς ἐκκλησίας" ὁ σωτήρ.

38,1: σημεῖον γοῦν ἡγεμονικωτάτης ἀρχῆς ὁ πῖλος ὁ ὑπὲρ αὐτήν· ἄλλως τε ἀκηκόαμεν, ὡς εἴρηται· "καὶ τοῦ Χριστοῦ κεφαλὴ ὁ θεός" "καὶ πατὴρ τοῦ κυρίου ἡμῶν Ἰησοῦ Χριστοῦ".

[64] Background texts: Ex. 28:4ff.; Sap. 18:24. Parallels: *Abr.* 205; *QE* II 85; cf. Josephus, *Antiq.* III 184-187.

[65] Cf. *Str.* V 106,3; 107,1; VI 138,5; 142,4-143,1; *Exc.* 10,1 (Sagnard, SChr. 23, p. 77 note 2); 10,3; 10,5; 11,4-12; 27,3; 27,5; cf. R. Cadiou, *Introduction au système d'Origène*, 1932, p. 34-35.

the number twelve.[66] Philo, following the Septuagint, does not mention any particular number, and he connects the bells with the harmony of earth and water. In Clement, they are linked with the timespan of one year. This year is associated with the 'acceptable year' of the Lord, whose arrival the bells sonorously announce. Heinisch[67] points out that a possible correspondance with Justin is formed by the sound if not the numbering. Justin interprets the sound of the twelve bells as the preaching of the twelve apostles.

This passage of Clement is characterized by highly individual, even unique interpretations. It may be merely that the sources he uses are no longer traceable, but on the other hand, he may not have been dependant on outside sources at all. Clement is clearly comfortable manipulating and interpreting numbers. Numerical patterns had, in any case, played an important role in Exodus, the underlying model for both Philo and Clement. Clement is able to modify numerical patterns and interpretations to suit his particular situation, program and taste.

There is no clear indication that Clement has used Philo directly here. Philo follows roughly the order of the Septuagint, but some of the numbers he picks up are different, and the mythological names are missing. Stählin makes his comparison on the basis of general themes like the robe representing the universe. Such cosmological imagery pervades the whole passage in Philo (cf. *VM* II 88, 135). Creation, however, is not discussed as such but in relationship to the Creator. In performing his functions, the high priest represents creation and order in the universe, and his example deserves imitation (*VM* II 134,135).[68]

Clement, on the contrary, speaks about the robe as the κόσμος αἰσθητός; this signifies a considerable shift from Philo, for whom the universe was the cosmos in its totality, both αἰσθητός and νοητός. When Philo discusses the sensible world, for example, in connection with the five pillars (*VM* II 81f.) or the logeion (*VM* II 127), he always pairs it with the noetic world. For Stählin, the dark color of the air is another reference to Philo; the darkness of the air also appeared earlier, in *Str.* V 32,3 (fr. 2.2), in connection with the colorful curtains. In the present case, Clement takes one of the stones to represent the moon; it cuts the air—a play on the name 'Artemis'—and thereby divides the air into bright and shady regions.

In *Str.* V 32,3 (fr. 2.2), there had been a clear dependence on Philo in a related matter, the colorful curtains, and the darkness idea therefore

---

[66] Justin, *Dial.* 42,1; Irenaeus, *Adv. Haer.* I 18,4.
[67] Heinisch, *Einfluss*, p. 235.
[68] Bréhier, *Idées*, p. 170-175.

must have formed part of the borrowing. In this passage, however, the parallel is much less evident; Philo, indeed, has mentioned on various occasions that the air is dark: *VM* II 88; *QE* II 85 (curtains); *VM* II 118 (robe); *Abr.* 205 (hemispheres). In the absence of any further points of comparison, however, the idea of the color could have been taken from any of them or even from other sources, since it was probably not limited to Philo and Clement.[69]

2.11   *Str.* V 37,5-38,1 - *VM* II 131.116?

For the translation see fr. 2.10

After discussing the meaning of the high priest's vestments (*VM* II 109-130), Philo deals with his headdress, which he calls κίδαρις, a kind of a persian turban.[70] Philo states that a turban instead of a diadem on the priest's head expresses the judgement that whoever is consecrated to God is superior to all others, not only to ordinary laymen but also to kings.[71]

Clement indicates that the gold hat, which he calls πῖλος, signifies the royal power of the Lord as head of the church; a small florilegium of texts from the epistles of St. Paul[72] that use the word 'head' forms the leitmotif for this passage; Christ is the head of the church, while God is the head of Christ. The theme of the 'head' also returns in the succeeding passage (*Str.* V 38,2.5.6).

Except from the general idea, self-evidently evoked by the elevation of the hat, no parallel with Philo can be found in Clement's handling of the image.

2.12   *Str.* V 38,2 - *VM* II 130?
VM II 122

V 38,2 "Moreover there was a chestpiece (peristetion) consisting of the ephod (epomis),[73] which is the symbol of work, and the logeion (logion);[74] the latter indicates the logos and is the symbol of heaven, made by the word, and subjected to Christ, the head of all things, inasmuch as it moves in the same way and in a like manner.

---

[69] Chrys. *SVF* II, *fr. phys.* 562, p. 177; Plut. *Mor.* 381D; cf. Le Boulluec, *Str.* V (SChr. 279), p. 171.

[70] Cf. Plut. *Vitae* 1025E (κίταρις).

[71] Background text: Ex. 28:37 (μίτρα); cf. Josephus, *Antiq.* III 172.

[72] Eph. 5:23; Col. 1:18 (cf. *Paed.* II 73,3; *Str.* III 103,3); Rom. 15:6; 1 Cor. 11:3; 2 Cor. 11:31.

[73] ἐπωμίς or ephod signifies the shouldercovering.

[74] λογεῖον or λόγιον signifies the breastplate.

V 38,3   *The* luminous *emerald stones, therefore, in the ephod, signify the sun and the moon,* the co-workers of nature.

V 38,4   The shoulder is, I think, the beginning of the arm. *The twelve stones set in four rows* on the breast, *describe for us the circle of the zodiac, in the four changes of the year.*

V 38,5   It was otherwise requisite that the law and the prophets, who represent the righteous in both Testaments, should be placed below the Lord's head. For we are justified in saying that the apostles were at once prophets and righteous, 'since one and the same Holy Spirit works in all'.

V 38,6   As the Lord is above the whole world, even above the world of thought, so the name engraven on the petalon has been regarded as being 'above all rule and authority'; and it was inscribed with reference both to the written commandments and the sensible manifestation (of Christ).

V 38,7   It is the name of God that is expressed; since the Son works, seeing the goodness of the Father, being called God Saviour, first principle of all things, which was modeled after the invisible God, the first and before the ages, and which moulds all things that came into being after it.'"[75]

In *VM* II 130 Philo deals with the meaning of the logeion or breastpiece; he makes the obvious link between logeion and logos (cf. *VM* II 125ff.; *Leg.* III 119; *Spec.* I 88). He explains the significance of the 'logeion' as follows; words do not have any value, if not followed by deeds in accordance with them. Therefore the logeion is fastened to the ephod or shoulderpiece, because the shoulder is considered to be a symbol of deeds and activity. This last image returns in other words in *Mut.* 193 as well; the shoulder is the symbol of labor.

Clement starts the next section with ναὶ μήν. In his version, the chestpiece consists of the ephod and the logeion. The idea of the shoulder evokes work,[76] and the logeion is explained through logos. In his continuation,

---

[75] *Str.* V 38,2-7: ναὶ μὴν τὸ μὲν περιστήθιον ἔκ τε ἐπωμίδος, ἥ ἐστιν ἔργου σύμβολον, ἔκ τε τοῦ λογίου (τὸν λόγον δὲ τοῦτο αἰνίσσεται) [ᾧ] συνέστηκεν καὶ ἔστιν οὐρανοῦ εἰκὼν τοῦ λόγῳ γενομένου, τοῦ ὑποκειμένου τῇ κεφαλῇ τῶν πάντων τῷ Χριστῷ <καὶ> κατὰ τὰ αὐτὰ καὶ ὡσαύτως κινουμένου.

38,3: οἱ οὖν ἐπὶ τῆς ἐπωμίδος σμαράγδου φωτεινοὶ λίθοι ἥλιον καὶ σελήνην μηνύουσι τοὺς συνεργοὺς τῆς φύσεως.

38,4: χειρὸς δέ, οἶμαι, ὦμος ἀρχή. οἱ δὲ ἐπὶ τῷ στήθει τέτραχα τεταγμένοι δώδεκα τὸν ζῳδιακὸν διαγράφουσιν ἡμῖν κύκλον κατὰ τὰς τέσσαρας τοῦ ἔτους τροπάς.

38,5: ἄλλως τε ἐχρῆν τῇ κεφαλῇ τῇ κυριακῇ νόμον μὲν καὶ προφήτας ὑποκεῖσθαι, δι' ὧν οἱ δίκαιοι μηνύονται καθ' ἑκατέρας τὰς διαθήκας· προφήτας γὰρ ἅμα καὶ δικαίους εἶναι τοὺς ἀποστόλους λέγοντες εὖ ἂν εἴποιμεν, ἑνὸς καὶ τοῦ αὐτοῦ ἐνεργοῦντος διὰ πάντων ἁγίου πνεύματος.

38,6: ὥσπερ δὲ ὁ κύριος ὑπεράνω τοῦ κόσμου παντός, μᾶλλον δὲ ἐπέκεινα τοῦ νοητοῦ, οὕτως καὶ τὸ ἐν τῷ πετάλῳ ἔγγραπτον ὄνομα "ὑπεράνω πάσης ἀρχῆς καὶ ἐξουσίας" εἶναι ἠξίωται, ἔγγραπτον δὲ διά τε τὰς ἐντολὰς τὰς ἐγγράφους διά τε τὴν αἰσθητὴν παρουσίαν.

38,7: ὄνομα δὲ εἴρηται θεοῦ. ἐπεί, ὡς βλέπει τοῦ πατρὸς τὴν ἀγαθότητα, ὁ υἱὸς ἐνεργεῖ, θεὸς σωτὴρ κεκλημένος, ἡ τῶν ὅλων ἀρχή, ἥτις ἀπεικόνισται μὲν ἐκ "τοῦ θεοῦ τοῦ ἀοράτου" πρώτη καὶ πρὸ αἰώνων, τετύπωκεν δὲ τὰ μεθ' ἑαυτὴν ἅπαντα γενόμενα.

[76] Cf. *Str.* V 37,2 (fr. 2.10) and V 38,4 (fr. 2.14).

Clement gives a Christological interpretation; the logeion is the symbol of heaven, made by the logos and submitted to Christ, the head of all. In spite of the associations shoulder/work and logeion/logos that the two writers have in common, no conclusive evidence for a direct dependance can be found; the associations are obvious, and since they are not formulated in very similar terms, they could derive from a common background, even though that background cannot be precisely defined.

Stählin mentions[77] that the distinction between chestpiece (περιστήθιον) and logeion is based on a misunderstanding since both words describe the same object. The cause for this confusion dates back to the Septuagint itself, because the Hebrew word חֹשֶׁן is represented by two different Greek words. In Ex. 28:4 for example, it is translated as περιστήθιον but in Ex. 28:15.22 as logeion. Philo used both words but did not understand them as two different things. Another distinction, according to Stählin, comes up in the imagery. In Philo, the shoulderpiece symbolizes heaven, while the breastpiece represents the stars. In another passage, *Spec.* I 94, however, Philo mentions the περιστήθιον as οὐρανοῦ μίμημα; this variation shows how the imagery of the various parts of the vestments of the high priest is not fixed even in Philo.

Be this as it may, it appears that Clement takes up the Philonic thread at *VM* II 122, rather than at *VM* II 130, as Stählin indicates. Clement's confusion about the chestpiece and logeion is hard to explain. It might be a matter of sloppiness in borrowing, a trait which Clement has displayed on other occasions. It could, alternatively, be a matter of confusion in the later manuscript tradition, considering the problems with ᾧ and κινούμενα, and the addition of καὶ proposed by Stählin.

2.13   *Str.* V 38,3 - *VM* II 122

For the translation see fr. 2.12

Philo first gives a tentative interpretation of the shoulderpiece as a representation of heaven. In support of this, he then presents what he calls a common view that the two circular emerald stones signify sun and moon. He himself prefers the interpretation that they represent the two hemispheres of the sky; just as the stones are equal to each other, so is the hemisphere above equal to that below the earth.[78]

In contrast with *Str.* V 37, 2ff., where he follows a different tradition, Clement here makes use of a piece of Philo. In his adaptation of the text,

---

[77] Stählin, BKV XIX, p. 151 note 10.
[78] Background text: Ex. 28:6ff.

he substitutes ἐπωμίς for the Philonic ἀκρώμιον and brings up the brightness of the emeralds while leaving out their number. Of the two symbolic options that Philo gives, Clement chooses the sun and the moon, entitling them 'co-workers of nature', while Philo had called them 'rulers of the day and night'. In a separate sentence, Clement, as he had previously, mentions the meaning of the shoulder as a symbol of work, calling it the beginning of the arm or hand (cf. fr. 2.10-2.14). The word 'co-workers' (συνεργούς) may be connected with this idea.

2.14   *Str.* V 38,4 - *VM* II 124

For the translation see fr. 2.12

After the shoulderpiece Philo deals with the stones on the breast.[79] They are distributed into four rows of three and signify the zodiac circle and the seasons of the year.[80]

Clement prunes Philo's description down to bare essentials; he omits the colors and the number three (cf. *Str.* V 35,7, fr. 2.9, where the zodiac is also mentioned). In interpreting the twelve stones, Clement adds a Christian dimension by bringing in the prophets and apostles in connection with the number twelve.[81] He tends to cling to the visual aspect of the image; the shoulderpiece and the breastpiece are literally put below the head as well as figuratively subordinated to it, since the verb ὑποκεῖσθαι is used twice (p. 352 1.3; 1.10).

A more general theme occurs in this connection, namely the unity of the old and the new covenant; both the prophets and the apostles are put on one level and brought into one continuous history of salvation. The line of thought is dear to Clement; its frequent appearance is stimulated by his opposition to the Marcionites.

Appendix:

Translation of *Str.* V 39,1 - 40,4

V 39,1   "Furthermore the logeion signifies the prophecy which cries by the Word and proclaims the judgment that is to come; since it is the same Word which prophesies and judges and discriminates all things.
V 39,2   And they say that the robe prophesied the ministry in the flesh by which he was made visible to the world directly.
V 39,3   So the high priest, putting off his consecrated robe—the world

---

[79] πρῶτον *VM* II 122; ἔπειτα *VM* II 124.
[80] Parallels: *VM* II 130; *Spec.* I 87; *QE* II 114.
[81] Cf. J. Daniélou, Les douze Apôtres et le Zodiaque, in *VigChr* 13 (1959), p. 21.

and the creation in the world are consecrated by him who assented that what was made was good—, washes himself and puts on the other tunic, a holy-of-holies one, so to speak, which is to accompany him into the adytum.

V 39,4 It signifies, as seems to me, that the levite is also Gnostic as the chief of the other priests—those bathed in water, and clothed in faith alone, and receiving their own individual abode—himself distinguishing the objects of the intellect from the things of sense, rising above the other priests, hasting to the entrance of the noetic realm, to wash himself from the things here below, not in water as formerly one was cleansed on being enrolled in the tribe of Levi, but already by the Gnostic Word.

V 40,1 But purified in his whole heart and having directed his mode of life to the highest pitch, grown beyond the size of the ordinary priest, briefly, being sanctified both in word and life, and having put on the bright array of glory, and having received the ineffable inheritance of that spiritual and perfect man, 'which eye has not seen and ear has not heard and which has not entered into the heart of man', having become son and friend, he is now replenished with insatiable contemplation face to face. For there is nothing like hearing the Word Himself, who by means of the Scripture inspires fuller intelligence.

V 40,2 For so it is said, 'And he shall put off the linen robe that he had put on when he entered into the holy place and shall lay it aside there and wash his body in water in the holy place and put on his robe'.

V 40,3 But in one way, as I think, the Lord puts off and puts on by descending into the realm of sense, and in another, he who through Him has believed puts off and puts on, as the apostle intimated, the consecrated stole.

V 40,4 Thence after the image of the Lord, the most appropriate were chosen from the sacred tribe to be high priests, and those elected to the kingly office and to prophecy were anointed.''[82]

---

[82] *Str.* V 39,1-40,4: καὶ μὴν τὸ λόγιον τὴν προφητείαν τὴν ἐκβοῶσαν τῷ λόγῳ καὶ κηρύσσουσαν καὶ τὴν κρίσιν τὴν ἐσομένην δηλοῖ, ἐπεὶ ὁ αὐτός ἐστι λόγος ὁ προφητεύων κρίνων τε ἅμα καὶ διακρίνων ἕκαστα.

39,2: φασὶ δὲ καὶ τὸ ἔνδυμα, τὸν ποδήρη, τὴν κατὰ σάρκα προφητεύειν οἰκονομίαν, δι' ἣν προσεχέστερον εἰς κόσμον ὤφθη.

39,3: ταύτῃ τοι ἀποδοὺς τὸν ἡγιασμένον χιτῶνα ὁ ἀρχιερεὺς (κόσμος δὲ καὶ ἡ ἐν κόσμῳ κτίσις ἡγίασται πρὸς τοῦ καλὰ συγκαταθεμένου τὰ γινόμενα) λούεται καὶ τὸν ἄλλον ἐνδύεται ἅγιον ἁγίου ὡς εἰπεῖν χιτῶνα, τὸν συνεισιόντα εἰς τὰ ἄδυτα αὐτῷ,

39,4: ἐμοὶ δοκεῖν ἐμφαίνων τὸν Λευίτην καὶ γνωστικὸν ὡς ἂν τῶν ἄλλων ἱερέων ἄρχοντα, ὕδατι ἀπολελουμένων ἐκείνων καὶ πίστιν ἐνδεδυμένων μόνην καὶ τὴν ἰδίαν ἐκδεχομένων μονήν, αὐτὸν διακρίναντα τὰ νοητὰ τῶν αἰσθητῶν, κατ' ἐπανάβασιν τῶν ἄλλων ἱερέων σπεύδοντα ἐπὶ τὴν τοῦ νοητοῦ δίοδον, τῶν τῇδε ἀπολουόμενον οὐκέτι ὕδατι, ὡς πρότερον ἐκαθαίρετο εἰς Λευιτικὴν ἐντασσόμενος φυλήν, ἀλλ' ἤδη τῷ γνωστικῷ λόγῳ.

40,1: καθαρὸς μὲν <οὖν> τὴν καρδίαν πᾶσαν, κατορθώσας δ' εὖ μάλα καὶ τὴν πολιτείαν ἐπ' ἄκρον, πέρα τοῦ ἱερέως ἐπὶ μεῖζον αὐξήσας, ἀτεχνῶς ἡγνισμένος καὶ λόγῳ καὶ βίῳ, ἐπενδυσάμενος τὸ γάνωμα τῆς δόξης, τοῦ πνευματικοῦ ἐκείνου καὶ τελείου ἀνδρὸς τὴν ἀπόρρητον κληρονομίαν ἀπολαβών, "ἣν ὀφθαλμὸς οὐκ εἶδεν καὶ οὖς οὐκ ἤκουσεν καὶ ἐπὶ καρδίαν ἀνθρώπου οὐκ ἀνέβη," υἱὸς καὶ φίλος γενόμενος, "πρόσωπον" ἤδη "πρὸς πρόσωπον" ἐμπίπλαται τῆς ἀκορέστου θεωρίας. οὐδὲν δὲ οἷον αὐτοῦ ἐπακοῦσαι τοῦ λόγου, πλείονα τὸν νοῦν διὰ τῆς γραφῆς ἐνδιδόντος.

40,2: λέγει γὰρ ὧδε· "καὶ ἐκδύσεται τὴν στολὴν τὴν λινῆν, ἣν ἐνδεδύκει εἰσπορευόμενος εἰς τὰ

3. Conclusions

3.1   In the last paragraphs (from *Str.* V 38,6 onwards), a syndrome that had occurred in embryonic form earlier emerges in its fully-fledged state; Christian allegories, which had seemed to be interjections, are revealed to be preludes to the decisive, concluding Christian interpretation. Individual elements of the description of the furnishings of the temple and the vestments are constructed in a way that seems symmetrical with the construction of the passage as a whole; each is concluded with a Christian allegory. The allegories vary in their emphasis in directions that might be characterized as salvational, Christological, Gnostic or eschatological.[83]

In the last paragraphs, Clement weaves in some colorful threads from the previous passages, like the 'petalon' in *Str.* V 38,6, the 'logeion' in *Str.* V 39,1, and the vestments as a whole in *Str.* V 39,3. The 'petalon', in which the name of God is engraved (cf. *Str.* V 34,5;fr. 2.5), is linked to the name of Christ with words drawn from St. Paul.[84] On the one hand, it shows Christ as the image of the invisible God and as the one who impresses his image on creation, while on the other hand, it shows him as the one who leads to salvation; salvation and creation are closely linked in this connection. The 'logeion' is defined as the word that speaks through the prophets and that will judge all things;[85] the unity of the history of salvation, in this case from a eschatological perspective, is thereby affirmed.

The interpretation of the vestments is expanded in a new direction. The high priest takes off his clothes, washes himself and puts on a special linen garment. The basic text for this description is Leviticus 16,[86] which substitutes the text of Exodus 28, on which Clement had drawn up to this point. Clement introduces a theme in which the words 'to wash', 'to take off' and 'to put on' clothes form the keywords.

Two parallel movements reveal themselves; on the one hand, there is an assimilation of the high priest with Christ; the image of changing

---

ἅγια, καὶ ἀποθήσει αὐτὴν ἐκεῖ. καὶ λούσεται τὸ σῶμα αὐτοῦ ὕδατι ἐν τόπῳ ἁγίῳ καὶ ἐνδύσεται τὴν στολὴν αὐτοῦ.''
40,3: ἄλλως δ', οἶμαι, ὁ κίριος ἀποδύεταί τε καὶ ἐνδύεται καπιὼν εἰς αἴσθησιν, ἄλλως ὁ δι' αὐτοῦ πιστεύσας ἀποδύεταί τε καὶ ἐπενδύεται, ὡς καὶ ὁ ἀπόστολος ἐμήνυσεν, τὴν ἡγιασμένην στολήν.
40,4: ἐντεῦθεν κατ' εἰκόνα τοῦ κυρίου ἀρχιερεῖς ἀπὸ τῆς ἁγιασθείσης ἤροῦντο φυλῆς οἱ δοκιμώτατοι καὶ οἱ εἰς βασιλείαν καὶ οἱ εἰς προφητείαν ἐκλεκτοὶ ἐχρίοντο.

[83] Cf. Mondésert, *Clément*, p. 182.

[84] Eph. 1:21; Phil. 2:9.

[85] Heinisch, *Einfluss*, p. 237f., points out that διακρίνων joints Ex. 28:15. 30: τὸ λογεῖον τῆς κρίσεως.

[86] Also Philo has used this biblical text in *Leg.* II 56 and *Somn.* I 216. He interprets the clothes that are layed off as the outside opinions and impressions with which the soul is clothed. For a comparable interpretation in Clement, see *Exc.* 27.

clothes suggests his descent into the realm of the senses. On the other hand, the Gnostic who has come to faith through Christ is the one who changes clothes. By the descent of Christ the ascent of the believer is made possible, and the hinge on which both movements turn is purification. The terminology alludes strongly to Baptism; the reference is made clear by a row of verbs; not only by 'wash', 'take off' and 'put on', but also by 'anoint'.[87]

A parallel for these last paragraphs can be found in another writing of Clement, *Exc.* 27, in which the entrance of the high priest is also discussed. F. Sagnard has given evidence for the parallel;[88] groups of analogous words are present in both passages. *Exc.* 27 discusses the ascent of the soul inspired by the logos up to the highest level, that of angels and archangels; the soul in its purified form is, as it were, spiritually incorporated in this part of the celestial hierarchy by the logos.[89] Leaving open the question whether the passage in *Exc.* 27 represents a heterodox position, as some would have it,[90] or Clement's own views, a clearcut difference between the two parallels is the focus on the incarnation of Christ and the reference to Baptism evident in *Str.* V 39 and 40. *Exc.* 27 does not address itself to either of these topics but merely to the ascent of the Gnostic soul up to the highest vision.

Thus the line of thought developed in fragmented form in our passage (*Str.* V 32-38) is a prelude to the following paragraphs (*Str.* V 39-40), in which Christ comes down,[91] undresses himself and dresses himself to sense perception and in which the Gnostic rises up, undresses himself and is newly dressed to see and to contemplate.

3.2   Before asking how Philo influenced Clement's line of thought, this line itself together with its digressions must be retraced. The starting point for the passage was the hidden meaning of things: that is, how and

---

[87] ἀποδύς, λούεται, ἐνδύεται, ὕδατι ἀπολελουμένων, πίστιν ἐνδεδυμένων μόνην, κατ' ἐπανάβασιν, καθαρός, ἐπενδυσάμενος, ἐχρίοντο. The first detailed report on the ritual of Baptism is found in Hippolytus, *Traditio Apostolica* 21, ed. Botte, 1963, p. 45-59; Dix 2nd ed., 1968, p. 33-39 n. 21-22; the Greek text of this passage, however, is lost so that a close comparison of words is not possible. Dix has pointed out that in the last paragraphs of *Exc.* (77-86) a ritual of Baptism that parallels the *Traditio Apostolica* is also presupposed; cf. Sagnard, *Exc.* (SChr. 23), App. F p. 230-239; for the terminology see also Hort and Mayor p. LV.

[88] Sagnard, *Exc.* (SChr 23), p. 117 note 4.

[89] *Exc.* 27,3.

[90] Lilla, *Clement*, p. 175ff.

[91] Méhat, *Étude*, p. 465, has the opinion that the high priest is not linked to Christ but to the gnostic; this is only partly right since the two concepts are connected; see also *Str.* V 40,3: ἄλλως δ', οἶμαι, ὁ κύριος...ἄλλως ὁ δι' αὐτοῦ πιστεύσας..., in which a clear division in two parts is perceivable.

why divine things were wrapped up in figures.[92] As an example of figurative language in the Bible, Clement offers the description of the furnishings of the temple and the vestments of the high priest. He presents this in a setting of symbolic speech among the Egyptians and Greeks, including both poets and philosophers.

This focus on the hidden explains why Clement stresses the distinction between the 'outsiders' for whom the deeper meaning of the biblical words is hidden and the 'insiders' who have access to it.[93] As in Philo, the description is divided into two parts, the furnishings of the temple and the vestments of the high priest. In Clement's introductory summary, he curiously fails to mention the temple as such; he promises instead the seven circuits around the temple, a subject that does not reappear again.

The parts of the temple on which Clement dwells are the covering, the veil, the altar of incense and its position, the five and the four pillars, the candlestick, the table, the ark and the golden figures. This design is roughly comparable to that of Philo and Josephus. This framework, however, is interrupted by some substantial digressions on the four and the five pillars (fr. 2.4 and 2.5). The numbers lead to an accumulation of allegorical associations like the five loaves from the miracle of the multiplication of the loaves and the fishes, the five senses and the incarnation of Christ, who has become visible for the five senses. A similar method is applied to the number four; the four covenants are evoked, the name of God in Hebrew (the tetragrammon), the name of God in Greek and the Gnostic, who on his way to gnosis conquers the πάθη ; the last allegory can be explained because πάθη are, like the virtues, connected with the number four. The digressions on the four and the five pillars are concluded by Christian interpretations that return in the important paragraphs at the end of the passage. The pillars are related, on the one hand, to the incarnation of Christ and, on the other, to the Gnostic at his entrance into the noetic realm.

In describing the candlestick and the table, Clement returns to his Philonic source. Following his usual method, he then continues with a Christological interpretation; the candlestick signifies the outward appearance of the cross, which is interpreted as the enlightenment that the believers receive through the ministry of the highest spiritual beings. The position of the table and the shew-breads signify the assembly of the spiritual body and the terrestrial church. In describing the ark and the golden figures, the Philonic scheme is abandoned in favor of one inspired

---

[92] Cf. *Str.* VI 125,1f.; Den Boer, *Allegorese*, p. 69ff.; Völker, *Wahre Gnostiker*, p. 18.
[93] *Str.* V 33,2f.; 33,4f.; 34,7; 35,5.

by various other sources.[94] Clement tries to sketch the outlines of the highest spiritual spheres through allegorical interpretations. The terms in which he approaches this lofty subject are tentative; he cautiously offers various alternatives. He leaves open whether the ark with the cherubim signifies the ogdoas or God. In any case (πλήν), as Clement puts it, it represents eternal rest in its various aspects, and the individual parts of the cherubim, in turn, have symbolic meanings related to this idea.

The high priest's robe, the second part of Clement's description, initially does not have a Philonic background. The stones on the breast and shoulders, seven in number, have a cosmological function and refer to creation. In an additional Christian interpretation, they signify the differences of the believers in rank. The melodious bells allude to the arrival of Christ, and the golden hat is connected simultaneously with the head and the power of Christ.

This idea is pushed further; Christ is mentioned in all his 'head' functions: as head of the church, head of law and prophets, head of creation and head of the universe. God is mentioned as the head of Christ, a relationship that remains quite vague in Clement and that is usually expressed through biblical quotations, here one from St. Paul.[95] Only from fr. 2.12 onward does Philo come to the surface again. The borrowing is followed by an interpretation that brings out the unity of the Bible. The law, the prophets and the apostles are all put under the 'head' of Christ, who has inspired the word of the Scripture as a whole.

3.3   Philo's immediate influence on Clement seems to be restricted to providing formal guidelines. While Clement passes over some of what he encounters along these guidelines, he stops at a few points of interest, which he adapts in an abbreviate, sketchy fashion.

Thus the borrowings fall into three blocks:

a) *Str.* V 32,2-33,3
b) *Str.* V 34,8-35,3
c) *Str.* V 38,2-38,4

Other references indicated by Stählin, like etymologies and commonplaces, are too vague to be considered valid parallels.

Clement takes over a few cosmological elaborations without placing the same emphasis on them that his source had. He remodels Philo's

---

[94] p. 350 l. 3: ὡς βούλονταί τινες.
    p. 350 l. 3-4: εἴτε, ὅπερ μᾶλλον.
    p. 350 l. 17: ἑρμηνεύεται.
    p. 350 l. 17-18: εἴτε...εἴτε.
[95] 1 Cor. 11:3.

cosmology in a Christological, Gnostic and eschatological sense; in the various concluding allegories, there is a continuous concern with the history of salvation. From these allegories we can infer Clement's own interests in the temple's furnishings and the high priest's vestments. They are centered on two complementary themes that form two sides of the same coin: the incarnation of Christ and the rise of the Gnostic to the higher regions. This higher realm is at times described according to the Gnostic perspective as ceaseless contemplation and at times as eternal rest, in which the highest spiritual beings reflect the divine reality.

Clement does not seem interested in cosmology as such and for that reason transforms the cosmology that had been, in part, transmitted through Philo. The universe and the construction of the universe are sanctified by Christ; in this connection Clement refers implicitly to Gen. 1:31, when he says that He (Christ) assents that what was made was good (*Str.* V 39,3).[96] Ultimately, the attire of the high priest represents the distribution of salvation, which had been made accessible to the world through the logos (Christ).[97]

Apart from Philo, other influences are demonstrably present; in part they are acknowledged explicitly. The influence of the Apocalypse and the Epistle to the Hebrews color Clement's descriptions from time to time. Noteworthy in this connection is the absence of the idea of sacrifice in Clement. In both Philo and the Epistle to the Hebrews it plays an important role; in the latter, as the unique offering of Christ himself. St. Paul also has a considerable importance, especially toward the end of the passage; the predominance of St. Paul is, however, generally characteristic of Clement's use of the Bible.

Jewish or Judeo-Christian influences, furthermore, make their appearance; they can be identified with a certain degree of probability through the use of alternative versions of the Septuagint. Speculation on numbers is in part drawn from Philo, but some of it may also be connected with traditional Early Christian sources; these latter passages tend to have a somewhat artificial flavor.[98] Influences from Gnostic exegesis may also be inferred; this material was presumably taken over from his opponents by Clement.

In summary, then, Philo supplies part of the structure through which Clement moves, in which he lingers and from which he digresses. This

---

[96] Cf. *Str.* II 53,2; VII 83,3; in this positive assessment of creation an anti-gnostic tendency is involved, cf. Völker, *Wahre Gnostiker*, p. 195; see also De Faye, *Clément*, p. 256ff.; R. B. Tollinton, *Alexandrine Teaching on the Universe, four lectures*, 1932; Marrou, *Paed.* I (SChr. 70), Introd. p. 37f., 58, speaks about an anthropocentric universe.

[97] *Str.* V 39,2.

[98] Cf. Méhat, *Kephalaia*, p. 240.

structure is a formal matter that does not determine the specific direction of his thought. The pole of attraction emerges clearly in the last paragraphs and is signalled by individual allegories throughout the whole passage.

CHAPTER SIX

THE SHORT SEQUENCES

1. Introductory remarks

Apart from the more extended sequences that have been analyzed in the previous chapters, four more concise sequences are examined here. They are put together in this chapter not because of their content, but because of their size. Their subject matter is only partly related. The first and the last sequence deal with the problem of knowledge of God and with the anthropomorphic way of speaking about God found in the Bible. The second sequence describes the ascent of the Gnostic soul on its way to contemplation; this passage presents an extensive disquisition on numbers and is characterized by a strongly ethical tone. The third sequence deals with the Gnostic soul in its relationship to God. All these passages have in common that they are built on biblical texts that had already been used by Philo.

The approach to the individual passages is similar to that of the preceding chapters. First a translation is given, which is followed by a schematic overview. The individual units are then analyzed within the context in which they appear. Finally, the two authors are compared. A more general conclusion like those provided in previous chapters was not feasible given the diversity of the material in this section.

1.2 Overview of the passages

2.1	*Str.* II 5,3-6,4	—	*Post.* 5-18
2.2	*Str.* II 46,2-52,4	—	*Congr.* 83-106; *Post.* 22-29
2.3	*Str.* V 67,4-68,3	—	*Sacr.* 95-100
2.4	*Str.* V 71,5-74,1(4)	—	*Post.* 14-20; *Somn.* I 63-66

2 Individual passages

2.1 *Str.* II 5,3-6,4 - *Post.* 5-18

II 5,1 "Accordingly, the Barbarian philosophy, which we follow, is really perfect and true. So it is said in the book of Wisdom: 'For he himself has given me the unerring knowledge of things, to know the constitution of the world', and so forth, down to 'and the natural properties of roots'. Among all these he comprehends natural science, which deals with all the things that have come into being in the world of sense.

II 5,2 And in continuation he alludes also to the spiritual things, when he continues: 'What is hidden or manifest I have known; for wisdom, the artificer of all things, taught me'. You have in brief the program of our philosophy.

II 5,3 The learning of these branches, when pursued with right conduct, leads through wisdom, the artificer of all things, *to the Ruler of all, something that is difficult to grasp* and *apprehend, since it always recedes and withdraws from him who pursues it.*

II 5,4 But he who is far off has come very near, oh ineffable marvel: 'I am a God who draws near', says the Lord. He is remote in essence, for how could what is begotten have ever approached the Unbegotten, but very near in *power*, by which he holds all things in his embrace.

II 5,5 'Shall one do things in secret, and shall I not see him?', Scripture says, for *the power* of God is always present, *taking hold* of us through the faculty of contemplation, beneficence and instruction.

II 6,1 Whence Moses, convinced that God is never to be known by human wisdom, says: *'Show yourself to me'* and he is pressed to enter *into the darkness, where God*'s voice *was, that is into the inaccessible and invisible conceptions of the Existent. For God is not in darkness or in space but above both space and time* and *pecularities of created things.*

II 6,2 Wherefore *neither is he* ever *in some particular part, since he contains all and is not himself contained by anything,* either by limitation or by section.

II 6,3 For 'what house will you build to me says the Lord'. But he has not even built one for himself, since he cannot be contained, and though heaven be called his throne, not even thus is he contained, but he rests delighted in the creation.

II 6,4 It is clear then that the truth has been hidden from us and if that has been already shown by one example, we shall establish it little after by several more.''[1]

---

[1] *Str.* II 5,1-6,4: ἡ μὲν οὖν βάρβαρος φιλοσοφία, ἥν μεθέπομεν ἡμεῖς, τελεία τῷ ὄντι καὶ ἀληθής. φησὶ γοῦν ἐν τῇ Σοφίᾳ "αὐτὸς γάρ μοι δέδωκεν τῶν ὄντων γνῶσιν ἀψευδῆ, εἰδέναι σύστασιν κόσμου" καὶ τὰ ἑξῆς ἕως "καὶ δυνάμεις ῥιζῶν." ἐν τούτοις ἅπασι τὴν φυσικὴν ἐμπεριείληφε θεωρίαν τὴν κατὰ τὸν αἰσθητὸν κόσμον ἁπάντων τῶν γεγονότων.

5,2: ἑξῆς δὲ καὶ περὶ τῶν νοητῶν αἰνίττεται δι' ὧν ἐπάγει· "ὅσα τέ ἐστι κρυπτὰ καὶ ἐμφανῆ ἔγνων· ἡ γὰρ πάντων τεχνῖτις ἐδίδαξέ με σοφία." ἔχεις ἐν βραχεῖ τὸ ἐπάγγελμα τῆς καθ' ἡμᾶς φιλοσοφίας.

5,3: ἀνάγει δὲ ἡ τούτων μάθησις, μετὰ ὀρθῆς πολιτείας ἀσκηθεῖσα, διὰ τῆς πάντων τεχνίτιδος σοφίας ἐπὶ τὸν ἡγεμόνα τοῦ παντός, δυσάλωτόν τι χρῆμα καὶ δυσθήρατον, ἐξαναχωροῦν ἀεὶ καὶ πόρρω ἀφιστάμενον τοῦ διώκοντος.

5,4: ὁ δὲ αὐτὸς μακρὰν ὢν ἐγγυτάτω βέβηκεν, θαῦμα ἄρρητον· "θεὸς ἐγγίζων ἐγώ," φησὶ κύριος· πόρρω μὲν κατ' οὐσίαν (πῶς γὰρ ἂν συνεγγίσαι ποτὲ τὸ γεννητὸν ἀγεννήτῳ;), ἐγγυτάτω δὲ δυνάμει, ᾗ τὰ πάντα ἐγκεκόλπισται.

5,5: "εἰ ποιήσει τις κρύφα", φησί, "τι, καὶ οὐκ ἐπόψομαι αὐτόν;" καὶ δὴ πάρεστιν ἀεὶ τῇ τε ἐποπτικῇ τῇ τε εὐεργετικῇ τῇ τε παιδευτικῇ ἁπτομένη ἡμῶν δυνάμει δύναμις τοῦ θεοῦ.

6,1: ὅθεν ὁ Μωυσῆς οὔποτε ἀνθρωπίνῃ σοφίᾳ γνωσθήσεσθαι τὸν θεὸν πεπεισμένος, "ἐμφάνισόν μοι σεαυτόν" φησὶ καὶ "εἰς τὸν γνόφον", οὗ ἦν ἡ φωνὴ τοῦ θεοῦ, εἰσελθεῖν βιάζεται, τουτέστιν εἰς τὰς ἀδύτους καὶ ἀειδεῖς περὶ τοῦ ὄντος ἐννοίας· οὐ γὰρ ἐν γνόφῳ ἢ τόπῳ ὁ θεός, ἀλλ' ὑπεράνω καὶ τόπου καὶ χρόνου καὶ τῆς τῶν γεγονότων ἰδιότητος.

6,2: διὸ οὐδ' ἐν μέρει καταγίνεταί ποτε ἅτε περιέχων οὐ περιεχόμενος ἢ κατὰ ὁρισμόν τινα ἢ κατὰ ἀποτομήν.

6,3: "ποῖον γὰρ οἶκον οἰκοδομήσετέ μοι;" λέγει κύριος· ἀλλ' οὐδὲ ἑαυτῷ ᾠκοδόμησεν ἀχώρητος

Schematic overview

Str. II 5,3	—	*Post.* 18	(paraphrase with literal elements)
Str. II 5,4(5)	—	*Post.* 20	(reminiscence)
Str. II 6,1	—	*Post.* 16	(biblical quotation)
Str. II 6,1	—	*Post.* 14	(biblical quotation and continuation)
Str. II 6,2	—	*Post.* 7	(quasi-literal citation)
Str. II 6,3-4	—	*Post.* 5	(reminiscence)

Philo, *Post.* 1-24

At the beginning of *De Posteritate*, Philo takes as his point of departure Genesis, 4:16a "Cain went out from the face of God". He rejects an anthropomorphic and overly literal interpretation of the 'face' of God (*Post.* 1-4). Similarly, he takes up the spatial implications of the passage; any 'place' of God does not have a three-dimensional locus because God contains everything and is not contained by anything (*Post.* 5-7);[2] a figurative interpretation is clearly necessary (*Post.* 7). Alluding to several biblical passages, Philo concludes that even if the wise man who is longing to see God does not fully realize this aim, the goal is sufficient in itself to give a foretaste of joy (*Post.* 21).[3]

The passages are a paraphrase of Ex. 20:21; "So see him enter into the darkness where God was", a quotation from Ex. 33:13; "He says, show yourself to me", and a quotation from Gen. 22:4; "He sees the place from afar". These texts give biblical shape to Philo's Platonizing conception of the soul on its way to attaining knowledge of God. It appears that all that can be said about God's nature can be contradicted by an opposite conception, and yet both terms may be simultaneously valid. Philo works with negative terminology; for example, God is ἀειδής, ἀόρατος and ἀσώματος. Yet examined more closely, his approach is really more antithetical than negative.

The nature of the universe is included in these conceptions of God and has an integral relationship to them. For example, in *Post.* 6-7 he says: "Yet God has left nothing empty...but has completely filled all things;

ὤν, κἂν "ὁ οὐρανὸς θρόνος" αὐτοῦ λέγηται, οὐδ' οὕτω περιέχεται, ἐπαναπαύεται δὲ τερπόμενος τῇ δημιουργίᾳ.

6,4: δῆλον οὖν ἡμῖν ἐπικεκρύφθαι τὴν ἀλήθειαν, ᾗ καὶ ἐξ ἑνὸς παραδείγματος ἤδη δέδεικται, μικρὸν δ' ὕστερον καὶ διὰ πλειόνων παραστήσομεν.

[2] Cf. Philo, *Conf.* 136; *Somn.* I 185; Past. Hermae 26 (*Mand.* 1,1), SChr. 53bis p. 144; Irenaeus, *Adv. Haer.* IV 20,2 (Hermas); *Dem.* 4; Clement, *Str.* VI 39,3 as quotation from *Kerugma Petrou*, E. Klostermann, *Apocrypha* I (Kleine Texte 30), p. 13-16; Orig., *Dial. c. Her.* 2, 12; cf. W. R. Schoedel, Enclosing not Enclosed, the early Christian doctrine of God, in *Early Christian Literature and the Classical Tradition* (in hon. R. M. Grant), 1979, p. 75-85; G. L. Prestige, *God in patristic Thought*, 1936, p. 32-33.

[3] See Colson V, p. 586 par. 7.

...he contains everything and is not himself contained by anything." In *Post.* 14: "For the cause of all is not in the darkness, nor locally in any place at all, but high above both place and time. For he has placed all creation under his control, and is contained by nothing but transcends all". In *Post.* 19: "... whereas the heavenly bodies as they go past moving objects are themselves in motion, God who outstrips them all, is motionless...he is at once close to us and far from us".

God's nature is impossible to fathom, even with a purely spiritual approach. Yet Philo speaks of other means of apprehending God beyond speculative knowledge: namely, through his powers (*Post.* 14,20) and through the divine words (*Post.* 18). By these powers, which Philo describes as formative (ποιητικός) and corrective (χολαστήριος), God takes hold of mankind. Contact with God may be obtained both through the creation of the cosmos and through the law; he is accessible and nearby, but an absolute knowledge is not possible, and in this respect he is remote.

Clement, *Str.* II 5-6

The perfect truthfulness of the βάρβαρος φιλοσοφία is exemplified with citations from the book of Wisdom. This truth encompasses knowledge of both sensible and spiritual reality. Wisdom connected with the right course of conduct leads ultimately to God. Following the quotations from Philo's *De Posteritate*, Clement declares that it is impossible to reduce God to a concept. Yet he is present in power and is therefore very near but concealed. The idea of the proximity of God is reinforced by a quotation from Jer. 23:23: "I am a God at hand and not a God far off." This power manifests itself in three ways: through contemplation, beneficence and instruction.

In these borrowings Clement orients himself on three biblical quotations in Philo; the texts are Ex. 20:21, 33:13 and Gen. 22:4. Clement replaces the last, which had been the centerpiece of the discussion of God's proximity and distance, with Jer. 23:23 (see above), and he adds the next verse, Jer. 23:24. This substitution may well have a purpose here. It certainly downplays God's remoteness and stresses his closeness and tends to give this emphasis to the whole discussion. When the issue of God's dwelling place comes up in the course of this discussion, Clement gives as an illustration Is. 66:1, a text that has been quoted in Acts 7:49; Philo himself does not quote the Bible here. According to the position of λέγει κύριος, the text seems to be brought in via Acts.[4]

---

[4] Cf. *Str.* V 74,5; on the contrary, *Str.* V 124,1.

To the material that he borrows from Philo Clement links a theme of his own: namely, the hidden character of truth. This theme is not identical with the hiddenness of God and the impossibility of apprehending the nature of God. Clement here assumes the latter as essentially self-evident (*Str.* V 5,4; 5,5). The concealment of truth is related to the imperfection of human knowledge. In addition, it has the paedagogical intention of training and stimulating a person who makes the effort to learn the truth.[5]

As appears from the schematic overview, these parts of *Stromateis* II 5 and 6 follow a sequence in borrowing from Philo. The first two phrases, 18-20, function as a unity, while the others are traversed in reverse order. This time Clement evidently did not go forward through his scroll of *De Posteritate* but turned it backwards.

Clement has chosen Philo as one jumping-off point from which to develop his thoughts, first, on how the human soul comes to God through wisdom and, second, on how to articulate the concept of God. He moves along the biblical markers seeded throughout Philo. He compresses Philo's elaboration and reinforces it with other biblical texts. The proximity of God is stressed more strongly than the idea of his remoteness; in this instance, remoteness is equivalent to the unknowability of God's nature, which is tacitly understood by Clement (*Str.* II 5,4; 5,5).

In these borrowings, the biblical texts are partially wrapped in scraps of Philonic elaboration. Some subtle alterations are made to the wording of this skimpy packaging; in Philo (*Post.* 20; cf. *Post.* 14), the powers through which God reaches mankind are in the plural (δυνάμεις); Clement, on the other hand, adapts this as a singular power of God (δύναμις) (*Str.* II 5,4; cf. *Str.* V 71,5). In another case, when Moses enters the cloud of darkness in which God is present (*Post.* 14), Clement changes 'God' into the 'voice of God' (*Str.* II 6,1). Again, Philo describes God as τὸ αἴτιον (*Post.* 14); Clement alters this to ὁ θεός (*Str.* II 6,1).[6]

Basically, both of them are working around the same issue: how to attain God by wisdom or knowledge. A shift appears when Clement infuses his own theme of the hidden character of the truth, an aspect of the problem that is entirely missing in this context in Philo.

2.2 *Str.* II 46,2-52,4 - *Congr.* 83-106
Post. 22-29

II 46,1 "To these three activities therefore, our philosopher attaches himself: first, contemplation; second, the performance of the precepts;

---

[5] *Str.* II 5,2; 6,4; 7,3; 8,1.
[6] Cf., however, *Str.* V 71,5, where Clement does take over πρῶτον αἴτιον.

third, the training of good men; these in concurrence, form the Gnostic. Whenever one of them is missing, knowledge limps.

II 46,2 Whence the Scripture says divinely: *'And the Lord spoke to Moses, saying, speak to the sons of Israel and you shall say to them, I am the Lord your God.*

II 46,3 *You shall not act according to the customs of the land of Egypt, in which you have dwelt, and you shall not act according to the customs of the land of Canaan, into which I bring you;*

II 46,4 *and in their usages you shall not walk. You shall perform my judgements and keep my precepts and walk in them: I am the Lord your God.*

II 46,5 *And you shall keep all my commandments and do them.* The man *that does them shall live in them; I am the Lord your God'.*

II 47,1 Whether then Egypt and the land of Canaan be the symbol of the world and of deceit or of passions and vice, the saying shows us what must be abstained from and what, being divine and not wordly, must be observed.''[7]

II 49,3 ''For the highest demonstration to which we have alluded as an objective acquired by understanding, produces faith by the adducing and opening up of the Scriptures to the souls of those who desire to learn; this might well be knowledge.

II 49,4 For if what is adduced in order to prove the point at issue is assumed to be true, as being divine and prophetic, manifestly the conclusion arrived at by inference from it will consequently be inferred truly, and rightly for us the demonstration might well be knowledge.[8]

II 50,1 *When* then *the memorial of the celestial and divine food* was commanded *to be consecrated in the golden pot, it was said, 'The omer was the tenth of the three measures'. For by the three measures* are indicated *three* means of judgement *in ourselves; sensation for objects of sense, language for spoken things, both names and words, and the mind for intellectual objects.*

II 50,2 The Gnostic, therefore, will abstain from errors in language and thought and sensation and action, having heard that 'he who looks in lust has committed adultery', and reflecting that 'blessed are the pure in heart for they shall see God', and knowing this, 'that not what enters into the mouth defiles but that what comes forth by the mouth defiles the man; for out of the heart proceed thoughts'.

---

[7] *Str.* II 46,1-47,1: Τριῶν τοίνυν τούτων ἀντέχεται ὁ ἡμεδαπὸς φιλόσοφος, πρῶτον μὲν τῆς θεωρίας, δεύτερον δὲ τῆς τῶν ἐντολῶν ἐπιτελέσεως, τρίτον ἀνδρῶν ἀγαθῶν κατασκευῆς· ἃ δὴ συνελθόντα τὸν γνωστικὸν ἐπιτελεῖ. ὅ τι δ᾽ ἂν ἐνδέῃ τούτων, χωλεύει τὰ τῆς γνώσεως.
46,2: ὅθεν θείως ἡ γραφή φησι· "καὶ εἶπεν κύριος πρὸς Μωυσῆν λέγων· λάλησον τοῖς υἱοῖς Ἰσραὴλ καὶ ἐρεῖς πρὸς αὐτούς· ἐγὼ κύριος ὁ θεὸς ὑμῶν·
46,3: κατὰ <τὰ> ἐπιτηδεύματα γῆς Αἰγύπτου, ἐν ᾗ κατῳκήσατε ἐν αὐτῇ, οὐ ποιήσετε· καὶ κατὰ τὰ ἐπιτηδεύματα γῆς Χαναάν, εἰς ἣν ἐγὼ εἰσάγω ὑμᾶς ἐκεῖ, οὐ ποιήσετε·
46,4: καὶ τοῖς νομίμοις αὐτῶν οὐ πορεύσεσθε· τὰ κρίματά μου ποιήσετε καὶ τὰ προστάγματά μου φυλάξεσθε, πορεύεσθαι ἐν αὐτοῖς· ἐγὼ κύριος ὁ θεὸς ὑμῶν.
46,5: καὶ φυλάξεσθε πάντα τὰ προστάγματά μου, καὶ ποιήσετε αὐτά. ὁ ποιήσας αὐτὰ ἄνθρωπος ζήσεται ἐν αὐτοῖς· ἐγὼ κύριος ὁ θεὸς ὑμῶν."
47,1: εἴτ᾽ οὖν κόσμου καὶ ἀπάτης εἴτε παθῶν καὶ κακιῶν σύμβολον Αἴγυπτος καὶ ἡ Χανανῖτις γῆ, ὧν μὲν ἀφεκτέον, ὁποῖα δὲ ἐπιτηδευτέον ὡς θεῖα καὶ οὐ κοσμικά, ἐπιδείκνυσιν ἡμῖν τὸ λόγιον.
[8] The optative plus ἄν in a main clause; cf. 4 Macc. 1:1. 5. 7. 8. 10; Acts 26:29; Hort and Mayor p. 365-373; irrealis Blass-Debrunner-Rehkopf, par. 385,1.

II 50,3 This is, as I think, *the true and just measure according to God* by which measurable things are measured: that is, the number ten, which comprehends man, that the three above-mentioned measures point out summarily.

II 50,4 The ten might be body and soul, the five senses, the faculty of speech, the power of reproduction, the intellectual or the spiritual faculty or whatever you choose to call it.

II 51,1 And we must, in a word, ascending above all the others stop at the mind, just as indeed in *the universe* we must *go beyond the nine parts*, the first consisting of the four elements put in one place *for equal interchange*, then *the seven wandering stars plus the one that wanders not, the ninth* part, to reach to the perfect number, *which is above the nine, the tenth* part, to the knowledge of *God*; to speak briefly, *desiring the Creator* beyond the creation.

II 51,2 Wherefore the tithes both of the epha and of the sacrifices were presented to God, and the *paschal* feast began on the tenth day, being *the transition from every passion and the entire realm of sense.*

II 51,3 The Gnostic is therefore fixed by faith, but he who thinks himself wise does not attach himself to the truth voluntarily, *moved as he is by unstable and wavering impulses.*

II 51,4 It is therefore reasonably written; '*Cain went forth from the face of God, and dwelt in the land of Naid, over against Eden'. Naid is interpreted as 'commotion' and Eden 'delight'*;

II 51,5 now faith and knowledge and peace are delight, from which he who has disobeyed is cast out, but he who thinks himself wise will not even begin with listening to the divine commandments; but self-taught, throwing off the reins, he plunges voluntarily into a billowing *commotion*, sinking down in mortal and created things from the knowledge of the uncreated, *holding various opinions at various times.*

II 51,6 'Those who have no guidance fall like leaves'; reason and the governing principle, remaining unmoved and directing the soul, is called its pilot. *For access to the Immutable is obtained by a truly immutable means.*

II 52,1 Thus '*Abraham was standing before the Lord and approaching spoke'*, and to Moses it is said: '*But (do) you stand there with me'.*

II 52,2 And the followers of Simon wish to be *assimilated* in manners to *the Standing* (τῷ Ἑστῶτι), whom they adore.

II 52,3 Faith, therefore, and the knowledge of the truth render the soul that chooses them always uniform and equable.

II 52,4 *Shifting*, changing and turning away is *congenial* to falsehood, as are *calmness* and rest and peace to the Gnostic.''⁹

---

⁹ *Str.* II 49,3-52,4: ἡ γὰρ ἀνωτάτω ἀπόδειξις, ἣν ἠνιξάμεθα ἐπιστημονικήν, πίστιν ἐντίθησι διὰ τῆς τῶν γραφῶν παραθέσεώς τε καὶ διοίξεως ταῖς τῶν μανθάνειν ὀρεγομένων ψυχαῖς, ἥτις ἂν εἴη γνῶσις.

49,4: εἰ γὰρ τὰ παραλαμβανόμενα πρὸς τὸ ζητούμενον ἀληθῆ λαμβάνεται, ὡς ἂν θεῖα ὄντα καὶ προφητικά, δῆλόν που ὡς καὶ τὸ συμπέρασμα τὸ ἐπιφερόμενον αὐτοῖς ἀκολούθως ἀληθὲς ἐπενεχθήσεται· καὶ εἴη ἂν ὀρθῶς ἡμῖν ἀπόδειξις ἡ γνῶσις.

50,1: Ἡνίκα γοῦν τῆς οὐρανίου καὶ θείας τροφῆς τὸ μνημόσυνον ἐν στάμνῳ χρυσῷ καθιεροῦσθαι προσετάττετο, "τὸ γόμορ" φησὶ "τὸ δέκατον τῶν τριῶν μέτρων ἦν". ἐν ἡμῖν γὰρ αὐτοῖς τρία μέτρα, τρία κριτήρια μηνύεται, αἴσθησις μὲν αἰσθητῶν, λεγομένων δὲ <καὶ> ὀνομάτων καὶ ῥημάτων ὁ λόγος, νοητῶν δὲ νοῦς.

50,2: ὁ τοίνυν γνωστικὸς ἀφέξεται μὲν τῶν κατὰ λόγον καὶ τῶν κατὰ διάνοιαν καὶ τῶν κατὰ

Schematic overview:

a)	*Str.* II 46,2-5	—	*Congr.* 86
b)	*Str.* II 47,1	—	*Congr.* 83
c)	*Str.* II 50,1	—	*Congr.* 100
d)	*Str.* II 50,3	—	*Congr.* 101*
e)	*Str.* II 51,1-2	—	*Congr.* 102-106
f)	*Str.* II 51,3-52,1	—	*Post.* 22-30; *Cher.* 12

a)   *Str.* II 46,2-5 - *Congr.* 86

In this part of *De Congressu*, which is basically a commentary on Gen. 16:1-6, Philo has reached verse 3, where Abraham, after dwelling ten years in the land of Canaan, takes Hagar as his wife. Philo offers the following interpretation; in the time of childhood we are governed by physical concerns, but on our way toward maturity the faculty of discerning between virtue and vice ripens. According to this moralizing scheme, Egypt, as country of childhood, symbolizes sense, and Canaan, as coun-

αἴσθησιν καὶ ἐνέργειαν ἁμαρτημάτων, ἀκηκοὼς ὅπως "ὁ ἰδὼν πρὸς ἐπιθυμίαν ἐμοίχευσεν," λαβών τε ἐν νῷ ὡς "μακάριοι οἱ καθαροὶ τῇ καρδίᾳ, ὅτι αὐτοὶ τὸν θεὸν ὄψονται," κἀκεῖνο ἐπιστάμενος ὅτι "οὐ τὰ εἰσερχόμενα εἰς τὸ στόμα κοινοῖ τὸν ἄνθρωπον, ἀλλὰ τὰ ἐξερχόμενα διὰ τοῦ στόματος ἐκεῖνα κοινοῖ τὸν ἄνθρωπον· ἐκ γὰρ τῆς καρδίας ἐξέρχονται διαλογισμοί."

50,3: τοῦτ', οἶμαι, τὸ κατὰ θεὸν ἀληθινὸν καὶ δίκαιον μέτρον, ᾧ μετρεῖται τὰ μετρούμενα, ἡ τὸν ἄνθρωπον συνέχουσα δεκάς, ἣν ἐπὶ κεφαλαίων τὰ προειρημένα τρία ἐδήλωσεν μέτρα.

50,4: εἴη δ' ἂν σῶμά τε καὶ ψυχὴ αἵ τε πέντε αἰσθήσεις καὶ τὸ φωνητικὸν καὶ σπερματικὸν καὶ τὸ διανοητικὸν ἢ πνευματικὸν ἢ ὅπως καὶ βούλει καλεῖν.

51,1: χρὴ δὲ ὡς ἔπος εἰπεῖν τῶν ἄλλων πάντων ὑπεραναβαίνοντας ἐπὶ τὸν νοῦν ἵστασθαι, ὥσπερ ἀμέλει κἂν τῷ κόσμῳ τὰς ἐννέα μοίρας ὑπερπηδήσαντας, πρώτην μὲν τὴν διὰ τῶν τεσσάρων στοιχείων ἐν μιᾷ χώρᾳ τιθεμένων διὰ τὴν ἴσην τροπήν, ἔπειτα δὲ τὰς ἑπτὰ τὰς πλανωμένας τήν τε ἀπλανῆ ἐνάτην, ἐπὶ τὸν τέλειον ἀριθμὸν τὸν ὑπεράνω τῶν ἐννέα, τὴν [δὲ] δεκάτην μοῖραν, ἐπὶ τὴν γνῶσιν ἀφικνεῖσθαι τοῦ θεοῦ, συνελόντι φάναι μετὰ τὴν κτίσιν τὸν ποιητὴν ἐπιποθοῦντας.

51,2: διὰ τοῦτο αἱ δεκάται τοῦ τε οἴφι τῶν τε ἱερείων τῷ θεῷ προσεχομίζοντο, καὶ ἡ τοῦ πάσχα ἑορτὴ ἀπὸ δεκάτης ἤρχετο, παντὸς πάθους καὶ παντὸς αἰσθητοῦ διάβασις οὖσα.

51,3: πέπηγεν οὖν τῇ πίστει ὁ γνωστικός, ὁ δὲ οἰησίσοφος ἑκὼν τῆς ἀληθείας οὐχ ἅπτεται, ἀστάτοις καὶ ἀνιδρύτοις ὁρμαῖς κεχρημένος.

51,4: εἰκότως οὖν γέγραπται· "ἐξῆλθεν δὲ Κάιν ἀπὸ προσώπου τοῦ θεοῦ καὶ ᾤκησεν ἐν γῇ Ναὶδ κατέναντι Ἐδέμ." ἑρμηνεύεται δὲ ἡ μὲν Ναὶδ σάλος, ἡ δὲ Ἐδὲμ τρυφή·

51,5: πίστις δὲ καὶ γνῶσις καὶ εἰρήνη ἡ τρυφή, ἧς ὁ παρακούσας ἐκβάλλεται, ὁ δὲ οἰησίσοφος τὴν ἀρχὴν οὐδὲ ἐπαΐειν βούλεται τῶν θείων ἐντολῶν, ἀλλ' οἷον αὐτομαθὴς ἀφηνιάσας εἰς σάλον κυμαινόμενον ἑκὼν μεθίσταται, εἰς τὰ θνητά τε καὶ γεννητὰ καταβαίνων ἐκ τῆς τοῦ ἀγεννήτου γνώσεως, ἄλλοτε ἀλλοῖα δοξάζων.

51,6: "οἷς δὲ μὴ ὑπάρχει κυβέρνησις, πίπτουσιν ὥσπερ φύλλα." ὁ λογισμὸς καὶ τὸ ἡγεμονικὸν ἄπταιστον μένον καὶ καθηγούμενον τῆς ψυχῆς κυβερνήτης αὐτῆς εἴρηται· ὄντως γὰρ ἀτρέπτῳ πρὸς τὸ ἄτρεπτον ἡ προσαγωγή.

52,1: οὕτως "'Ἀβραὰμ ἑστὼς ἦν ἀπέναντι κυρίου καὶ ἐγγίσας εἶπεν'" καὶ τῷ Μωυσεῖ λέγεται "σὺ δὲ αὐτοῦ στῆθι μετ' ἐμοῦ."

52,2: οἱ δὲ ἀμφὶ τὸν Σίμωνα τῷ Ἑστῶτι, ὃν σέβουσιν, ἐξομοιοῦσθαι <τὸν> τρόπον βούλονται.

52,3: ἡ πίστις οὖν ἥ τε γνῶσις τῆς ἀληθείας αἰεὶ κατὰ τὰ αὐτὰ καὶ ὡσαύτως ἔχειν κατασκευάζουσι τὴν ἑλομένην αὐτὰς ψυχήν.

52,4: συγγενὲς δὲ τῷ ψεύδει μετάβασις <καὶ> ἐκτροπὴ καὶ ἀπόστασις, ὥσπερ τῷ γνωστικῷ ἠρεμία καὶ ἀνάπαυσις καὶ εἰρήνη.

try of adolescence, vice. The holy word, which knows exactly where the native land of our mortal race is located, sets before us what we should do and what is good. Philo drops the passage from Lev. 18:1-5 into this setting, and he adds that true life is the life of the person who walks in the judgements and ordinances of God. He concludes in *Congr.* 88 that only after a proper interval of time, expressed by 'ten years', can man profitably desire paideia.

In Clement, the borrowed passage, which forms a quotation within a quotation, covers Lev. 18:1-5. The passage is identifiably from Philo rather than directly from the Septuagint for several reasons; it occurs in a series of borrowings from Philo, Clement is the only Early Christian writer to draw on this passage, and it has the same overall length as in Philo. The wording of the passage varies in minor ways from the Septuagint in a way that also reveals the Philonic origin. In Lev. 18:5, however, an additional influence is required to explain a variation that goes beyond Philo; Septuagint: ἃ ποιήσας ἄνθρωπος ζήσεται ἐν αὐτοῖς; Philo: ὁ ποιήσας αὐτὰ ζήσεται ἐν αὐτοῖς; Clement: ὁ ποιήσας αὐτὰ ἄνθρωπος ζήσεται ἐν αὐτοῖς. Clement offers a combination of the two; this could simply be a conflation, but it also reflects a quotation of the Septuagint in the N.T.; in several codices of Gal. 3:12, one finds; ὁ δὲ νόμος οὐκ ἔστιν ἐκ πίστεως, ἀλλ' ὁ ποιήσας αὐτὰ ἄνθρωπος ζήσεται ἐν αὐτοῖς.

b)   *Str.* II 47,1 - *Congr.* 83

The position of this fragment has already been discussed in a).

The biblical background plays a clear role; from this background Philo builds up a coherent, if variable multi-level picture. Egypt at times signifies πάθη, in other cases σῶμα or γεῶδες σῶμα; the two may also coexist.[10] For Philo, Canaan signifies vice. In his description of the soul's passage from Egypt (the emotions) to Canaan (vice), Canaan is linked to adolescence.[11]

Clement gives a free reminiscence of the Philonic etymologies. He leaves the choice open (εἴτε/εἴτε); one may interpret the image either by κόσμος and ἀπάτη or by πάθη and κακία.[12] He consistently replaces Philo's word

---

[10] Parallels in Philo: *Congr.* 20 (as characteristic of the μέση παιδεία); *Congr.* 85 (as πάθος of childhood); *Congr.* 118 (revolt against God); *Congr.* 163f.

[11] Parallels: *Congr.* 81-88, 121.

[12] For a parallel within the *Stromateis* of the etymology Egypt equals cosmos, see *Str.* I 30,4; II 88,2; VII 40,2.

σῶμα with κόσμος, as we have seen above.[13] ἀπάτη represents an extension
of the etymology that is not found in Philo. The explanations of names
have been used by Clement as equivalencies that are self-evident; they
are employed as commonplaces, often being interjected almost
arbitrarily, and lack the freshness and functionality that they have in
Philo's explanations. Clement starts the passages in *Str.* II 46,1 with a
program of the Gnostic, whom he calls 'our philosopher'; he is occupied
with three activities: contemplation, performance of the precepts and forming of good men.

The quotation from Lev. 18:1-5 has been used as reinforcement of the
second activity, that of following precepts. Thereafter, Clement takes up
a suggestion from the ζήσεται in the biblical text, and restates his Gnostic
program. A polemical intention is perceptible; Clement seems to direct
himself against an anti-nomistic tendency. He stresses that the law works
for Hebrews and their neighbors, who he puts on the same level. In his
explanation, Clement says that *we ourselves* are the neighbors for whom,
as for the Hebrews, life means training and education. The law remains
equally valid for both. The emphasis suggests that this passage derived
from Philo is being applied with a highly contemporary significance.

Following the divine precepts leads to the search for God and is closely
linked to the latter (*Str.* II 47,4). For this effort to know God, a variety
of terms drawn from disparate traditions, like θεωρία and ἐποπτική
(ἐπιστήμη), are used in an almost synonymous way. A striking aspect of
his treatment of gnosis and the Gnostic is his very tentative terminology,
exemplified by his use of ἄν with the optative (see St-Fr. p. 138, ll. 12,
13, 17 (24); p. 139, ll. 8, 11).

c)   *Str.* II 50,1 - *Congr.* 100

After preliminary allusions to the number ten (*Congr.* 81 onwards), Philo
attacks it directly in *Congr.* 89; the 'crucial' examples are given. These
examples from the Pentateuch illustrate the perfection of the number.
Noah was the tenth descendant from Adam; Abraham appeared as the
tenth warrior against the nine kings, and a tithe was presented as a
thank-offering for his victory (*Congr.* 90-93). Thus, according to Philo,
the number of ten is connected with God and the number nine with the
mortal human race.

He digresses on the subject of the tithe; a tenth part of all first-fruits
is an obligatory offering; this injunction applies to everything the earth
has to offer, whether animals or fruit, and, in an original development,

[13]   see p. 35.

also to whatever lives in mankind, whether sensible or spiritual. As one
of his examples of the number ten, Philo quotes Ex. 16:36; "The gomor
was the tenth part of three measures." Philo gives life to this seemingly
obscure metrological formula by relating it, as a kind of corollary, to the
divine mandate to preserve the manna in a golden jar, which had occurred nearby (Ex. 16:32ff.). On this basis he is able to construct a powerful
allegory; the three measures of fine flour signify things of sense, of speech
and of thought, of which, as it were, a tithe has to be offered (*Congr.*
100-101).

Clement's excerpt from this material forms a nearly literal quotation
centered on Ex. 16:36. Some minor alterations are made to the Philonic
component: turning τὸ μνημεῖον into τὸ μνημόσυνον, changing καθιεροῦτο
into καθιεροῦσθαι because of the requirements of the grammatical construction, and making changes in the word order. Clement abbreviates
on his way and gives an interpretation: ἐν ἡμῖν γὰρ αὐτοῖς τρία μέτρα, τρία
κριτήρια μηνύεται,....

After a digression about pistis, gnosis and apodeixis (*Str.* II 48-49), in
which the tone is strongly colored by a display of philosophical argumentation,[14] this Philonic borrowing is dropped very abruptly into the verbal
flow. Any reader must be completely mystified by the relationship it has
to the preceding section. The only relationship, in fact, seems to be that
Clement is quoting in sequence from Philo's *De Congressu* and feels
prompted to resume the process at this point.

He then develops the borrowing independently by interpreting the
senses, language and mind in an ethical way; the Gnostic has to refrain
from transgressions in sensation, speech and thought as well as in overt
action. This line of thought is reinforced by some evangelical texts (Mt.
5:8.28; 15: 11. 18).

d)   *Str.* II 50,3 - *Congr.* 101

For the contents of this passage of *De Congressu*, see the previous section (c).

Clement has compressed phrases from two of Philo's sentences into one
of his own. Based on the text of Ex. 16:36, Clement first mentions the
number three and then passes over to ten, the perfect number. He maintains that the latter binds a human being together, and he designates as
man's ten constituent parts the body, soul, five senses, language, pro-

---

[14] For the terminology cf. J. C. M. van Winden, Le commencement du dialogue entre
la foi et la raison, in *Kyriakon* (Mél. J. Quasten), 1970, I, p. 205-213; Osborn, *Philosophy*,
p. 146ff.

creation and spiritual faculties. In *Str.* VI 134,2, the anthropological treatment of the number ten is modified slightly; man's components are the five senses, speech, procreation, the spiritual faculty infused at the creation, the reasoning part of the soul and, last and tenth, the distinctive character of the holy spirit that comes through faith. In this latter passage, soul and body are missing, and spiritual faculties are more strongly articulated.

Comparison between Philo and Clement c) and d)

With the help of various biblical texts,[15] Philo gives a dossier on the number ten; his examples are not always easy to understand, but they are in some sense interrelated. They are at least a selection of texts of the Bible connected both with this number and with tithing. He then links man's faculties to these concepts. From αἴσθησις, λόγος and νοῦς, the last also termed 'man inside man' or 'the immortal within the mortal' (*Congr.* 97), have to be offered tithes to God, who gives fertility to reason.

He thus applies the biblical examples as stepping stones in a theological movement that follows the reciprocal relationship of man and God, who is assimilated to the number ten. Divine generosity must be answered through ritual gratitude and honor in both the material and the spiritual sense. The interpretation extends the rules of the law theologically, and therefore lacks a purely ethical component in spite of the many imperatives affirmed.

In Clement, the connections between the biblical quotations and the interpretation are strained to the limit. Only with the text of Philo in the background is it possible to retrace the jumps in thought, especially that from the number three to the number ten. Clement interprets three by αἴσθησις, λόγος and νοῦς, and he links them with sins (ἁμαρτήματα); in doing this, he gives a strong ethical accent to his treatment. The perfect number ten, moreover, is linked to mankind, which is held together by ten elements. These different foci make it clear that the liturgical and theological interpretation of Philo is replaced by a more ethical and anthropological interest.

e)   *Str.* II 51,1-2 - *Congr.* 102-106

On the basis of two biblical texts (Ex. 29:40; Lev. 6:13) in which a tithe of flour is prescribed for offering, Philo gives an 'explication raisonnée'

---

[15] Ex. 16:36; 29:40; Lev. 6:13.

of the numbers ten and nine. Ten indicates once more perfection and the sphere of God while nine represents the world of sense. To reach this perfect number and to worship God, the number nine has to be surpassed. He connects the numbers to cosmology. The universe is composed of nine parts, of which heaven has eight: the planets, of which one is motionless while the other seven move through space. The ninth part is formed by three natural elements that are connected: namely, earth, water and air. Most people honor the nine parts and the world that is formed from them, but he who reaches perfection honors God, the tenth, who is above the nine and is their maker.

In *Congr.* 106 he begins a new series of examples that elucidates the meaning of ten, in this case without connecting it with tithing. He starts with the Passover (πάσχα), which he interprets as the passover of the soul crossing from the realm of sense and passion to the tenth, which is the realm of the mind and of God. The biblical background of this example is Exodus 12:3, in which the sacrifice of a young sheep on the tenth day of the month is prescribed.

In Clement, the passage consists of a paraphrase of his Philonic example. Various words or groups of words are taken over unaltered or with only minor variations, like ὑπεραναβαίνοντας (-τες in Philo); τὰς ἑπτὰ τὰς πλανωμένας τήν τε ἀπλανῆ ἐνάτην (different order in Philo); τὸν ὑπεράνω τῶν ἐννέα; διὰ τοῦτο; παντὸς πάθους καὶ παντὸς αἰσθητοῦ διαβάσις. Sometimes Clement substitutes equivalents within the Philonic matrix: for example, κτίσις (ἔργον in Philo); τὴν ἴσην τροπήν (μία συγγένεια τροπὰς in Philo); ποιητής (τεχνίτης in Philo). Units that are spread out in different sentences in Philo are compressed to one single phrase in Clement. Significant distortions occur because of this telescoping, as in the treatment of the Passover. In Philo, it had heralded a new and discrete series, while Clement attaches it almost as it were absent-mindedly to the previous material and then drops it abruptly without the development it had had in Philo.

A shift in meaning occurs in his use of τέλειος. In Philo, it indicates the perfect human being, who in contrast with the mass honors God, the tenth. Clement does not take τέλειον as referring to man but attaches it to ἀριθμόν, the perfect number ten. The perfect ten does not correspond directly to God, as it had on various occasions in Philo, but instead to reaching the *knowledge* of God. Another alteration occurs in the description of the heavenly bodies. Philo starts with the stars and descends to the earthly elements: earth, water and air. Clement, on the contrary, rearranges the order; he starts explicitly (πρώτην μὲν τήν) with the lowest unit, which he subdivides into four unspecified units that we can easily reconstruct as earth, water, air and fire, and then proceeds in ascending order.

In general then, Philo describes the universe as nine-partite in descending order from celestial to terrestrial; the perfect man jumps over this hierarchy in a contrary, ascending movement to the tenth position. The numbers ten and one form a pairing because the tenth is simultaneously the perfect multiplicity and the One, namely the Creator. Clement describes the world in an ascending line, beyond which mankind rises, without mentioning a descent. The image of the reciprocal movement and the equalization of one and ten is, therefore, dispensed with. He does mention the Creator, but does not give him the qualification of μόνος. God, moreover, as ultimate objective is displaced by the knowledge of God.

f) *Str.* II 51,3-52,1 - *Post.* 22-28; *Cher.* 12

f1)	*Str.* II 51,3	—	*Post.* 22
f2)	*Str.* II 51,4	—	*Post.* 1; *Cher.* 12
f3)	*Str.* II 51,5	—	*Post.* 25
f4)	*Str.* II 51,6	—	*Post.* 27b
f5)	*Str.* II 52,1	—	*Post.* 27a
f6)	*Str.* II 52,1-4	—	*Post.* 28-30

The treatise *De Posteritate* begins with a quotation from Gen. 4:16: "And Cain went out from the face of God and dwelt in the land of Naid over against Eden." In *Post.* 22ff., Philo interprets the country to which Cain is going as 'tossing'. He compares this state (in both senses of the word) with a person who is dependent on wavering and unsettled impulses like a ship that is tossing at the mercy of the stormy sea. He then moves on to a favorite theme that God stands firmly and represents rest, while creation, on the other hand, is subject to continuous movement and change.

He continues to elaborate the theme with other biblical quotations (Deut. 28:65,66; 21:23) that are connected by an emphasis on the verb to hang (κρεμάννυμι), which is connected with floating, unstable conditions. Man is described in his ambiguity; the foolish man (ἄφρων) is directed towards creation, always on the move without a fixed principle, while the man of worth is inclined to God, the unchanging one. By way of other biblical texts that share an emphasis on the word to stand (ἵστημι) (Gen. 18:22; Deut. 5:31), Moses and Abraham are taken as examples for the steadfast soul who has access to the unchanging God and who stands close to the divine power.

From a technical point of view, Clement's borrowings consist of three disconnected fragments that are almost literal quotations (f1, f3, f4) and three literal quotations that contain a biblical text (f2, f5, f6). Generally Clement follows the order of his source, but one disruption occurs in f2, where he jumps backwards in a way that has on occasion been seen elsewhere.[16] He introduces the beginning of Philo's treatise (*Post.* 1 / Gen. 4:16) as a clarification of the previous quotation, which thereby receives its necessary setting. It is as if he suddenly realized that material he had omitted was, in fact, essential. Unlike *Post.* 1, Clement continues the biblical quotation with the etymologies of the names Naid and Eden. These etymologies do occur elsewhere in *De Posteritate*, including a passage a few lines later, but only in another book of Philo, *Cher.* 12, are they directly linked with this biblical text, and Clement's treatment here may have ultimately been inspired by it.

Clement makes a few alterations. He replaces πρόσοδος with προσαγωγή, and he leaves out ψυχῇ, which had been connected with ἀτρέπτῳ,[17] and θεόν, which had been connected to τὸν ἄτρεπτον; instead of the latter he fills in with τὸ ἄτρεπτον. As a result, the remains of Philo's sentence are more apophtegmatic and neutral in character. In addition to these literal quotations, characteristic words from *De Posteritate* are also scattered through the passage: *Str.* II 51,5/ *Post.* 22, κυμαινόμενον; *Str.* II 51,6 / *Post.* 22, ἄπταιστον; *Str.* II 52,4 / *Post.* 29, μετάβασις; *Str.* II 52,4 / *Post.* 23,24,28 ἠρεμία; *Str.* II 52,4 / *Post.* 24, ἀνάπαυσις; *Str.* II 52,2 / *Post.* 23, τῷ Ἑστῶτι. Other words recall *De Posteritate* only somewhat less specifically: *Str.* II 51,3 / *Post.* 22,24 οἰησίσοφος/ἄφρων, φαῦλος; *Str.* II 52,4 / *Post.* 28, γνωστικός/σπουδαῖος. Similar images may occur, like *Str.* II 51,6, which can be compared with the end of *Post.* 22. The diction of the whole passage is evidently inspired by these parts of Philo.

From the point of view of the content, the dependency is just as strong. Clement begins with the statement that the Gnostic is fixed through faith; the fool, on the contrary, does not have a grip on the truth, and he is therefore moved hither and thither. The scheme of loose and fixed, connected with a double-sided image of man is taken over from Philo. The limits to the dependency are, however, just as evident; after establishing the double-sided anthropological scheme, Clement moves off on his own. He is not so interested in spinning out the contrast between God and creation or in describing God as unchangeable and the 'standing' one (*Post.* 23 τῷ ἑστῶτι, ἑστώς).

A bit further on (*Str.* II 52,2) Clement applies this latter term to a totally different context when he says that the followers of a certain Simon adore the 'Standing' (Ἑστώς), to whom they want to be

---

[16] see p. 107.
[17] L reads ἀτρέπτως.

assimilated. The concept of assimilation can also be found in Philo (*Post.* 23); apparently Clement came across this association in reading Philo but did not adapt it to God within a contrast of God and the human soul but to a sectarian movement.[18] Once again Clement's attention seems to move in an almost capricious way. The effect is evidently connected with his associative way of thinking. Because we have the text of Philo at hand we can retrace some of the verbal basis for Clement's intellectual acrobatics.

There is, of course, a basic tension created by the different orientation of Clement and his source; Clement's interest is clearly directed to man and not to God. If he refers to God it is almost incidental and connected with the two biblical quotations, Gen. 18:22; Deut. 5:31, that he has taken over from Philo.

It is worth noting that the two other biblical quotations in Philo are not quoted by Clement. In these texts the crucial word is κρεμάννυμι (to hang or to be uncertain), which is used as a term of calamitous misfortune: Deut. 28:(65),66; "your life shall be hanging before your eyes", and Deut. 21:23; "he who hangs on a tree is cursed of God." We may assume that there are serious grounds for a Christian author to avoid mentioning these texts in this kind of setting. They (or one of them) had been incorporated in an already-traditional collection of testimonia in which the word κρεμάννυμι plays a significant role. Daniélou has shown how this collection had given new dimensions to the theology of salvation.[19]

Within the Philonic scheme fixed/loose, Clement focuses primarily on mankind and its choice, which is directed toward the ascent to God. This ascent is made possible by faith and knowledge (γνῶσις) of the truth. These two combine to give stability to the soul. Philo's contrast between God and creation turns in Clement to the opposition between gnosis and false gnosis. Philo's emphasis on the concept of God is shifted to the Gnostic or the Gnostic soul.

---

[18] A. Hilgenfeld, *Die Ketzergeschichte des Urchristentums*, 1884, repr. 1963, p. 181ff; H. Waitz, Simon Magus in der altchristlichen Literatur, in *ZNtW* 5 (1904), p. 141; for the concept of standing and stability see: M. A. Williams, *The immovable race* (Nag Hammadi Studies, vol. 29), 1985; the standing one and Simon Magus: Lampe s. v. ἵστημι A 1b; J. M. A. Salles-Dabadi, *Recherches sur Simon le Mage*, [CRB 10] (1969); J. Fossum, *The name of God and the angel of the Lord*, 1985, p. 121.

[19] See also Gal. 3:13; cf. *Str.* V 72,3; J. Daniélou, Typologie et allégorie chez Clément d'Alexandrie, in *StPatr.* IV (TU 79), 1961, p. 52ff.; E. des Places, Un thème platonicien dans la tradition patristique; le juste crucifié, in *StPatr* IX, 3 (TU 94), 1966, p. 30-40; W. C. van Unnik, Der Fluch des Gekreuzigten; Deut. 21,23 in der Deutung Justins des Martyrers, in *Theologia Crucis-Signum Crucis* (Festschr. E. Dinkler), 1979, p. 483-499.

2.3   Str. V 67,4-68,3 - Sacr. 95-100

V 67,1   "Now the sacrifice which is acceptable to God is unwavering detachment from the body and its passions. This is the real, true piety.

V 67,2   And it might be that, on this account, philosophy is rightly called by Socrates the practise of death. For he who neither employs his eyes in the exercise of thought nor draws anything from his other senses, but uses pure mind itself to apprehend things, practises the true philosophy.

V 67,3   This is, then, the import of the five years of silence prescribed by Pythagoras, which he enjoined on his disciples: that, abstracting themselves from the objects of sense, they might with the mind alone contemplate the Deity...It was from Moses that the eminent Greeks drew these philosophical tenets.

V 67,4   For *he commands burnt offerings to be skinned and divided into parts*. For the Gnostic soul must be consecrated to the light, stript of the hide of matter, devoid of the frivolousness of the body and of all the passions, *which are acquired through vain and lying opinions*, and divested of the lusts of flesh.

V 68,1   But most men, *clothed with what is perishable like snails*,[20] *and rolled all round in a ball in* their excesses, *like hedgehogs*, entertain the same ideas of the blessed and immortal God *as of themselves*.

V 68,2   But it has escaped their notice, though they be near us, *that* God *has bestowed on us ten thousand things in which He does not share: birth, being Himself unborn; food, He wanting nothing; and growth, He being always equal; and long life and happy death, He being immortal and incapable of growing old*.

V 68,3   *Therefore* let no one imagine that *hands and feet*, mouth and eyes, *going in and coming out, anger* and threats are said by the Hebrews to be *passions of God*. By no means! But that some of these expressions are used more sacredly in an allegorical sense, which, as the discourse proceeds, we shall explain at the proper time."[21]

---

[20]   Philo here chooses an unfortunate image, since the snail is clad in a highly permanent shell.

[21]   *Str.* V 67,1-68,3: Θυσία δὲ ἡ τῷ θεῷ δεκτὴ σώματός τε καὶ τῶν τούτου παθῶν ἀμετανόητος χωρισμός. ἡ ἀληθὴς τῷ ὄντι θεοσέβεια αὕτη.

67,2: καὶ μή τι εἰκότως μελέτη θανάτου διὰ τοῦτο εἴρηται τῷ Σωκράτει ἡ φιλοσοφία· ὁ γὰρ μήτε τὴν ὄψιν παρατιθέμενος ἐν τῷ διανοεῖσθαι μήτε τινὰ τῶν ἄλλων αἰσθήσεων ἐφελκόμενος, ἀλλ' αὐτῷ καθαρῷ τῷ νῷ τοῖς πράγμασιν ἐντυγχάνων τὴν ἀληθῆ φιλοσοφίαν μέτεισιν.

67,3: τοῦτο ἄρα βούλεται καὶ τῷ Πυθαγόρᾳ ἡ τῆς πενταετίας σιωπή, ἥν τοῖς γνωρίμοις παρεγγυᾷ, ὡς δὴ ἀποστραφέντες τῶν αἰσθητῶν φιλῷ τῷ νῷ τὸ θεῖον ἐποπτεύοιεν. ** παρὰ Μωυσέως τοιαῦτα φιλοσοφήσαντες οἱ τῶν Ἑλλήνων ἄκροι.

67,4: προστάσσει γὰρ "τὰ ὁλοκαυτώματα δείραντας εἰς μέλη διανεῖμαι", ἐπειδὴ γυμνὴν τῆς ὑλικῆς δορᾶς γενομένην τὴν γνωστικὴν ψυχὴν ἄνευ τῆς σωματικῆς φλυαρίας καὶ τῶν παθῶν πάντων, ὅσα περιποιοῦσιν αἱ κεναὶ καὶ ψευδεῖς ὑπολήψεις, ἀποδυσαμένην τὰς σαρκικὰς ἐπιθυμίας, τῷ φωτὶ καθιερωθῆναι ἀνάγκη.

68,1: οἱ δὲ πλεῖστοι τῶν ἀνθρώπων τὸ θνητὸν ἐνδυόμενοι καθάπερ οἱ κοχλίαι καὶ περὶ τὰς αὐτῶν ἀκρασίας ὥσπερ οἱ ἐχῖνοι σφαιρηδὸν εἰλούμενοι περὶ τοῦ μακαρίου καὶ ἀφθάρτου θεοῦ τοιαῦτα οἷα καὶ περὶ αὐτῶν δοξάζουσιν.

68,2: λέληθεν δ' αὐτούς, κἄν πλησίον ἡμῶν τύχωσιν, ὡς μυρία ὅσα δεδώρηται ἡμῖν ὁ θεός, ὧν αὐτὸς ἀμέτοχος, γένεσιν μὲν ἀγένητος ὤν, τροφὴν δὲ ἀνενδεὴς ὤν, καὶ αὔξησιν ἐν ἰσότητι ὤν, εὐγηρίαν τε καὶ εὐθανασίαν ἀθάνατός τε καὶ ἄγηρως ὑπάρχων.

68,3: διὸ καὶ χεῖρας καὶ πόδας καὶ στόμα καὶ ὀφθαλμοὺς καὶ εἰσόδους καὶ ἐξόδους καὶ ὀργὰς καὶ ἀπειλὰς μὴ πάθη θεοῦ τις ὑπολάβῃ παρὰ Ἑβραίοις λέγεσθαι, μηδαμῶς, ἀλληγορεῖσθαι δέ τινα ἐκ τούτων τῶν ὀνομάτων ὁσιώτερον, ἃ δὴ καὶ προϊόντος τοῦ λόγου κατὰ τὸν οἰκεῖον καιρὸν διασαφήσομεν.

Schematic overview

a)	*Str.* V 67,4	—	*Sacr.* 84
b)	*Str.* V 68,1	—	*Sacr.* 95
c)	*Str.* V 68,2-3	—	*Sacr.* 98,100,96

a) *Str.* V 67,4 - *Sacr.* 84

Philo offers an interpretation of the prescription in Lev. 2:14 that the offering of first fruits has to be new, roasted, sliced and finely ground (*Sacr.* 76); 'sliced' or 'divided' he takes to mean a careful analysis and classification of thoughts, and 'pounded' means persistent practice and exercise of what the mind has grasped (*Sacr.* 82-88). Philo enriches the context with an excerpt from Lev. 1:6: "when the burnt offering[22] has been skinned, it shall be divided into its limbs." He interprets this related prescription to mean that the soul should be seen bare and without a skin of false conjectures and that it should then be 'divided' as its members demand.

The 'whole' (ὅλον) evoked by 'burnt offering' (ὁλοκαύτωμα) is virtue. This adds a further level of abstraction to the interpretation. The division, whether of the soul or of the virtuous soul, distinguishes prudence, temperance, courage and justice. The whole and the parts are closely linked with each other. This structure is then applied in a similar way to the idea of reason so that the ethical interpretation flows into an intellectual one; reason must be trained by being divided under the proper headings by arguments and demonstrations; it will thereby be relieved from disorder and obscurity.

From this speculation on the soul, virtues and reason, Clement selects only the soul. The soul is qualified with the title γνωστικός, and is linked to a discussion of the passions rather than of virtues. Philo's word σκεπασμάτων (*Sacr.* 84) is reflected by Clement with τῶν παθῶν.[23] The soul is described as a willing instrument of carnal lusts, whose corporeal aspect is stressed emphatically.[24] The soul therefore must be stripped both from materiality and passions, so that it can be consecrated to the light in its naked form.

---

[22] Both Philo and the LXX have it in the singular, Clement in the plural.

[23] Lilla, *Clement*, p. 86 note 2, observes a contradiction in Clement because he takes over these Stoically-tinted terms from Philo, and by doing so he contradicts his own view on πάθος.

[24] *Str.* V 67,4: τῆς σωματικῆς φλυαρίας; τῶν παθῶν πάντων; τὰς σαρκικὰς ἐπιθυμίας.

In Philo, the whole system, which departs from a cluster of biblical texts, seems to work within a context of logic, ethics and anthropology; practicing the virtues is an extension of the use of reason.

Clement, on the contrary, takes over a fraction of Philo's arguments. This fraction, which, as usual, is centered on a biblical quotation, is placed into a purely ethical framework. This framework is based on the contradiction between the sphere of the σῶμα and the πάθη and the sphere of the νοῦς, and to a degree it dictates the selection of material.[25]

b)   Str. V 68,1 - Sacr. 95

The problem of God swearing an oath, a subject evoked by Ex. 13:11-13 (Sacr. 89), is dealt with in an apologetic perspective by Philo from Sacr. 91 onwards. This divine action must be seen as a concession to the human incapacity to form a valid conception of God; Philo states with the words of Num. 23:19 that God is not like man. He then develops the themes of differences between man, God and human conceptions of God (Sacr. 95,96). As an illustration of human limitations, he gives the images of the snails and the hedgehog; mortal man cannot step outside himself in his conceptions. Blessed and immortal things are conceived in terms of man's own nature.

A scrap of this passage of Philo leaps abruptly into Clement's work. One of the biblical texts, (Num. 23:19), a favorite of Philo, is left out, while the other is taken over. What remains is repeated almost literally; he varies it only by adding ἀκρασίας and θεοῦ. By stressing human excess, the first of these insertions, on the other hand, allows the ethical outlook of Clement to come into sharper focus, and it changes Philo's idea that mankind is locked in himself. The second addition changes Philo's indirect way of speaking about God into a more direct one; 'the blessed' and 'the immortal' becomes the blessed and immortal God.[26]

c)   Str. V 68,2-3 - Sacr. 98,100,96

Philo, who is thoroughly explaining Ex. 13:11-13, deals in Sacr. 97 with its beginning:[27] ''if God gives such and such to you, you shall separate

---

[25] Elsewhere a difference between ethical theory and ethical practice has also been observed; see p. 114f. above. It may be that a different attitude to the Stoa is involved, as Lilla, Clement, p. 86 note 2, points out. It also may be connected with a different position towards the law. For Philo, ethical behaviour is much less a problem because it is already fixed and ordained. Unlike Clement who has to allegorize the law and who is looking for a basis of ethical practice.

[26] Cf. Str. V 68,3 πάθη θεοῦ / Sacr. 96, πάθη τοῦ αἰτίου; Str. II 6,1 φωνὴ τοῦ θεοῦ/ Post. 14 τὸ αἴτιον.

[27] See also, Sacr. 89.

them'' (Ex. 13:11). In his interpretation, he restates a familiar theme; man can give only what is already given by God. In 98-100, God's giving is extended explicitly to the gifts of nature, and a distinction is made between ἀδιάφορα and ἀγαθά. Nature means the divine power that establishes all these things; in this formulation, nature is practically equivalent to God. The second part of the biblical verse, which is focused on the idea of separation, Philo takes as an injunction to separate the concept of God from the lower, more profane and more human thoughts about him. Speaking about God anthropomorphically means improper use of words, an error that comes about through the weakness of human beings.

Philo gives a special turn to the gifts of nature. Some of the specifically good gifts are distinguished sexually; the male group is generative and conceiving and the female group is travailing and bringing to birth. In *Sacr.* 102-103, these gifts are adapted to the working of the soul and its response to nature's gifts, which is also characterized sexually. The male offspring of the soul represents the good things εὐπάθεια and ἀρετή while the female part is less fortunately allotted κακία and πάθος.[28]

Clement paraphrases the idea of the divine gifts from *Sacr.* 98 and telescopes previous and succeeding thoughts from the Philonic passage into it without their original articulation (*Sacr.* 100,96). An alteration occurs (πάθη) τοῦ αἰτίου in Philo (*Sacr.* 96) turns into (πάθη) τοῦ θεοῦ in Clement (*Str.* V 68,3). More striking, however, is the exchange of nature (φύσις) for God (*Sacr.* 98 - *Str.* V 68,2). Philo had repeatedly equated physis as originating power with God;[29] this fits partly into an Aristotelian tradition[30] and partly into a Stoic tradition that knows physis as principle of growth in the universe.[31] Clement was well-acquainted with the definitions of physis in the different schools and must have intentionally avoided leaving it equivalent to God.[32]

Another point of difference is the treatment of anthropomorphisms in speaking about God. Philo accepts them as inevitable, arguing that this improper use of language comes about through human weakness.[33] Cle-

---

[28] R. A. Baehr, *Philo's use of the categories male and female*, 1970; for the concept of εὐπάθεια, cf. J. Dillon and A. Terian, Philo and the Stoic doctrine of εὐπάθεια, in *SPh* 4 (1976-77), p. 17-24.

[29] Leisegang s. v. θεός 3: θεός est φύσις vel hac voce intelligitur; R. A. Horsley, The law of nature in Philo and in Cicero, in *HThR* 71 (1978), p. 35-59.

[30] Arist. *Met.* 1014 b 16; *Cael.* I 4, 270b; 271 a 33; I 11, 291 b 13.

[31] For example, Seneca, *De benef.* IV 7; C. J. de Vogel, *Greek Philosophy*, 1950-1959, vol. III, p. 66.

[32] *Str.* V 100,4; Fragm. IV in St-Fr III p. 219, ll. 19,26; see also Ch. VIII p. 226.

[33] see Colson II, p. 486 par. 121; Runia, *Philo*, p. 438.

ment, on the other hand, argues that anthropomorphic images of God must be allegorized because God is not subject to πάθη. He does not accept anthropomorphisms but instead presents a technical solution for dissolving them.

2.4   *Str.* V 71,5-74,1 - *Post.* 14-20; *Somn. I* 64-66

V 71,4   "Form and motion, standing, throne, place, right or left of the father of the universe are not at all to be conceived, although it is written so. But what each of these means will be shown in its proper place.

V 71,5   *The* first *cause is not then in space but above both space and time* and name and conception. Therefore also Moses says: *'Show yourself to me'*, intimating *most clearly* that God is not capable of being *taught*, or expressed in speech by man. For the *inquiry is formless and invisible*, but the grace of knowledge is from Him by the Son.

V 72,1   Most clearly Solomon shall testify to us, speaking thus: 'The prudence of man is not in me, but God gives me wisdom and I know holy things'.

V 72,2   Now Moses, describing allegorically the divine prudence, called it the 'tree of life', planted in paradise; this paradise may be the world, in which all things proceeding from creation grow.

V 72,3   In it also the Word becoming flesh blossomed and bore fruit and gave life to those who had tasted of his graciousness, since it was not without the tree that He came to our knowledge. For our life was hung on it, in order that we might believe.

V 72,4   And Solomon again says: 'It is a tree of immortality to those who take hold of it'.

V 72,5   Wherefore he says: 'Behold, I set before your face life and death, to love the Lord your God and to walk in His ways and hear His voice and trust in life. But if you transgress the statutes and the judgments which I have given you, you shall be destroyed with destruction. For this is life and the length of your days, to love the Lord your God'.

V 73,1   Again: *'Abraham, when coming to the place that God told him of, looking up on the third day, sees the place from afar'*.

V 73,2   For the first day is that which is constituted by the sight of good things, and the second is the desire of the soul for the best;[34] on the third, the mind perceives spiritual things, for *the eyes of understanding are opened* by the teacher who rose on the third day. The three days may be the mystery of the seal,[35] by which one believes in Him who is really God.

V 73,3   It is consequently from afar that he sees the place. For the region of God is *hard to attain*; God whom Plato called the region of ideas, having learned from Moses that He is a place which contains all kinds of things and their totality.

V 73,4   But it is seen by Abraham from a distance, of course, because of his being in the realm of generation, and he is initiated by an angel next to him.

---

[34] <τῶν> ἀρίστων St; ἀρίστης L; ἡ ψυχῆς <τῆς οὐσίας τῆς> ἀρίστης ἐπιθυμία Fr; cf. *Protr.* 117,1.
[35] Of baptism.

V 74,1   For that reason the apostle says: 'Now we see as through a mirror, but then face to face', *by those sole, pure and incorporeal applications of the intellect.'*[36]

Schematic overview

*Somn.*I 61-71

In *Somn.*I 61, Philo interprets the word τόπος, basing himself on the phrase ἀπήντησε τόπῳ from Gen. 28:11, but reinforcing his ideas with

---

[36] *Str.* V 71,4-74,1: σχῆμα δὲ καὶ κίνησιν ἢ στάσιν ἢ θρόνον ἢ τόπον ἢ δεξιὰ ἢ ἀριστερὰ τοῦ τῶν ὅλων πατρὸς οὐδ' ὅλως ἐννοητέον, καίτοι καὶ ταῦτα γέγραπται· ἀλλ' ὃ βούλεται δηλοῦν αὐτῶν ἕκαστον, κατὰ τὸν οἰκεῖον ἐπιδειχθήσεται τόπον.

71,5: οὔκουν ἐν τόπῳ τὸ πρῶτον αἴτιον, ἀλλ' ὑπεράνω καὶ τόπου καὶ χρόνου καὶ ὀνόματος καὶ νοήσεως. διὰ τοῦτο καὶ ὁ Μωυσῆς φησιν "ἐμφάνισόν μοι σαυτόν", ἐναργέστατα αἰνισσόμενος μὴ εἶναι διδακτὸν πρὸς ἀνθρώπων μηδὲ ῥητὸν τὸν θεόν, ἀλλ' ἢ μόνῃ τῇ παρ' αὐτοῦ δυνάμει γνωστόν. ἡ μὲν γὰρ ζήτησις ἀειδὴς καὶ ἀόρατος, ἡ χάρις δὲ τῆς γνώσεως παρ' αὐτοῦ διὰ τοῦ υἱοῦ.

72,1: σαφέστατα δὲ ὁ Σολομὼν μαρτυρήσει ἡμῖν ὧδέ πως λέγων· "φρόνησις ἀνθρώπου οὐκ ἔστιν ἐν ἐμοί, θεὸς δὲ δίδωσί μοι σοφίαν· ἅγια δὲ ἐπίσταμαι."

72,2: αὐτίκα τὴν φρόνησιν θείαν ἀλληγορῶν ὁ Μωυσῆς "ξύλον ζωῆς" ὠνόμασεν ἐν τῷ παραδείσῳ πεφυτευμένον, ὃς δὴ παράδεισος καὶ κόσμος εἶναι δύναται, ἐν ᾧ πέφυκεν τὰ ἐκ δημιουργίας ἅπαντα.

72,3: ἐν τούτῳ καὶ ὁ λόγος ἤνθησέν τε καὶ ἐκαρποφόρησεν σὰρξ γενόμενος καὶ τοὺς γευσαμένους τῆς χρηστότητος αὐτοῦ ἐζωοποίησεν, ἐπεὶ μηδὲ ἄνευ τοῦ ξύλου εἰς γνῶσιν ἡμῖν ἀφῖκται· ἐξεκρεμάσθη γὰρ ἡ ζωὴ ἡμῶν εἰς πίστιν ἡμῶν.

72,4: καὶ ὅ γε Σολομὼν πάλιν φησίν· "δένδρον ἀθανασίας ἐστὶ τοῖς ἀντεχομένοις αὐτῆς."

72,5 διὰ τοῦτο λέγει· "ἰδοὺ δίδωμι πρὸ προσώπου σου τὴν ζωὴν καὶ τὸν θάνατον, τὸ ἀγαπᾶν κύριον τὸν θεὸν καὶ πορεύεσθαι ἐν ταῖς ὁδοῖς αὐτοῦ καὶ τῆς φωνῆς αὐτοῦ ἀκούειν καὶ πιστεύειν τῇ ζωῇ· ἐὰν δὲ παραβῆτε τὰ δικαιώματα καὶ τὰ κρίματα ἃ δέδωκα ὑμῖν, ἀπωλείᾳ ἀπολεῖσθε· τοῦτο γὰρ ἡ ζωὴ καὶ ἡ μακρότης τῶν ἡμερῶν σου, τὸ ἀγαπᾶν κύριον τὸν θεόν σου."

73,1: πάλιν· "ὁ Ἀβραὰμ ἐλθὼν εἰς τὸν τόπον ὃν εἶπεν αὐτῷ ὁ θεὸς τῇ τρίτῃ ἡμέρᾳ ἀναβλέψας ὁρᾷ τὸν τόπον μακρόθεν."

73,2 πρώτη μὲν γὰρ ἡ δι' ὄψεως τῶν καλῶν ἡμέρα, δευτέρα δὲ ἡ ψυχῆς <τῶν> ἀρίστων ἐπιθυμία, τῇ τρίτῃ δὲ ὁ νοῦς τὰ πνευματικὰ διορᾷ, διοιχθέντων τῶν τῆς διανοίας ὀμμάτων πρὸς τοῦ τῇ τρίτῃ ἡμέρᾳ διαναστάντος διδασκάλου. εἶεν δ' ἂν καὶ αἱ τρεῖς ἡμέραι τῆς σφραγῖδος μυστήριον, δι' ἧς ὁ τῷ ὄντι πιστεύεται θεός.

73,3: μακρόθεν οὖν ἀκολούθως ὁρᾷ τὸν τόπον· δυσάλωτος γὰρ ἡ χώρα τοῦ θεοῦ, ὃν χώραν ἰδεῶν ὁ Πλάτων κέκληκεν, παρὰ Μωυσέως λαβὼν τόπον εἶναι αὐτόν, ὡς τῶν ἁπάντων καὶ τῶν ὅλων περιεκτικόν.

73,4: ἀτὰρ εἰκότως πόρρωθεν ὁρᾶται τῷ Ἀβραὰμ διὰ τὸ ἐν γενέσει εἶναι, καὶ δι' ἀγγέλου προσεχῶς μυσταγωγεῖται.

74,1: ἐντεῦθεν ὁ ἀπόστολος "βλέπομεν νῦν ὡς δι' ἐσόπτρου" φησί, "τότε δὲ πρόσωπον πρὸς πρόσωπον", κατὰ μόνας ἐκείνας τὰς ἀκραιφνεῖς καὶ ἀσωμάτους τῆς διανοίας ἐπιβολάς.

Literature: Daniélou, Typologie, p. 50-54; Völker, *Wahre Gnostiker*, p. 92ff.; De Faye, *Clément*, p. 222f.

other biblical texts in which the word occurs. He distinguishes first a place that is filled by a material form (σῶμα), then the place of the divine word (ὁ θεῖος λόγος), which is filled by God with incorporeal powers (ἀσώματοι δυνάμεις), and finally the place of God himself. This is called 'place' because God contains everything and is contained by nothing; in that sense He himself is a place. Philo then quotes Gen. 22:3,4, which also had been used in *Post.* 17 and was later to reappear in Clement. Philo's two versions of the verses differ slightly from each other as well as from the Septuagint. The reading in *Post.* 17 varies from the Septuagint more than does that of *Somn.* I 64. Clement's adaptation of the biblical text is clearly derived from *Post.* 17.

For Philo, the Genesis text had presented an apparent contradiction; how can someone who has already reached a place be able simultaneously to see the same place from afar? Philo gives a two-part solution to the difficulty; 'place' first means the divine logos and then God before the logos (*Somn.* I 65). The person who reaches the first (the logos) under the guidance of wisdom only sees the second (God) from afar. This person is not capable of contemplating God; he sees only that God is far away from all created things (*Somn.* I 66). God, however, sends his λόγοι as helpers for virtuous people to heal and to strengthen them through training (*Somn.* I 69). Some paragraphs later, Philo again uses the image of the divine logos, this time in the singular; it offers itself as a travelling companion to the lonely soul (*Somn.* I 71).[37]

The passages dealing with the locality of God in *De Posteritate* and *De Somniis* may be concerned with the same subject, but they approach it from different angles. In *De Posteritate*, the place (τόπος) is described from the viewpoint of the soul in ascent and in contemplation. In *De Somniis*, the problem was posed as a more theoretical problem in the definition of God.

An ambiguity in the interpretation of τόπος can be observed that stems from Philo's two contradictory starting points; on the basis of biblical sources, God is, on the one hand, described as place who stays in relationship to the person He meets; this relationship between God and man is clarified particularly by the revelation of God to the patriarchs. On the basis of philosophical conceptions, God is, on the other hand, defined in impersonal, conceptual terms like ἀόρατος and ἀκατάληπτος. These two approaches remain juxtaposed in Philo. By adding intermediary powers, he seems to suggest a solution that can soften the above-mentioned ambiguity. In an absolute sense it is impossible to know God; man cannot proceed further than knowing *that* God exists while remaining

---

[37] προτείνω: (literally) it stretches forward.

ignorant of *what* he is. In terms of relationship, however, a contact is established.[38]

Although it is not entirely fair to say that the first option, namely, the impossibility of seeing or knowing God, is un-biblical, the Pentateuch does approach the problem differently. The Bible is not interested in posing theoretical problems involving means of knowledge nor in developing theoretical solutions to them; the concept of knowledge and knowing is simply out of place in the narrative world of the Pentateuch. This is clearly a critical moment for Philo in his dealing with the two traditions: that is, as he tries to graft a Greek shoot onto a Jewish stem; in order to be recognizable and understandable to the Greek world to which he belongs, he must reconcile its conceptuality with the personalized, relational matrix of the Bible.

Clement's introduction and the first borrowing from *Post.* 14-16

Clement starts in *Str.* V 71,1 in a perspective apparently quite different from that of Philo. He takes up the distinction between the small and the great mysteries; the first have the function of education and preparation; the latter move into real contemplation.[39] Clement has the movement toward contemplation proceed in ascending stages. He distinguishes a first phase, that of purification, which he connects with confession (a possible reminiscence of Baptism). The second phase moves toward contemplation by means of intellectual abstraction; this deductive reasoning means sifting diversity of conceptions from the unified core, a process that ultimately leads to the discernment of unity; this reductive method is analogous to the negative way of approaching the concept of God that was wide-spread in philosophical circles of Clement's time.[40] With them, Clement declares that divine reality can be known only in a negative sense: not by what it is but by what it is not (*Str.* V 71,3). The ultimate unity or objective achieved through the process is not conceived as a localized point (σημεῖον) but a position in thought. Some of the philosophical wording in this formulation, as Stählin has pointed out,[41] may ultimately derive from Aristotle.

Clement then 'translates' the spiritual process into Christological terms; the object of contemplation becomes Christ, who appears as a

---

[38] Sandmel, *Philo*, p. 91; Runia, *Philo*, p. 436f.

[39] Dependence on Philo in a more general sense is, however, present; see chapter VII on *Str.* IV 3,1.

[40] Cf. Le Boulluec, *Str.* V (SChr. 279), p. 244ff.

[41] Cf. *Str.* VI 90,4; see also Arist. *De Anima* I 4, 409 ab; *Anal. post.* I 27, 87 a 36; Nicom. Geras. *Introd. arithm.* II 3.

mediator of divine revelation. In the final phase, the soul progresses by means of sanctification to a divine abyss or infinite opening: τὸ ἀχανές ἁγιότητι (*Str.* V 71,3; cf. *Str.* V 81,3, where the abyss is called βυθός). Clement expands some of the epistemological problems he had dealt with the help of Philo's terminology. It is impossible to know God; He can be apprehended only through his power, δύναμις,[42] which exists in the gift of knowledge by the Son.

He moves into the question of anthropomorphisms that had engaged Philo; biblical formulations, like form, throne or place, should not be understood in conventional earthly terms; Clement promises to come back to this issue at a more convenient moment.[43]

The argumentation around the locality of God might have been evoked by Clement's preoccupation with certain ideas of the Valentinians, as Alain Le Boulluec pointed out. They connected the concept of locality with the demiurge and the negative powers linked with him (cf. *Exc.* 34,1-2; 38,1-3; 39). This may well explain why Clement fastens on the problem of locality in his selection from Philo; Clement's concern with the Valentinian problem also seems underlined by the qualification of χώρα τοῦ θεοῦ as region of ideas in *Str.* V 73,3; the concept, it might be noted, ̦ultimately derives from Plato, but also has Philonic implications.[44]

Christological exposition in *Str.* V 72

Between the first borrowing from *Post.* 14-16 and the second one from *Post.* 18-20, Clement sandwiches a paragraph in which he improvises on the theme of the tree of knowledge and the tree of life. This insertion is extensively analysed by Jean Daniélou;[45] Clement associates the tree of life in paradise[46] with the incarnate word that flowers and bears fruit. The tree of life also is connected with the wood of the cross. In varying Deut. 28:66, Clement says that the life of man is hung in order to come

---

[42] Note, singular.

[43] Cf. *Str.* V 68,3; Méhat, *Étude*, p. 36ff., has tabulated 33 passages in which Clement promises to clarify the issue at a more appropriate time.

[44] See chapter VII on *Str.* IV 3,1; Clement mentions Plato in *Str.* V 73,3 by name; this citation, however, is linked to a need, not felt by Philo, to put labels on and to set thoughts in an 'official' context; Jaap Mansfeld has observed that Clement seems to perceive himself in front of an ignorant audience more than Philo does.

[45] Daniélou, *Typologie*, p. 50ff.; Idem, La vie suspendue au bois, in *Études d'exégèse Judéo-Chrétienne* (ThH. V), 1966, p. 53-75.

[46] For parallels in Philo (*Leg.* I 18, 59; III 17, 52; *Plant.* 10; *QG* I 11), see Daniélou, *Typologie*, p. 50f.

to belief; the use of the verb χρεμάννυμι is striking in this connection,[47] and the biblical text from which the formulation derives presumably belongs to a collection of testimonia, as Daniélou has pointed out.

With a few images, Clement is able to evoke a complexity of theological ideas. Traces of the imagery can be found in predecessors like Barnabas, Justin and Irenaeus.[48] The gifts of faith and knowledge are connected with the crucified Christ. Human beings are put in the footsteps of Christ in suffering to come to life, and they are led to the tree of knowledge. Clement illustrates the ideas of life connected with death and man's free choice in the matter by quoting Deut. 30:15-20, a passage that seems to belong to traditional material as well.[49]

Resumption of *Post.* 17-20

With the traditional word πάλιν, Clement moves back to Philo. He starts with the Philonic rendering of Gen. 22:3-4 and allegorizes on the phrase 'on the third day'. In a Platonizing distinction, the first day is interpreted as the sight of good things; the second shows the desire of the soul for the best, and the third day, the contemplation of spiritual things.[50] Clement applies Philo's words to describe this contemplation as illumination, and he projects it to the resurrection of Christ on the 'third day'. In a similar way, he adds another allegory, introduced by the usual formulation εἶεν δ'ἂν καί..., that alludes to the ritual of Baptism.[51] Layers of association are supperposed densely on the brief biblical phrase in a method that is comparable to Philo's, namely, by subdividing a text and building in successive steps on each unit.

The next unit is concerned with the second half of the text, the 'place from afar'. According to Clement, Moses, for whom God is a 'place', finds a successor in Plato, who calls God the 'place of the ideas'. In *Str.*

---

[47] Daniélou has given a survey of the usage of Deut. 28:66, a text that may already belong to a collection of testimonia used from Melito of Sardis onwards; Daniélou, Typologie, p. 52. Philo has also employed the text in the environment of *Post.* 24, not in *Post.* 8-9, as Daniélou, Typologie, p. 53, indicates, in explaining move versus rest; in this explanation χρεμάννυμι signifies to be floating, unstable, insecure.

[48] Tree of life-Jesus: Justin, *Dial.* LXXXVI 1. 4; tree of life-cross: Ignatius, *Trall.* XI 2; Justin, *Apol.* I 55,3; tree of life-gnosis: Clement: hoc loco. An interesting parallel can also be found in *Ev. Ver.* 18,24-26, which adapts the imagery to the gnosis; see, Puech, Quispel, van Unnik, *The Jung Codex*, 1955, p. 116; χρεμάννυμι (Deut. 28:66): *Paed.* II 73,3; further Melito of Sardis, *Pasc.* 444; Irenaeus, *Dem.* 79; *Adv. Haer.* IV 10,2; V 18,3; Tertullian, *Adv. Iud.* 13,11; Cyprian, *Testim.* II 20.

[49] Cf. *Str.* II 12,1; Irenaeus, *Adv. Haer.* IV 39,1; for individual verses see *BiPatr* I, p. 119f.

[50] Cf. *Symp.* 210-211; *Phaedr.* 251-256.

[51] See σφραγίς, chapter IV, p. 39.

IV 155,2, Clement had already made this thought explicit; there χώρα ἰδεῶν is made equivalent to νοῦς and νοῦς to God. The idea can also be found in Philo's *De Somniis* (*Somn.* I 65ff.), where the place is now the divine logos, now God before the logos. The equation of place of God and χώρα ἰδεῶν is not necessarily derived from Philo,[52] but on this occasion it is likely to be. Clement has connected the thought to the Jewish apologetic position that Plato is dependent on Moses. Both Clement and Philo, moreover, link the equation to Gen. 22:3-4. The use of this biblical text is in itself important testimony for influence from Philo since Clement is the only Christian writer of his day to do so.[53]

In explaining the words 'from afar' Clement takes up the technique of a pseudo-dialogue; an affirmation is made that seems to imply a previous question; he states *but of course* (*Str.* V 73,4) he was seeing from a distance. He then explains that Abraham's condition of being at a distance was due to his attachment to created things (ἀτὰρ εἰκότως πόρρωθεν ὁρᾶται τῷ Ἀβραὰμ διὰ τὸ ἐν γενέσει εἶναι). A mediating figure of an angel is transposed by Clement from a somewhat later verse (Gen. 22:11) to initiate Abraham. A beloved text of St. Paul (I Cor. 13,3) underlines how clear this ultimate vision becomes while a quotation from *Post.* 20 specifies that the contact is pure and incorporeal.[54]

Clement also cites Plato as one who offers an incorporeal method of attempting to perceive God and paraphrases *Republic*, VII,532a-b. In his exposition against material perceptions or definitions of God, he returns to Moses; he did not permit images in the temple and led the people to an idea of God through the veneration of His name. The Gnostic Moses made clear, according to Clement, that God is unlimited (ἀπερίληπτος), invisible (ἀόρατος) and not to be circumscribed (ἀπερίγραπτος) (*Str.* V 74,4).

Philonic influence

Clement returns to the Philonic idea of locality in *Str.* V 74,5 when he says that the temple of God should not be conceived in terms of a concrete place. As an example, he cites Is.66:1, a text that had already been used in *Str.* II 6,3.[55] Judging by the position of λέγει κύριος, Clement probably quotes it via Acts 7:49, in which the verse from Isaiah appears.

---

[52] See chapter VII, on *Str.* IV 155,2; cf. *Str.* V 16,3.
[53] See *BiPatr* I, p. 83.
[54] In Philo negative, in Clement positive.
[55] *Str.* V 74,5: ἀλλὰ γοῦν κωλύων ὁ λόγος τάς τε τῶν ἱερῶν κατασκευὰς καὶ τὰς θυσίας ἁπάσας τὸ μὴ ἔν τινι εἶναι τὸν παντοκράτορα αἰνίσσεται δι' ὧν φησι· "ποῖον οἶκον οἰκοδομήσετέ μοι; λέγει κύριος. ὁ οὐρανός μοι θρόνος" καὶ τὰ ἑξῆς.
See above, p. 151.

In the succeeding passage, *Str.* V 78,3, another reminiscence of Philo emerges through a reference to Ex. 20:21. This text, as mentioned above, formed the substratum for *Post.* 14ff., which had been taken over by Clement in *Str.* II 6,1.[56] It is, moreover, cited by no other author of his time. In this case, Clement gives a different interpretation of γνόφος; God stands in the darkness because the unbelief and the ignorance of the masses blocks off the truth. With the help of Ex. 19:12, the masses are identified as those to whom it was not allowed to ascend the mountain with Moses (*Str.* V 78,2). This interpretation is related to a favorite theme of Clement: namely, the concealment of truth from the multitude. Philo does not cite Ex. 19:12 nor does he offer the kind of interpretation Clement does, instead he links the darkness (γνόφος) to the darkness of God's nature, which is formless, invisible and incorporeal.

Comparison between Philo and Clement

As in *Str.* II 5-6, Clement harks back to *Post.* 14-20 in his description of the knowledge of God. While in *Str.* II 5-6 Philo's sequence was reversed, it is here followed in a forward progression. It is noteworthy that Clement borrows from the same passage of Philo in two different ways. A few Philonic words or sentences are common to both treatments; he uses the phrase οὔκουν ἐν τόπῳ τὸ πρῶτον αἴτιον ἀλλ' ὑπεράνω καὶ τόπου καὶ χρόνου....; he quotes from Ex. 33:13; he repeats the word δυσάλωτος; he also links Is. 66:1, not cited by Philo, to the idea of the locality of God (see *Str.* II 5-6).

Clement presents the borrowings from Philo in this passage in a more philosophical tone than they had been in *Str.* II 5-6; the role of Plato in creating this environment is explicitly cited (*Str.* V 73,3; 74,2). He is, in addition, more heavily preoccupied with the question of τόπος/χώρα (*Str.* V 71,5; 73,1; 73,3; 74,4; 74,5). As in *Str.* II 5-6, the impossibility of knowing God is affirmed. God can only be perceived through his δύναμις. Unlike Philo, this is understood as a singular phenomenon (see *Str.* II 5-6). Clement interprets δύναμις as the gift of knowledge by the Son (*Str.* V 71,5). He elaborates this idea by inserting the Christological passage about the tree of life (*Str.* V 72) between the borrowings from Philo.

The second block, *Str.* V 73,1-74,1, continues on the theme of locality. *De Posteritate* was clearly the basis for Clement's borrowing here, but the version of the same material in *De Somniis* must have run through the back of his mind. A few parallels in *Somn.* I 64-66 are strikingly close. For

---

[56] See above, p. 150.

example, περιέχομαι (*Str.* V 73,3 - *Somn.* I 64) and the idea that Abraham is linked to created things (*Str.* V 73,4 - *Somn.* I 66); Gen. 22:3 is also mentioned in *Somn.* I 64.

ἀτὰρ εἰκότως πόρρωθεν... (*Str.* V 73,4) might be related to the question that Philo puts in both *De Posteritate* and *De Somniis* in connection with the Genesis text: "he sees the place from afar". In Philo's words, the question is "How can it be far off if he is already there". By his choice of words, Clement almost seems to be giving an answer to Philo's question. This phenomenon, a kind of implicit dialogue with his source, has been noted elsewhere.[57]

δι' ἀγγέλου in *Str.* V 73,4 can be paralleled with λόγοι (*Post.* 18) or δυνάμεις (*Post.* 14.20). By transposing Philo's 'powers' to one angel, Clement brings the story back to the biblical proportions.[58] It is, however, clear throughout these borrowings that Clement wants to avoid the divine powers in the plural by using the singular (cf. *Str.* V 71,5; 73,4; also *Str.* II 5,4; 5,5).

Clement quotes literally the phrase κατὰ (μόνας) ἐκείνας τὰς ἀκραιφνεῖς καὶ ἀσωμάτους τῆς διανοίας ἐπιβολάς, but he uses it to mean something quite different. Philo stated in a negative way that even with the pure spiritual contact of understanding we cannot touch God. Clement adapts this positively to reinforce the words of St. Paul. To I Cor. 13:12—"now we see as in a mirror but then face to face"—Clement attaches Philo's "with the pure spiritual contact of understanding".[59] This seems to be an intentional misunderstanding by Clement; it is as if he found Philo's words too beautiful not to misapply.

---

[57] See p. 44.

[58] Osborn, *Philosophy*, p. 41f.

[59] 1 Cor. 13:12; R. Mortley, The Mirror and 1 Cor. 13,12 in the Epistemology of Clement of Alexandria, in *VigChr* 30 (1976), p. 109-120; Mortley, p. 118-119, does not discuss the influence of Philo in *Str.* V 74,1.

CHAPTER SEVEN

THE ISOLATED REFERENCES

Introductory remarks

As stated in chapter one above,[1] many of the references to Philo listed in Stählin's index do not form part of a sequence of borrowings, and their assessment is more problematic than that of the more securely Philonic material previously examined. These isolated citations in Stählin's index will be reviewed and graded in terms of the likelihood of their derivation from Philo; an A signifies certain dependence (quotation); a B means probable dependence (paraphrase and reminiscence with support from the context); a C represents a case in which dependence is unprovable, and a D signifies non-dependence on Philo.

A question mark in this chapter, in contrast with those in the previous chapters, means that the reference in the register of Stählin or in the additions made by his successors does not offer any correspondence with the passage in Philo. Occasionally it has been possible to retrace the passage that was evidently intended, and in these cases, the correction is supplied.

All the references in Stählin's register to the *Stromateis* will be reviewed. A telegraphic style will be used for the isolated references; an exhaustive treatment of every possible parallel will not be presented because of the large quantity of material involved. It is important, however, to survey the material as a whole since a comprehensive survey is a better tool for testing and a better basis for further exploration than a partial one is. When a high degree of completeness has been achieved, it will be possible to quantify the relationships not only between the differing levels of value in the register but also between the differing weights that the various themes taken from Philo have in Clement's work; what was most important to Clement in Philo can emerge with much greater certainty and balance. To gain a comprehensive survey, the material from the extensive sequences will also be reviewed and graded; in these cases, each individual component of the sequence will be rated on its own so that most elements will receive an A, but some with less securely identifiable material will receive a B or C.

---

[1] See p. 22.

The final calculations resulting from this review, which are tabulated in chapter VIII,[2] are based on the sum of individual Philonic parallels in the *Stromateis*. Every calculation, however, is dependent on the way in which one divides the various units, and the exact numbers should not be taken in too absolute a sense. In particular, a sequence falls apart in a number of units, but these units can be distinguished in various ways, and these different methods produce different totals. The organization of Stählin's register determines the basic guidelines for an accounting, but it is possible to subdivide or combine some of these citations in various ways. Stählin himself calculated more than 300 borrowings, as he mentions in the introduction to his German translation.[3] According to our calculations, there are 205 individual units in the *Stromateis*.

Book I

Str. I 1,2   —   Somn. II 134   D

Clement juxtaposes παῖδες σωμάτων-ψυχῆς δὲ ἔγγονοι οἱ λόγοι. In Philo, good thoughts are, as it were, ἔγγονοι of the young soul in training. Stählin gives a reference to Plato, *Symp.* p. 209 ad; *Phaedr.* p. 278a; *Theaet.* p. 150d and Arist. *Eth. Nic.* IX 7,3 p. 1168 A 1-3. Philo and Clement have in common that there is no reminiscence of Plato's maieutics; this is not valid for the passage from the *Phaedrus*. Clement and Philo take over different motifs. Clement stays within the idea of the written word; Philo speaks of good thoughts and their 'brothers'. There is no positive indication of a borrowing from Philo. Clement seems to have borrowed the idea of the written word from Plato directly.

Str. I 1,3   —   Prob. 13   B

The general drift is the same in Philo and Clement; wisdom must be transmitted ungrudgingly. Both use κοινωνικὸν (subst. neutr.) as an attribute of σοφία and not of a person (cf. *Str.* II 87,2 in a Philonic context). In Ps.Plato *Def.* p. 411e the same is again valid, but the word κοινωνικός has a different meaning: namely, social equality. σοφία seems not to be linked to κοινωνικός elsewhere.

Str. I 12,2   —   Gig. 25   D

A proverbial comparison that appears in a comparable context, but there is no indication that Clement borrows it from Philo.

---

[2] see p. 223.
[3] Not only in the *Stromateis* but throughout Clement's works, see Stählin, BKV VII, p. 17.

Str. I 19,1-2	—	*Migr.* 15	?
		Conf. 15	
Str. I 21,2	—	*Her.* 15	?
		Abr. 15	
Str. I 28-32	—	(see chapter II) 7	A
		4	B
		2	C
Str. I 29,6	—	*Dec.* 8	D

A biblical commonplace in a different context; Clement does not speak, as does Philo, of the children of the πόρνη.

Str. I 38,4	—	*Conf.* 159	C

Cf. Clement, *Str.* I 32,4; V 10,3; VI 55,4. The combination στοχασμός—ἀλήθεια is relatively rare in both authors (Philo 3x, Clement 4x). In Clement, its context deals with the relationship between Greek philosophy (στοχασμός) and Christian truth (ἀλήθεία).[4] In Philo the two are regularly opposed to one another;[5] cf. *Op.* 72; *Ebr.* 167; *Somn.* I 23; *Spec.* IV 50; this opposition also appears in the text to which Stählin refers, *Conf.* 159, in which στοχασμός has a negative tone. In that sense the comparison is not felicitous. Better would be a reference to *Spec.* I 38, in which a usage similar to Clement's occurs. In this case, στοχασμός is not opposite, but comes in a second place after the perception of truth (φαντασίας δ'ἀληθοῦς δεύτερά ἐστιν εἰχασία καὶ στοχασμός..). In the context Philo also discusses philosophy. Dependence, however, still does not seem proven.

Str. I 67,3	—	*VM* II,4	?
Str. I 72,4	—		D

The mentioning of Philo's name; cf. *Str.* I 31,1; 153,2; II 100,3.

Str. I 100,1	—	*Agr.* 14-15	C

Cf. *Str.* I 28,4 (chapter II p. 00) and VI 81,1.

---

[4] Cf. Le Boulluec, *Str.* V (SChr. 279), p. 67-69.
[5] πολέμιος, in the meaning of 'hostile', see Liddell and Scott.

Str. I 100,2	—	*Fuga* 57	?
Str. I 150-182	—	(see chapter III) 9	A
		2	B
		3	C
Str. I 168,2	—	*Conf.* 171	B

Cf. Plato, *Protag.* 324b; 325c; *Gorgias* 480cd; 525b; Philo, *Sacr.* 27.131; *Agr.* 40; *Conf.* 171; *Spec.* II 196; Clement, *Str.* I 171,1.4; 173,5; VI 99,2; Chrys. *fr. mor.*332, *SVF* p. 81. The words διόρθωσις and ἐπανόρθωσις are practically synonymous, but the authors have their preferences; διόρθωσις: Plato 1x, Philo 1x, Clement passim; ἐπανόρθωσις: Plato 3x, Philo passim, Clement 1x. κατόρθωμα does not include the idea of improvement, but of good life; cf. Philo, *Sacr.* 131; *VM* I 154; Orig. *Princ.* III 1,23. The combination of κόλασις and διόρθωσις only occurs in Philo, Clement (2x) and Chrysippus (a fragment, however, that is totally reconstructed on the basis of Clement); later it occurs in Julianus Apost. *Or.* 3. Context: Philo deals with God's goodness and severity, which is an aspect of his lawgiving and thus his beneficial power; Clement states that the good law is also severe. Both have been influenced by Plato, who did not pair these two words. Plato asks if the judge who condemns is just and therefore good. The two authors found the idea of measure (μέτριος) in Plato; the distinction between guilt that can or cannot be justified; if the guilty person is not improved by punishment, then at least bystanders will be improved through seeing it. It would appear that Clement draws on Plato directly: the comparison with the doctor is emphasized more than might be expected from Philo's fugitive allusion; the summary of the punishments does not fit into his context, and the word παράδειγμα appears. Yet because of the formulation of the question and the pairing of the two words, it is clear that Clement also has Philo in mind. The setting, moreover, is Philonic, see chapter III p. 49; Clement has been inspired by Philo to the point of taking over some of his words, but he also carries the argument a step further.

Str. I 182,2-3	—	*QG* III 42	B

Cf. Philo, *Conf.* 137; *Mut.* 29; *Abr.* 121; *VM* II 99; Clement, *Protr.* 26,1; *Str.* I 167,1; IV 151,3. Clement knows various derivations for the word θεός, a.o.: θεός-θεσμός, see *Str.* I 167,1; θεός-τίθημι/θέσις, hoc loco; θεός-θέω, see *Protr.* 26,1; *Str.* IV 151,3 (cf. Plato, *Crat.* 397d). Also in Philo the accepted derivation θεός-τίθημι occurs, see *Conf.* 137; *Mut.* 29; *VM* II 99.[6]

---

[6] Cf. Schmid-Stählin I 2 (*HA* VII. 1. 2), p. 614 Anm. 5; Heinisch, *Einfluss*, p. 88f.; Prestige, *God in Patristic Thought*, 1936, p. 1f.; Den Boer, *Allegorese*, p. 75; Treu, *Etymologie*, p. 92f.

A reminiscence of Philo is likely because both use the word διακόσμησις/διακοσμέω in the etymology (*Abr.* 121; *VM* II 99), both have the same interpretation of Gen. 17:4 (*QG* III 42) and in both authors God is called διαθήκη (*QG* III 42).

Book II

Str. II 5-6	—	(see chapter VI) 6	A

Str. II 9,4	—	*Congr.* 140	D

A Stoic commonplace, cf. Clement, *Str.* II 47,4; 76,1; VI 54,1.

Str. II 14,2	—	*Fug.* 10	D

A philosophical-historical commonplace.

Str. II 18,4	—	*VM* I 162; II 4	C

Cf. Clement, *Str.* I 167,3; *Str.* II 19,2; *Str.* II 100,1. A conception that also occurs in Neo-Pythagorean circles: in Diotogenes, who is hard to date, probably first century B.C.; also in Musonius, first century A.D. In *Str.* I 167,3 it is applied to Moses and occurs in a Philonic context; for the idea without this terminology see *Str.* II 100,1.[7]

Str. II 20,1*-2	—	*Congr.* 51	B
		Abr. 57	

Cf. Clement, *Paed.* I 57,2; *Str.* II 99,3 (chapter IV above). The three patriarchs, Abraham, Isaac and Jacob, are described allegorically. Abraham is φίλος: cf. Jas.2:23; Philo, *Sobr.* 56; Clement, *Paed.* III 42,3; *Str.* II 103,2; *Str.* IV 105,3; 106,1 (from 1 Clem. *Ad Cor.* 10,1; 17,2).[8] Jacob (Israel) is ὁρῶν; also Clement, *Paed.* I 77,2; *Str.* I 31,4; IV 169,1; *Exc.* 56,5. This derives from Philo, see: *Ebr.* 82; *Congr.* 51; *Abr.* 57. Isaac is called ἱερεῖον, cf. Philo, *Sacr.* 110. The first (Abraham) is a common Jewish and Christian allegory; the second (Jacob) only occurs in Philo, while the third (Isaac) is not to be found in Philo, but belongs to a Jewish

---

[7] W. Richardson, Νόμος Ἔμψυχος: Marcion, Clement of Alexandria and St. Luke's Gospel, in *StPatr.* (TU 81), 1962, p. 191.

[8] For Abraham, see E. Fascher, Abraham φυσιολόγος und φίλος θεοῦ, in *Mullus* (Festschr. Theodor Klauser *JAC* E1), 1964, p. 111-124; for 1 Clemens, see Zahn, *Suppl. Clem.*, p. 151f.; Knopf, *Ap. Väter*, p. 59 note 1; Stählin, BKV VIII, p. 146 note 3.

and Christian tradition.[9] The combination of reminiscences, which are creatively recomposed by Clement, makes dependence probable for all three.

Str. II 27,2	— *Post.* 26	C
	Abr. 14	
	QG I 79	

Cf. Clement, *Str.* II 41,1; also Ps.Plato, *Defin.* 416c.[10] A philosophical formula: with ἀγαθοῦ in the singular, Clement stands closer to Ps.Plato than to Philo, who repeatedly speaks of ἀγαθῶν; in *Str.* II 41,1, however, Clement does use the plural. κτῆσις is proper to Clement. It is hard to determine if Clement borrows this thought via Philo. The argument in favor: Clement borrowed from this part of *Post.* elsewhere (see chapter VI, *Str.* II 51,3).

Str. II 28,2	— (incorrect, actually *Str.* II 28,3)	

Str. II 28,3	— *Deus* 55	C
	Plant. 106	

Cf. Clement, *Paed.* I 97,3; *Str.* II 81,1 (Philonic context); V 68,2 (Philonic context); VI 39,3 (*Kerugma Petri*); VII 14,5; 31,6; also Just.*Dial.* 23,2. It belongs to a Jewish apocalyptic tradition. Clement is not interested in the description of the abstract concept of God, but of God's relationship to people.

Str. II 41,2	— *QG* I 17	D

A philosophic commonplace attributed to several people (Zeno, Pythagoras). Unlike Philo, Clement does not mention an author but presents it as his own. The contexts are different.[11]

Str. II 46-52	— (see chapter VI) 6	A
Str. II 54,4	— *VM* II 228	?
Str. II 61,4	— *Somn.* I 247.248	A

---

[9] Barnabas 7,3; Melito of Sardis, *Pasch.* 431,499; Irenaeus, *Adv. Haer.* IV 5,4; Tertullian, *Adv. Marc.* III 18,2; *Adv. Iud.* 10,6; 13,20; cf. J. Daniélou, *Sacramentum Futuri*, 1950, p. 110-111.

[10] Bultmann, art. ἐλπίς, in *TWNT* II, p. 515ff.

[11] A. Otto, *Die Sprichwörter und sprichwörtlichen Redensarten der Römer*, 1890, repr. 1964, p. 26.

A paraphrase with literal components; ἐπιστραφεῖσαν diverges from the Septuagint-version of Gen. 19:26 (ἐπέβλεψεν), but parallels Lk. 17:31. The usage of διορᾶν and (especially) στήσας is striking: a typically Philonic word in a comparable context.[12] In the development of the allegory Philo and Clement go different ways. In Philo the motif is the στήλη, which is melted (by the rain) if one is not directed towards knowledge or virtue. In Clement the human condition is the subject; if one looks back to wordly values, one will be unable to proceed further. The στήλη is explained in a positive sense (in *Protr.* 103,4, however, it is negative). There might be a polemical overtone directed against the negative explanation of Philo.

Str. II 69,4-70,1   —   *Migr.* 127f.   B

The concept of following God in combination with Gen. 12:4a. The pairing is unique in both Philo and Clement. Clement's use of the first half of the biblical verse is the earliest in the Christian tradition.

Str. II 70,3   —   *QG* I 82   A

QG I 82 forms the basis for Clement here; the texts are literal equivalents. In both Philo and Clement, the context deals with virtues, and for both moral conversion effects improvement of life;[13] cf. Philo, *Abr.* 17-18, where Philo develops Enoch as an example of μετάνοια, on the basis of Gen. 5:24.

Str. II 71,3   —   *Migr.* 8   B

A Jewish apologetic tradition; the combination of γνῶθι σεαυτὸν and πρόσεχε σεαυτῷ in reference to Moses makes dependance likely.[14]

Str. II 72,1   —   *Spec.* II 185   D

A Stoic definition of χαρά, see Diog. Laert.VII 116, *SVF* III 431; Andronicus, περὶ παθῶν 6, *SVF* III 432. This type of definition of virtues and vices is well-known to Clement, see *Paed.* I 101,1.[15]

---

[12] App. Colson V, p. 605 par. 244.

[13] Früchtel, Griechische Fragmente, p. 112f.; Camelot, *Str.* II (SChr. 38), p. 89 note 8.

[14] γνῶθι σεαυτόν in general: P. Courcelle, *Connais-toi toi-même; de Socrate a Saint-Bernard*, 1974-1975, p. 39-43 (Philo); p. 77-80 (Clement); A. J. Festugière, *Le Dieu cosmique*, 3, 1940, p. 579-581; H. Jonas, *Gnosis und spätantiker Geist*, 1954, t. II, p. 42; A. Nazzaro, Il gnoti seauton nell'epistemologia filoniana, in *Annali della Facolta di Lettere e Filosofia di Napoli* XII, 1969-1970, p. 49-86.

[15] M. Spanneut, *Le stoïcisme des pères de l'église, de Clément de Rome à Clément d'Alexandrie* (PSorb 1), p. 234f.

Str. II 78-100   —   (see chapter IV) 27   A

                                                                1   B

Str. II 100,3   —   *VM* I 22   A

It is notable that Clement mentions Philo here by name (as a Pythagorean) and cites one of his writings.[16] He presents Philo's words freely and adds the words γυμναὶ παθῶν; instead of ἐπιστήμη, ἀλήθεια is inserted, an alteration that makes it impossible to use καινοτομέω, which has been replaced by εὐστοχέω. The context is Philonic, see chapter IV, p. 72; 107.

Str. II 100,4-101,1   —   *Migr.* 131.127   B

Cf. Philo, *Leg.* II 22; Clement, *Str.* V 94,6; 95,1; Chrys. *fr. mor.* 9, *SVF* III p. 4. Clement links ὁμοίωσις to the idea of following God and to Deut. 13:5; this biblical text only occurs once in Philo (to reinforce ἕπομαι θεῷ) and twice in Clement; the other occasion on which Clement uses the text is also within a Philonic context. The philosophical idea κατὰ τὴν φύσιν ζῆν, here ascribed to the Stoics by Clement, must derive from Philo because of this combination of factors. Clement's attitude towards the Stoic concept is different from Philo's. Clement polemizes against people who label God as φύσις.[17]

Str. II 102,6   —   *Opif.* 69   C

Cf. Clement, *Str.* II 38,5; V 94,4; VI 114,4 (a combination of Gen. 1:26 with νοῦς and the idea of dissimilarity). Gen. 1:26 is the starting point for both; image and similitude are not distinguished. Both writers stress that image and similitude must not be conceived in a corporeal form but in the νοῦς which has a dominant function (ἡγεμών, ἄρχω).[18] Both are polemic, but against different targets; Philo opposes an anthropomophic conception of God; to overstate the case, Clement attacks theomorphic ideas of humans.[19]

---

[16] Cf. *Str.* I 31,1; *Str.* I 72,4 as Pythagorean; *Str.* I 153,2.

[17] Mondésert, *Clément*, p. 169; see also chapter VIII p. 226.

[18] Unlike Irenaeus, who relates it to the whole human being; cf. A. Orbe, *Antropologia de San Ireneo*, 1969, p. 108-110; Orbe identifies dependency between Philo and Clement but does not mention these specific texts.

[19] A. Mayer, *Das Gottesbild im Menschen nach Clemens von Alexandrien* (StAns 15), 1942, p. 33; Mondésert, *Clément*, p. 171 note 2.

Str. II 103,2 — *Sobr.* 55 D

Cf. Clement, *Paed.* III 12,4; *Str.* II 20,2, see above. A Jewish and Christian commonplace; the influence of Philo is unprovable and improbable here.

Str. II 105,1 — *Spec.* IV 101 B

Cf. Lev. 11:7; Deut. 14:8. ἐγκράτεια, connected with the prohibition against the consumption of pork. The prohibition is taken literally rather than allegorized. As justification, Clement cites the good flavor, which, as it were, 'drips' from it. Although the argumentation is different, the idea may well derive from Philo. Clement is the first of his days to use the underlying biblical texts. Cf. *Paed.* III 73,3; *Str.* II 67,3; V 51,2; VII 33,1.

Str. II 105,3 — *Spec.* IV 110f. D

Also in Lev. 11 (see previous text) ὗς (vs. 7) is followed by τῶν ἐν τοῖς ὕδασιν (vs. 9). Clement continues the argument while Philo allegorizes.

Str. II 106,2 — *Congr.* 79 ff. B

For the concept and the words γαστρὸς καὶ τῶν ὑπὸ γαστέρα κρατητέον, see *Str.* I 30,2 (chapter II); there it occurs in a Philonic setting.

Str. II 106,3 — *Agr.* 142 D
  QG I 41

Cf. Diog. Laert. II 85;86; Eus. *P.E.* XIV 18,32; Plut. *Mor.* 673B; 786C; 1087E; 1122E, cf. Epic. *fragm.* 411. A philosophical-polemical commonplace. There is no indication that Clement borrows from Philo. In *Agr.*, Philo is unaware of the unfavourable tone of the formula.

Str. II 110,4-111,4 — *Plant.* 11-12 B
  Leg. II 22-23
  Her. 137-138
  Deus 43 (35-48)

Cf. Chrys. *fr. phys.* 714, *SVF* II p. 205; Orig.*De Orat.*6,1. A chain of Stoic commonplaces about the tripartition of ἕξις, φύσις, ψυχή, connected with ὁρμή and φαντασία. In Philo (*Deus* 46-48), the high rank of man is expressed within the theme of κίνησις; mankind has a voluntary movement in which the (lower) δύναμις may be freely used. Clement adapts this to express the relationship between πάθη as κίνησις and its control. The larger contexts are different in Philo and Clement while the smaller are similar. Unless this whole complex occurs elsewhere, dependency seems likely.

Str. II 141,5   —   *Contempl.* 62   B

Cf. Plato, *Leges* VI p. 774; Philo, *Abr.* 136; *Spec.* III 39. Both express Plato's idea that the polis is damaged by a lack of children. The wording σπάνις ἀνδρῶν also occurs in Dem. *Or.* 25,31 and Aeneas Tact.40,4. Both Philo and Clement link the shortcoming to the unwillingness to beget children, whether through pederasty or enkratism. Both might have derived σπάνις ἀνδρῶν from Demosthenes, but this is improbable because he was not speaking about the destruction of marriage; for that reason the influence seems to have come from Philo.

Str. II 143,2   —   *Ebr.* Fr. 6   B

A comparison between farmers, who are supposed to be sober when they sow, and the procreation of man.[20]

Book III

Str. III 36,5   —   *Somn.* II 117.118   D

Cf. 2 Macc. 5:21; Herod. VII 54; Isocr. *Paneg.* (IV) 89. Clement, presumably, has the text of 2 Macc. in mind and adds a complement; he gives a moral interpretation. The idea of rising above nature also occurs in 2 Macc., Philo and Isocrates. Clement has no words in common with Philo.

Str. III 44,3   —   *QG* I 11   B

Cf. Philo *Op.* 53. What the eye is in the body, knowledge is in the mind. Presumably a philosophical commonplace, see also Arist. *Topic.* I 17 p. 108a 11; *Eth. Nic.* I 4 p. 1096b 29; Celsus in Origen, *Contra Celsum* VII 45. The texts of Philo and Clement, however, are closely related. See Früchtel, *Griechische Fragmente*, p. 113.

---

[20] The passage is linked by Früchtel to a fragment of Philo, which had been identified by P. Wendland, *Neuendeckte Fragmente Philos*, 1891, p. 23f.

Str. III 45,3   —   *Dec.* 58   C
                             Spec. I 112

Cf. Plato, *Rep.* 546a; *Phd* 95d; *Phl.* 55a; Arist. *Phys.* V 5 p. 229b 13; Galenus, *De San.* I. A common philosophic concept in a stylized formula; the concept exists in Plato. Philo (*Spec.* I 112) has about the same compact phrase.

Str. III 57,3   —   *VM* II 69   B

Cf. Ex. 24:18; 34:28; Deut. 9:9.18. A midrash on the story of Moses (on the mountain). Both take the idea of fasting from Ex. or Deut. In Philo, Moses did not think about eating and drinking. Clement goes a step further; Moses did not suffer from hunger or thirst. Both deal with ἐγκράτεια in the context and in both the idea of χάρις θεοῦ occurs.

Str. III 83,2   —   *VM* II 84   D
                             Spec. III 33.109
                             Aet. 66
                             Legat. 56

Cf. Clement, *Str.* IV 150, 2. Apparently a fixed metaphor. Philo indicates twice that he is quoting, although the source is unclear.[21] Clement treats it as a self-evident equivalent to the womb.

Str. III 87,4   —   *Dec.* 119   C

Cf. *Str.* VI 147,4 (no reference to Philo is made here). An almost identical thought applied in a totally different way. The replacement of ὑπηρέτης by διάκονος may be explained by the fact that Clement frequently uses ὑπηρέτης in an unfavourable sense.

Str. III 90,1   —   (incorrect, actually *Str.* III 90,3)

Str. III 90,3   —   *Jos.* 43   D

Cf. Deut. 23:18; Philo, *Spec.* III 51. They have only the word πιπράσκω in common (in Philo, *Spec.* III 51): a general reference to a law or custom among the Jews.[22]

---

[21] Colson IX, p. 231 note a.
[22] Colson VI, p. 162; VII, p. 507.

Str. III 95,2   —   *QG* I 53   D

The material comes to Clement by way of Cassianus.[23] Stählin refers to Philo because of the same explanation of Gen. 3:21, but without Cassianus's enkratic dualism.

Str. III 99,1   —   *Jos.* 59   B
                                   Ebr. 220.224
                                   Mut. 68

Cf. Plato, *Theaet.* 150c; ἄγονος σοφίας were words applied by Socrates to himself as an explanation of his maieutic. Clement (ἄγονος ἀληθείας) and Philo attach them to a biblical eunuch and interpret them allegorically; the word ἄγονος in this sense is rare. The step from the phrase of Socrates to a contemptuous usage in connection with an εὐνοῦχος could only have been made by a non-Greek. Of Abraham the contrary has been said by Philo; he was οὐκ ἄγονος σοφίας (*Mut.* 68).

Book IV

Str. IV 3,1   —   *Sacr.* 62   B

Cf. Philo, *VM* I 62; *Cher.* 49; *Abr.* 120ff.; *Leg.* III 100; Clement, *Str.* I 15,3; V 71,1; VII 27,6. The mention of the greater and lesser mysteries forms a metaphoric comparison, which is used ironically in Plato, *Gorgias* 497c. In Middle Platonism it is treated as a topos and indicates the distinction between preparatory knowledge that precedes philosophy and philosophy itself. In Clement, it is transposed into a Christian sense. Cf. Plut. *Vitae* 668A; *Mor.* 382D; Chrys. *fragm.* 42, *SVF* II, p. 16/34-17/2 in Plutarch; Iambl. *Protr.* cap. 2; Albinus, *Did.* p. 182,8f. The formulation of *Str.* IV 3,1 (varying word order aside) is highly similar to *Sacr.* 62; the contexts are also comparable. Both have πρό instead of πρίν as in Plato. The doubling of μυηθέντες μυστηρίων seems unique. In Philo, both μικρὰ and μεγάλα μυστήρια are actually προπαιδεία of the concept of God. In Chrysippus and Plutarchus, the same holds true for the latter; i.e., the μεγάλα μυστήρια, but not for the former, the μικρὰ μυστήρια.[24]

---

[23] About whom the only source seems to be Clemens *Str.* III.
[24] Bornkamm in *TWNT* IV, p. 815 note 54, p. 816/3; Lilla, *Clement*, p. 190; Dillon, *Middle Platonists*, p. 300; Le Boulluec, *Str.* V (SChr. 279), p. 242; Wyrwa, *Platonaneignung*, p. 123f.

Str. IV 5,3   —   *Gig.* 64   B

Cf. Num. 20:17; Philo, *Post.* 101f.; *Deus* 159; *Migr.* 146; *Spec.* IV 168; *QG* IV 226; Clement, *Str.* VII 73,5; 91,5. The story of the royal way from Numbers is transposed by Philo to the way of wisdom and true philosophy. Clement seems to have taken over this image from Philo; there is no indication that it is a commonplace; Clement is the first of his day to quote Num. 20:17. In favor of direct dependence are *Str.* IV 5,3, ὄντως - *Gig.* 64, τῷ ὄντι, and the metaphoric congruities between *Str.* VII 73,5 and *Deus* 159.[25]

Str. IV 38,3   —   *Post.* 71   D

A proverb, in which there is scarcely any similarity in terminology between Philo and Clement.[26]

Str. IV 49,4-56,4   —   *Probus* 22; 96; 105ff.   B

Str. IV 49,4 — *Probus* 22

Eurip. *Fr.* inc. 958; quoted also by Plut. *Mor.* 34B as from Euripides. The quotation is identical both in Philo and Clement.

Str. IV 50,1 — *Probus* 96

Cf. Ambros. *Ep.* 37,34. This fragment represents the category of 'tall stories' about philosophers. Compared to Philo it forms a paraphrase with literal components. A larger part of the story of the death of Calanos is preserved in the letter of Ambrose. The story is also described in Strabo XV 1.68.

Str. IV 56,1-4 — *Probus* 105-109

The subject is steadfastness under torture. Various examples, parallels for which exist in other authors, are mentioned by Clement; cf. Plut. *Mor.* 1051 D; 1126 DE; Diog. Laert.IX 27,59; Cicero, *Tusc.* II 52; Tert. *Apol.* 50; Dio Chrys. 37,45. No literal dependence on Philo occurs in this fragment.

---

[25] Michaelis in *TWVT* V, p. 60ff; J. Passcher; 'Η ΒΑΣΙΛΙΚΗ ΟΔΟΣ, 1931; Völker, *Fortschritt*, p. 35 note 1; Pohlenz, *Philon*, p. 461.

[26] Otto, *Sprichwörter*, p. 316.

Conclusion of *Str.* IV 49,4-56,4; a sequence reveals itself and some of the words in the first two fragments are literally comparable. Since the parallels are traditional material like poetic quotations and 'tall stories' of philosophers, a judgment about dependence must be made cautiously. On the one hand, it is possible that both Philo and Clement use a common source independently. On the other hand, it cannot be excluded that Clement is dependent on Philo directly and that he gives hiw own development towards the end of the passage. In favor of the latter option is the sequence in which the material occurs.

Str. IV 59,5   —   *Leg.* II 38   D

A general statement without kinship in words or ideas.

Str. IV 117,4   —   *Agr.* 130   C

The contexts are totally different. In both authors the word μωμοσκόπος occurs only once. According to Stephanus-Dindorf, *Thes. gr.* s.v., the only early occurrences are in Philo and Clement.

Str. IV 150,2   —   *VM* II 84   D
                                              Spec. III 33.109
                                              Aet. 66

Cf. Clement, *Str.* III 83,2. A quotation from an unknown author (*Aet.* 66); Philo does not feel obliged to specify his source.[27] Clement presents it as a self-evident equivalent for the womb.

Str. IV 151,3   —   *Conf.* 137   D

Cf. Plato, *Crat.* 397d; Clement, *Protr.* 26,1; *Str.* II 5,4; V 81,3. Etymology θεός, see *Str.* I 182,2-3.

Str. IV 155,2   —   *Cher.* 49   C

Philo, *Opif.* 20; *Post.* 18; cf. Plut. *Mor.* 882D (θεός is here equivalent to νοῦς, not to χώρα). For the concept see Clement, *Str.* IV 159,2 p. 318/31ff. Based on a Middle Platonic commonplace. It cannot be proven

---

[27] Colson IX, p. 231a.

that Clement's combination of God as νοῦς or λόγος with χώρα ἰδεῶν derives from Philo, but cf. *Str.* V 73,3.[28]

Str. IV 155,3	— QG IV 2	D
	Somn. I 233	

There is no indication that Philo was the intermediary for this borrowing from Homer. The Homeric material may have been in common usage in philosophical schools and may have been derived from that tradition. Philo made the effort to look it up in Homer himself, Clement manages to mix in a bit of Plato. The contexts are totally different in the two.[29]

Str. IV 158,2-3	— *Spec.* I 112f.	D

Cf. Lev. 21:2-3; both reflect the text of Lev. (Philo also adds vs. 11-12). Philo takes it literally while Clement interprets uncleanness as referring to sin caused by unbelief. Nothing in the context suggests a borrowing from Philo.[30]

Str. IV 161,1	— QG IV 99	B

Cf. Philo, *Post.* 133. An elaboration of Gen. 24:16 based on doubling the significance of παρθένος, which is explained as virginity of body and soul. The length of the biblical verse 16a is the same as in *QG*, and again Clement is the first of his day to quote this verse.[31]

Str. IV 161,2	— *Ios.* 57	D
	Flacc. 135	

Cf. Aristeas, *Epist.* 216, 261 (without εἰρήνη); 1 Clem. 61,1; 65,1[32]. In Philo the group of words has a secular implication, connected with political tranquility. In 1 Clem. it is transposed to the church and by Clement to the individual condition. The etymology in the first part of the sentence, Rebecca equals δόξα, is not to be found in Philo.

---

[28] Cf. chapter VI, p. 173f.; A. Méhat, Le "lieu supracéleste" de Saint Justin à Origène, in *Forma Futuri* (Mél. Mich. Pellegrino), 1975, p. 292 note 35; Wolfson, *Philosophy*, p. 267; Le Boulluec, *Str.* V (SChr. 279), p. 85, 252.

[29] For borrowings from Homer in general, see Gussen, *Leven in Alexandrië*, passim; Daniélou, *Message*, p. 73-101; G. Glockmann, *Homer in der frühchristlichen Literatur bis Justinus* (TU 105), 1968; Zeegers-vander Vorst, *Citations*, passim.

[30] For literal use of the individual laws by Philo, see chapter IV above.

[31] Mercier, *QG* (FE 34A), p. 49.

[32] R. Knopf, *Die Apostolische Väter* (HNT, Erg.-Bd) p. 147; Foerster, in *TWNT* II, p. 409.

Str. IV 161,3   —   *Leg.* III 79   D

Cf. Gen. 14:18; Hebr. 7:1,2. Material readily available via Hebr.[33]

Str. IV 162,2   —   (incorrect, actually *Str.* IV 161,2)

Str. IV 163,1   —   *Plant.* 17.20   B

Cf. Clement, *Protr.* 63,4.; ultimate source Plato, *Tim.* 90a-d. Clement puts the thematic material, which Philo had borrowed directly or indirectly from Plato, in a different perspective;[34] the corporeal also contributes to contemplation. The terminology in Philo and Clement is too closely related to be a coincidence.

Str. IV 163,4   —   *Leg.* I 72   D
                                    QG I 13

Cf. Plato, *Def.* 411d; Albinus, *Did.* 182,32-34. Ultimately derived from Plato; Clement's wording is closely related to Albinus, though in shortened form. All three have συμφωνία in contrast with Plato. Clement did not have to borrow it from Philo.[35]

Str. IV 169,1   —   *Ebr.* 82   B
                                    Congr. 51
                                    Abr. 57

Cf. Clement, *Paed.* I 77,2; *Str.* I 31,4; II 20,2; *Exc.* 56,5. See under *Str.* II 20,2.

Book V

Str. V 8,5-7   —   *Cher.* 4-7   A

Cf. Philo, *Leg.* III 83; *Gig.* 62-64; *Mut.* 66; *Abr.* 82; *QG* III 43. Clement, *Str.* VI 138,2. Etymologies of Abraham and Abram. Largely a literal quotation interrupted by an excursus that deals with the possibilities of

---

[33] G. Bardy, Melchisédech dans la tradition patristique, in *RB* 35 (1926), p. 496-509; 36 (1927) p. 24-45; J. Daniélou, *Bible*, p. 196-201.
[34] Runia, *Philo*, p. 323ff.
[35] Früchtel, Clemens und Albinus, in *PhW* 57 (1937), p. 592; Völker, *Wahre Gnostiker*, p. 291; Lilla, *Clement*, p. 80.

understanding: ἀναβλέψας εἰς τὸν οὐρανόν (Gen. 15:5). ἐξειλεγμένος represents an alteration (Philo: ἐπειλημμένος, but *Gig.* 64: ἐξειλεγμένος).[36]

Str. V 22 — *Contempl.* 16 C

Cf. (χρόνου φείδου) Max. Sos. in Stobaeus III,173. A proverb.

Str. V 30,5 — *Prob.* 13 D

Cf. Plato, *Phaedr.* 247a; Philo, *Spec.* II 249; reminiscences: *Fug.* 62.74; *Leg.* I 61; III,7; Clement, *Str.* V 19,2. Clement quotes verbatim from Plato.[37]

Str. V 31,2 — *Prob.* 2 C

Cf. Clement, *Str.* IV 5,3; VII 91,5. A partial list from Diog. Laert. VIII 17. The expression is used by others as well.[38] A dependence on Philo is hard to prove. It might have been traditional in protreptic education.

Str. V 32-40 — (see chapter V) 9 A
5 C

Str. V 52,5 — *Leg.* II 99 A
Somn. II 267.269

Cf. Philo, *Agr.* 82f; *Ebr.* 111. Ex. 15:1 is linked with πάθη and ἡδοναί. Clement is the only Christian writer of his day who quotes this biblical verse. The passage strongly recalls two places in Philo where not only the biblical text is used but also the qualifications of πάθος are comparable: namely, πολυσκελές, κτηνῶδες and ὁρμητικόν.

Str. V 53,2 — *Deus* 157 see the following[39]
Agr. 37

Str. V 53,2-4 — *Det.* 6-9 B
Somn. I 219-225

---

[36] Cohn (C-W), Prol. I, p. LX; Harl, *Heres* (FE 15), p. 158.
[37] Petit, *Probus* (FE 28), p. 14 note 1.
[38] For other sources and literature, see Petit, *Probus* (FE 28), p. 137 note 5; Le Boulluec, *Str.* V (SChr. 279), p. 133.
[39] Früchtel (Add. St-Fr sub p. 362) bases his comparison on ποικίλος χιτών and λάκκος; even better is a comparison of the allegorical interpretation as a whole: ποικίλος χιτών connected with the story of Joseph.

Cf. Gen. 37:23-24; Clement is the first of his day to quote the verses separately; for this biblical quotation in Philo, see *Ios.*14. The figure of Joseph is treated in an ambivalent way by Philo[40] because of his role as statesman and his stay in Egypt. The multi-colored coat first indicates unstable knowledge, which he has because of his position, and then becomes a key for interpreting his personality. As a person, Joseph can be linked in a negative sense to φιλοπαθής, φιλοσώματος and the ἡδονή (*Deus* 17; 111). Clement develops this ambivalence in a positive sense by allegorizing the multi-colored garment as γνῶσις (cf. *Paed.* II 113,3, where the garment of Christ alludes to wisdom). The well and the removal of the coat are worked out independently (*Str.* V 53,3). In another interpretation, the multi-colored coat signifies ἐπιθυμίαι. This can derive from Philo's negative characterization of Joseph. Philo does not, however, use the word ἐπιθυμία. The double direction of Philo's allegory has taken root in Clement. The positive side is developed as γνῶσις and the negative as ἐπιθυμία; the two allegories stand next to one another without being connected.

Str. V 65,2	—	*Deus* 55	D
		Mut. 14	
		Somn. I 184	

General platonizing concepts; dependence not demonstrable.

Str. V 67,4-68,3	—	(see chapter VI) 3	A

Str. V 71,5-74,4	—	(see chapter VI) 4	A

Str. V 78,2	—	*Leg.* III 141-142	B
		VM II 70-71	

Moses's ascent of the mountain linked with contemplation or initiation: the combination seems to be found only in Philo.[41] Ex. 19:12.20 appear in Clement but not in Philo.

Str. V 78,3	—	*Post.* 14	B

Cf. Ex. 20:21; Philo, *Mut.* 6-7; *VM* I 158; Clement, *Str.* II 6,1; V 71,5, see chapter VI above. Clement has certainly derived the equation of

---

[40] Colson/Earp X, p. 351-357.
[41] Le Boulluec, *Str.* V (SChr. 279), p. 258.

γνόφος with the invisible God from Philo,[42] yet they have hardly any words in common. Philo works this out in *Mut.* 6-15, where he speaks (in 14-15) about the impropriety of names for God and where he uses the word ἄρρητον. According to the *BiPatr.*, Ex. 20:21 is used only by Philo in the above-mentioned places and by Clement in this place and in *Str.* II 6,1 (see chapter VI above).

Str. V 79,4   —   *Op.* 171-172   C

Cf. Plato, *Tim.* 31a. An almost literal quotation from Plato. The unity of the world is connected with the unity of God. Note the shift of οὐρανός and κόσμος. The formula is a topos; there is no definite evidence that Philo has influenced Clement here.

Str. V 80,3   —   *Sacr.* 59-62   A

Cf. Gen. 18:6; Ex. 12:39; Philo, *Sacr.* 62; *Spec.* II 158. Clement has inaccurately summarized Philo. Philo uses two allegories: that of Mamre (three measures of meal; God and his two powers) and that of the unleavened bread from the story of Exodus. In Clement, all this is compressed into one, but the 'powers' do not relate to their new context. It is a literal quotation from *Sacr.* 60 with an insertion (ἀζύμους) from *Sacr.* 62.

Str. V 81,3   —   *Conf.* 137   B

Cf. Philo, *Plant.* 7; *Congr.* 152; *Aet.* 66; Clement, *Str.* II 5,4; 113,2; *Exc.* 7,3; Irenaeus, *Adv. Haer.* IV 20,6.[43] John 1:18 and the concept of κόλπος play a considerable role in Valentinian gnosis, where interest tends to focus on the emanation of the aeons *from* the bosom (cf. *Exc.* 7,3; also, Irenaeus, *Adv. Haer.* I 1,1; *Gospel of the Egyptians*, 40,1, Robinson p. 195; idem 42-43, Robinson p. 196). Yet one passage from Valentinus[44] is closely related: Epiph. *Haer.* 31,2. The word ἐγκολπίζω in this religious sense occurs only once in Philo and Clement.[45] The first part of the sentence (with τινὲς) refers to the Gnostics, and the question arises whether or not the second part also reflects their ideas. Against this influ-

---

[42] H. Ch. Puech, La ténèbre mystique chez le Pseudo-Denys l'Aréopagite et dans la tradition patristique, in *En quête de la Gnose* I, 1978, p. 134-135.

[43] Sagnard, *Exc.* (SChr 23), p. 69, notes 3-4; A. Orbe, *En los alberos de la exegesis iohannea* (Estudios Valentinianos II), 1955, p. 156-157; Völker, *Wahre Gnostiker*, p. 480f.

[44] In Epiphanius, *Haer.* 31,5, GCS Epiph. I (Holl), p. 392.

[45] Philo 3x, Clement 1x without this significance.

ence is the phrase ὡς ἄν, which is characteristic of Clement,[46] and the formula τὰ πάντα ἐγκεκόλπισται, which also appears in *Str.* II 5,4. Clement has probably borrowed the formula from Philo; he alters τὰ ὅλα into τὰ πάντα, which had been used by Philo some lines before.

Str. V 81,5   —   *Post.* 3   D

A philosophic commonplace with some individual nuances.

Str. V 82,1   —   *Legat.* 6   C

Cf. Justin, *Apol.* II 6,1; Theophilus, *Aut.* I 3; Max. Tyr. *Or.* II 10; Cicero, *Nat. Deorum* I 12,30. The impropriety of applying names to God is a topos found both in philosophical currents and in the Christian apologists. Elements of the idea also appear in Philo.

Str. V 93,4-94,2   —   *Opif.* 13-16;25*;26*;   B
                                        29;36;38;55

Cf. Gen. 1:1.2a.3. A Platonizing interpretation of Genesis. Similarities are: μονάς as the first day; the number six connected with procreation; linking the words ἀρχέτυπος, ἀπεικονίζω (Clement, εἰκών) and παράδειγμα. Gen. 1:2a occurs both in *Opif.* 29 and *Str.* V 93,5, see also V 90,1; this part of the biblical verse is not used elsewhere in Philo. The idea of a visible and an invisible creation (*Opif.* 29ff.; *Str.* V 93,5f.) also occurs in Theophilus, *Aut.* II 13. Clement offers a capsule version of *Opif.*, including both the basic philosophical structure and the biblical texts.[47] The whole passage is scarcely intelligible without Philo in the background.

Str. V 94,2-6   —   *Opif.* 139   B
                                    Leg. I 31ff.; 39
                                    Her. 231

A Platonizing interpretation of Genesis: there are vague verbal similarities to Philo, but no single Philonic passage serves as basis. The similarities represent altered reminiscences.[48] Philo, moreover, exploits

---

[46] Cf. Sagnard, *Exc.* (SChr. 23), Introd. p. 50.
[47] Runia, *Philo*, p. 169f.
[48] Le Boulluec points out that Clement, in contrast to Philo, does not differentiate between Gen. 1:26-27 and Gen. 2:7, Le Boulluec, *Str.* V (SChr. 279), p. 303.

Plato tacitly in a description of the creation of mankind; Clement explicitly points out the analogies between the Bible's account and Plato's (especially *Timaeus* 30cd).

Str. V 94,6-95,1   —   *Migr.* 127f.;131   B

A general philosophic idea (ὁμοίωσις) in combination with a biblical text (Deut. 13:5). Clement is the first of his days to quote this verse. Dossier, see *Str.* II 100,4. The passage as a whole, *Str.* V 93,4-95,4, moves from a clear Philonic influence to a general Philonic tone. As often happens the Philonic source is diluted as Clement proceeds with the idea.

Str. V 105,2   —   *Ios.* 126   D

Cf. Plato, *Rep.* VII p. 521c; *Phaedo* p. 95d. No clear parallel with Philo presents itself.

Str. V 106,3   —   *Deus* 12   C

Cf. Philo, *Mut.* 179-180. Λειμών as σφαῖρα ἀπλανής linked with the number seven. Clement goes on, as usual, to the number eight. In the complex of problems around hebdoas and ogdoas it is important to consider influences from Gnosticism, where the number eight has a special prominence; compare Clement's treatment of the temple and the high priest[49] and *Str.* VI 139,4-145,5. Here the construction on seven and eight echoes Plato (*Rep.* X 616b), and Philo's influence is hard to prove.[50]

Str. V 134,1   —   *Deus* 157   ?

Book VI

Str. VI 31,4   —   *Somn.* I 141   C

The powerful ψυχαί moving between God and the world are discussed in a comparable context. Clement speaks about natural powers and Philo about souls.

---

[49] *Str.* V 36,3, see chapter V, p. 133.

[50] Since much is altered between Plato and Clement, Le Boulluec suggests the influence of Philo here, Le Boulluec, *Str.* V (SChr. 279), p. 326; see also *Corp. Herm.* XI 19; further Daniélou, *Théologie*, p. 134; *Message*, p. 120; Sagnard, *Gnose*, p. 378-382; Helderman, *Anapausis*, p. 141.

Str. VI 32,3-4   —   *QE* II 45.47   D

Cf. 1 Tim. 6:16; Aristob.in Eus. *P.E.* VIII 10, 12-17. The passage *Str.* VI 32,3-33,1, which is based on fragments from Exodus, is as a whole more influenced by Aristobulos than by Philo; see specifically the quotation from the former in *Str.* VI 32,5-33,1. The σάλπιγγες ἄνευ ὀργάνων, *Str.* VI 32,3, also go back to Aristobulos; see Eus. *P. E.* VIII 10,5. In common with both Aristobulos and Philo is the contamination of the burning bush (Ex. 3) and the fire on Mount Sinai (Ex. 19-20). The Greek fragments of *QE* II 45. 47 do not offer many other points of contact;[51] Philo has the image of the fire as divine δύναμις but allegorizes in a different way. The comparable word ἀπρόσιτος is here attached to the mountain and not, as in Clement, to the light; cf. 1 Tim. 6:16.

Str. VI 33,2-5   —   *Decal.* 33-35   D

Popular tales of acoustical illusions in remote places.[52] For the first story see also Plut. *Mor.* p. 419E.

Str. VI 34, 1-3   —   *Migr.* 47-48   B

Cf. Clement, *Str.* VI 45,1. The concept of the voice of God as a sound without form is linked to Deut. 4:12b. Philo stresses the difference between hearing and seeing; seeing the word of God means seeing with the eye of the soul. Clement develops the idea that God is able to produce a sound beyond natural possibilities. Clement is the one and only writer of his day to quote, like Philo, Deut. 4:12; the fact makes dependence probable.[53]

Str. VI 60,3   —   *Leg.* III 190-191   B

Cf. Gen. 25:26; 27:36. An etymology of the name of Jacob based on the biblical texts. More than one passage of Philo is comparable. πτερνίζω-πτερνιστής: *Leg.* II 99; *Sacr.* 42.135; *Migr.* 200; *Her.* 252; *Somn.* I 171; *Leg.* I 61; *Leg.* II 89.99; *Leg.* III 15.93.180; *Mut.* 81. The etymology is usually interpreted in a ethical way in connection with πάθη or κακία. Clement presupposes the etymology and attaches it to the elected as υἱοὶ τοῦ Ἰακώβ.[54] The tradition passes on by way of Origen to later times.[55]

---

[51] Petit, *QE* (FE 33), p. 269.
[52] Mondésert, *Clément*, p. 171 note 3.
[53] Mondésert, *Clément*, p. 171 note 3.
[54] Heinisch, *Einfluss*, p. 110.
[55] For example *CoJoh* I 35, 260; Lampe s. v. πτερνίζω and πτερνιστής.

Str. VI 78,3   —   *Congr.* 142   D

Cf. Chrys. *Fr. Mor.* 197, *SVF* III p. 197. Two related but somewhat different philosophical commonplaces.

Str. VI 80,3   —   *QG* III 3   A

Cf. Philo, *Spec.* II 45; III 1. A description of the soul that is elevated and travels around the heavens. The texts are partly literal equivalents. Philo deals with the physiologos, Clement with the Gnostic.[56]

Str. VI 81,4   —   *Agr.* 14ff.   C

Cf. *Str.* I 28,4; I 100,1[57]

Str. VI 84,5-6   —   *Congr.* 88.90   D
                                Post. 173

Str. VI 84,7-85,4   —   *QG* I 91   A

All the elements are present in Philo's *QG* I 91, cf. also (compared to *Str.* VI 85,4) *Opif.* 108f.; *QG* II 2,5; IV 27. None of these numerical serieses, however, fits in with Clement's text as well as *QG* I 91 does.[58] Clement gives an abbreviation of his Philonic example. Unless the relevant text of *QG* should prove to be an interpolation,[59] dependence is certain.

Str. VI 86,2   —   *VM* II 128   D

There are similarities in wording but probably coincidental ones; the terms are generally used in technical descriptions. Philo is describing the logeion of the high priest, Clement the ark in the context of Gen. 6:14-16.

---

[56] Recorded in the apparatus fontium St-Fr, sub p. 471, 27-29, but not mentioned in the Index or Addenda etc.; cf. Früchtel, Griechische Fragmente, p. 114.

[57] Cf. Albinus, in C. F. Herrmann, *Plato* VI, p. 162, 19f.; Früchtel, Clemens Al. und Albinus, in *PhW* 57 (1937) p. 591; M. Pohlenz, *Klemens*, p. 111 note 1.

[58] K. Staehle, *Die Zahlenmystik bei Philon*, 1931, p. 81-82; F. E. Robbins, The tradition of Greek arithmology, in *CPh* 16 (1921), p. 97-123; Idem, Arithmetic in Philo Judaeus, in *ibidem* 26 (1931), p. 343-361; O. Arndt, Zahlenmystik bei Philo; Spielerei oder Schriftauslegung, in *ZRGG* 19 (1967), p. 167-171; H. Moehring, Arithmology as an exegetical tool in the writings of Philo of Alexandria, in *SBL Seminar papers* (1978, series 13), p. 191-227; for *QG* IV 27, cf. Früchtel, Griechische Fragmente, p. 114; a Jewish element in this arithmetic material is the reference to Nu. 8:24 and the seven months'children.

[59] The identical treatment makes one suspicious since Clement hardly ever quotes literally; he normally varies or abbreviates; Méhat, *Kephalaia*, p. 241 note 2.

Str. VI 93,1   —   *Migr.* 184-186   C
                              Somn. I 53-57

Cf. Clement, *Str.* V 8,5; VI 80,3 (Abraham); also, Tat. *Or. ad Gr.*
27,2-3;[60] Irenaeus *Adv. Haer.* II 28,2. Clement knew Philo's allegorization of Abram/Abraham, and the beginning of *Str.* VI 93,1: τί γὰρ ὄφελος
εἰδέναι τὰς αἰτίας... may allude to it. In all probability, however, Clement's basic concern is a traditional Jewish and Christian preoccupation
with the utility of a scientific research in general (here Philo limits himself
to astronomy).

Str. VI 110,3   —   *Decal.* 66   C

Cf. Deut. 4:19; Justinus, *Dial.* 121,2. Instead of faith, God has given the
sun, the moon and the stars to honor as a way for the heathen not to
become fully irreligious. Justin also uses Deut. 4:19 in this sense, stressing even more strongly than does Clement the positive role of the cult of
the heavenly bodies. Clement has no words in common with Philo, but
comparable is the idea of the lesser error and the veneration of the servants rather than the master.

Str. VI 125,5   —   *Abr.* 208   D

Cf. Sext.Emp. *Adv. Mathem.* IX 124.

Str. VI 132,3   —   *Migr.* 93   B
                              Contempl. 78

The concept of the σῶμα τῶν γραφῶν occurs both in Philo and Clement.
The latter starts with a double presentation of Moses's earthly end as an
assumption and a burial, a conception whose source must have been the
Assumptio Moysis.[61] This concept presupposes that Clement knew Philo's
double image. In Clement's formulation it is composed of the λέξεις and
the ὀνόματα, which are opposed to the διάνοιαι. In Philo, the basic idea
is presented in terms of the opposition between a σῶμα that is composed
of τὰς ῥητὰς διατάξεις and a ψυχή that is its invisible comprehension. This
interpretive structure, which is passed on by Origen to later periods and
which was to play such an important role in hermeneutics, must have
been borrowed by Clement from Philo, in so far as available evidence
indicates.[62]

---

[60] E. J. Goodspeed, *Die ältesten Apologeten*, 1914, p. 293.
[61] A. H. Charles, *APOT* II, p. 408.
[62] Schweizer s.v. σῶμα, in *TWNT* VII, p. 1052.

Str. VI 134,1   —   *Her.* 167   B

Cf. Clement, *Str.* VI 136,4. The dichotomy of the soul is related to the
two tables of Moses. This division is also present in St.Paul (2 Cor. 3:3)
but there differently applied to both the tables of stone and the fleshly
tables of the heart.

Str. VI 134,2   —   *Mut.* 111   D

The number ten is related to the senses; the usual five senses are joined
by the voice, procreation, the spirit working in creation (Gen. 2:7), the
hegemonikon and the Holy Spirit; see also *Str.* II 50,3-4, a slightly different version in a Philonic context. Cf. Chrys. *fr. phys.* 827ff., *SVF* II
p. 226. The construction, though usually connected with other numbers,
is presumably a Stoic commonplace, which is also related to the number
seven by Philo.[63]

Str. VI 136,4   —   *Her.* 167   B

Cf. *Str.* VI 134,1

Str. VI 138,2   —   *QG* III 43   A

The light of truth is the spirit of God enabling one to obtain knowledge
of real existences.[64] The texts of Philo and Clement are closely related;
Clement offers an abbreviated version of Philo's words.

Str. VI 139,4-145,5   —   *Leg.* I 2-20   B

Introduction. In this passage in which the ten commandments are
interpreted, Clement is mainly occupied with the commandment to
keep the seventh day as a day of rest. The number seven is the focus
of attention, but six and eight are also taken up. As appears from
other passages in which numbers form points of reference[65] a complex of sources lie behind his thoughts. In several places, Aristobulos
is present; *Str.* VI 137,4-138,4; 141,7-142,1.4.[66] In Stählin's annota-

---

[63] *Opif.* 117; *Leg.* I 11; *Det.* 168; *QG* I 75; Heinisch, *Einfluss*, p. 102ff. (numbers 7 and
10); Pohlenz, *Philon*, p. 453.

[64] Cf. Früchtel, Griechische Fragmente, p. 114.; Mercier, *QG* (FE 34A), p. 98.

[65] See chapter V, passim; cf. A. Quacquarelli, Recupero della numerologica per la
metodica dell'esegesi patristica, in *Annali di Storia dell'Esegesi* 2 (1985), p. 235-249.

[66] N. Walter, *Der Thoraausleger Aristobulos* (TU 86), 1964, p. 3, 30 note 5, 74 note 2,
106, 169.

tions, Philo, especially his *Opif.* and *Leg.*, is the second most important source. Delatte[67] is opposed to the 'onesidedness' of Stählins references, and he contests Philo's share in this passage. Delatte has, moreover, pointed out other parallels, among which are Gnostics, particularly Marcos, who is known through Irenaeus, *Adv. Haer.* I 14,7. How far Philo is involved will be investigated section by section, keeping in mind the arguments brought into the discussion by Delatte. A conclusion will be added after the individual sections have been examined. A consecutive sequence of borrowings in the proper sense does not occur, and so the passage is included in this chapter rather than the preceding.

Str. VI 139,4   —   *Leg.* I 4   B

The number six in the creation in six days is interpreted in an allegoric sense as the directions of movement of living creatures, as had Philo. Liking the number six to the directions of movement is a philosophical commonplace.[68] Philo stresses the living creatures with the words ὀργανικὸν σῶμα. In Clement, they are probably indicated by the term γενικώταται; the combination of both the commonplace and the interpretation makes dependence probable.

Str. VI 140,1   —   *Leg.* I 15   C

Cf. Philo, *Opif.* 99f.; *Her.* 170; *VM* II 210. A Pythagorean commonplace; the number seven is ἀμήτωρ; Clement interprets it as sabbath (also Philo, *VM* II 210-212) and ἀνάπαυσις.[69]

Str. VI 141,7   —   *Leg.* I 5   B

A Jewish topos: namely, the idea that God does not stop creating. It appears in Aristobulos, in Eus. *P.E.* XIII 12,11. Aristobulos is satisfied with an answer about the order of creation while Philo and Clement carry the question a step further and focus on a concept of God. For Philo it consists of ποιεῖν, for Clement of ἀγαθοεργεῖν.[70] This extension of the discussion in both Philo and Clement is strongly suggestive of influence.

---

[67] A. Delatte, *Études sur la littérature pythagoricienne*, 1915, p. 231-247 (Clement).

[68] Cf. Mart. Capella VII 736; Colson I, p. 148; Delatte, *Études*, p. 234f.

[69] Delatte, *Études*, p. 236 more parallels; for ogdoas, see Le Boulluec, *Str.* V (SChr. 279), p. 149; A. Dupont-Sommer, *La doctrine gnostique de la lettre 'Waw' d'après une lamelle araméenne inédite*, 1946, p. 40-50; Sagnard, *Gnose Val.*, p. 366, 378.

[70] A rare word, cf. *Str.* VI 159,4 (ἀγαθοποιέω), but then of people. For the fragment of Aristobulos, see H. Schenkl, in *RMP* 66 (1911), p. 400ff.; Walter, *Thoraausleger*, Aristobulos Fr. 5, Register p. 265.

Str. VI 142,2   —   *Opif.* 13   C
                                  Leg. I 2*

A Jewish topos; everything is created at once, but the various days
are mentioned because of the order. Aristobulos, in Eus. *P.E.* XIII
12,11-12 also presents this reasoning. Clement adds that not
everything is similar in value, an observation that is missing in both
Aristobulos and Philo.

Str. VI 142,4   —   *Leg.* I 2   B

God does not need time; with creation time also came into existence.
Philo and Clement have a very similar thought expressed in slightly
different terms. Philo speaks of χόσμος and Clements of χτίσις.[71] The
thought is a continuation and elaboration of *Str.* VI 142, 2, in which
the problem of simultaneity and various days of creation was brought
up. Philo and Clement carry the idea further than Aristobulos, in
whose admittedly few remaining fragments this issue is not
discussed. (Note: *Str.* VI 142,4 end, p. 504 1.17-18 literally from
Aristobulos (*P.E.* XIII 12, 13), cf. *Str.* V 107,1(-4), with the same
words).

Str. VI 143,1   —   *Leg.* I 8   C

Cf. Philo, *Opif.* 114f.; *Spec.* II 57. In the explanation of the number
seven, Clement brings in the 'protoctistes' and the heavenly bodies,
including the planets, the Pleiades, the Great Bear and the moon.
Without the 'protocistes'[72] the development on seven is a
commonplace, also used by Philo. His treatment of the theme in *Leg.*
offers all these various celestial entities; the other parallels in Philo
offer a selection.

Str. VI 143,2   —   *Opif.* 101   C

A probable topos concerning the four phases of the moon; no literal
parallels in Philo, but the same phenomenon is described.

Str. VI 144,2   —   *Leg.* I 12   C

Cf. Philo, *Opif.* 119. A probable topos describing the seven senses;
no words in common; Clement is closer to *Leg.*

---

[71] Clement alters χόσμος, see chapter II, p. 35; chapter VI, p. 156f.
[72] See chapter V (*Str.* V 35,1), p. 128ff.

Str. VI 144,3-6   —   *Opif.* 104   C

A fragment of Solon, cf. Anatolios *peri dekados*, in *Monac. Graec.* 384 f.58v;[73] Presumably this fragment had been used by Aristobulos, who could have found it in a Pythagorean anthology on numbers.[74] That Aristobulos included this fragment may be concluded from Clement, *Str.* V 108,1, where Solon is mentioned in connection with a quotation from Aristobulos; this seems to be an allusion to the very fragment of Solon that Clement quoted in book VI! Given the variety of sources available, it cannot be proven that Clement derived the Solonic fragment via Philo.

Str. VI 145,1   —   *Leg.* I 13   C

Cf. Philo, *Op.* 125. A topos in which the number seven is connected with the process of a disease.

Str. VI 145,4-5   —   *Leg.* I 20-21   B

Cf. Philo, *QG* I 1. Some words are the same or have the same root. χρόνῳ, ποιεῖν, ὑπολάβωμεν, ἀόριστον (*QG* I 1; *Leg.* I 20, διορίζων); striking is the reference to Gen. 2:4: ὅτε ἐγένετο. Dependence on Philo seems very probable.[75]

Conclusion of *Str.* VI 139,4-145,5: Aristobulos is certainly present in some of the passages (*Str.* VI 137,4-138,4; 141,7-142,1.4 and possibly in the fragment of Solon 144,3-6); Delatte's conclusion, however, that the passage as a whole could have been based on Aristobulos seems unlikely.[76] There are clear indications that Clement used Philo in *Str.* VI 145,5 and to a lesser degree in VI 139,4; 141,7; 142,4. Delatte is right that Clement has drawn on other sources in treating the number eight; this number does not play any role in Philo. The remaining passages are mostly commonplaces, but given the many Philonic parallels, it cannot be excluded that Clement used Philo as his main source. In fact, the combination of cases of probable dependence and cases of possible though not strictly probable dependence reinforce one another and

---

[73] G. Borghorst, *De Anatolii fontibus*. Berl. Diss. 1905; herausg. von J. L. Heiberg, *Annales intern. d'histoire*. Congrès de Paris 1900 5a section; Diehl, fr. 19.

[74] Philo may also have used this putative anthology; Stählin, BKV XIX, p. 338 note 1; Walter, *Thoraausleger*, p. 169; Le Boulluec *Str.* V (SChr. 279), p. 329.

[75] Früchtel, Griechische Fragmente, p. 114; Petit, *QG* (FE 33), p. 41; J. C. M. van Winden, The first fragment of Philo's Quaestiones in Genesim, in *VigChr* 33 (1979), p. 313-318.

[76] Against Delatte, *Études*, p. 233.

build a strong position in favor of believing that Philo lies behind this passage as a whole. If Clement used Philo as his point of departure, parallels in *Leg.* are closer to Clement's text than those from *Opif.* The only material in *Opif.* that is unparalleled in *Leg.* is the fragment from Solon. Although Clement follows no strict sequence from *Leg.*, the parallels all seem to be drawn from the first twenty paragraphs. The general context for this material in clement and his Jewish predecessors is the creation in six days and the seventh day. The theological implications of this issue are more developed in Philo than they are in Aristobulos. Traces of this extension can be found in Clement as well.

Str. VI 168,3	—	*Her.* 259	B
		QG IV 196	

Clement takes over aspects of Philo's idea that the prophet is a musical instrument who is played on by God and who therefore has no command over his own words; cf. Philo, *Migr.* 84. Since the image does not occur elsewhere,[77] it seems probable that Philo's influence is at work. This conception of ecstatic inspiration, in fact, is heavily loaded with negative associations in the Christian tradition because of its association with Montanism; cf. Miltiades (in Eus. *HE* V 17,1-3), who polemizes against ecstasy; also Origenes, *Princ.* III 3,4.

Book VII

Str. VII 2,1	—	*VM* II 67	B

Cf. Philo, *Abr.* 50; *Virt.* 184. The veneration of the true God. Clement uses the doubling θεοφιλής and φιλόθεος only here and shortly thereafter (*Str.* VII 3,6; 4,1). Philo offers the probable point of departure; the contexts are also comparable: Clement, τὸν τῷ ὄντι θεὸν—Philo, τὸ πρὸς ἀλήθειαν ὄν, and Clement, θρησκεύοντα—Philo, θεραπεύειν/θεραπείαν.

Str. VII 3,1-4	—	*Contempl.* 1f.	C

Cf. Clement, *Paed.* I 1,1. Some similarity in ideas, but no unmistakable points of contact.

---

[77] See Lampe s.v. ὄργανον.

Str. VII 9,3-4   —   *Opif.* 141   D

A magnet and its various rings of force; the image is already classic; cf.
Plato, *Ion* 533de, where the power of the Muses (θεία δύναμις) is compared
to the magnet. In Philo, man becomes weaker the farther he moves from
his source of strength while Clement does not touch that aspect but
speaks of the attraction of the Holy Spirit (cf. *Str.* II 26,2, where he again
uses the image but with a different development). Both Clement and
Philo drew the image from Plato.

Str. VII 16,6*   —   *Her.* 231   C

Cf. Plato, *Rep.* X 597e; A.Orbe calls attention to this passage.[78] A
Platonizing interpretation of Genesis turning around the image of God
(Gen. 1:26-27). Both Clement and Philo are dependent on Plato; the title
παμβασιλεύς that Clement attributes to God suggests immediate influence
from Plato. This term makes only one certain appearance in Clement (in
Str. VII 54,4 it is a conjecture of von Wilamowitz-Moellendorf).

Str. VII 19,4-20,2   —   *Congr.* 79f.   D

Cf. Clement, *Str.* I 30,1; 93,5; VI 80,1ff. See chapter II sub I 30,1, where
it occurs in a Philonic context.

Str. VII 40,2   —   *Congr.* 20   C

The etymology of Egypt.[79]

Str. VII 44,6   —   *Deus* 93   B

εὔθικτος (Hort and Mayor: quick, ready, usually with the tongue, but
also with the eye or other faculty); it occurs a few times in Philo (*Leg.* I
55; *Post.* 79.80; *Deus* 93; *Legat.* 57.168), however, in combination with
προσβολή, only in *Deus* 93. In Clement, εὔθικτος with this meaning of
quick or clever appears only here. Liddell and Scott lists only Philo as an
example of the combination ε. with π. Clement was probably inspired by
that previous use of the word. In Philo, it signifies the natural disposition
for rapid insight; in Clement, it refers to the condition of the Gnostic.[80]

---

[78] A. Orbe, *Antropologia de san Ireneo*, 1969, p. 108.
[79] See chapter II; cf. Colson/Earp X, p. 303c; Treu, Etymologie, p. 200; J. Munck,
Christus und Israel, *Acta Jutlandica* XXVIII, Aarhus, 1956, p. 49 Anm.
[80] A shift from quick witted to gnostic.

Str. VII 53,1-2   —   *Cher.* 14-15   D
                              QG IV 204

An ethical commonplace with no evidence for direct dependence.[81]

Str. VII 64,6   —   *Somn.* I 167   D
                              Abr. 52

A commonplace (see *Str.* I 31,5) with no evidence for direct dependence.

Str. VII 70,1   —   *Contempl.* 34   C

In Philo, the image is closely linked to the story that deals with the way of construction of the monastery of the Essenes. Clement uses the combination θεμέλιος and ἐγκράτεια only here and in *Str.* II 105,1 (where Philonic influence is present; the idea without θεμέλιος also: *Str.* II 80,4-5). In Philo, however, θεμέλιος is frequently used in combination with the virtues.[82] Influence is hard to fix precisely.

Str. VII 73,5   see   *Str.* IV 5,3   B

Str. VII 74,1   —   *Leg.* III 250   C
                              QG I 150

The combination of τρίβολοι and σκόλοπες occurs only once in Clement and is apparently not found in other writers. Related combinations not only appear in Philo but also have an extensive biblical background. τρίβολοι cf. Gen. 3:18; 2 Ki. 12:31; Pr. 22:5; Ho. 10:8; Mt. 7:16; Hebr. 6:8. σκόλοπες: Nu. 33:55; Si. 43:19; Ho. 2:8; Ez. 28:24. ἄκανθαι: Jer. 4:3; Ez. 28:24; Mt. 7:16; 13:7.22; Hebr. 6:8. Clement and Philo have in common their application to the vices.

Str. VII 91,5   —   see *Str.* IV 5,3   B

Str. VII 105,4   —   *Plant.* 134   C

The etymology of the name of Judas, here, however, not 'Ιούδας but 'Ιουδαία! (see also under Ch. II, *Str.* I 31,6, there within a Philonic context).[83]

---

[81] Cf. Colson II, p. 482, app. par. 15.
[82] See Indices Leisegang and Mayer s. v.
[83] Heinisch, *Einfluss*, p. 111; Colson/Earp X, p. 357.

Str. VII 109,2-110,1   —   *Agr.* 142ff.   D

Cf. Clement, *Paed.* III 76,1f; *Str.* V 51,4. A traditional Jewish and Early Christian theme incorporated within a section largely borrowed from Irenaeus *Adv. Haer.* V 8,3.[84]

Book VIII

Str. VIII 32,2   —   *Somn.* II 164-168   D

With the exception of ὀργή there are no words in common; the idea is distantly related.

---

[84] Dossier, see Hort and Mayor, p. 192-193.

CHAPTER EIGHT

CONCLUSIONS

1. Introductory remarks

The *Stromateis* of Clement of Alexandria are one of the first approaches to the problems of fundamental and therefore systematic theology from a Christian point of view. The work tries to establish relationships between, on the one hand, Hellenistic culture and philosophy and, on the other, Scripture and Christian faith. Clement was well equipped to undertake the enterprise of bridging these opposites since he was evidently a highly educated and erudite man[1] with access to the resources of the most famous library of antiquity. Yet he was not the first to approach this mediating task; he had been preceded by the Jew Philo, who had paved the way of Hellenization for Christian thinkers.[2] Philo's role was well-recognized even in antiquity: he was praised by later theologians like Eusebius, Jerome and Augustine for his trail-blazing work and he was heavily used by many other authors like Origen, Ambrose and the Cappadocian fathers in a tradition reaching on to later times.[3]

Philo had adapted concepts from the Platonic and Stoic heritage for the explanation of Scripture. The latter consisted for him almost exclusively of the five books of Moses, the Pentateuch. Only occasional references are made to other biblical books, like those of the prophets, the Psalms, or the books of wisdom, while the Pentateuch is interpreted almost line by line. It is uncertain if Philo was the first Jewish writer to make this kind of a systematic attempt to link Platonizing concepts and the Stoic interpretative method to the explanation of the Bible. Philo seems to have occupied an exceptional position within Judaism;[4] he has little in com-

---

[1] Marrou, *Paed.* (SChr 70), Introd. p. 67ff.

[2] H. Chadwick, Philo and the beginnings of Christian thought, in *The Cambridge History of Later Greek and Early Medieval Philosophy* ed. A. H. Armstrong, 1967, p. 137-192; S. Sandmel, *Philo of Alexandria*, an introduction, 1979, p. 148-163 (Philo and Christianity); M. Alexandre, *Congr.* (FE 16), Introd. p. 83-97 (esp. the influence of *Congr.* on the Christian authors from Clement onwards).

[3] Cf. Cohn, in C-W I, p. LXXXXVff. (Testimonia de Philone eiusque scriptis). Once again it must be pointed out that Philo's writings were preserved and transmitted by Christians, not by Jews; only in the 16th century did Jews start to show interest in Philo, cf. Sandmel, *Philo*, p. 14 note 24.

[4] Sandmel, *Philo*, p. 127ff.,147.

mon either with earlier Jewish apologetic writers, some of whom are known from fragments preserved in Clement and Eusebius, or with the Judaism of Midrash and Talmud. Students of Philo have attempted to distinguish his various types of exegesis and to connect them with earlier traditions; it is evident that he drew on different antecedent traditions, but in the absence of substantial evidence, it is of dubious value to speculate about the scope and the literary level of preceding work. Philo, on the other hand, exploited an important and relatively recent development in philosophy; a phase in Platonic thought that is called Middle Platonism and that probably originated in Alexandria some generations earlier. His interpretative method is unlikely to antedate this development.

Many of Philo's writings survive, with only a few represented as fragments; he and Origen can be rated as the two most productive authors of Alexandria. It appears that Clement refers to the majority of the thirty-two known treatises: namely, twenty-five of them, that means seventy percent of Philo's works. This figure is arrived at on the basis of the parallels between Clement and Philo that are rated with an A or B in chapter seven above: that is, those parallels that reveal a certain or probable dependence on Philo. The books from which Clement quotes literally or almost literally in sequential and coherent passages in the *Stromateis* are, however, limited in number; they consist of *De Posteritate* (12x), *De Congressu* (15x), *De Vita Mosis* (22x), *De Virtutibus* (27x). Other certain references to Philo occur only in isolation. In addition to the above-named works, they derive from *Legum Allegoriae, De Cherubim, De Sacrificiis Abelis et Caini, De Somniis* and *Quaestiones in Genesim;* the last source, however, is problematic.[5] The number of treatises that Clement consulted carefully as direct sources is, therefore, relatively limited. He apparently had knowledge of a larger quantity of Philo's works, but he has drawn on them from memory in a less scrupulous way. The two forms of reference suggest interesting problems for Clement's working methods. In the case of relatively meticulous use of Philo, he may either have had the scrolls themselves before him, or else he worked from notes.

---

[5] Philo's *QG* and *QE* have been transmitted to later times indirectly in an Armenian translation, which probably dates from the 5th century. In addition, a number of Greek fragments have been identified, which are preserved in catenae and anthologies. A minor part is handed down in an ancient latin translation (for the editions, see above p. 232). One of the many problems connected with the *QG* and *QE* is the uncertainty about the previous text on which the Armenian translation is based. In most cases a comparison is not possible because the Greek is missing. Mistranslations in passing from the Greek to the Armenian may have taken place. Also the Greek of the text on which the Armenian is based may have been interpolated and modified, for example, under the influence of Christian writers.

Any excerpts, capsule versions or outlines must have been made by Clement himself. He infuses the borrowings into his own text in such an appropriate way, and he displays such an accurate knowledge of what his source was saying in the environment of the borrowed material that it is hardly conceivable that he was working from a pre-existing anthology.

2. The method of investigation reviewed

The extensive register of Stählin, which was later enriched by Früchtel/Treu, provided a rugged and intractable terrain; it had to be landscaped, weeded and pruned. In this research, therefore, one of the first objectives was to find a consistent method for assessing the raw material. In a preliminary phase, the register was rearranged from its traditional organization in terms of Philo's works to a listing based on their order in Clement. A distinction then came to the fore quickly: that between the sustained and the scattered borrowings. The sustained passages with their numerous borrowings derived from a single book of Philo showed a curious associated phenomenon; in shorter or longer form, a progression usually appeared in Clement's borrowings that reflected the material's original order in Philo. In one case, conversely, the order was regressive. The phenomenon, which has been called 'sequence', appeared in its clearest form in *Str.* II 78-100[6], where Clement went through Philo's treatise *De Virtutibus* from beginning to end. Every page of the treatise, had it been in the form of a book, would have been represented by a few lines. It goes without saying that this working method has consequences for the content; while the borrowed material seems almost to give body to its new setting, parts cannot be taken over in fragmentary form without distorting the intention of the original whole.

The sustained passages show Clement drawing on Philo with unique clarity and reveal the most characteristic aspects of his exploitation of this source. They thereby became a measuring rod for assessing, in the narrower sense, the material in the register, and, in the larger sense, important aspects of the relationship between the two writers. Because the sustained passages showed a standard pattern, that of sequenced borrowing from one single Philonic treatise, they were treated in a similar way. In separate chapters for each major sequence, the borrowed material was compared with the original and the contextual setting in both writers was reviewed. In addition, isolated, unsequenced parallels had been identified; these were described in the seventh chapter above. Unlike the sus-

---

[6] chapter IV above.

tained passages they proved to be of varying degrees of value, and it was much more difficult to establish a reliable system to rate them. It would have been possible to develop an elaborate system of distinctions, but a relatively limited number of categories (four) was selected to render the raw material manageable and more easily surveyed. From this method it was at last possible to quantify the relationship between certain, probable and uncertain dependence as well as to determine the incidence of non-dependence among the previously indexed parallels. The first and last possibilities (designated A and D) are the clearest and easiest to decide, and the results are the most reliable. In the intermediate situations (cases B and C, of either probable or unprovable dependence), it is easier either to misplace the emphasis or to remain in the realm of uncertainty. Even if a passage is not demonstrably dependent, dependence does theoretically remain possible. Yet the shifts between B and C probably tend to balance one another statistically. The numbers, moreover, should not be taken in too absolute a sense since this, like every tabulation, is dependent on the criteria of arrangement. In spite of these restrictions, it has seemed possible to create a manageable instrument with which a number of essential questions can be assessed: what was Clement's technique in borrowing from Philo, what were his purposes, and what were the criteria for his selections.

Compared to the methods discussed in the first chapter, that employed here does not attempt to review the theology of either Clement or Philo in a broad sense. This study, moreover, does not attempt to enter into some aspects of their thoughts deeply or systematically. Only those problems are discussed that are connected with the parallel passages under examination. This is a limitation of the method and one can even consider it a shortcoming; the benefits, however, are that the abundant parallel material was rendered digestable and a possible basis for further research was created.

A methodical starting point was formed by the more technical aspects of borrowing, and only thereafter were the substance and the meaning of the material reviewed. First, the true parallels had to be circumscribed and the alterations had to be defined, and only thereafter could the contents be compared. In previous literature on the subject, one of the stumbling blocks to a satisfying description of the relationship between the two writers appeared to be the ways in which they were compared. Content was generally made the starting point while efforts to work from a more formal or technical base, on the other hand, were not carried through as far as they could have been. The methodological problem involved here is related to a more general one in studies of comparison that transgresses the borders of this particular study; the problem is that of comparing two authors to one another without introducing ideas that are inessential, irrelevant or even alien to them. By first comparing words and phrases on a strictly technical basis a solid framework for further advances is created. Passages were analysed in detail, and attention was directed to the construction of sentences and to the usage and meanings of words. The passages were then compared for shifts of grammar or vocabulary. The borrowings were next reviewed within Clement's own line of thought. The question was raised of what Clement's intentions had been in absorbing this material into his own work. An underlying conviction was that by knowing his intentions a clearer view might be obtained about Clement's own contribution to the borrowed material. In the larger sense, this perspective is equivalent to an insight into the varying operation of Jewish and Christian hermeneutics.

In this way the formal transpositions were evaluated on the basis of their content. When a similar phenomenon turned up several times, a pattern could be defined. To accurately delimit these patterns it was necessary to study the borrowed material as a whole. The investigations were limited, however, to the *Stromateis* where Philo was most frequently alluded to and where he, indeed, played a dominant role among the sources, but the same method could well be applied to the rest of Clement's works.

It was preferable to work through the method consistently since a comparison is easier to make when each unit of analysis has a similar framework. In the course of this study, it became evident that Clement did not always use Philo for the same reason. These variable motives make it more difficult to discover patterns in the content. Clement may lean on Philo in a traditional apologetic theme, or he may use him polemically. His polemical intentions, moreover, are not always the same. Yet in spite of these varying circumstances, the method brought to the fore a consistently biblical component that was relevant not only for the form but also for the content. In dealing with Clement's criteria for selecting material from Philo, this biblical element will be discussed more extensively.

In summary then, the method of investigation has been to review and to assess the large body of potentially Philonic material. Clement's technique of working has been examined at close range in cases of certain Philonic borrowing. Attempts have been made to give a clearer view of Clement's intentions in this process, to characterize his method of selection and to uncover hermeneutic distinctions and alterations. Whether or not this approach achieves its intended objectives is up to the reader to decide.

3. Clement's technique of borrowing

As mentioned above, the existence of continuous sequences was most surprising. Méhat has already called attention to this phenomenon, but he has not worked out the consequences of this discovery for all possible passages.[7] Mondésert has pointed out a similar process at work in the biblical citations.[8] At the beginning of each chapter the sequences are presented in a schematic way. The four major sequences are dealt with in individual chapters while four shorter progressions are treated together in a single chapter. To have a balanced comparison with the isolated references, individual units within the sequences are rated by the same standards as the isolated ones are. This rating is tabulated in chapter VII. A total number of 206 putative borrowings were examined; 86 formed parts of sequences, and 120 were isolated units.

Beyond the mere fact of a progression and a derivation from one book in Philo, all the sequences are characterized by literal correspondences between Philo and Clement. Two passages, *Str.* IV 49,4-56,4 and *Str.* VI 139,4-145,5, showed features of the sequential ones; they are not, however, grouped among them but are dealt with in the seventh chapter, dedicated to the isolated references. In the first passage there is a sequence, and words are literally comparable, but since the comparanda are groups of traditional material like poetic quotations and stories about philosophers, a judgment about dependence must be made cautiously. It is possible that Philo forms the underlying source for Clement, but it is also conceivable that both have drawn on a pre-existing anthology, which could have stemmed from a school tradition. The second of these 'dubious sequences' presents a more complicated situation; the references are mainly formed by commonplaces, and literality is largely absent. Ultimately, the two passages have been given a B (for possible dependence), but they have not been included among the other sequences because of these major dissimilarities.

From a technical point of view, some repeated phenomena can be identified. In all instances, the original Philonic example is considerably abbreviated. Abbreviated fragments from successive paragraphs may present a condensed form of a section of Philo. On one occasion Clement explicitly announces the principle of abbreviation; at the beginning of his account of Moses's life-story, Clement says "His family and his deeds and life are reliably related by the scriptures themselves, but have nevertheless to be stated by us *as briefly as possible.*" He did not, moreover, worry excessively about accusations of plagiarism since Clement's phrase

---

[7] Méhat, *Kephalaia*, p. 242.
[8] Mondésert, *Clément*, p. 73.

"by us" actually means with the words of Philo. Another characteristic of his technique is the abrupt way that material borrowed from Philo jumps into his text. These discontinuities give a strange flavor to his sentences and lead to illogical turns of thought. In these various ways, therefore, Philo's original text is nearly always presented in a damaged and defective form. Repeatedly, confusion and disorder appear; words are shifted strangely, and sentences are chopped into cryptic fragments.

The development of Clement's thought would be entirely incomprehensible in these sections if Philo's text was not at hand. This applies not only to the readers of today but must also have held true for his own contemporaries. The readers for whom the *Stromateis* were intended may well have had some knowledge of the underlying texts of Philo. The material that forms the basis for the *Stromateis* could well have been presented as part of a course of study; the teacher's basic notes could have functioned independently in a educational situation, and he presumably provided some explanation himself. The *Stromateis* as we know them cannot have been these notes, as some have proposed; in spite of their difficulties, they are well composed and polished writings. Apparent traces of the direct or spontaneous use of language have been pointed out, but these arguments are inconclusive since in the Greek of Clement and other writers of his period many artificial devices are employed. It is hard to determine whether the use of spoken language is a rhetorical device or records an actual situation.[9]

One cannot say that Clement did his work badly or amateurishly. In spite of his cut-and-paste technique, his illogical insertions and his abrupt transitions, there are clever and ingenious inventions as well. Clement was capable of subtly turning the words of Philo to serve his own purposes. Material was transposed in converted and rearranged form. An impressive ability to vary and juggle words manifests itself persistently. Characteristic of his technique is also the way that borrowings tend to move away from their source in a distinct pattern. Clement often started in a relatively literal fashion, but quotation tended to turn into reminiscence or even less as he went on. Via introductory or transitional phrases one can pick up the thread of the Philonic source again. Various techniques thus tend to weave themselves into a single passage.

A curious technique is the 'jump backwards'. Occasionally Clement started his borrowing well into Philo's treatise, then leaped back to the beginning and thereafter proceeded in a steady forward direction. The phenomenon has a psychological or even practical explanation; if one author wants to use another's text, the book or scroll will be taken and

---

[9] Méhat, *Étude* p. 321ff., 283ff.

leafed through. In the course of the search for a specific text, the adaptor may become so interested that not only the passage he had in mind but also other material that just struck his eye is taken over. The new discoveries can be developed more extensively than the original objective and may be recorded in a telegraphic style or in brief notes. This procedure is clearly taking place in the backward jumps of the *Stromateis*. The phenomenon makes it almost possible for the spectator of today to look over the shoulder of an ancient author at work.

Another distinctive technique occurs when Clement addresses himself to his source. This implied dialogue makes it clear that Clement questions his model and uses it critically; he keeps his source at a certain distance. The implied dialogue may take the form of a conjunction or an adverb that turns the borrowed material into a hypothesis rather than an assertion. He may likewise frame it as an interrogative sentence. These additions, which are usually quite short, have a considerable effect on the content of the borrowing.[10] In this case as well, the transformations can be understood only if the Philonic substratum is at hand.

Another distinctive manner of composing could be called a process of accumulation. This process is characteristic of Clement's working method in general; it is found when citations from other authors as well as Philo are involved. It is often an associative way of working in which one word, as it were, evokes the other without being supported by a logical connection; various layers of imaginative thought are piled on each other. This occurs particularly in the construction of allegories. Schematically described, Clement usually has a biblical starting point; a first layer of allegories is introduced, in our case derived from Philo, and thereafter other interpretations follow that may either have been taken over from other sources or invented by Clement himself. He usually closes with a distinctly Christian allegory. The link between the images is often vague, frequently no more than a specific number, around which the allegories are grouped.

In general, then, Philo is used in a sketchy way by Clement, and in the sequences, while the degree of sketchiness may vary, the borrowings form a kind of framework or template on which Clement works. In spite of the free elaboration on his model many aspects of the process of borrowing retain an almost physical presence, as we watch the writer at his desk turning through his source manuscript. An analysis of his techniques of borrowing also provides a clue to the understanding of his motives in using Philo.

---

[10] see p. 110.

4. Parallel and diverging intentions

At the end of the second chapter it was asked whether it was possible to appraise the influence of Philo on Clement.[11] This question took shape as a choice between two alternatives; did Philo give direction to Clement's thought, or did Philonic borrowings merely form a flavorful filling for the capacious *Stromateis*? In the light of this study it now seems possible to provide an answer or perhaps answers. A positive response seems merited where the intentions of the two coincide, but, as could be seen from the sustained passages, Clement did not always work according to a uniform plan. Clement proved to have objectives similar to Philo's in some cases, but in others he used Philo's words for quite dissimilar purposes. Literal borrowing, which appears in both situations, does not always mean that the thoughts of both authors actually tend in the same direction.[12]

In the allegory of Hagar and Sarah, analyzed in chapter two, Clement directs himself to fellow Christians who reject Greek culture and philosophy. He uses Philo polemically to answer this rejection. He chooses Philo especially when the latter had linked an allegorical interpretation of a biblical passage to a philosophic scheme. These combinations have been frequent foci of Clement's attention in the isolated references as well, where numerous examples occur.[13] The intentions of Philo and Clement are kindred; Philo also had to defend the value and justify the attraction of Greek culture against the suspicions of his coreligionists.[14] Clement seems to have a sharper tone than Philo did in this defence; this sharpness seems evident in his image of the prostitute, which is not found in Philo. The differing tones reflect the difference between measured apology and combative polemics. Yet the situations are similar enough to make the relationship very substantial.

In the various borrowings from Philo's *De Virtutibus*, examined in chapter IV, a polemic intention is present as well. In these cases, followers of Marcion, who wanted to make a distinction between the law of Moses and faith in Christ, are the implied antagonists. Clement defends the belief in one God who is the same and indivisible from beginning to end. To demonstrate that the law of Moses is not contrary to faith, Clement allegorizes all its prescriptions that are offered to him by Philo's treatise. Curiously enough, Philo does not allegorize in *De Virtutibus*; for him, the various rules can stand as they are. In this case Cle-

---

[11] chapter II, p. 47.
[12] Osborn, *Beginnings*, p. 12, 279.
[13] See overview, p. 224.
[14] Alexandre, *Congr.* (FE 16), p. 79ff.

ment exploits Philo for entirely different purposes and for benefits that
Philo could not have suspected. Philo's general intention may have been
to make clear to the outside world that Jewish laws and usages were not
asocial or unfriendly towards others.[15] Clement cites the same laws and
prescriptions to convince his Christian opponents of the unity of law and
faith.

In addition to using him in polemics against anti-philosophic groups
and against followers of Marcion, Clement calls on Philo's help, as discussed in chapter three, to retell the life story of Moses. He thus engages
in a traditional type of Jewish biblical interpretation. Burton Mack, who
distinguishes several major types of interpretation in Philo,[16] calls this
type encomium, "...a kind of description of the patriarchs which retells
the biblical story in such a way as to minimize or overlook offensive traits
or deeds and idealize those which can illustrate certain virtues. Because
the old stories are changed in this way one may certainly see a kind of
interpretation achieved here. But this interpretation is accomplished
without setting up a contrast between the biblical text and the interpretation." To a degree Clement's approach here fits well into the tradition
of encomium; he retells the story with the words of Philo yet without
departing far from the biblical background. Clement leans on Philo in
both the narrative part, in which dependency is very close, and in its continuation, in which he makes use of him in a more schematic way. In this
latter section, Moses's functions as a prophet and lawgiver are taken
over, but his function as a high priest is, however, left out. Clement,
moreover, takes new steps in developing the functions of lawgiver and
prophet. Philo's purpose in writing the *De Vita Mosis* may have been to
give a first introduction of Jewish ideas to sympathetic pagans. Clement's
intentions are apologetic as well; they present a traditional argument that
maintains that Hebrew philosophy is older than any other wisdom and
that Plato is dependent on the Jewish law written in Greek. The one
apology is dependent on the other even in spite of the shifts in focus. By
taking over Philo's *Life of Moses* in abbreviated form Clement plays a considerable role in transmitting the Jewish-Hellenistic tradition to later
times.[17]

In chapter five above, in which the functions of the temple and the
vestments of the high priest were described, Philo provides, as in the

---

[15] *Virt.* 141.

[16] Mack, in *SPh* 3, p. 81ff.

[17] For Philo's intentions, see Arnaldez, Mondésert a. o., *VM* I (FE 22), p. 13; for the
continuous tradition, see Gregory of Nyssa, *The Life of Moses*, trans. A. J. Malherbe/E.
Ferguson, 1978, Introd. p. 6.

story of Moses, a formal guideline. Once again the Philonic material parallels the Bible so closely that Philo seems almost to have served as a cursory or alternative biblical reading for Clement. Along this Philonic-biblical line Clement projects his own further interpretations. There are elements drawn from many other sources in this passage as well, since the theme of the temple and the clothing of the high priest has a long tradition. As in previous Christian interpretations, the high priest is equivalent to Christ. In a novel way, Clement introduces the interpretative concept of the descent of Christ and the ascent of the Gnostic soul; the two movements are described as the nucleus of the history of salvation.

Some of the same patterns surface again in chapter six (VI 2; VI 3), where the theme of spiritual ascent was observed. In the background text here Philo also alludes to the ascent of the soul, as does Clement. The symbolism of numbers again plays a major role, as it had in the discussion of the temple. In both passages, however, the two writers diverge in their intentions in much the same way. The theocentric and cosmologic outlook of Philo is turned in a salvational and anthropological direction in Clement.

The concept of God was another occasion for Clement to consult Philo. As pointed out in chapter six (VI 1; VI 4), he borrows Philo's words to give a further elaboration of this concept. Burton Mack has distinguished the anti-anthropomorphic apology, to which he counts the Philonic passages, as a major type of interpretation.[18] "This kind of interpretation does not appear to have produced a systematic corpus of interpretation of the Pentateuch as a whole, but does occur regularly where anthropomorphic statements about God are encountered in the Pentateuch....Philo often uses these traditional topoi to argue for the necessity of allegorical interpretation of the Pentateuch, but this appears a later rationale." Philo has linked the anthropomorphic way of speaking about God in the Bible with the philosophical problem of the possibility (or rather impossibility) of knowing God. In this sense, he was Clement's predecessor, since it is along this same line that Clement has proceeded. In Clement, the anthropomorphic way of speaking does not appear to have been a focus of attention. From the passages dealt with in chapter six, his point seems to turn around how it is possible to obtain knowledge of God and how God's locality must be understood. The intentions of Philo and Clement are similar in an overall sense, but the emphasis is different; Clement, for example, changes the word *God* into *knowledge of God* on several occasions.

---

[18] Mack, in *SPh* 3, p. 81.

In this way Clement has taken over various themes, most of them apologetic, from Philo. Some were traditional, and they stay traditional in Clement's treatment. They are transposed from a Jewish to a Christian setting but remain closely related in their basic roles. Other ideas are used by Clement for his own purposes. In all cases, as will be discussed *infra*, shifts in content occur. Even in these highly Philonic passages, Clement reveals his own themes, as it were, between the lines. This infiltration was not limited to one single passage but was a pervasive technique throughout. These characteristic messages are the unity of the Old and the New Testament, the difference between believers and unbelievers and the intentional concealment of the truth.[19]

Throughout all the varying purposes for which Philo is used, one constant manifested itself clearly: namely, the focus on the biblical texts. This phenomenon is not, however, a question of Clement's intentions in adapting Philo but is related to his criteria for selecting material from him. The question of intentions approaches the problem of borrowing from a broader contextual setting, while the problem of selection emerges from a narrower focus on the transposed material itself.

5. Clement's criteria for selection

In both the sustained and the isolated passages, again and again biblical quotations form part of the material taken over from Philo. The presence of a biblical background, in fact, appears to be a key element in Clement's selection. The tabulation in the following section demonstrates the frequency with which this embedded biblical material is passed from the one writer to the other. As pointed out above in the analyses of the sustained passages, Clement sometimes leaps from one biblical text to the next in Philo so that his use of Philo amounts to a kind of doubled borrowing.[20] This practice gives Clement's loose organization an extra element of jumpiness. The biblical excerpt is frequently identical in both writers; that is, the quotation begins and ends with the same words, even when it is only fragmentary. Clement, moreover, was often the first Christian writer to introduce some of these texts and frequently the only one of his time to use them. In some cases this biblical material presents unusual elements whose purpose or meaning is not at all obvious; this obscurity makes dependence on Philo seem all the more probable; why else would he have chosen such a text than from the fact that Philo cites it? In the isolated references particularly, the uniqueness of the quotation was a decisive argument for dependence. In the more traditional biblical

---

[19] Den Boer, *Allegorese*, p. 69ff.
[20] See chapter II (2. 4), p. 32.

texts, identity of the excerpt and its combination with a specific theme could tip the balance in favor of a Philonic origin. Recurrent is the fact that Clement selects texts from the Old Testament incorporated in Philo that had already been taken over in the New Testament. The 'resonance' of these texts probably played a considerable role in Clement's selection.

The biblical material is not always given in the form of a quotation; sometimes it is only a paraphrased biblical story or a generic biblical reminiscence. This material fits into two patterns that correspond to two different functions. Clement may use Philo simply to retell the biblical story or parts of it (chapters three and five above); here the tenor of the passage hardly differs from that of the Bible itself. At other times, Philo has provided pre-selected combinations of texts that could be used in an argumentation or interpretation (chapters two, four and six above). In both cases, Philo is treated as if he had been a cursory reader; Clement goes through Philo as if relevant biblical texts had been underlined expressly for his benefit.

Clement's principles of selection from Philo have been assessed on the basis of passages that are rated with an A or B. A more accurate idea of the role of the Bible has been formed in relation to distinctive themes. A distinction has been made between passages in which the interpretation of Scripture is central and those in which philosophical-theological considerations are dominant.[21] The distinction is a formal one; in reality, of course, the texts give a more nuanced picture in which the two are not always easily distinguished. Yet this articulation reflects the two main streams from which Clement's selection is nourished.

In the following section where the results of this research are tabulated, the figures are revealing about the relative importance of the various principles involved in Clement's selections from Philo. The calculations are based on a total of 205 parallels. The passages that are rated with an A or a B are 125. In 35 of these cases the Bible is interpreted allegorically. Another 26 cases involve biblical interpretation but do not make use of the allegorical method. Counting these two categories together, Clement employs Philo for biblical interpretation on a total of 61 occasions; this corresponds to nearly half of all borrowings (49%).

The allegorical methods used by Clement are described in the individual chapters and were referred to briefly in the section on his technique of borrowing.[22] A biblical element to which little attention has been given in this study is formed by formulaic interpretations of names; these are usually termed etymologies. The interpretation of names was

---

[21] See schematic survey p. 223f.
[22] See p. 214ff.

very common in antiquity, not only in Jewish and Christian circles but
also in the Greek world. Clement has taken over various of these traditional etymologies of classical origin,[23] and it is not surprising that Philo
was an eagerly-used source in the interpretation of Hebrew names.
These Hebrew etymologies, however, present a very mixed bag, and
tracing their origins is by no means simple or certain. For good reasons
it has been supposed that various traditions had already come together
in Philo. This becomes clear through the fact that some of the
etymologies suppose a good knowledge of Hebrew while others, on the
contrary, reveal a weak and faulty command of the language. Another
group seems to have been invented by Philo, while others are due to Clement himself.[24] Most of the etymologies in our comparisons occur not in
isolated passages but in extended, securely Philonic contexts. At times
the parentage is revealed by a change from a full and vivid statement in
Philo to a truncated and stereotyped rendition in Clement. Etymologies
can also be enlarged; Clement may supply further alternatives, which are
of uncertain parentage.[25] These etymologies, in any case, make up a
substantial presence within the biblical stream.

The second main stream is formed by borrowings that focus on
philosophical or theological concepts. They amount to 59 of the 125
instances. No distinction is made between theology and philosophy
because Clement does not make such a distinction himself. The largest
percentage (21 cases) turns around ways of speaking about God; twelve
of these cases are linked with the biblical background while in nine the
concept of God occurs in isolated form. After the concept of God, Clement's attention is drawn (in descending order of frequency) to ideas
about knowledge and wisdom and then to Platonizing interpretations of
Scripture, in which the Bible functions as illustration of the philosophical
concept; thus for example, the two-part division of the soul is compared
to the two tables of the law of Moses. Slightly less frequent are borrowings that describe ascent and contemplation or homoiosis and following
God. Even in the philosophical stream, 31 of the total of 59 cases are
linked in one way or another to a biblical background: that is, in half of
the occurrences. Thus Philo has also been Clement's teacher in the
application of philosophical thoughts to biblical material as he had been
in the realm of more strict biblical interpretation. A few borrowings
involve the virtues and various other themes, as can be seen in the following tabulation. A final component is formed by philosophical
classifications.

---

[23] Treu, Etymologie, p. 192ff.
[24] A. Hanson, Philo's etymologies, in *JThS* XVIII (1967) p. 128-139.
[25] *Str.* I 31,6.

In conclusion, it seems fair to say that the interpretation of Scripture has been Clement's most important focus of attention in the writings of Philo. Next in importance are a number of philosophical and theological concepts, of which the concept of God was the most strongly represented. In this last category as well, half of the cases have biblical connections. The total of borrowings involving biblical quotations or biblical reminiscences, in fact, proves to be three-quarters of the total, and the importance of a biblical background for Clement's selection could hardly be more strikingly evident.

6. Schematic survey

6.1.   Total number of units   205   (listed in chapter VII)

Sequences	86		
A	69		
B	10	A + B	= 92%
C	7	C	= 8%
Isolated references	119		
A	7		
B	39	A + B	= 39%
C	32		
D	41	C + D	= 61%
?	6		
Totals	205		
A	76		
B	49	A + B	= 61%
C	39		
D	41	C + D	= 39%

6.2.1. General division of themes

(* means: in combination with biblical material)

Sequences	A + B = 79		Total
philos./theol. conceptions		14	
	*	13	27
biblical interpretations	*	52	52
Isolated references	A + B = 46		
philos./theol. conceptions		14	
	*	18	32
biblical interpretations	*	9	9
rest		5	5

6.2.2. Subdivision of themes

Sequences	A + B = 79		Total
philos./theol. conceptions		27	
God		8	
	*	7	15

knowledge/wisdom		2	
	*	1	3
ascent/contemplation		2	2
images	*	2	2
categories		1	
	*	1	2
virtues		1	
	*	2	3

Isolated references	A + B =	46	Total
philos./theol. conceptions		32	
God		1	
	*	5	6
knowledge/wisdom		6	6
ascent/contemplation		1	
	*	1	2
homoiosis/following		3	3
elucidations		2	
	*	3	5
images		1	
	*	3	5
categories		1	1
virtues		2	
	*	3	5

6.3.   Division of themes in totals and percentages

Sequences and isolated references		A + B	= 125	Total	
philos./theol. conceptions	28		= 22%		
	* 31		= 25%	59	= 47%
of which: God	9		= 7%		
	* 12		= 10%		
biblical interpretations				61	= 49%
of which: allegorical	* 35		= 28%		
non-allegorical	* 26		= 21%		
rest	5		= 4%	5 =	4%
Total use of the Bible	*			92 =	74%

7. Themes and shifts in meaning

In examining the individual passages, both additions to and alterations of the borrowed Philonic material were identified. Setting aside subjects that turn up only once, regular patterns emerge in the way Clement reshapes Philonic themes. The principal common topics are the concept of God, the creation of the cosmos, the position of the law, the virtues and wisdom.

7.1 God and creation

In the narrative parts, as in the story of Moses and that of the Midianite women,[26] God appears to be much more active in Philo's treatment than in Clement's. God has a combative role; he intervenes to save the unity of the people; he has national features and acts in agreement with providence and according to a clear plan. In the non-narrative parts, in which the philosophical tone is accentuated, Philo and Clement are much closer to each other. They present a concept of God that has similar features although there still are some shifts of emphasis. In Philo, for example, the liturgical element is stressed; his God has to be honored and served. Philo also struggles more overtly with the language of the Bible in places where God is spoken about in anthropomorphic terms.[27] The difficulty or impossibility of transposing this biblical language into philosophical terminology is addressed squarely.

In comparable passages in Clement, a more abstract approach emerges. Repeatedly the Philonic concept of God was turned into the idea of the knowledge of God. In dealing with the problem of anthropomorphisms, Clement takes over a few aspects of Philo's treatment without giving them real coherence. Honor and service to God are played down by Clement in favor of rational knowledge. From his Jewish predecessor, however, he learns that this knowledge has to be considered a gift. The powers with which God manifests himself to mankind are consistently translated by Clement into the singular, thereby converting them into a single power. It is striking that the concept of logos hardly plays any role in the passages in which Clement leans on Philo. On one of the few occasions in which the logos is discussed, its appearance is self-evident; the logeion as part of the clothing of the priest is allegorically interpreted as logos. Repeatedly, Clement gives all these themes a Christological dimension. He adapts the logeion in this way, and the alteration of δυνάμεις into the singular δύναμις is likewise determined by a Christological intention; in creation, the Philonic powers actively maintaining contact between God and the created world are reduced to a singular power, which Clement centers on Christ.

Philo has a wide range of alternatives for the name of God: God, Lord, Monad, The One, The Really Existent, That Which Is, He Who Is, The First Cause.[28] Clement tends simply to adopt θεός. In one instance θεός is replaced by κύριος; the latter might reflect either the title of Christ or

---

[26] See p. 79ff.

[27] See note 18 above.

[28] Sandmel, *Philo* p. 91ff.; Dillon, *Middle Platonists*, p. 155; N. A. Dahl and A. F. Segal, Philo and the Rabbis on the Names of God, in *JSJ* 9 (1978), p. 120.

that of God in the Septuagint. Calling God ἀπαθής represents a shift away from Philo and may be connected with a later development in Middle Platonic thinking, a development that took place under the influence of the Stoa.[29]

Another intentional shift occurs when Clement replaces the word φύσις with θεός. The ideas behind this change are decidedly complex, and it is necessary to review the background briefly. In Philo, God and φύσις are very closely related and are treated as equivalents. This equivalence is connected with Philo's idea that the creation of the cosmos is the first and fundamental revelation of God. The order and organization of the cosmos reflects the divine order, which is by implication the order of the divine logos. Not only does the cosmos reflect the logos but, as noetic reality, the cosmos also *is* the divine logos in its creative power.[30] By contemplating the cosmic order the soul can advance as far as possible toward the contemplation of God. The cosmos and the human soul thereby lie in each other's extension; the human soul is a microcosm that is built up according to the same principles as the macrocosm. Philo's most evident contribution to this line of thought is that the creator, who is at the same time lawgiver, has conceived the law in harmony with the order of creation. Like the logos, the law is not only supposed to be an immanent factor in God's conception[31] but an active principle in creation. Philo has attempted in this way to bring the Jewish law, as source of philosophical activity, into relation with philosophical conceptions; in other words, to link the story of creation in Genesis with Greek philosophy.

Clement alters Philo's words in ways that give them a new perspective. While Philo can use φύσις as equivalent for God, Clement obviously tries to avoid this equation. The reason that Clement replaces the word φύσις is, however, not entirely because of a rejection of Philo's doctrine per se. In *Str.* II 10,2; 115,1-2; IV 89,4 and *Exc.* 54-57,[32] he denies that salvation comes from nature. Clement polemicizes openly against followers of Valentinus and Basilides and attacks their ideas, or at least his vision of their ideas, in which pneumatici will find natural salvation. This polemical attitude of Clement may well be the explanation why Clement avoids φύσις here as a tainted word and replaces it with θεός. Apart from the verbal substitution, there is a notable conceptual change as well. This stems from their changing interpretations of the history of creation.

---

[29] See chapter I (Lilla) p. 17; chapter IV (2. 2) p. 74ff.

[30] J. C. M. van Winden, The world of ideas in Philo of Alexandria, an interpretation of *De Opificio Mundi* 24-25, in *VigChr* 37 (1983), p. 211.

[31] Van Winden, see previous note, p. 209.

[32] Cf. Irenaeus, *Adv. Haer.* I 6; II 29,2.

As for Philo, the revelation for Clement lies in creation and in the word of God, but it also lies in the Son. Clement's Christological focus intervenes repeatedly to create major structural differences from Philo's system. In chapter V above, Philo's cosmological intentions were transformed by Clement in a similar way; because of the role of Christ, the history of creation is converted into a history of salvation. Such transformations evidently have consequences for the concept of God itself.

The central position that God has in Philo, shifts in Clement in favor of Christ, who takes over the salvational and personal aspect of divine operation; he is called image of God and is presented as the object of the highest contemplation. This shift may be the reason why Clement's concept of God takes on a rather abstract and impersonal tone; this flavor is further accentuated by adding his theme of concealment of truth. An intentional obscurity around the concept of God is created by this highly individual interest of Clement. His Philonic passages, however, include only a fraction of all the passages in which he speaks about God. They represent, so to speak, only some of the frames, whose images can be corrected or completed by the rest of the film. It is not enough to suppose, as some have done,[33] that Clement merely consolidates and renames the Philonic concept of the powers of God, the δυνάμεις, the λόγοι or the λόγος, by superposing a Christological meaning; the centre of gravity within the concept of God itself seems to have shifted.

7.2 Law, virtues and knowledge

Philo links the Greek idea that right understanding leads to right behaviour with the Jewish premise that the standards for right behaviour are given in the Pentateuch. The law of Moses consists of prescriptions and rules in which all the virtues are incorporated. Unlike so much biblical material dealt with by Philo, these prescriptions are not to be allegorized, a fact that is related to the law's central position. The divinity of the law is posited; as has been pointed out above, it is given in accordance with the unwritten law of nature. By knowing and following the law one can achieve knowledge of God as far as is possible in human terms.

Clement, who's thoughts are comparable schematically, has built up his scheme from different components. Differently from Philo, the law is not the basis of his thinking but has a subordinate role. It forms a preparation for knowledge and wisdom in the same way that philosophy

---

[33] For example Wolfson, *Philosophy*, p. 177ff.; 204ff.

does. Clement accepts the law and defends it against people who want
to get rid of the law in a kind of exaggerated Paulinism. More than once
Clement emphasizes the idea that the law educates to Christ without,
however, rejecting the law. In the shift from νόμος to λόγος, which has
been dealt with in chapter IV above, the educating role of the law is discussed. The law leads to Christ, but simultanuously is given and
accomplished by Christ. Following the example of Philo, Moses is put on
the stage by Clement as lawgiver, shepherd and prophet but is rather
quickly replaced in these roles by Christ. The function of the high priest,
to which Philo dedicates a large section of his book on Moses, is completely left aside by Clement, since this role has such clearly
Christological implications in the Christian realm.

There is no trace of a negative attitude toward the law in Clement. He
defends the position of the law against the attacks of the followers of Marcion. He does not, moreover, echo the negative valuations that are well
known from other Christian writers, nor does he interpret the law
exclusively as a prefiguration of Christ.[34] Yet Clement has to face difficulties in dealing with the law similar to those other Christian writers
before him had. How is it possible to incorporate and interpret the diversity of Jewish rules and prescriptions in the books of Moses: prescriptions
like the prohibition against eating pork, against a man's wearing
women's clothes or against muzzling an ox while it is treading out the
corn. Unlike Philo, Clement's solution in dealing with these prescriptions is to allegorize them.

From the material under discussion, it is difficult to define what
substitute Clement offers for the virtues that for Philo are based in the
law. Filling a void left by a fulfilled law is a problem of which an
awarenes, in a general sense at least, already emerges in the theology of
St. Paul, when he declares freedom from the law as a matter of principle
and substitutes for it the general precept of loving each other. The question is for Clement, as it had been in earlier days, where to find the standards for normal everyday life? As it appears from the *Paedagogue*, the
Stoa was of considerable influence in assessing standards and values,
particularly in a negative sense. Marrou has pointed out that ethics in
Clement are transfigured by adding a Christian perspective. On the one
hand, the range of virtues that derive from the Greek world can be
extended infinitely; when the Christian transposition takes place, on the
other hand, Clement's ethics are limited to the idea of following Christ,
the incarnate Word, as enjoined in the Gospels.

---

[34] For example in Tertullian, who has a rather rigoristic and anti-Jewish approach,
with perhaps the exception of *Adv. Marcionem*, the law is interpreted almost exclusively
as a prefiguration of Christ.

In Clement the concept of virtue is strongly assimilated to his concept of wisdom. Marrou has termed this rational ethics.[35] In the Philonic borrowings, Clement repeatedly replaces virtue with knowledge, while in Philo the two had equal value. The outlines of the process by which either the rational soul or the Gnostic reach the highest knowledge are basically similar in Philo and in Clement. In this process, however, the position of the law is shifted; for Philo, it represents the point of departure and forms the basis for the concepts of virtue and of God. For Clement, the basis is Christ and following or imitating Christ, and the final objective of knowledge is also conceived in a Christological sense, while the law has a preparatory function. When Clement draws the line of ascent to the ultimate goal, he projects it, in the cognitive realm, toward the knowledge of God and, in the realm of virtuous action, toward the ultimate form of following Christ: martyrdom. Martyrdom represents an element in Clement's theology whose importance can hardly be overestimated; in the passages that he takes over from Philo, however, it does not play a significant role.[36]

8. Final remarks

All the variations and alterations that have been touched on above in the concept of God, in creation, in the position of the law, in knowledge and virtues have in common an important component of Christology. In their schematic outline, the tracks along which knowledge and wisdom can be achieved seem comparable. In both writers the subdivision of the human soul is described in similar terms. These are, however, almost peripheral matters when the final goal, an even more fundamental issue, appears to be conceived so differently. In a certain sense, Clement did not need Philo for drawing these general pathways; he was aware of other philosophical traditions in which these mechanisms could have been found. Philo, however, was his master in the use and interpretation of the Pentateuch, skills that other traditions did not provide. In addition, Philo's vision that made it possible to link philosophical concepts with the biblical message was of great influence; this vision itself must be considered as ''a step of monumental significance in the history of thought, a step with greater consequences for the development of philosophy and religion than its author could possibly have foreseen.''[37] On this track Philo found a follower in Clement; the latter hungrily swallowed Philo's

---

[35] Marrou, *Paed.* I (SChr. 70), p. 60.
[36] Particularly in *Str.* IV; the only occasion on which it occurs in this context, see p. 76f.
[37] Runia, *Philo*, p. 544.

words and eagerly absorbed his thoughts; he used Philo's inventions and misused them to provide his own. Many of the twisting threads of Clement's theological thinking are taken from Philo but they are woven into a very different tapestry.

BIBLIOGRAPHY

1) The works of Clement

Comprehensive editions and indices

Sylburg F. *Clementis Alexandrini Opera Graece et Latine*, ed.D.Heinsius, Coloniae, 1688
Potter J. *Clementis Alexandrini Opera quae Extant*, 2 vols with latin translation, Oxonii, 1715; reprinted by Migne PG 8 and 9, Parisii, 1857, 2nd ed. 1890-1891
Stählin O. *Clemens Alexandrinus erster Band; Protrepticus und Paedagogus* (GCS 12), Leipzig, 1905, 3d ed.U.Treu, Berlin, 1972
Stählin O. *Clemens Alexandrinus zweiter Band; Stromata Buch I-VI* (GCS 15), Leipzig, 1906, 4th ed. U.Treu, Berlin, 1985
Stählin O. *Clemens Alexandrinus dritter Band; Stromata Buch VII und VIII; Excerpta ex Theodoto; Eclogae Propheticae; Quis dives salvetur; Fragmente* (GCS 17), Leipzig, 1909, 2nd ed.L.Früchtel and U.Treu, Berlin, 1970
Stählin O. *Clemens Alexandrinus vierter Band; Register* (GCS 39), Leipzig, 1936, partial 2nd.ed. U.Treu, Berlin, 1980
Biblia Patristica; index des citations et allusions bibliques dans la littérature patristique, I, Paris, 1975

Individual editions, translations and commentaries

Wilson W. *Clement of Alexandria* (ANCL 4, 12, 22, 24), London, 1867-1872; repr. (ANFa 2), New-York, 1887
Hort F.J.A. and Mayor J.B. *Clement of Alexandria, Miscellanies Book VII. The Greek text with Introduction, Translation, Notes, Dissertations and Indices*, London, 1902
Butterworth G.B. *Clement of Alexandria, Exhortation to Greeks, The rich man's salvation, To the newly baptized* (Loeb Classical Library 92), London, 1919
Bardy G. *Clément d'Alexandrie*, (Les moralistes chrétiens), 2nd ed., Paris, 1926
Stählin O. *Clemens von Alexandreia, Ausgewählte Schriften* (BKV, zweite Reihe, vols 7, 8, 17, 18, 19, 20), München, 1934-1938
Casey R.P. *The Excerpta ex Theodoto of Clement of Alexandria* (StD 1), London, 1934
Overbeck F., *Titus Flavius Klemens von Alexandreia. Die Teppiche*, ed.C.A.Bernoulli and L.Früchtel, Basel, 1936
Cataudella Q. *Protreptico ai Greci*, Torino, 1940
Sagnard F. *Extraits de Théodote* (SChr 23), Paris, 1948
Mondésert C. and Plassart A. *Le Protreptique* (SChr 2), 2nd ed., Paris, 1949
Mondésert C. and Caster P. *Les Stromates. Stromate I* (SChr 30), Paris, 1951
Mondésert C. and Camelot P. *Les Stromates. Stromate II* (SChr 38), Paris, 1954
Oulton J.E.L. and Chadwick H. *Alexandrian Christianity; selected translations of Clement and Origen with Introduction and Notes*, (LCC II), London, 1954
Marrou H.I. and Harl M. *Le Pédagogue I* (SChr 70), Paris, 1960
Mondésert C. and Marrou H.I. *Le Pédagogue II* (SChr 108), Paris, 1965
Mondésert C., Matray C. and Marrou H.I. *Le Pédagogue III* (SChr 158), Paris, 1970
Boulluec A. Le and Voulet P. *Les Stromates. Stromate V* (SChr 278/279), Paris, 1981
Nardi C. *Clemente Alessandrino, Estratti profetici-Eclogae propheticae* (BiblPatristica IV), Firenze, 1985
Pini G. *Stromati. Note di vera filosofia* (Lett.crist. delle origin. Testi XX), Roma, 1985

2) The works of Philo

Only the main editions of Philo's works are mentioned. For the individual editions, translations and commentaries, see Runia, *Philo*, p. 461ff.

Comprehensive editions, translations and indices

Mangey T. *Philonis Judaei opera quae reperiri potuerunt omnia*, 2 vols with latin translation, Londinii, 1742
Cohn L. and Wendland P. *Philonis Alexandrini opera quae supersunt*, 6 vols, Berolini, 1896-1915
Leisegang J. *Indices ad Philonis Alexandrini opera* (Cohn-Wendland vol.7), Berolini, 1926-1930
Cohn L., Heinemann I., Adler I. and Theiler W. *Philo von Alexandreia; die Werke in deutscher Übersetzung*, 7 vols, Breslau/Berlin, 1909-1964
Mayer G. *Index Philoneus*, Berlin, 1974
Colson F.H. and Whitaker G.H. *Philo* (Loeb Classical Library), 10 vols, London, 1929-1962
Earp J.W. *Philo* (Loeb Classical Library Indices to vols I-X, vol.X, p.189-520), London, 1962
Arnaldez R., Pouilloux J., Mondésert C. *Les Oeuvres de Philon d'Alexandrie*, 35 vols, Paris, 1961-
Biblia Patristica. Supplément Philon d'Alexandrie, Paris, 1982

The Armenian texts

Aucher J.B. *Philonis Paralipomena Armena*, Venetiis, 1826
Marcus R. *Philo* (Supplement Loeb Classical Library), 2 vols, London, 1953-1962
Mercier C. *Quaestiones et solutiones in Genesim I-VI* (Les oeuvres de Philon d'Alexandrie vol.34A-B), Paris, 1979-1984
Terian A. *Philonis Alexandrini De animalibus*, Chico California, 1981

3) General bibliography

Aland B., Marcion, Versuch einer neuen Interpretation, in *ZThK* 70 (1973), p. 420-447
Alexandre M., La culture profane chez Philon, in *PAL*, Paris, 1967, p. 105-129
Andresen C., Justin und der mittlere Platonismus, in *ZNtW* 44 (1952/53), p. 157-195
——, *Logos und Nomos; die Polemik des Kelsos wider das Christentum* (AKG 30), Berlin, 1955
Amir Y., *Die hellenistische Gestalt des Judentums bei Philon von Alexandrien*, Neukirchen, 1983
Apostolou G., *Die Dialektik bei Klemens von Alexandria* (EHS 20), Frankfurt a/M., 1980
Arndt O., Zahlenmystik bei Philo; Spielerei oder Schriftauslegung, in *ZRGG* 19 (1967), p. 167-171
Arnim H. von, *Stoicorum Veterum Fragmenta*, 4 vols, Leipzig, 1903-1924, repr. Stuttgart, 1964
Arnou R., Platonisme des Pères, in *DThC* XII (1933), c. 2258-2392
Auf der Mauer H. J. and Waldram J., Illuminatio Verbi Divini-Confessio Fidei-Gratia Baptismi, in *Fides Sacramenti, Sacramentum Fidei* (in hon. P. Smulders), Assen, 1981, p. 41-95

Baer R. A., *Philo's use of the categories male and female* (ALGHJ 9), Leiden, 1970
Balthasar H. U. von, Le mysterion d'Origène, in *RSR* 26 (1936), p. 513-526; 27 (1937), p. 38-64
——, *Geist und Feuer*, Salzburg, 1938
Bardy G., *Clément d'Alexandrie* (Les moralistes chrétiens), Paris, 1926
——, Melchisédech dans la tradition patristique, in *RB* 35 (1926), p. 496-509; 36 (1927), p. 24-45
——, *Littérature grecque chrétienne*, Paris, 1928
——, L'église et l'enseignement pendant les trois premiers siècles, in *RevSR* XII (1932), p. 1-28

——, *La spiritualité de Clément d'Alexandrie* (VS Suppl. 39), p. 81-104; 129-145

——, *La vie spirituelle d'après les Pères des trois premiers siècles*, rev. ed. Tournai 1968, Paris, 1935

——, Aux origines de l'école d'Alexandrie, in *RSR* 27 (1937), p. 65-90

——, Pour l'histoire de l'école d'Alexandrie, in *Vivre et Penser*, 1942, p. 80-109

——, art. Apatheia, in *DSp* I, c. 727-246, Paris, 1937

——, *La conversion au Christianisme durant les premiers siècles*, Paris, 1949

Bartelink G. J. M., Einige Bemerkungen über die Meidung heidnischer oder christlicher Termini in dem frühchristlichen Sprachgebrauch, in *VigChr* 19 (1965), p. 194-209

——, *Het vroege christendom en de antieke cultuur*, Muiderberg, 1986

Bauckham R., The fall of the angels as the source of philosophy in Hermias and Clement of Alexandria, in *VigChr* 39 (1985), p. 313-330

Bauer W., *Wörterbuch zu den Schriften des Neuen Testaments*, 5th ed., Berlin/New York, 1971

Berchmann, *From Philo to Origen; Middle Platonism in transition*, Chico Calif., 1985

Bernard J., *Die apologetische Methode bei Klemens von Alexandrien; Apologetik als Entfaltung der Theologie*, Leipzig, 1968

Bianchi U., (ed.) *La Tradizione dell'Enkrateia; motivazioni ontologiche e protologiche* (Atti del Congresso Internazionale, 20-23 aprile 1982), Roma, 1982

Bickerman E., The Septuagint as translation, in *Studies in Jewish and Christian history* 1 (Leiden 1976), p. 167-200

Bigg Ch., *The Christian Platonists of Alexandria*, Oxford, 1886, repr. Hildesheim/New York, 1981

Bitter R. A., *Vreemdelingschap bij Philo van Alexandrië; een onderzoek naar de betekenis van* πάροικος, Utrecht, 1982

Blair H. A., A method of exposition in the *Stromateis* of Clement of Alexandria, in *Studia Biblica* I (1978), p. 41-47

——, Allegory, Typologie and Archetype in, *StPatr* 17/1 (1982), p. 263-267

——, *The kaleidoscope of truth; types and archetypes in Clement of Alexandria*, Worthing, 1986

Blaß F. W., Debrunner A., Rehkopf F., *Grammatik des neutestamentlichen Griechisch*, 14th ed., Göttingen, 1976

Böhlig A., Zum Proverbientext des Clemens Alexandrinus, in *ByF* 3 (1968), p. 73-79

Boer W. den, *De allegorese in het werk van Clemens Alexandrinus*, Leiden, 1940

——, Hermeneutic problems in Early Christian literature, in *VigChr* 1 (1947), p. 150-167

——, Allegory and History, in *Romanitas et Christianitas* (in hon. J. H. Waszink), Leiden, 1973, p. 15-28

Børresen K. E., L'usage patristique de métaphores féminins dans le discours sur Dieu, in *RThL* 13 (1982), p. 205-220

Borgen P., *Bread from heaven; an exegetical study of the concept of manna in the Gospel of John and the writings of Philo*, Leiden, 1965

——, Philo of Alexandria, in *Jewish Writings of the Second Temple Period* (ed. M. Stone), Assen, 1984, p. 233-282

Botte B., La vie de Moïse par Philon, in *Cahiers Sioniens* 8 (1954), p. 173-180

Boulluec A. Le, Exégèse et polémique antignostique chez Irénée et Clément d'Alexandrie; l'exemple du centon, in *StPatr* 17/2 (1982), p. 707-712

——, *La notion d'hérésie dans la littérature grecque IIe-IIIe siècles* (EtAug), t. I De Justin à Irénée, t. II Clément d'Alexandrie et Origène, Paris, 1985

Bousset W., *Jüdisch-Christlicher Schulbetrieb in Alexandria und Rom; literarische Untersuchungen zu Philo und Clemens von Alexandria, Justin und Irenäus*, Göttingen, 1915

Boyancé P., Études philoniennes, in *REG* 76 (1963), p. 64-109

Bradley D. J. M., The transformation of Stoic ethic in Clement of Alexandria, in *Aug* XIV (1974), p. 41-66

Brambillasca G., Citations de l'écriture sainte et des auteurs classiques dans le *Protreptikos* de Clément, in *StPatr* XI (1972), p. 8-12

Braun H., Der Hebräerbrief (Handb. zum NT 14), Tübingen, 1984

Bréhier E., *Les idées philosophiques et religieuses de Philon d'Alexandrie*, Paris, 1908

——, *Chrysippe et l'ancien stoïcisme*, Paris, 1910, reed. Paris/London, 1971

Broek R. van den, Niet-gnostisch christendom voor Clemens en Origenes, in *NedThT* 33 (1979), p. 287-299

——, The Authentikos Logos; a new document of Christian Platonism, in *VigChr.* 33 (1979), p. 260-286

Brontesi A., *La soteria in Clemente Alessandrino*, Roma, 1972

Broudéhoux J. P., *Mariage et famille chez Clément d'Alexandrie*, Paris, 1970

Butterworth G. W., Clement of Alexandria and art, in *JThS* 17 (1915/16), p. 68-76

Cadiou R., *Introduction au système d'Origène*, Paris, 1932

——, *La jeunesse d'Origène*, Paris, 1935

Camelot P. Th., Les idées de Clément d'Alexandrie sur l'utilisation des sciences et de la littérature profane, in *RSR* 21 (1931), p. 38-66

——, Clément d'Alexandrie et l'utilisation de la philosophie grecque, in *RSR* 21 (1931), p. 541-569

——, *Foi et Gnose; introduction à l'étude de la connaissance mystique chez Clément d'Alexandrie* (ETHS 3), Paris, 1945

——, Clément d'Alexandrie et l'Ecriture, in *RB* 53 (1946), p. 242-248

Campenhausen H. Frhr. von, *Kirchliches Ambt und geistliche Vollmacht in den ersten drei Jahrhunderten* (BHTh 14), Tübingen, 1953

——, *Die griechische Kirchenväter*, Stuttgart, 1955

——, *Die Entstehung der christlichen Bibel*, Tübingen, 1968

Casey R. P., Clement of Alexandria and the beginnings of Christian Platonism, in *HThR* 18 (1925), p. 39-101

——, Clement and the two divine logoi, in *JThS* 25 (1924), p. 43-56

Castincaud F., *Les citations d'auteurs grecs profanes dans le Pédagogue de Clément d'Alexandrie* (mémoire pour la maîtrise, Poitiers), 1976

Cataudella Q., Citazioni bacchilide in Clemente Alessandrino, in *Forma Futuri* (In onore di M. Pellegrino), Torino, 1975, p. 119-125

Cazeau J., Philon d'Alexandrie, exégète, in *ANRW* II 21.1 (1984), p. 156-226

Chadwick H., *Alexandrian Christianity* (The Library of Christian Classics 2), Philadelphia, 1954, (Clement of Alexandria p. 15-165)

——, St. Paul and Philo of Alexandria, in *Bull. of the John Rylands Library* 48 (1966), p. 286-307

——, *Early Christian Thought and the Classical Tradition; studies in Justin, Clement and Origen*, Oxford, 1966

——, Philo and the beginnings of Christian Thought, in *The Cambridge History of later Greek and early Medieval philosophy* (ed. A. H. Armstrong), Cambridge, 1967, p. 137-192

——, *The Early Church* (*The Pelican History of the Church 1*), London, 1967

——, art. Florilegia, in *RAC* 7 (1969), c. 1131-1160

Chantraine P., *Dictionnaire étymologique de la langue grecque*, Paris, 1968-1977

Charles R.H. (ed.), *The Apocrypha and Pseudepigrapha of the Old Testament in English*, 2 vols, Oxford, 1913

Christ W., Philologische Studien zu Clemens Alexandrinus, in *ABAW*. PPK 21, Abt III, München, 1901, p. 457-526

Christiansen I., *Die Technik der allegorischen Auslegungswissenschaft bei Philo von Alexandrien*, Tübingen, 1969

Clark E. A., *Clement's use of Aristotle; the Aristotelian contribution to Clement of Alexandria's refutation of Gnosticism*, New York, 1977

Clark F. L., Citations of Plato in Clement of Alexandria, in *TPAPA* 33 (1902), p. 12-20

Classen C. J., Der platonisch-stoische Kanon der Kardinaltugenden bei Philo, Clemens Alexandrinus und Origenes, in *Kerugma und Logos* (Festschr. C. Andresen), Göttingen, 1979, p. 68-88

Cohn L., Zur indirekten Überlieferung Philos und die älteren Kirchenväter, in *JPTh* 18 (1892), p. 475-492

Collomp P., Une source de Clément d'Alexandrie et des homélies pseudo-Clémentines, in *Revue de Philologie* 37 (1913), p. 19-46

Colpe C., Von der Logoslehre des Philon zu der des Clemens von Alexandrien, in *Kerugma und Logos* (Festschr. C. Andresen), Göttingen, 1979, p. 89-107

Colson F. H., Philo on education, in *JThS* 18 (1917), p. 151-162

Copelloti L., L'influsso di Filone su Clemente nell'esegesi biblica (diss.), Torino, 1956

Courcelle P., *Connais-toi toi-même de Socrate à Saint Bernard*, 3 vols, Paris, 1974-1975

Cross F. L., *The early Christian Fathers*, London, 1960

Crouzel H., Les sources bibliques et l'enkrateia chrétienne, in *La tradizione dell'enkrateia* (ed. U. Bianchi), Roma, 1985, p. 505-526

Dahl N. A. and Segal A. F., Philo and the Rabbis on the names of God, in *JSJ* 9 (1978), p. 1-28

Dalbert P., *Die Theologie der hellenistisch-jüdischen Missionsliteratur unter Ausschluss von Philo und Josephus*, Hamburg, 1954

Daniélou J., La typologie d'Isaac dans le christianisme primitif, in *Bib* 28 (1947), p. 363-393

——, *Sacramentum Futuri* (ETH), Paris, 1950

——, *Bible et Liturgie*, 2nd ed., Paris, 1951

——, *Les anges et leur mission, d'après les Pères de l'Église*, Dinant, 1953

——, *Théologie du judéo-christianisme* (Histoire des doctrine chrétiennes avant Nicée I), Tournai, 1958

——, *Philon d'Alexandrie*, Paris, 1958

——, Les douze Apôtres et le Zodiaque, in *VigChr* 13 (1959), p. 14-21

——, *Message Évangélique et culture hellénistique aux IIe et IIIe siècles* (Histoire des doctrines chrétiennes avant Nicée II), Tournai, 1961

——, Typologie et allégorie chez Clément d'Alexandrie, in *StPatr* 4 (1961), p. 50-57

——, La tradition selon Clément d'Alexandrie, in *Conferenze patristiche II serie: Studia Ephemeridis 'Augustinianum' 10*, Roma, 1972, p. 5-18

Deiber A., *Clément d'Alexandrie et l'Égypte* (*Mémoires de l'institut français du Caire, X*), Cairo, 1904

Dekkers E., *Tertullianus en de geschiedenis van de liturgie*, Brussel, 1947

Delatte A., *Études sur la littérature pythagoricienne* (BEHE. H 217), Paris, 1915

Diels H., *Doxographi Graeci*, Berlin, 1879, 1965⁴

Dillon J. and Terian A., Philo and the doctrine of εὐπάθειαι, in *SPh* 4 (1976-1977), p. 17-24

——, *The Middle Platonists; a study of Platonism 80 B.C. to A.D. 220*, London, 1977

——, Eudorus und die Anfänge des Mittelplatonismus, in *Der Mittelplatonismus* (ed. Cl. Zintzen), Darmstadt, 1981, p. 3-32

Dölger F. J., Σφραγίς, Paderborn, 1911

——, Die Symbolik der Achtzahl in der sonstigen Literatur des christlichen Altertums, in *AuC* 4 (1934), p. 165-182

——, Zur Symbolik des altchristlichen Taufhauses, in *AnCl* 4 (1934), p. 153-187

Dörrie H., Die Stellung Plutarchs im Platonismus seiner Zeit, in *Philomathes* (in hon. P. Merlan), 's-Gravenhage, 1971, p. 36-56

——, Zur Methodik antiker Exegese, in *ZNtW* 65 (1974), p. 121-138

——, *Platonica Minora*, München, 1976

Drummond J., *Philo Judaeus or the Jewish-Alexandrian philosophy in its development and completion*, 2 vols, London, 1888

Ebenharter A., Die Ecclesiastikuszitate bei Klemens von Alexandrien, in *ThQ* 93 (1911), p. 1-22

Echle H. A., *The terminology of the sacrament of regeneration according to Clement of Alexandria* (diss.), Washington, 1949

Egan J., Logos and emanation in the writings of Clement of Alexandria, in *Trinification of the world* (in hon. E. Crowe), 1978, p. 176-209

Eizenhöfer L., Die Siegelbildvorschläge des Clemens von Alexandreia und die älteste christliche Literatur, in *JAC* 3 (1960), p. 51-69

Ellis E. E., *Prophecy and Hermeneutic*, Tübingen, 1978

Elter A., *De gnomologiorum graecorum historia atque origine commentatio*, Bonn, 1893-1895
Ernst W., *De Clementis Alexandrini Stromatum libro VIII qui fertur*, Göttingen, 1910
Études sur le Judéisme hellénistique (Lectio divina 119), ed. R. Kuntzmann et J. Schosser, Paris, 1984
Eijk A. H. C. van, The Gospel of Philip and Clement of Alexandria; gnostic and ecclesiastical theology on the resurrection and the eucharist, in *VigChr* 25 (1971), p. 94-120

Fascher E., Der Logos-Christus als göttlicher Lehrer bei Clemens von Alexandrien, in *TU* 77 (1961), p. 307-320
——, Abraham φυσιολόγος und φίλος θεοῦ, in *Mullus* (Festschr. Th. Klauser, JAC E1), Münster, 1964, p. 111-124
Faye E. de, Les *Stromates* de Clément d'Alexandrie, in *RHR* 36 (1897), p. 307-320
——, *Clément d'Alexandrie; étude sur les rapports du Christianisme et de la philosophie grecque au IIe siècle* (BEHE. R), 2nd ed., Paris, 1906
Ferguson J., *Clement of Alexandria*, New York, 1974
Festugière A. J., *L'idéal religieux des Grecs et l'Evangile*, Paris, 1932
——, *La Révélation d'Hermès Trismégiste*, Paris, 1949-1954; 1. *L'astrologie et les sciences occultes*, 2nd ed., Paris, 1954; 2. *Le Dieu cosmique*, Paris, 1949; 3. *Les doctrines de l'âme*, Paris 1953; 4. *Le Dieu inconnu et la gnose*, 2nd ed., Paris, 1954
Floyd W. E. G., *Clement of Alexandria's treatment of the problem of Evil* (OTM), Oxford, 1971
Fortin E. L., Clement of Alexandria and the esoteric tradition, in *StPatr* IX,3 (TU 94), 1966, p. 41-56
Fossum J., *The name of God and the angel of the Lord*, Utrecht, 1985
Fraser P. M., *Ptolemaic Alexandria*, 3 vols, Oxford, 1972
Frend W. H. C., *Martyrdom and persecution in the early church*, Oxford, 1965
——, *The rise of Christianity*, London, 1984
Früchtel L. Nachweisungen zu Fragmentensammlungen II, in *PhW* 56 (1936), p. 14-39
——, Literarisch-historische Einführung, in F. Overbeck *Die Teppiche* (ed. C. A. Bernouilli and L. Früchtel), Basel, 1936
——, Griechische Fragmente zu Philons *Quaestiones in Genesim*, in *ZAtW* 55 (1937), p. 108-115
——, Clemens Alexandrinus und Albinus, in *PhW* 57 (1937), p. 591-592
——, Neue Zeugnisse zu Clemens Alexandrinus, in *ZNtW* 36 (1937), p. 81-90
——, Clemens Alexandrinus und Theodoretus von Kyrrhos, in *PhW* 59 (1939), p. 765-766
——, Beiträge zu Clemens Alexandrinus (*Strom.* I 7), in *Würzb. Jahrb. für Altertumswiss.* 2 (1947), p. 148-151
——, art. Clemens Alexandrinus, in *RACh* 2 (1955), p. 182-188
Früchtel U., *Die kosmologische Vorstellungen bei Philo von Alexandrien* (ALGHJ 2), Leiden, 1968

Gabrielsson J., *Über die Quellen des Clemens Alexandrinus*, 2 vols, Upsala, 1 1906; 2 1909
Gahbauer F. R. G., Die Erzieherrolle des Logos Christus in der Ethik des Klemens von Alexandrien auf dem Hintergrund des (mittel) Platonismus und stoischen Anthropologie, in *MThZ* 31 (1980), p. 296-305
Geffcken J., *Zwei griechische Apologeten*, Leipzig, 1907
Gemoll W., Xenophon bei Clemens Alexandrinus, in *Hermes* 52 (1918), p. 105-107
Gigon O., Die Erneuerung der Philosophie in der Zeit Ciceros, in *EH* III, Genève, 1955, p. 25-61
Glockmann G., *Homer in der frühchristlichen Literatur bis Justinus* (TU 105), 1968
——, Spuren Justins bei Clemens Alexandrinus, in *Helikon* 15/16 (1975-1976), p. 401-407
Goodenough E. R., The political philosophy of hellenistic Kingship, in *YCS* 1 (1928), p. 55-102
——, Philo's Exposition of the law and his *De Vita Mosis*, in *HThR* 27 (1933), p. 109-125

——, *By Light, Light; the mystic Gospel of Hellenistic Judaism*, New Haven, 1935, repr. Amsterdam 1969

——, *The politics of Philo Judaeus*, New Haven, 1938

——, *An introduction to Philo Judaeus*, Oxford, 1940

Grant R. M., *The letter and the Spirit*, London, 1957

——, *Gnosticism and Early Christianity*, London, 1959

——, Early Alexandrian Christianity, in *ChH* 40 (1971), p. 133-144

——, The Stromateis of Origen, in *Epektasis* (mél. J. Daniélou), Paris, 1972, p. 285-292

Guéroud O. and Jouquet P., *Un livre d'écolier du IIIe siècle avant J.-Chr.*, Cairo, 1938

Gussen P. J. G., *Het leven in Alexandrië volgens de cultuurhistorische gegevens in de Paedagogus (boek II en III) van Clemens Alexandrinus*, Assen, 1955

Guthrie W. K. C., *A history of Greek philosophy*, 6 vols, Cambridge, 1962-1981

Hanson A., Philo's etymologies, in *JThS* 18 (1967), p. 128-139

Hanson R. P. C., *Allegory and Event; a study of the sources and significance of Origen's interpretation of Scripture*, London, 1959

Harl M., *Origène et la fonction révélatrice du Verbe incarné* (PatSor 2), Paris, 1958

——, Cosmologie grecque et représentations juives dans l'oeuvre de Philon d'Alexandrie, in *PAL*, 1967, p. 189-203

Harnack A. von and Preuschen E., *Geschichte der altchristliche Literatur bis auf Eusebius*, I *Überlieferung*, Leipzig, 1893; II *Chronologie*, Leipzig, 1904; new ed. by K. Aland, Leipzig, 1958

Harnack A. von, *Lehrbuch der Dogmengeschichte*, 3 vols, 4th ed., Tübingen, 1909, repr. 1964

——, Die Terminologie der Wiedergeburt und verwanten Erlebnisse in der ältesten Kirche, in *TU* 42,3 (1918), p. 97-143

——, *Die Mission und Ausbreitung des Christentums in den ersten drei Jahrhunderten*, 2 vols, 4th ed., Leipzig, 1924

——, *Marcion, das Evangelium vom unbekannten Gott* (TU 45), 2nd ed., Leipzig, 1924

Hatch E. and Redpath H. A., *A concordance to the Septuagint*, 2 vols, Oxford, 1897, repr. Graz, 1975

Hausherr I., *Nous du Christ et voies d'oraison* (OrChrA 157), Roma, 1960

Hay D. M., Philo's references to other allegorists, in *SPh* 6 (1979-1980), p. 41-75

Hegermann M., *Die Vorstellung vom Schöpfungsmittler im hellenistischen Judentum und Urchristentum*, Berlin, 1961

Heinemann I., *Philons griechische und jüdische Bildung*, Breslau, 1932

Heinisch P., *Der Einfluss Philo's auf die älteste christliche Exegese; Barnabas, Justin und Clemens von Alexandreia*, Münster, 1908

Helderman J., *Die Anapausis im Evangelium Veritatis* (Nag Hammadi Studies 18), Leiden, 1984

Helmbold W. C. and O'Neil E. N., *Plutarch's Quotations* (PhMon 19), Oxford, 1959

Hellinger S., *Weibliche Aspekte im Gottesbild? Untersuchungen zu Clemens von Alexandria*, Basel, 1981

Héring J., *Étude sur la doctrine de la chute et de la préexistence des âmes chez Clément d'Alexandrie* (BEHE. R 38), Paris, 1923

Heussi C., Die *Stromateis* des Clemens Alexandrinus und ihr Verhältnis zum *Protreptikos* und *Pädagogos*, in *ZWTh* 45 (1902), p. 465-512

Hilgenfeld A., *Die Ketzergeschichte des Urchristenrums*, Leipzig 1884, repr. 1963

——, *Judentum und Judenchristentum; eine Nachlese zu der Ketzergeschichte des Urchristentums*, Leipzig 1886, repr. 1966

Hitchcock F. R., Did Clement of Alexandria know the *Didache*?, in *JThS* 24 (1923), p. 397-401

Hoek A. van de Bunt-van den, Origenes' *De Principiis* in tweevoud, in *Bijdr* 38 (1977), p. 199-203

——, Aristobulus, Acts, Theophilus, Clement making use of Aratus' *Phainomena*: a peregrination, in *Bijdr* 41 (1980), p. 290-299

——, Milk and honey in the theology of Clement of Alexandria, in *Fides Sacramenti-Sacramentum Fidei* (in hon. P. Smulders), Assen, 1981, p. 27-39

Hoek A. van den, Mistress and Servant; an allegorical theme in Philo, Clement and Origen, in *Origeniana Quarta* (Innsbrucker theologische Studien 19, ed. L. Lies), Innsbruck-Wien, 1987, p. 344-349

——, The concept of σῶμα τῶν γραφῶν in Alexandrian theology, forthcoming

Hoffmann R., Die Einheit von Theorie und Praxis bei Klemens von Alexandrien, in *Die Antike im Umbruch* (ed. S. Otto), München, 1974, p. 37-64

Horn H. J., Antakolouthie der Tugenden und die Einheit Gottes, in *JAC* 13 (1970), p. 5-28

——, Zur Motivation der allegorischen Schriftexegese bei Clemens Alexandrimus, in *Hermes* 97 (1969), p. 439-496

Hozakowski V., *De chronographia Clementis Alexandrini*, Münster, 1896

Ivánka E. von, *Plato Christianus; Übernahme und Umgestaltung des Platonismus durch die Väter*, Einsiedeln, 1964

Jacobson H., *The Exagoge of Ezechiel*, Cambridge, 1983

Jacoby F., *Die Fragmente der griechischen Historiker*, Berlin 1924, repr. Leiden, 1950-1964

Jaeger W., *Early Christianity and the Greek Paideia*, Cambridge (Mass.), 1962

Jaubert A., *La notion d'alliance dans le Judaïsme aux abords de l'ère chrétienne*, Paris, 1963

Jervell J., *Imago Dei, Gen. 1,26f. im Spätjudentum, in der Gnosis und in den paulinischen Briefen*, Göttingen, 1960

Joly R., *Christianisme et philosophie; études sur Justin et les Apologistes grecs du deuxième siècle*, Bruxelles, 1973

Junod E., Un écho d'une controverse autour de la pénitence; l'histoire de l'apôtre Jean et du chef des brigands chez Clément d'Alexandrie (*Quis dives* 42, 1-15), in *RHPR* 60 (1980), p. 153-160

Kannengiesser C., Philon et les Pères sur la double création de l'homme, in *PAL*, p. 277-297

Kappelmacher A., *Zur Tragödie der hellenistischen Zeit* (Wiener Studien 44), Wien, 1924/25

Karpp H., *Probleme altchristlicher Anthropologie; biblische Anthropologie und philosophische Psychologie bei den Kirchenvätern des dritten Jahrhunderts* (BFChTh 44,3), Gütersloh, 1950

——, Die Bußlehre des Klemens von Alexandrien, in *ZNtW* 43 (1950/51), p. 224-242

Kasher M., *Encyclopedia of Biblical interpretation*, New York, 1953-

Kittel G., (ed.) *Theologisches Wörterbuch zum Neuen Testament*, 11 vols, Stuttgart, 1933-1979

Knauber A., Die patrologische Schätzung des Clemens von Alexandrien bis zu seinem neuerlichen Bekanntwerden durch die ersten Druckeditionen des 16. Jahrhunderts, in *Kyriakon* (Festschr. J. Quasten), Münster, 1970, I, p. 289-308

Koch H., War Klemens von Alexandrien Priester?, in *ZNtW* 20 (1921), p. 43-48

Koch H., *Pronoia und Paideusis* (AKG 22), Berlin, 1932

Kovács J. L., *Clement of Alexandria and the Valentinian Gnostics* (diss. Columbia Univ. New York), 1978

Krämer H. J., *Der Ursprung des Geistmetaphysik*, Amsterdam, 1964

Krause W., *Die Stellung der frühchristlichen Autoren zur heidnischen Literatur*, Wien, 1958

Kretschmar G., Ein Beitrag zur Frage nach dem Ursprung der frühchristliche Askese, in *ZThK* 61 (1964), p. 27-67

Ladaria L. F., *El espiritu en Clemente Alejandrino; estudio teològico-antropològico*, Madrid, 1980

Lampe G. W. H., *A Patristic Greek Lexicon*, Oxford, 1961

——, *The Seal of the Spirit*, 2nd ed., London, 1967

Lazzati G., *Introduzione allo studio di Clemente Alessandrino*, Milano, 1939

Lebreton J., Le désaccord de la foi populaire et de la théologie savante dans l'Eglise chrétienne du IIIe siècle, in *RHE* 19 (1923), p. 481-505; 20 (1924), p. 5-37

——, La théorie de la connaissance religieuse chez Clément d'Alexandrie, in *RSR* 18 (1928), p. 457-488

——, La théologie de la Trinité chez Clément d'Alexandrie, in *RSR* 34 (1947), p. 55-76, 142-179

——, art. Clément d'Alexandrie, in *DSp* II,1 (1953), c. 950-961

Lebreton J. and Zeiller J., *Histoire de l'église; depuis les origines jusqu'à nos jours* (ed. A. Fliche and V. Martin), t. II, Paris, 1935

Leisegang H., *Der Heilige Geist*, Leipzig, 1919

Leo F., Bemerkungen zu den neuen Bruchstücken Menanders, in *NGWG. PH*, Berlin, 1907, p. 320ff.

Lewy H., *Sobria ebrietas* (Beih. ZNtW 9), Berlin, 1929

Liddell H. G., Scott R. and Jones H. S., *A Greek-English Lexicon*, 9th ed., Oxford 1966

Lieske A., *Die Theologie der Logosmystik bei Origenes* (MBTh 22), Münster, 1938

Lietzmann H., *Die Geschichte der alten Kirche* II, Leipzig/Berlin 1936

Lilla S. R. C., *Clement of Alexandria; a study in Christian Platonism and Gnosticism* (OTM), Oxford, 1971

Loofs F., *Leitfaden zum Studium der Dogmengeschichte*, 6th ed. (ed. K. Aland), Tübingen, 1959

Lot-Borodin M., La doctrine de la déification das l'église grecque jusqu'au XIe siècle, in *RHR* 105-107 (1931-1933)

Lubac H. de, "Typologie" et "Allegorisme", in *RSR* 34 (1947), p. 180-226

——, *Exégèse médiévale*, Paris, 1959-1964

Lucchesi E., *L'usage de Philon dans l'oeuvre exégétique de Saint Ambroise* (ALGHJ 9), Leiden, 1977

Luneau A., *L'histoire du salut chez les Pères de l'église* (ThH 2), Paris, 1964

Maas W., *Unveränderlichkeit Gottes; zum Verhältnis vom griechisch-philosophischer und christlicher Gotteslehre*, München, 1974

Mack B. L., Exegetical traditions in Alexandrian Judaism; a program for the analysis of the Philonic Corpus, in *SPh* 3 (1974/75), p. 71-112

——, Weisheit und Allegorie bei Philo von Alexandrien, in *SPh* 5 (1978), p. 57-105

——, Philo Judaeus and exegetical traditions in Alexandria, in *ANRW* II 21.1 (1984), p. 227-271

Malingrey A. M., *Philosophia; étude d'un groupe de mots dans la littérature grecque des Présocratiques au IVe siècle après J. C.*, Paris, 1961

Mansfeld J., Heraclitus, Empedocles and others in a Middle Platonist cento in Philo of Alexandria, in *VChr* 39 (1985), p. 131-156

Marcus R., Jewish and Greek elements in the LXX, in *Louis Ginzberg Jubilee Volume*, New York, 1945, p. 227-245

Marrou H. I., *Saint Augustin et la fin de la culture antique*, 2nd ed., Paris, 1949

——, Humanisme et Christianisme chez Clément d'Alexandrie, in *EH* III, Genève, 1955, p. 183-200

——, *Histoire de l'éducation dans l'Antiquité*, 2nd ed., Paris, 1950; (english translation) *A history of education in Antiquity*, London, 1956

——, Morale et Spiritualité dans le *Pédagogue*, in *StPatr* II (1957), p. 538-546

——, art. Diatribe, II Christliche, in *RACh* III (1957), c. 997-1009

——, La théologie de l'histoire dans la Gnosis Valentinienne, in *Le Origini dello Gnosticismo* (ed. U. Bianchi), Leiden, 1967, p. 215-226

Marsh H. G., The use of ΜΥΣΤΗΡΙΟΝ in the writings of Clement of Alexandria with special reference to his sacramental doctrine, in *JThS* 37 (1936), p. 64-80

Martin J., *Antike Rhetorik* (HAW II,3), München, 1974

May G., Platon und die Auseinandersetzung mit den Häresien bei Klemens von Alexandrien, in *Platonismus und Christentum* (Festschr. H. Dörrie, JbAC Erg. 10), Münster, 1983, p. 123-132

Mayer A., *Das Gottesbild im Menschen nach Clemens von Alexandrien* (StAns 15), Roma, 1942

McCue J. F., Conflicting versions of Valentinianism? Irenaeus and the *Excerpta ex Theodoto*, in *The rediscovery of Gnosticism I*, Leiden, 1980, p. 404-416

Meeks W. A., The Divine Agent and His Counterfeit in Philo and the Fourth Gospel, in *Aspects of Religious Propaganda in Judaism and Early Christianity* (ed. E. Schüssler Fiorenza), Notre Dame, 1976, p. 43-67

Mees M., *Die Zitate aus dem Neuen Testamen bei Clemens von Alexandrien* (Quad. di Vet. Chr. II), Bari, 1970

——, Jetzt und Dann in der Eschatologie des Klemens von Alexandrien, in *Aug* 18 (1978), p. 127-137

Méhat A., "Pénitence seconde" et péché involontaire" chez Clément d'Alexandrie, in *VigChr* 8 (1954), p. 225-233

——, Remarques sur quelques passages du IIe Stromate de Clément d'Alexandrie, in *REG* 69 (1956), p. 41-49

——, "Apocatastase", Origène, Clément d'Alexandrie, Act. 3,21, in *VChr* 10 (1956), p. 196-214

——, Les ordres d'enseignement chez Clément d'Alexandrie et Sénèque, in *StPatr* II (TU 64), 1957, p. 351-357

——, *Étude sur les 'Stromates' de Clément d'Alexandrie* (PatSor 7), Paris, 1966

——, *Kephalaia; recherches sur les materiaux des 'Stromates' de Clément d'Alexandrie et leur utilisation* (thèse compl. dactyl.), 1966

——, Θεός 'Αγάπη; une hypothèse sur l'object de la gnose orthodoxe, in *StPatr* IX (TU 94), 1966, p. 82-86

——, L'hypothèse des "Testimonia" à l'épreuve des *Stromates*; remarques sur les citations de l'Ancien Testament chez Clément d'Alexandrie, in *La Bible et les pères* (Coll. de Straßbourg 1-3 Oct. 1969), Paris, 1971

——, Clément d'Alexandrie et les sens de l'Ecriture, in *Epektasis* (Mél. J. Daniélou), Paris, 1972, p. 355-365

——, Le "lieu supracéleste" de Saint Justin à Origène, in *Forma Futuri* (Mél. Mich. Pellegrino), Torino, 1975

——, Vraie et fausse gnose d'après Clément d'Alexandrie, in *The rediscovery of Gnosticism* (SHR 41/1), Leiden, 1980, p. 426-433

Mendelson A., A reappraisal of Wolfson's method, in *SPh* 3 (1974/75), p. 11-26

——, *Secular education in Philo of Alexandria*, Cincinnati, 1982

Merki H., Ὁμοίωσις Θεῷ; von der platonischen Angleichung an Gott zur Gottähnlichkeit bei Gregor von Nyssa (Paradosis 7), Freiburg, 1952

——, art. Ebenbildlichkeit, in *RAChr* 4 (1958), p. 467-479

Merlan Ph., Greek Philosophy from Plato to Plotinus, in *The Cambridge History of later Greek and Early Medieval Philosophy* (ed. A. H. Armstrong), Cambridge, 1970, p. 11-132

Moehring H., Arithmology as an exegetical tool in the writings of Philo of Alexandria, in *SBL Seminar papers* (Series 13) 1, p. 191-227

Mohr R. D., *The Platonic cosmology* (PhAnt 42), Leiden, 1985

Moingt J., La gnose de Clément d'Alexandrie dans ses rapports avec la foi et la philosophie, in *RSR* 37 (1950), p. 195-251, 398-421, 537-564; 38 (1951), p. 82-118

Molland E., Clement of Alexandria on the origin of Greek philosophy, in *SO* 15/16 (1936), p. 57-85

Mondésert Cl., Le symbolisme chez Clément d'Alexandrie, in *RSR* 26 (1936), p. 158-180

——, *Clément d'Alexandrie; introduction à l'étude de sa pensée religieuse à partir de l'Écriture* (Theol. 4), Paris, 1944

——, À propos du signe du temple; un texte de Clément d'Alexandrie, in *RSR* 36 (1949), p. 580-584

——, Vocabulaire de Clément d'Alexandrie, le mot λογικός, in *RSR* 42 (1954), p. 258-265

Mondin B., *Filone e Clemente*, Torino, 1968

——, Fede cristiana e pensiero greco secondo Clemente Alessandrino, in *Evangelizzazione e cultura* II, 1976, p. 132-142

Monte Peral L. A., *Akataleptos Theos; der unfassbare Gott* (ALGHJ 16), Leiden, 1986

Moreschini C., Note ai perduti Stromata di Origene, in *Origeniana Quarta* (Innsbr. theol. Studien 19, ed. L. Lies), Innsbruck-Wien, 1987, p. 36-44

Mortley R., *Connaissance religieuse et herméneutique chez Clément d'Alexandrie*, Leiden, 1972
——, The mirror and 1 Cor. 13,12 in the epistomology of Clement of Alexandria, in *VChr* 30 (1976), p. 109-120
——, L'historiographie profane et les Pères, in *Paganisme, Judaïsme, Christianisme* (Mél. M. Simon), Paris, 1978, p. 315-327
——, The theme of silence in Clement of Alexandria, in *JThS* XXIV (1973), p. 197-202
——, *From word to silence; I The rise and fall of the Logos, II The way of negation Christian and Greek*, Bonn, 1986
Moulton J. H. and Milligan G., *The Vocabulary of the Greek Testament illustrated from the papyri and other non-literary sources*, London, 1930, repr. 1949
Mras K., Die Stellung der *P. E.* des Eusebius im antiken Schrifttum, in *AAWW* 93 (1956), p. 209-217
Munck J., *Untersuchungen über Klemens von Alexandreia* (FKGG 2), Kopenhagen-Stuttgart, 1933
——, Christus und Israel; eine Auslegung von Röm. 9-11, in *Acta Jutlandica* XXVIII (1956); engl. ed. *Christ and Israel; an interpretation of Romans 9-11*, Philadephia, 1967

Nardi C., *Il battesimo in Clemente Alessandrino; interpretazione di Eclogae propheticae 1-26* (Studia Ephemerides "Augustinianum" 19), Roma, 1984
Nauck A. and Snell B., *Tragicorum Graecorum Fragmenta* 1-2, Göttingen, 1971-1981
Nautin P., Notes sur le *Stromate* I de Clément d'Alexandrie, in *RHE* 47 (1952), p. 618-631
——, Pantène, in *Tome commémoratif du Millénaire de la Bibliothèque patriarcale d'Alexandrie* (Publications de l'Institut d'études orientales de la bibliothèque patriarcale d'Alexandrie), Alexandrie, 1953, p. 145-153
——, Notes critiques sur le *Stromate* I de Clément d'Alexandrie, in *RHE* 47 (1952), p. 618-631
——, Notes critiques sur le *Stromate* II de Clément d'Alexandrie, in *RHE* 49 (1954), p. 835-841
——, *Lettres et écrivains chrétiens des IIe et IIIe siècles*, Paris, 1961
——, Une citation méconnue des *Stromates* d'Origène, in *Epektasis* (Mél. J. Daniélou), Paris, 1972, p. 373-374
——, Les citations de la *Prédication de Pierre* dans Clément d'Alexandrie, Strom. VI 39-41, in *JThS* 25 (1974), p. 98-105
——, Les fragments de Basilide sur la souffrance et leur interprétation par Clément d'Alexandrie et Origène, in *Mélanges d'histoire de religions offerts à Henri-Charles Puech*, Paris, 1974, p. 393-403
——, La fin des *Stromates* et les *Hypotyposes* de Clément d'Alexandrie, in *VChr* 30 (1976), p. 268-302
Nazzaro A. V., *Recenti studi Filoniani (1963-1970)*, Napoli, 1973
Nestle E. and Aland K., *Novum Testamentum Graece*, Stuttgart, 1979[26]
Newman J. H. Card., *Apologia pro vita sua, being a history of his religious opinions*, new impr., London, 1904
Nikiprowetzky V., La spiritualisation des sacrifices et le culte sacrificiel au temple de Jérusalem chez Philon d'Alexandrie, in *Sem* 17 (1967), p. 97-116
——, L'exégèse de Philon d'Alexandrie, in *RHPhR* 53 (1973), p. 309-329
——, *Le commentaire de l'Ecriture chez Philon d'Alexandrie* (ALGHJ 11), Leiden, 1977
—— / Solignac A. de, Philon d'Alexandrie / Philon chez les pères, in *DSp* XII 1, Paris, 1984, c. 1352-1374
——, *Hellenica et Judaica, hommage à Valentin Nikiprowetzky* (ed. A. Caquot, M. Hadas-Lebel et J. Riaud), Leuven/Paris, 1986
Norden E., *Die antike Kunstprosa vom VI Jahrhundert vor Chr. bis in die Zeit der Renaissance*, 2 vols, Leipzig, 1898, 5th ed. Darmstadt, 1958
——, *Agnostos Theos*, Leipzig, 1913, reed. Darmstadt, 1974

Orbe A., Teologia bautismal de Clemente Alejandrino, segun *Paed.* I 26,3-27,2, in *Greg* 36 (1955), p. 410-448

——, *Estudios Valentinianos I; hacia la primera teologia de la procesion del Verbo* (AnGr 99), Roma, 1958

——, *Antropologia de San Ireneo*, Madrid, 1969

Osborn E. F., *The philosophy of Clement of Alexandria* (TaS 3), Cambridge 1957

——, Teaching and writing in the first chapters of the *"Stromateis"* of Clement of Alexandria, in *JThS* 10 (1959), p. 335-343

——, *The beginnings of Christian Philosophy*, Cambridge, 1981

——, Clement of Alexandria; a review of research, 1958-1982, in *The Second Century* 3/1 (1983), p. 219-244

——, Logique et exégèse chez Clément d'Alexandrie, in *Lectures anciennes de la Bible* (Cahiers de Bibl. Patr. 1), Straßbourg, 1987, p. 169-190

Otto A., *Die Sprichwörter und sprichwörtlichen Redensarten der Römer*, Leipzig, 1890, repr. Hildesheim, 1964

Oulton J. E. L., Clement of Alexandria and the *Didache*, in *JThS* 41 (1940), p. 177-179

Pade P. B., Λόγος θεός; *Untersuchungen zur Logos-Christologie des Titus Flavius Clemens von Alexandrien*, Roma, 1939

Passcher, J., Ἡ ΒΑΣΙΛΙΚΗ ΟΔΟΣ; *der Königsweg zur Wiedergeburt und Vergöttung bei Philon von Alexandreia*, Paderborn, 1931

Paulsen D., Ethical individualism in Clement of Alexandria, in *CTM* 43 (1972), p. 3-20

Pearson B. A., Philo and Gnosticism, in *ANRW* II 21.1 (1984) p. 456-476

Pelikan J., *The Emergence of the catholic tradition (100-600)*, Chicago, 1971

Pellegrino M., *La catechesi cristologica di S. Clemente Allesandrino*, Milano, 1939

Pelletier A., Le grand rideau du vestibule du Temple de Jérusalem, in *Syr* 35 (1958), p. 218-226

——, La tradition synoptique du Voile déchiré, in *RSR* 46 (1958), p. 161-180

Pépin J., *Mythe et allégorie; les origines grecques et les contestations judéo-chrétiennes*, Paris, 1958, 1976²

——, *Théologie cosmique et théologie chrétienne*, Paris, 1964

——, Remarques sur la théorie de l'exégèse allégorique chez Philon, in *PAL*, p. 131-167

——, La vraie dialectique selon Clément d'Alexandrie, *Epektasis* (Mél. J. Daniélou), Paris, 1972, p. 375-383

——, Clément d'Alexandrie, les catégories d'Aristote et le fragment 60 d'Héraclite, in *Concepts et catégories dans la pensée antique* (BHPh ed. P. Auberque), 1980, p. 271-284

Peterson E., *Frühkirche, Christentum und Gnosis*, Freiburg, 1959

Places E. des, Un thème platonicien dans la tradition patristique, le juste crucifié, in *StPatr* IX 3 (1966), p. 30-40

——, *Platonismo e tradizione cristiana*, Milano, 1976

——, *Eusèbe de Césarée commentateur; Platonisme et Écriture Sainte* (ThH 63), Paris, 1982

Pohlenz M., *Philon von Alexandreia* (NAWG 1942/1), Göttingen, 1942, p. 409-487

——, *Klemens von Alexandreia und sein hellenisches Christentum* (NAWG 1943/3), Göttingen, 1943, p. 103-180

——, *Die Stoa; Geschichte einer geistigen Bewegung*, 2 vols, Göttingen, I 1984⁶, II 1980⁵

Prestige C. L., Clement of Alexandria *Stromata* 2,8 and the meaning of 'hypostasis', in *JThS* 30 (1929), p. 270-272

——, *God in Patristic Thought*, London, 1936

Prümm K., Glaube und Erkenntniss im zweiten Buch der *Stromata* des Klemens von Alexandria, in *Schol* 12 (1937), p. 17-57

Prunet O., *La morale de Clément d'Alexandrie et le Nouveau Testament* (EHPhR 41), Paris, 1966

Puech H. Ch., La ténèbre mystique chez Pseudo-Denys l'Aréopagite et dans la tradition patristique, in *EtCarm* 23 (1938), p. 33-52

——, La Gnose et le temps, in *ErJb* 20 (1951), p. 57-113

——, Quispel G. and Unnik W. C. van, *The Jung Codex*, London, 1955

Quacquarelli A., I luoghi communi contra la retorica in Clemente Alessandrino, in *RSFil* 4 (1956), p. 456-476

——, *Indirizzi e metodi nella scuola Antinicena*, Brescia, 1962
——, *L'ogdoade patristica e suoi riflessi nella liturgia e nei monumenti*, Bari, 1973
——, Recupero della numerologica per la metodica dell'esegesi patristica, in *Annali di Storia dell'Esegesi* 2 (1985), p. 235-249
Quasten J., Der gute Hirt in hellenistischer und frühchristlicher Logostheologie, in *Festschrift I. Herwegen*, Münster, 1938, p. 51-58
Quatember F., *Die christliche Lebenshaltung des Klemens von Alexandrien nach seinem Pädagogus*, Wien, 1946
Quispel G., Philo und die altchristliche Häresie, in *ThZ* 6 (*1949*), p. 429-436
——, Origenes and the Valentinian Gnosis, in *VigChr* 28 (1974), p. 29-42

Rahlfs A., (ed.) *Septuaginta*, 2 vols, Stuttgart, 1935⁹
Rahner H., Taufe und geistliches Leben bei Origenes, in *ZAM* 7 (1932), p. 205-232
Rahner K., Le début d'une doctrine des cinq sens spirituels, in *RAM* 13 (1932), p. 113-145
Resch A., *Agrapha*; ausserkanonische Schriftfragmente (TU 15/3), Leipzig, 1906, repr. Darmstadt, 1974
Reynolds L. D. and Wilson N. G., *Scribes and scholars; a guide to the transmission of Greek and Latin literature*, 2nd ed., Oxford, 1974
Richard M., art. Florilèges spirituels grecs, in *DSp* V, c. 476-512
Richardson W., The Philonic Patriarchs as Νόμος ἔμψυχος, in *StPatr* I (TU 63), 1957, p. 512-525
——, Νόμος ἔμψυχος; Marcion, Clement of Alexandria and St. Luke's Gospel, in *StPatr* VI (TU 81), 1962, p. 191-196
——, The basis of ethics; Chrysippus and Clement of Alexandria, in *StPatr* IX (TU 94), 1966, p. 87-97
Riedinger R., Zur antimarkionitischen Polemik des Klemens von Alexandreia, in *VigChr* 29 (1975), p. 15-32
Rist J. M., *Stoic philosophy*, Cambridge, 1969
Ritter A. M., Christentum und Eigentum bei Klemens von Alexandrien auf dem Hintergrund der frühchristlichen Armenfrömmigkeit und der Ethik der kaiserzeitlichen Stoa, in *ZKG* 86 (1975), p. 1-25
——, Klemens von Alexandrien, in *Gestalten der Kirchengeschichte I* (ed. M. Greschat), Stuttgart/Berlin, 1984, p. 121-133
Robberts H., Christian philosophy in Clement of Alexandria, in *Philosophy and Christianity* (ded. to H. Dooyeweerd), Kampen, 1965, p. 203-211
Robbins F. E., The tradition of Greek arithmology, in *CPh* 16 (1921), p. 97-123
——, Arithmetic in Philo Judaeus, in *CPh* 26 (1931), p. 345-361
Roberts L., The literary form of the *Stromateis*, in *The second century* 1 (1981), p. 211-222
Rüther T., *Die sittliche Forderung der Apatheia in den beiden ersten christlichen Jahrhunderten und bei Klemens von Alexandrien* (FThSt 63), Freiburg, 1949
Runia D. T., History of philosophy in the grand manner; the achievement of H. A. Wolfson, in *PhilRef* 49 (1984), p. 112-133
——, The structure of Philo's allegorical treatises; a review of two recent studies and some additional comments, in *VigChr* 38 (1984), p. 209-256
——, *Philo of Alexandria and the Timaeus of Plato* (PhAnt), Leiden, 1986
Russell D. A. *Plutarch*, London, 1973

Sagnard F., *La gnose valentinienne et le témoignage de Saint Irénée* (EPhM 36), Paris, 1947
Salles-Dabadi J. M. A., *Recherches sur Simon le Mage* (CRB 10), Paris, 1969
Sandmel, S., Parallelomania, in *JBL* 81 (1962), p. 1-13
——, *Philo of Alexandria; an introduction*, New York, 1979
——, Philo Judaeus, an introduction to the man, his writings and his significance, in *ANRW* II 21.1 (1984), p. 3-46
Savon H., *Saint Ambroise devant l'exégèse de Philon le Juif*, 2 vols, Paris, 1977
——, Saint Ambroise et saint Jérôme, lecteurs de Philon, in *ANRW* II 21.1 (1984), p. 731-759

Scham J., *Der Optativgebrauch bei Klemens von Alexandrien in seiner sprach- und stilgeschichtlichen Bedeutung; ein Beitrag zur Geschichte des Attizismus in der altchristlichen Literatur*, Paderborn, 1913

Schneider C., *Geistesgeschichte des antiken Christentums*, 2 vols, München, 1954

Schmölle K., *Läuterung nach dem Tode und pneumatische Auferstehung bei Klemens von Alexandrien* (MBTh 38), 1974

Schmoller A., *Handkonkordanz zum griechischen Neuen Testament*, Stuttgart, 1960[12]

Schoedel W. R., Enclosing not Enclosed, the early Christian doctrine of God, in *Early Christian literature and the classical tradition* (in hon. R. M. Grant), 1979, p. 75-85

Schubart W., art. Alexandria, in *RACh* I (1950), c. 271-283

Schürer E., *Geschichte des jüdischen Volkes im Zeitalter Jesu Christi*, Leipzig, 1901-1909, repr. Hildesheim, 1964; *The History of the Jewish people in the age of Jesus Christ (175 BC-AD 135); a new english version...by G. Vermes and F. Millar*, 4 vols, Edinburgh, 1973-1987

Schwanz P., *Imago Dei als christologisch-anthropologisches Problem bis Clemens von Alexandrien*, Halle, 1970

Schwartz J., Philon et l'apologétique chrétienne du second siècle, in *Hommage à André Dupont-Sommer*, Paris, 1971, p. 497-507

Schwyzer H. R., review of Clemens Alexandrinus, II, *Stromata* Buch I-VI, hrsg. von Otto Stählin 3. Aufl. neu hrsg. von Ludwig Früchtel, in *Gn* 37 (1965), p. 484-490

Seeberg E., *Lehrbuch der Dogmengeschichte* I, Leipzig, 1922

Seeseman, Das Paulusverständnis des Clemens Alexandrinus, in *ThStKr* 107 (1936), p. 312-346

Segal A. F., *The powers in heaven; early Rabbinic reports about Christianity and Gnosticism*, Leiden, 1977

Sevenster J. N., *Het verlossingsbegrip bij Philo, vergeleken met de verlossingsgedachte van de synoptische evangeliën*, Assen, 1936

Siegfried C., *Die hebräischen Worterklärungen des Philo und die Spuren ihrer Einwirkung auf die Kirchenväter*, Magdenburg, 1863

——, *Philon von Alexandreia als Ausleger des Alten Testaments*, Jena, 1875, repr. Amsterdam, 1970

Simon M., *Verus Israel*, Paris, 1948, repr. 2nd ed. Paris, 1984

Simonetti M., *Profilo storico dell'esegesi patristica*, Roma, 1981

Smith M., *Clement of Alexandria and a secret Gospel of Mark*, Cambridge (Mass.), 1973

Smith R. W., *The art of rhetoric in Alexandria; its theory and practice in the ancient world*, Den Haag, 1974

Smulders P., A quotation of Philo in Irenaeus, in *VigChr* 12 (1958), p. 154-156

——, Dogmengeschichtliche und lehramtliche Entfaltung der Christologie, in *MySal* III/1 (1970), p. 389-476

Spanneut M., *Le Stoïcisme des Pères de l'église, de Clément de Rome à Clément d'Alexandrie* (PSorb 1), Paris, 1957; 2nd ed., 1968

Staats R., Ogdoas als ein Symbol für die Auferstehung, in *VigChr* 26 (1972), p. 29-52

Staehle K., *Die Zahlenmystik bei Philon*, Leipzig, 1931

Stählin O., *Clemens Alexandrinus und die Septuagint* (Gymn. Progr.), Nürnberg, 1901

——, Clemens von Alexandrien und die Gnosis, in *Die pädagogische Hochschule* 1 (1929), p. 98-105

Stein E., *Die allegorische Exegese des Philo aus Alexandrien*, Giessen, 1929

Steneker H., *ΠΕΙΘΟΥΣ ΔΗΜΙΟΥΡΓΙΑ; observations sur la fonction du style dans le Protreptique de Clément d'Alexandrie* (GrChrPr,3), Nijmegen, 1967

Stelzenberger J., *Die Beziehung der frühchristlichen Sittenlehre zur Ethik der Stoa*, München, 1933

——, Über Syneidesis bei Klemens von Alexandria, in *MTZ* 4 (1953), p. 27-33

Stemplinger E., *Das Plagiat in der griechischen Literatur*, Leipzig/Berlin, 1912

Stephanus H., *Thesaurus Graecae Linguae*, Paris, 1831-1865

Steur K., *Poimandres en Philo* (diss. Nijmegen), Purmerend, 1935

Stone M. E. (ed.), *Jewish writings of the second temple period; apocrypha, pseudepigrapha, Qumran sectarian writings; Philo, Josephus* (CRINT II 2), Assen, 1984

Tardieu M., La lettre à Hipparque et les réminiscences pythagoriciennes de Clément d'Alexandrie, in *VigChr* 28 (1974), p. 241-247

Tcherikover V., *Hellenistic civilization and the Jews*, Philadelphia, 1959

Telfer W., Bees in Clement of Alexandria, in *JThS* 28 (1926/27), p. 167-168

Tengblad E., *Syntaktisch-stilistische Beiträge zur Kritik und Exegese des Clemens von Alexandrien*, Lund, 1932

Terian A., *Philonis Alexandrini De Animalibus*, Chico Calif., 1981, Introduction, p. 3-63

Theiler W., *Die Vorbereitung des Neoplatonismus*, 2nd ed., Berlin/Zürich, 1964

——, Philon von Alexandrien und der Beginn des kaiserzeitlichen Platonismus, in *Parusia* (Festschr. J. Hirschberger), Frankfurt, 1965, p. 199-218

——, *Forschungen zum Neuplatonismus* (QSGP 10), Berlin, 1966

Timothy H. B., *The Early Christian apologists and Greek philosophy, exemplified by Irenaeus, Tertullian and Clement of Alexandria*, Assen, 1973

Tollinton R. B., *Clement of Alexandria; a study in Christian liberalism*, 2 vols, London, 1914

——, *Alexandrian teaching on the Universe*; four lectures, London, 1932

Torjesen K. J., *Hermeneutical procedure and theological method in Origen's exegesis*, Berlin/New York, 1986

——, Pedagogical soteriology from Clement to Origen, in *Origeniana Quarta* (IThSt 19), Innsbruck/Wien 1987, p. 370-379

Torm F., Das Wort γνωστικός, in *ZNtW* 35 (1936), p. 70-75

Treu U., Etymologie und Allegorie bei Klemens von Alexandrien, in *StPatr* IV (1961), p. 191-211

Trisoglio F., Filone Alessandrino e l'esegesi cristiana; contributo alla conoscenza dell'influsso esercitato da Filone sul IV secolo, specificamente in Gregorio di Nazianzo, in *ANRW* II 21.1 (1984), p. 588-730

Tsermoulas J. M., *Die Bildersprache des Klemens von Alexandrien*, Cairo, 1934

Tsirpanlis C. N., Creation and history in the thought of Clement of Alexandria, in *Diakonia* 12/3 (1977), p. 1-9

Unnik W. C. van, Opmerkingen over het karakter van het verloren werk van Clemens Alexandrinus "Canon Ecclesiasticus", in *NAKG* 33 (1942), p. 49-61

——, *De ἀφθονία van God in de oudchristelijke literatuur* (MNAW. L 36/2), Amsterdam/London, 1973

——, Der Fluch des Gekreuzigten; Deut. 21,23 in der Deutung Justins des Martyrers, in *Theologia Crucis-Signum Crucis* (Festschr. E. Dinkler), Münster, 1979, p. 483-493

Valentin P., Héraclite et Clément d'Alexandrie, in *RSR* 46 (1958), p. 27-29

——, Two notes on Irenaeus, in *VigChr* 30 (1976), p. 201-213

Verdenius W. J., Christianiserende en historische Plato-interpretatie, in *NedThT* 8 (1954), p. 129-143

Vermender J. M., De quelques répliques à Celse dans le *Protreptique* de Clément d'Alexandrie, in *REAug* 23 (1977), p. 2-17

Viscido, Similitudini tratte dal mondo animale in Clemente Alessandrino, in *VetChr* 18 (1981), p. 383-392

Völker W., *Das Vollkommenheitsideal des Origenes* (BHTh 7), Tübingen, 1931

——, *Quellen zur Geschichte der christlichen Gnosis* (SQS 5), Tübingen, 1932

——, *Fortschritt und Vollendung bei Philo von Alexandrien*, Leipzig, 1938

——, *Der wahre Gnostiker nach Clemens Alexandrinus* (TU 57), Berlin, 1952

——, Die Verwertung der Weisheits-Literatur bei den christlichen Alexandrinern, in *ZKG* 64 (1952-53), p. 1-33

——, Basilius *Ep.* 366 und Clemens Alexandrinus, in *VigChr* 7 (1953), p. 23-26

Vogel C. J. de, *Greek Philosophy*, 3 vols, Leiden, 1950-1959

——, À la recherche des étapes précises entre Platon et le Néoplatonisme, in *Mn* 4/7 (1954), p. 111-133

——, Der sogenannte Mittelplatonismus, überwiegend eine Philosophie der Diesseitigkeit, in *Platonismus und Christentum* (Festschr. H. Dörrie), Münster, 1983, p. 277-302

——, Platonism and Christianity, a mere antagonism or a profound common ground?, in *VigChr* 39 (1985), p. 1-62

Vogt K., 'Man worden': een aspect van vroeg-christelijke anthropologie, in *Conc(N)* (1985/6), p. 66-76

Wagner W. H., A Father's fate; attitudes toward and interpretations of Clement of Alexandria, in *JRH* 6 (1971), p. 209-231

Waitz H., Simon Magus in der altchristlichen Literatur, in *ZNtW* 5 (1904), p. 121-143

Walter N., Der angebliche Chronograph Julius Cassianus; ein Beitrag zu der Frage nach den Quellen des Clemens Alexandrinus, in *Studien zum neuen Testament und zur Patristik* (Festschr. E. Klostermann, TU 77), Berlin, 1961, p. 177-192

——, *Der Thoraausleger Aristobulos* (TU 86), Berlin, 1964

——, Zur Überlieferung einiger Reste jüdisch-hellenistischer Literatur bei Josephus, Clemens und Euseb, in *StPatr* VII (1966), p. 314-320

——, Jüdisch-hellenistische Literatur vor Philon von Alexandrien unter Ausschluß der Historiker, in *ANRW* II 20.1/2, Berlin/New York, 1987, p. 67-120

Waszink J. H., Der Platonismus und die altchristliche Gedankenwelt, in *EH* III, Genève, 1955, p. 137-179

——, Bemerkungen zum Einfluss des Platonismus im frühen Christentum, in *VigChr* 19 (1965), p. 129-162

——, *Biene und Honig als Symbol des Dichters und der Dichtung in der griechisch-römischen Antike* (Rheinisch-Westfälische Akademie der Wissenschaften, Geistesw. Vorträge G 196), Opladen, 1974

——, *Opuscula selecta*, Leiden, 1979

Weiss H. F., *Untersuchungen zur Kosmologie des hellenistischen und palestinischen Judentums* (TU 97), Berlin, 1966

Wendland P., *Quaestiones Musonianae, De Musonio Stoico Clementis Alexandrini aliorumque auctore*, Berlin, 1886

——, *Neuendeckte Fragmente Philos*, Berlin, 1891

——, *Philo und die kynisch-stoïsche Diatribe*, Berlin, 1895

——, Philo und Clemens Alexandrinus, in *Hermes* 31 (1896), p. 435-456

——, *Die hellenistisch-römische Kultur in ihren Beziehungen zu Judentum und Christentum* (HNT 1,2), Tübingen, 1907

Whittaker J., Plutarch, Platonism and Christianity, in *Neoplatonism and Early Christian thought* (in hon. A. H. Armstrong), London, 1981, p. 50-63

——, *Studies in Platonism and the Patristic Thought* (CollStSer 201, Varior. repr.), London, 1984

Wieneke J., *Ezechielis Judaei poetae Alexandrini fabulae quae inscribitur 'Exagoge' fragmenta*, Münster, 1931

Wiese H., *Heraklit bei Klemens von Alexandria*, Kiel, 1963

Williams M. A., *The immovable race* (Nag Hammadi Studies 29), Leiden, 1985

Wilson R. McL., The early history of the exegesis of Gen. 1:26, in *StPatr* I (TU 63), Berlin, 1957, p. 423-437

——, Philo of Alexandria and Gnosticism, in *Kairos* 14 (1972), p. 213-219

Winden J. C. M. van, Le commencement du dialogue entre la foi et la raison, in *Kyriakon* (In hon. J. Quasten), Münster, 1970, I, p. 205-213

——, *An Early Christian Philosopher, Justin Martyr's Dialogue with Trypho, Chapters One to Nine* (PhP 1), Leiden, 1971

——, Quotations from Philo in Clement of Alexandria's *Protrepticus*, in *VigChr* 32 (1978), p. 208-213

——, The first fragment of Philo's *Quaestiones in Genesim*, in *VigChr* 33 (1979), p. 313-318

——, The world of ideas in Philo of Alexandria; an interpretation of *De Opificio Mundi* 24-25, in *VigChr* 37 (1983), p. 209-217

Witt R. E., The Hellenism of Clement of Alexandria, in *CQ* 25 (1931), p. 195-204

——, *Albinus and the history of Middle Platonism*, Cambridge, 1937, repr. 1971

Wolfson H. A., *Philo; foundations of religious philosophy in Judaism, Christianity and Islam*, 2 vols, Cambridge (Mass.), 1947, 2nd ed. 1962

——, Clement of Alexandria on the generation of the Logos, in *Church History* 20 (1951), p. 3-11

——, *The Philosophy of the Church Fathers* I, Cambridge (Mass.), 1956, 3d ed. 1970

Wyrwa D., *Die christliche Platonaneigung in den Stromateis des Clemens von Alexandrien* (AKG 53), Berlin/New York, 1983

Wytzes J., Paideia und Pronoia in the works of Clemens Alexandrinus, in *VigChr* 9 (1955), p. 148-158

——, The twofold way I; Platonic influences in the work of Clement of Alexandria, in *VigChr* 11 (1957), p. 226-245

——, The twofold way II; Platonic influences in the work of Clement of Alexandria, in *VigChr* 14 (1960), p. 129-153

Ysebaert J., *Greek baptismal terminology; its origins and early development*, Nijmegen, 1962

Zandee J., *The teachings of Silvanus and Clement of Alexandria; a new document of Alexandrian theology* (MEOL 19), Leiden, 1977

Zeegers-vander Vorst N., *Les citations des poètes grecs chez les apologistes chrétiens du IIe siècle*, Louvain, 1972

Ziegler K., art. Plagiat, in *RECA*, Hlbd. 40, c. 1956-1997

——, art. Plutarchus von Chaironeia, in *RECA* 41, c. 636-962

INDEX

1. Scriptural Index

2. Index of passages from Philo

3. Index of passages from Clement

4. INDEX OF PASSAGES IN OTHER ANCIENT AUTHORS

DATE DUE

JAN 06 1994		
MAY 04 98		
JUN 1 2 2000		